Capitalism, The American Em[pire] [and]
Globalization

Kenneth E. Bauzon

Capitalism, The American Empire, and Neoliberal Globalization

Themes and Annotations from Selected Works of E. San Juan, Jr.

palgrave
macmillan

Kenneth E. Bauzon
St. Joseph's College—New York
Brooklyn, NY, USA

ISBN 978-981-32-9082-2   ISBN 978-981-32-9080-8 (eBook)
https://doi.org/10.1007/978-981-32-9080-8

Jointly published with De La Salle University Publishing House
The print edition is not for sale in the Philippines. Customers from the Philippines please order the print book from: De La Salle University Publishing House.
ISBN of the Philippines edition: 978-971-555-677-4

© The Editor(s) (if applicable) and The Author(s), under exclusive license to Springer Nature Singapore Pte Ltd. 2019
This work is subject to copyright. All rights are solely and exclusively licensed by the Publisher, whether the whole or part of the material is concerned, specifically the rights of translation, reprinting, reuse of illustrations, recitation, broadcasting, reproduction on microfilms or in any other physical way, and transmission or information storage and retrieval, electronic adaptation, computer software, or by similar or dissimilar methodology now known or hereafter developed.
The use of general descriptive names, registered names, trademarks, service marks, etc. in this publication does not imply, even in the absence of a specific statement, that such names are exempt from the relevant protective laws and regulations and therefore free for general use.
The publisher, the authors and the editors are safe to assume that the advice and information in this book are believed to be true and accurate at the date of publication. Neither the publisher nor the authors or the editors give a warranty, expressed or implied, with respect to the material contained herein or for any errors or omissions that may have been made. The publisher remains neutral with regard to jurisdictional claims in published maps and institutional affiliations.

This Palgrave Macmillan imprint is published by the registered company Springer Nature Singapore Pte Ltd.
The registered company address is: 152 Beach Road, #21-01/04 Gateway East, Singapore 189721, Singapore

*For Kuya Leslie
for instilling in me a sense of history since youth
and for his invaluable contribution promoting
historical studies in the Philippines*

Preface

In an essay with a contested authorship (because it was published unsigned; exponents assert either John O'Sullivan, Editor, or muckraking journalist Jane McManus Storm Cazneau as author), entitled "Annexation," in the July–August 1845 issue of *United States Magazine and Democratic Review*, the author lamented the foreign interference of countries like England and France in the conduct of United States (US) foreign relations. The complaint singled out, in part, these countries particularly with regard to the westward expansion of the country through a series of acquisitions-by-treaty and by expulsions and forced removals of Native Americans the most infamous of which was the 1830 Indian Removal Act giving the national government the authority to transfer the native American population living east of the Mississippi River to designated reservations in the west, known popularly as the Trail of Tears; at the same time, the article was highly critical of those opposed to the impending annexation of Texas, e.g., Henry Clay who claimed that such an annexation would be damaging to democracy, into the Union. The article bewailed this foreign interference by the identified foreign countries which were doing so:

> ...for the avowed object of thwarting our policy and hampering our power, limiting our greatness and checking the fulfillment of our *manifest destiny* to overspread the continent allotted by Providence for the free development of our yearly multiplying millions. ("Annexation" 2, italics added)

Since Mexico gained its independence from Spain in 1821, the main problem of its leaders was consolidating central control over the country's expansive territory and enforcing its laws, which included prohibition of slavery, over its diverse population. Their effort failed when the slave-owning elites of the Mexican state of Texas, seeking to maintain the same socioeconomic system that sustained their status and power, declared independence and sought to join the Union, a goal finally attained in 1845 through congressional annexation. This US act led directly to the outbreak of the US-Mexican War lasting until 1848 when, upon Mexico's humiliating defeat, Mexico was forced to agree to the onerous terms of the Treaty of Guadalupe, that year. This treaty compelled Mexico, among other provisions, to relinquish any claim over fifty-five percent of its original territory, including what are now known as the states of New Mexico, Arizona, Utah, California, and portions of Colorado and Wyoming. The acquisition of these territories by the US seemed to validate the belief of Sam Houston, one of the leaders of the Texas secessionist uprising, who believed that the United States was destined to possess "all of Mexico" and that Americans have a "birthright" to claim the entire North American continent as their own. With the above-mentioned territories having been acquired as a matter of "manifest destiny," as claimed in the first-ever recorded use of this phrase in the above-cited article, what else is there for the proponents of American imperialism to acquire beyond the shores of California or Colorado as one looked into the vast expanse of the Pacific? Would "manifest destiny" be similarly asserted over the Pacific? How would such "manifest destiny" be actually fulfilled? For whose benefits and at whose expense?

This work seeks to provide some answers to these and related questions. Others, no doubt, have previously endeavored to supply answers, some more comprehensive than what I offer here. However, this work contains features unique to itself. As such, it may complement some while challenging others. The conceptualization of this project alone sets it apart from the rest, including those which it may complement, notably those that offer an alternative narrative other than official or mainstream versions of historical events as exemplified by Howard Zinn's now-classic *A People's History of the United States 1492—Present* (1995 revised and updated edition). While it deals with historical subjects, it does not conform to the strict narrative format that one may expect. It selects certain themes, explores the ideas behind these themes, and seeks to identify the motives, the forces, and the effects inherent in the events or consequences that these ideas have given rise to. Another unique feature of this work are the constant annotations from selected works of E. San Juan Jr. (henceforth, San Juan), a noted literary and cultural theorist whose works have become ubiquitous—hard not to notice—in his own field of comparative literature that even someone like myself, professionally trained in political science, cannot help but pay attention. The annotations are a form of intervention on the part of San Juan in the discussion especially at critical junctures—ranging in subjects that crisscross such fields as cultural studies, political science, philosophy, political thought, sociology, and history in a cross-disciplinary fashion—wherein San Juan offers his critical insight, interpretation, and meaning to assist the reader make sense of these events.

That San Juan is of Philippine ancestry is less important than the fact that his intellectual contributions—universal in appeal, encyclopedic in scope, critical in style and commitment, and composed virtually during his entire adult life and deserving of recognition as Philippine national treasure—are his own modest attempt to stitch together and make coherent a form of understanding of reality that is as total as he could possibly make it in his lifetime—particularly in its historical, cultural, and ideological manifestations—that would otherwise be loose, disparate, incoherent and, therefore, less meaningful because of their lack of connection with the whole. The third feature of this work is its attempt to preserve and recognize San Juan's historical materialist approach not only to literary and cultural criticism but also to those other fields that have already been mentioned and, perhaps, more. San Juan's use of this approach has been consistent, uncompromising, and sustained, exemplified by one of his early poems as an undergraduate, entitled, "Man is a Political Animal," published in the *Philippine Collegian*, student organ at the University of the Philippines, in its July 25, 1957 issue (San Juan 1957). Composed in the Vorticist style of Wyndham Lewis, and just as the original group of Vorticists in 1914 unsettled the Victorian sensibilities in England, San Juan's poem was composed in the wake of the enactment of the McCarthyist Anti-Subversion Act in the same year, putting a chill to academic freedom in the Philippines as a former US colony; the poem itself proved embarrassing enough to the University Administration that it was promptly censored, nay, condemned by leading personalities of the time like Amado Daguio, famed Filipino writer and Republic Cultural Heritage recipient; Ramon Tapales, Dean of the College of Arts and Sciences; and no less than Enrique Virata, President of the University. San Juan's faithful adherence to the tenets of historical materialist approach is demonstrated most recently by the publication of his very latest labor of love, too late for use in the present work, published in Pilipino, entitled *Kontra-Modernidad; Mga Pagsubok sa Projekto ng Mapagpalayang Pagbabago* (2019) (roughly and not an official translation, *Counter-Modernity; The Challenges of the Project for Change Towards Liberation*). However, the significance of this work is in its use of the Pilipino language which, while it may have been in response to comradely critique from some quarters of the Philippine literary community that he has not written enough in the national language of his country of origin, nonetheless, upholds and respects the tradition of this language as an organic tool in the project for national emancipation. This conforms with the emergence of San Juan as being organic to the neocolonial period in which he grew and ardently opposed; his continued existence is defined by a challenge to the assertion by the US empire for normality, as a matter of presumed manifest destiny, and a resistance to the world order that goes by this empire's own rules, because that claim to normalcy is but a construction and its victims, far from being abstract, are real live human beings who, as agents of their own selves, are not obliged to feel normal about their victimhood and whose freedom is yet to dawn. San Juan expressed his identification and solidarity with these victims in bringing about this dawning when he wrote, in a semi-autobiographical OpEd in a Manila newspaper in 2012, writing of his memory as an undergraduate student: "…mine is a prismatic and selective affair, conditioned by what I am now as an unfinished project… caught between a dead world and one struggling to emerge" (San Juan 2012).

While San Juan's consistency and fidelity to the historical materialist approach have been notable by themselves, weathering the suppressive periods of McCarthyism and the Cold War, many writers of San Juan's generation (along with mine too, albeit a step younger, if I may so add), have effectively remained quiet or have evolved intellectually into something that deflects from any red-baiting charge of being a "communist," a "Marxist," and the like. Consequently, academic disciplines throughout much of the Cold War period until quite recently have been dominated by functionalism and formalism, or their respective "neo-" variants and counterparts in related disciplines, whose proponents have found in them a safe haven from the persecution to which their Marxist colleagues have been subjected. Even a cursory look at the problem of racism in the US would note how it has been turned benign and subsumed into a variant of functionalism called critical race theory or conflict theory which, while avoiding the class dimension of the problem, has spawned such solutions as multiculturalism or race analysis without class. However, as noted in one of the chapters below, there has been an observable "return to class" with an appreciable recognition of the historical materialist approach what with the failure of the mainstream approaches to account for trends that are undemocratic, the rise of intolerant groups, the twin phenomena of persistent poverty and inequality with the ubiquitous accumulation of wealth—under the rules of neoliberalism—on the part of the Top One percent of the global population, not through hard work but, rather, through the stroke of a pen, and the sheer anomaly of a state that wants to foster multiculturalism—popular especially among members of the liberal class—within its own society while the same state engages in its own self-righteous acts of gratuitous violence abroad disguised as a war on terror causing unrecompensed death, destruction, and displacement upon a massive number of people, while perfecting the art and science of interrogation and torture in the process; and, without tolerance and with an authoritarian streak, foists its own philosophy of development on others wishing to experiment on other approaches, while it aids and abets its own surrogate allies in the starvation of a population (e.g., in the case of Yemen) or the ethnic cleansing of another (e.g., in the case of Palestine), collective forms of barbarism against these peoples of color. Surely, something is amiss that could not be explained merely by repeating the tenets of modernization theory or functionalism or multiculturalism or by any of the dominant theoretical approaches that have occupied academic discourse in the social sciences during the past half-a-century.

As alluded to above, the revival of the Marxist critical tradition has been noticeable in various disciplines. In the field of literary criticism, this revival is exemplified by the publication of Barbara Foley's *Marxist Literary Criticism Today* (2019), coming after decades of virtual hiatus (with the exception of San Juan) in the field. In its advertisement, Foley's book is described as follows: "In the first introduction to Marxist literary criticism in decades, Barbara Foley argues that Marxism continues to offer the best framework for exploring the relationship between literature and society. She lays out in clear terms the principal aspects of Marxist methodology—historical materialism, political economy, and ideology critique—as well as key debates about the nature of literature and the goals of literary criticism and pedagogy." In the book's Prologue, Foley herself opens with the following words: "Marxism is at once a method of socioeconomic analysis and a call for revolutionary social transformation. It is also an interpretive framework indispensable to an understanding of the relationship between literature and society— and thus, more generally of the connections between ideas, attitudes, and emotions on the one hand and their grounding in historical forces on the other" (Foley). Clearly, thus, historical materialism holds the prospect for an integrated critical understanding of reality that invites practitioners from every discipline; offers a basis for a cross-disciplinary collaboration in lieu of the parochial compartmentalization that has characterized the relations between and among academic disciplines for some time; and, holds the key to providing a possible solution to the persistent problem of inhumanity among humans.

A note on the genesis of this project. This work is both an edited and an expanded version of a project began in the spring of 2015. It was originally intended for a special issue of *Kritika Kultura* dedicated to the works of San Juan for publication the following year, in its Issue No. 26 under the inspired and exemplary editorship of Charlie Samuya Veric. *Kritika Kultura* is a refereed online journal of cultural and literary studies at the Ateneo de Manila University in Quezon City, Philippines. As the completed project was well in excess of the maximum allowable for individual contributions to the special issue, only the first part dealing with themes on the development of capitalism in the seventeenth century up until the Spanish–American War of 1898 could be included. Thus, the excess parts, which included discussions on the US colonization of the Philippines, the racialized nature of the US state, and the structures and principles of neoliberal globalization, languished for a while until the prospect of publishing with Palgrave Macmillan came along. Then, it had to be re-structured and significantly expanded. The result is the current version.

The inspiration for the approach of using annotations, however, came from a source over a century old. In 1888, Dr. Jose Rizal, who would be the Philippines' foremost hero, began his search at the British Museum for a book, entitled, in Spanish, *Sucesos De Las Islas Filipinas* (roughly, *Historical Events of the Philippine Islands*), written by one Dr. Antonio Morga. Rizal eventually found a copy, in two volumes, published in Mexico City by Casa de Geronymo in Balli in 1609. Rizal's interest was in learning how Morga, an influential lay historian and colonial bureaucrat of his time, narrated the history of Spanish colonial administration of the Philippine Islands, the motives behind this colonization, how the Filipinos were portrayed, and the factors attributed for their apparent socioeconomic backwardness. Based on his own research and accumulated knowledge, Rizal then went about the laborious process of annotating the book which, upon completion, he published in Paris in 1889 with the imprint of Garnier Hermanos. Rizal deemed his annotations essential to correcting Morga's views about the Filipinos, their pre-conquest civilization up until 1532, the nature of Spanish colonial policies, and practices, and how these had contributed to the social and economic backwardness of the Filipinos. Without, perhaps, intending it, Rizal had, in fact, through his annotations, written the country's first systematic history from the Philippine viewpoint.

As an impressionable high school student reading Rizal's annotations, I learned early on how even a well-intended work of scholarship like Morga's could have a distorting effect on history. Rizal's earnest efforts at annotating Morga may not have been as famous as his two novels, *Noli Me Tangere* (*Touch Me Not*, 1887), and *El Filibusterismo* (*Subversion*, 1891), but being exposed to Rizal's method nonetheless left an indelible impression on me about the value of history-writing as a vocation. As Morga himself explained in his work, he endeavored at impartiality; yet, Rizal noted that Morga's presuppositions underlined his interpretations and colored his conclusions.

In the same vein, the history being offered here, highlighting the interventions by San Juan at certain junctures in the narration is intended to offer an alternative meaning of history that would otherwise be different without such interventions. Any measure of satisfaction on the part of the reader would be regarded as success. Otherwise, I take full responsibility for any and all shortcomings.

New York, NY, USA Kenneth E. Bauzon
May 2019

References

San Juan, E., Jr., "Man Is a Political Animal" (Poem), *Philippine Collegian*, July 25, 1957.

_____, "Remebrance (sic) of Things Almost Past by An English Major in U.P. (1954–58)", *Manila Times*, March 4, 2012 (Brackets added). Available in: https://www.pressreader.com/@Sonny_Juan/csb_L0zQjf3TvXh9jl-Dbkb dJQjA9aoHqRUmY4P7WHqRRbHnAaDAfuG0og0W4cXya27B?fbclid= IwAR0WOOyGz70ZRWVidDp8xqCpEdYWPdHY1rU3YH9aZnV0ij76ty MIQ-VMzwk.

Acknowledgements

The broad conception for this work began with a contribution to the Special Issue No. 26 (2016) of *Kritika Kultura*, a refereed online journal of cultural criticism of the Ateneo de Manila University, in Quezon City, Philippines, dedicated to the life and works of Prof. E. San Juan Jr. That contribution became foundational to, albeit different from, the present work. With the end in view of preparing a monograph-length manuscript, work continued in earnest. By the fall of 2018, the manuscript, albeit still in raw form, was largely finished. It was at around that time when I was fortuitously contacted by Professor Nassef Manabilang Adiong of the University of the Philippines. A dynamic and exceptional scholar, Dr. Adiong currently serves as Chief Editor of the *International Journal of Islam in Asia* and of the *Islam in the Philippines Publication Series* of the De La Salle University Publishing House, and recently as Chevening Fellow at the Oxford Center for Islamic Studies in Great Britain. My subsequent correspondence with Dr. Adiong has been providential in that it led to a reference, via correspondence, to Professor Jonathan Bayot, Director of the De La Salle University Publishing House, and to Palgrave Macmillan. Thus, it is to Dr. Adiong first and foremost that I offer my heartfelt gratitude for opening the door for the possibility of a publication, and to Professor Bayot and Palgrave Macmillan for their respective decisions, following their requisite reviews, to endorse publication by their respective organizations.

Thoughts contained in this work have been years in gestation. Particularly meaningful have been the intellectually engaging conversations I have had with my colleagues in the Department over many years. To them, I extend my sincere appreciation for their candor and intelligence in sharing their expertise, particularly with Professors Raymond D'Angelo, Chair, and Mirella Landriscina, both sociologists, pertaining largely to race and class; with Professor Richard Torz, economist, pertaining to economic policy and inequality; and, with Professor Stephen Rockwell, political scientist, about the role of US Presidents in the shaping of colonial policy in the Philippines and in the administration of Native Americans, with their implications on the US "pacification" of the Muslim Filipinos.

To Professors E. San Juan Jr. and Delia Aguilar, my gratitude for their abiding friendship over many decades, and for their exemplary lives as intellectual-activists providing inspiration to current and future generations, including the present work.

To Ms. Meridith L. Murray, my appreciation for the competent and invaluable service she provided in preparing the Index.

Last but not least, my eternal gratitude to family members Drs. Leslie and Aurora Bauzon for their lifetime of selfless dedication to my professional success, and to Rosaida, for her affection, support, and understanding as well as for being my source for daily inspiration more than she realizes.

It goes without saying that none of the above are responsible for the views or interpretations expressed herein and that nothing is implied or inferred that they share the same in any way. Any remaining errors that lurk in the following pages are solely my responsibility.

Queens, New York   Kenneth E. Bauzon
June 2019

Contents

1 **Introduction** — 1
   The Problematic of Postcolonialism — 2
   Enlightenment and Empire — 4
   Enlightenment to Neoliberal Globalization — 9
   The Present Task — 14
   References — 20

2 **Background to Colonialism** — 23
   Early Capitalism as Subject of Study — 23
   Colonialism and Racism — 24
   Capitalism and the State — 26
   References — 30

3 **The American Empire in the Pacific** — 31
   Justifications and Rationalizations — 31
   Exploration of the Pacific, and the Pathology of Violence: The Case of the Malolo Massacre — 33
   The Claim to Exceptionalism, Pretext to Imperialism — 53
   1898—The Nexus of Global Events: The Spanish–American War of May 1898, the Philippine Revolution of June 1898, and the Expansion of the US Empire — 59
   References — 73

4	**Denials and Betrayals, Conquest and Capitulation**	77
	The State of the Philippine Revolution at the Point of US Intervention	77
	The Assassination of Bonifacio, the Pact of Biak-na-Bato, and Exile	79
	The Manipulation and Betrayal of Aguinaldo	81
	Aguinaldo Returns from Exile, Proclaims Philippine Independence	85
	Dewey's Plausible Deniability	88
	References	97
5	**The Philippine–American War, 1899–1913, and the US Counterinsurgency and Pacification Campaign**	101
	Pacification of a People "Sitting in Darkness"	101
	Racial Dimension of Pacification	110
	Pacification of Moroland	116
	Laying the Foundation for Racialized State Violence	151
	Laying the Foundation for Colonial Education	153
	References	167
6	**The Cold War and the Post-Cold War Hegemony**	171
	Hegemony Based on Capital Accumulation and Labor Extraction	172
	State of Permanent Warfare	174
	Principles and Institutional Structures of Neoliberal Globalization	176
	Uneven Development and Neoliberal Globalization	180
	References	187
7	**The Racialized State**	191
	Knowledge Production and the Cold War in the United States	191
	Rise of the Neoliberal Pedagogy	194
	The Fetish of Multiculturalism	199
	Denial of Historical Materialism and the Postcolonial Retreat	203
	The Problematization of Race Without Class in the United States	207
	The Recovery of Class, and the Class Basis of Racism	214
	Prognosis	221
	References	237

8	**Teleology in History and Intellectual Responsibility**	241
	The Contemporary State of the World	242
	Recapping Neoliberalism's Rules, and Implications	251
	US Militarism and the Threat of Nuclear Annihilation	254
	Prying Open "Emerging Markets": Corporations as Imperial Tools	258
	Contesting Empire and the Role of Emancipatory Movements	260
	References	261
References		263
Index		285

CHAPTER 1

Introduction

> Any society is founded on the interaction between humans and the natural world in order to transform it according to human needs. The conceptual tools developed in the Marxist tradition enable us to analyze this interaction, to engage in a conceptual mapping of the ensemble of interconnections and the laws of motion that render social phenomena intelligible and open to alteration. Materialist critique adopts a self-reflexive account of the varied interconnections, avoiding any tendency to reify the separations and contacts between different elements of the whole. In this process, the analyst or knower is also examined as part of the critique of the conflict of class ideologies. What this critique foregrounds is the totality of the dynamic contradictions animating class society, not only the major contradictions between the productive forces and social relations, etc., but also the tension between the system of needs of any social formation and the objective circumstances subtending it that underlie class conflict and its myriad sublimations. It is only within this synthesizing framework, complicated by layered mediations, that agency can acquire its measured effectivity.
>
> E. San Juan, *Imperialism and Revolution* (2007)

The Problematic of Postcolonialism

In a 1994 essay, the late Arif Dirlik, extraordinarily gifted historian, mentor, and friend, opened with the question: "When exactly... does the 'postcolonial' begin?" The question was a quote from fellow cultural theorist Ella Shohat, in her probing 1992 essay on postcolonialism, a school of thought in cultural criticism which began its career in the early 1980s but which, by the time of Shohat's essay, had already acquired its orthodox status. The phenomenal ascendancy of postcolonialism to become, in a short period of time, accepted and be part of the Establishment, even to be embraced by conservatives and the corporate community, "has less to do," according to Dirlik, "with its rigorousness as a concept or with the new vistas it has opened up for critical inquiry than it does with the increased visibility of academic intellectuals of Third World origin as pacesetters in cultural criticism"[1] (Dirlik, 329). With this acknowledgment, Dirlik's response to the original question posed, partially facetious, he admits, is: "When Third World intellectuals have arrived in First World academe" (Dirlik, 329).

But the more serious side to Dirlik's response to Shohat's query is one that deserves more attention. Not only does it have bearing to the current work which distinctly bears the stamp of the Third World both on its authorship and its subject; it also provides the critical context with which its purpose may be understood. Near the conclusion of his essay, Dirlik comes back to the question and offers this more profound response, which is: "the emergence of global capitalism, not in the sense of an exact coincidence in time but in the sense that the one is a condition for the other" (Dirlik, 352). This loose consensual reciprocity is indicated by the "absence" of any meaningful criticism on the part of postcolonial intellectuals directed at global capitalism. Dirlik describes this absence as "truly remarkable [because] this relationship, which pertains not only to cultural and epistemological but also to social and political formations, is arguably less abstract and more direct...." (Dirlik, 352). "To put it bluntly," Dirlik concludes, "postcoloniality is designed to *avoid* making sense of the current crisis and, in the process, to cover up the origins of postcolonial intellectuals in a global capitalism of which they are not so much victims as beneficiaries" (Dirlik, 353).

The description of global capitalism offered by Dirlik in his essay exactly a quarter of a century ago remains prescient. He distinguished contemporary global capitalism from the Eurocentric capitalism whose colonialism pretty much directly "worked over" (his phrase) the Third World during the past three centuries. Today, global capitalism serves as a concrete, rather than abstract, basis for a global structuring principle not centered on any one state wherein a private, unaccountable, profit-seeking but state-aided entity—the transnational corporation (TNC)—sees the Third World not as an abstract theme, as postcolonial language would reduce it to, but, rather, as concrete location for "emerging markets" to be exploited but which, as Dirlik views it, as sites also of struggles and resistance, a view complemented by San Juan when he wrote: "Whenever there is imperial domination in any form, historical experience teaches us that *there will always be a 'Third World' subject of resistance and dialectical transcendence*" (San Juan 1995) (italics added). The appearance of TNCs as major international actors occurs at the transformation of the division of labor characterized by "increased spatial extension as well as speed of production to an unprecedented level" (Dirlik, 348). "These same technologies," Dirlik adds, "have endowed capital and production with novel mobility, seeking maximum advantage for capital against labor as well as freedom from social and political interference.... For these reasons, analysts perceive in global capitalism a quantitative difference from past, similar practices – indeed, a new phase of capitalism" (Dirlik, 348–349).

The ascendancy of global capitalism as a global structuring force has had several discernible manifestations, each one related to all others. One of these is the phenomenon of global migration of labor impelled by poverty and oppression at the country of origin and the expectation of better income at the destination. Some governments like that in the Philippines have adopted as official policy the export of warm bodies motivated by the expectation of migrant remittances to boost domestic revenue. Other places, like in Central America, have seen conflicts imposed on peasants and the urban poor to maintain centuries-old land tenure system maintained by a native aristocracy in alliance with generals armed and trained by the United States (US) in the art of counterinsurgency. These are exacerbated by neoliberal rules—including punishing structural adjustment programs, privatization, and trade liberalization—overseen by such institutions as the World Bank, the World Trade Organization (WTO), and regional permutations as the Central American Free Trade Agreement—Dominican Agreement (CAFTA—DR), and the Trans-Pacific Partnership (TPP) all of which prohibit, through their respective charters, the enactment of protectionist national laws that might impede "free trade" under the principle of harmonization which seeks to conform national laws with neoliberal global trading rules overseen and enforced by the WTO. Along with harmonization rules, trading charters also grant investor rights to corporations and diminish whatever rights are there for workers, health and safety standards for consumers, and safeguards for a sustainable environment. In many of the above cases, the work of "economic hit men" has preceded formal negotiations designed to ensnare leaders into accepting terms that, in the end, cede their respective countries' sovereign claim over their resources; failing that, jackals have taken their toll on more than one occasion.

These and similar machinations, repeated and enforced all over the world, have contributed to the common perception, perpetuated by intellectuals in First World academes, not the least of whom are political scientists, that the Westphalian state system has become obsolete. What these observers have failed to note is that while national boundaries are being rendered porous and the sovereignty of smaller states is constantly being battered down, the imperial US state has evolved to a point where it is able to maintain its autonomy from these vicissitudes; not only that, it has managed to maintain a global hegemony—in its political, military, and economic manifestations—as though its maintenance is dependent on the dissolution of the sovereignty o f all others, except that of its close allies and surrogates. Because its power is second to none at this moment in its history, it has been able to summon at will its disciplinary authority at the world stage, defining its own rules and undermining any shred of international law governing civilized behavior. It has become law unto itself. To understand how this current situation has come to be, I suggest that we discuss and bring to light the thoughts and ideas that have provided its essential foundation, commencing with the Enlightenment.

Enlightenment and Empire

In the lead chapter of my 1991 book, I wrote the following: "Knowledge about society has been among the main goals of philosophers and social scientists, especially since the advent of the Enlightenment. Modern science has its origins during this period… Whereas before, the method of learning was speculative and ritualistic based on the assumption that a cosmic and social order determined the nature of human destiny, the modern period is rooted in the optimistic belief that human nature is shaped by man himself. If, therefore, man goes about constructing a society according to his image of it and exploits all the resources at his command, he can control nature, regularize his behavior, and predict the outcome" (Bauzon 1991, 3).

The subject of the Enlightenment and its relationship to empire has, unfortunately, eluded generations of critical scholarly scrutiny for at least the following three reasons, as follows: (1) Focus on the political and social thought of Enlightenment thinkers has traditionally concentrated on their ideas on politics, society, the nature of man, and reason or rationality—represented by Cartesian dualism alluded to in the above quote—being assumed to be uniquely endowed to man; (2) Foci on these and related subjects by various thinkers have been of a Eurocentric nature emphasizing, wittingly or unwittingly, the accomplishments and superiority of European civilization, and the deterministic conflation between mankind's future with European progress; and (3) contemporary commentators and interpreters who admire Enlightenment thinkers for their advocacy of individual freedom, in a political sense, often conflate it with nary a doubtful thought with free markets, or capitalism. In other words, the principles and practices of capitalism are deemed consonant with those of democracy. Consequently, the study of Enlightenment social and political theory has often allowed to slip by thoughts and ideas that rationalized colonialism, seen as a natural extension of man's endeavor to exploit "all resources at his command" but which, in its essence, is undemocratic (Bauzon 1991, 3). Further, colonialism was seen as a vehicle to assert the universality of Enlightenment values through the "civilizing" process and the taking up of the so-called White Man's Burden or as embodied in the French civilizing mission. Meanwhile, the expansion of liberal rights and the supposed improvement in the quality of life among Europeans within Europe proper were generally celebrated apart from and without regard to the violence and plunder being inflicted at the edges of the empire.

Typical of Enlightenment thinkers was John Locke, a liberal darling of the West whose ideas about political representation, separation of powers, and the right of citizens to rise up against a tyrannical government have found their way enshrined into Western—including United States—constitutions and laws. What has not gained equal attention has been his economic ideas justifying, in today's language, the privatization and commodification of the commons, acquisition of property through, among others, the enclosure movement; his racist predisposition toward indigenous peoples in the New World who, in his view, were lacking both in the capacity to reason and to labor; and his contributions to the flourishing of the slave-plantation complex. I make note of these in my 2016 article wherein I wrote, in reference to Chapter V of his 1690 essay, *Second Treatise on Government*, dealing with the subject of property: "Locke quite literally and figuratively unlocked the mystery of how to turn the commons, which he acknowledged as God's gift to all of humanity, into private property. He writes, in Section 26: 'God, who hath given the world to men in common hath also given them *reason* to make use of it to the best advantage of life, and convenience'" (Bauzon 2016, 416) (italics added). Further, Locke developed his conception of money, essential to the then-budding mercantile trade, as a representation of value created by labor as well as a means to facilitate acquisition and appropriation of property, especially in the New World, in which the indigenous population—or Native Americans—would be the primary victims. "The native Americans," I wrote further in the same piece, "were simply not meant to be served by this conception of appropriation, for the necessary twin brother of this is the dispossession of the native peoples" (Bauzon 2016, 417).

Locke was not the only prominent Enlightenment thinker justifying colonialism and empire. In 1752, David Hume wrote, in an essay on commerce: "The greatness of a state, and the happiness of its subjects, how independent soever they may be supposed in some respects, are commonly allowed to be inseparable with regard to commerce; and as private men receive greater security, i n the possession of their trade and riches, from the power of the public, so the public becomes powerful in proportion to the opulence and extensive commerce of private men" (Hume). Further down in the same essay, Hume adds: "As the ambition of the sovereign must entrench on the luxury of individuals, so the luxury of individuals must diminish the force, and check the ambition of the sovereign… The same method of reasoning will let us see the advantages of foreign commerce, in augmenting the power of the state, as well as the riches and happiness of the subject" (Hume).

The two above quotes from Hume exemplify and validate my earlier observation that the liberties that Europeans have come to enjoy have been seen to be codependent with their ability to carry out foreign commerce, which has brought them opulence. Further, as Hume openly suggests, the success of the state and the well-being of its subject are intertwined, with the latter presumed to have the ability to "check the ambition" of the former. Hume, thus, clearly identified himself not only as a proponent of commerce but also, as Singapore-based scholar Onur Ulas Ince describes, in an illuminating essay, as "champion of modern commercial civility" (Ince 2018, 108). The description of Hume by Ince is not by happenstance. It reflects the emerging debate during Hume's time among intellectual circles in Europe regarding the relationship between liberal ideas, on the one hand,

and commercial activities particularly with regard to slavery and the use of force as empire expanded, on the other. To Ince, this represented Hume's "conundrum" which Ince explains as follows: "Hume's writings on commerce and empire provide us with a window onto the challenges posed to metropolitan conceptions of commercial civility by imperial instantiations of commercial incivility in the eighteenth century" (Ince 2018, 108). Here, Ince contends that the "colonial plantation slavery" was one such instance that challenged Hume's conception of civil commerce. This practice, Ince writes, "constituted at once a powerful engine of global commerce *and* an uncivil institution that contravened the conventions of modern European civility that global commerce had made possible." Ince, however, found a loophole in Hume's logic which allowed him essentially to resolve this conundrum without much intellectual anguish. As Ince explains in the rest of his essay: "I maintain that Hume treated slavery principally as a moral and political problem, disavowing its economic centrality to the modern world of global commerce. This took the form of diverting attention from the modern, commercial incarnation of slavery (the colonial-capitalist plantation), and confining the discussion of this practice almost exclusively to its ancient, feudal or Asiatic variants" (Ince 2018, 109).

One might say, as Ince also does, that Hume's critique of slavery represents at that time the typical "liberal critique" of that institution as well as that of the empire that it sustained. By diverting attention, as Ince suggests, to its "ancient, feudal or Asiatic variants," it had little rationale to stop it nor did it mitigate the violence that accompanied the growth and expansion of empire, failing to recognize the inevitable entwinement between global commerce and empire, and between liberalism and capitalism. Despite the emerging critique of empire, particularly as the eighteenth-century manifestations of the Enlightenment came around, European empires, relying on their unmitigated use of force and on their respective trading companies which they have chartered, continued to encroach not only along the Atlantic but also in South and Southeast Asia, strengthening the global capitalist network designed to facilitate the extraction of raw materials, the transfer of wealth, and the remaking of the subject colonies after the European image. As to the prevalence of "barbarism" that accompanied the growth of these empires, the British most notably, Ince, offers a sobering observation to help his readers, including myself, make sense of it in the following words: this barbarism "represented neither a temporal relapse into more primitive attitudes of cruelty nor a spatial exodus from the domain of civility that was coextensive with Western Europe. Rather than an anomaly to Western commercial civility, *it constituted a dynamic internal to the historical emergence of global capitalist relations within the politico-legal framework of colonial empires*"[2] (Ince 2018, 133–134) (italics added). This barbarism was not lost on Fyodor Dostoyevsky who also noted, in his travels to Europe, the moral malaise that the Western Europeans seemed to embrace despite advances in knowledge and concomitant economic progress. Through the words of the character of Mikhail Osipovich Rakitin, a seminary student, conversing with another character, Alyosha (Karamazov), in an early draft of *Brothers Karamazov* (1880), published the year before his death, Karamazov captured the essence if not the irony of the Enlightenment, at least on the part of those that conflated it with colonialism and progress, in the following words: "Well then, eliminate the people, curtail them, force them to be silent. Because the European Enlightenment is more important than people" (as quoted in Treadgold, 207).

That the opulence achieved by Europe and, later, North America owing to the growth of their industry has been undeniable. Further, the expansion of European mercantile trade with the rest of the world alongside the conquest and colonization of other people's lands, aided by the state as illustrated by the enactment of British navigation laws, has also been a well-established fact. The so-called free trade has not been the success it was without state intervention in behalf of merchants, traders, manufacturers, and, in general, the capitalist class. The Invisible Hand was a mere figment of Adam Smith's imagination. As legal historian Michael E. Tigar notes, the tradition of state intervention in commerce has been a carryover from feudal times through Middle Ages when merchants lobbied their respective principalities to enact laws favorable to the rising merchant class, laws which later evolved to be part of Western international law. This was exemplified by the Crusaders—the Templars in particular—seeking state protection of the trade routes they had either seized or developed, along with the bounty they had accumulated. (Tigar, 35). With the advent of the modern era dominated by Enlightenment ideas on human progress, along with the formal abolition of feudalism throughout Europe, e.g., the 1789 decree of the French National Assembly, and the 1804 Napoleonic Code, both seeking lineage with Charlemagne's 1215 Magna Carta. Giving his imprimatur to evolving marriage between the state and commerce, French magistrate Charles de Secondat Montesquieu offered the following words, as quoted by Tigar:

The natural effect of commerce is to bring peace... The spirit of commerce brings with it that of frugality, economy, moderation, work, wisdom, tranquility, law, and order.... In order to maintain the spirit of commerce, it is necessary that the principal citizens engage in it themselves, and that its spirit rule alone, unhindered by any other, and that all the laws favor it. (as quoted in Tigar, 219)

Thus, at least in the four centuries since the Enlightenment began, and among the European states, extensive laws were passed, institutions were created, practices were established, and rationales were elaborated that facilitated and justified the extraction of wealth from the peripheries of empire to its center. Karl Marx wrote his astute observation of this process in Chapter 31, Volume 1 of his *Capital* (1867) in the following words: "The discovery of gold and silver in America, the extirpation, enslavement and entombment in mines of the aboriginal population, the beginning of the conquest and looting of the East Indies, the turning of Africa into a warren for the commercial hunting of black skins, signalised the *rosy dawn* of the era of capitalist production" (Marx) (italics added).

Enlightenment to Neoliberal Globalization

Having identified Hume as an example of a liberal critic of slavery (of a distant sort), and of imperialism (though not so much of the inevitable capitalist commerce that ensued from it), does not imply that criticisms were confined to him and/or his contemporaries, among whom was Edmund Burke. Burke, as member, in 1781, of the Select Committee of the Commons investigating the actuation of the British East India Company, excoriated the company for its arrogant and "plunderous" practices in the Asian subcontinent (Ince 2018, 133). In fact, over a century earlier, a Jewish dissident intellectual, born to Jewish merchant-parents fleeing as refugees from persecution of the Catholic Inquisition in Portugal to Holland, and then banished from his own Jewish community for his unconventional—even heretical—views, Baruch (also Benedict de) Spinoza (1632–1677) became a source of such criticisms manifest throughout his works, chief of which was his *Ethics* (1677), reputed to be one of the masterpieces to come out of the Enlightenment period, written as his way of demystifying the interrelationships between nature, man, and God. In combating what he regarded as superstitions during his time, and promoting reason, he postulated, among others, that God is nature, deemed as a metaphysical rather than as matter. He also rejected the notion that God took on a human form for the reason that the human body, just like the rest of nature, is the extension of God's essence. What has made Spinoza salient to contemporary thinkers, after about two centuries of obscurity following his death, has been his political views—as a political scientist—and, in particular, his views on democracy, laws, the concept of "multitude," and the role it plays in the shaping of a political order. In his *Political Treatise* (published posthumously in 1677), Spinoza declares that his aim was to explore the possibilities by which a "commonwealth" may be "so ordered that, whether the people who administer them are led by reason or by an affect, they *can't* be induced to be disloyal *or* act badly." His personal experience with the "people" or the "multitude," used in his treatise as a central conceptual framework, was given real meaning when the de Witt brothers, Johan and Cornelius, personal friends to Spinoza, were lynched in August 1672 at a courthouse in the Hague, not far from his home. Johan was, at the time, the de facto head of state of the Dutch Republic, and Cornelius was a successful career naval officer, scoring repeated victories against the British navy while serving as Deputy to Admiral Michiel de Ruyter, remembered as one of the most skilled naval officers in Dutch history. After having been at the helm of the Dutch ship of state guiding it to what is referred to as the Dutch Golden Age, characterized by the dominance of the Dutch East India Company of the trade routes to and from Asia, the de Witt brothers succumbed to the long-standing rivalry between the so-called Orange monarchists, Calvinist in their orientation, on the one hand, and the republican-oriented merchant class, to which the de Witt brothers were identified, on the other. The hysteria against the de Witt brothers and the state that they led had them as scapegoat and accused of treason for the weakened state of readiness against the twin threats of imminent British invasion from sea and French incursion by land. The spectacle of a lynch mob apparently impressed negatively upon Spinoza, and this challenged his desire to establish a "community of free men" (Melamed and Sharp, 5). Nonetheless, in his *Political Treatise*, he dedicated himself to resolving the problem of controlling passions and harnessing them (these passions) toward common good, leading him to develop his principle of *conatus* (power). But just as he was concerned with controlling the passions of the multitude, he was particularly concerned with the passions of political leaders and statesmen that lead them to corruption and who disrespect the law, sacrificing common interest for their private ends and turning "civil order into a state of hostility" (as quoted in Melamed and Sharp, 6).

Spinoza's thoughts have, interestingly, taken center stage in the trilogy of works by Michael Hardt and Antonio Negri commencing with *Empire* (2000), followed by *Multitude* (2004), and, finally, *Commonwealth* (2009). In this massive undertaking, Hardt and Negri have sought to explain and help their readers make sense of contemporary neoliberal globalization. In the first of their trilogy, *Empire*, Hardt and Negri describe the concept of empire in a way that might surprise many. In their Preface, they open with the words: "Empire is materializing before our eyes" yet they do not associate this with any territorially based empire as it was in the previous three centuries. Rather, they explain that "[a]long with the global market and global circuits of production has emerged a global order, a new logic and structure of rule – in short, a new form of sovereignty. Empire is the political subject that effectively regulates these global exchanges, the sovereign power that governs the world" (Hardt and Negri 2000, vi). They then make the qualification that while the sovereignty of the rest is diminishing, reduced to surrogacy, the sovereignty of this empire, deterritorialized as we speak, is increasing and "has taken a new form, composed of a series of national and supranational organisms united under a single logic of rule. This new global form of sovereignty is what we call Empire" (Hardt and Negri 2000, xii). They deny that the United States is the center of this new imperialist project. With this emergent new order along with its "enormous powers of oppression and destruction," one should not despair. Hardt and Negri assure us that "[t]he passage to Empire and its processes of globalization offer new possibilities to the forces of liberation. Globalization, of course, is not one thing, and the multiple processes that we recognize as globalization are not unified or univocal" (Hardt and Negri 2000, xv). The multitude has a task to do:

> Our political task, we will argue, is not simply to resist these processes but to reorganize them and redirect them towards new ends. The creative forces of the multitude that sustain empire are also capable of autonomously constructing a counter-Empire, an alternative political organization of global flows and exchanges. The struggles to contest and subvert Empire, as well as those to construct a real alternative, will thus take place on the imperial terrain itself – indeed, such new struggles have already begun to emerge. (Hardt and Negri 2000, xv)

Hardt's and Negri's deployment of concepts from Spinoza is duly acknowledged, most notably the concepts of sovereignty, democracy, and multitude. Hardt and Negri restate an axiom that Spinoza has observed, i.e., that the form of government is of little consequence—be it monarchy, aristocracy, or democracy—because in the final analysis "only one" ends up ruling: the monarch for the monarchy, the few for the aristocracy, and the many for democracy (Hardt and Negri 2004, 328). In this respect, sovereignty as a dominant concept in traditional political philosophy serves as "the foundation of all" because "one must always rule and decide" (Hardt and Negri 2004, 329). However, a surprising turn occurs when it comes to applying Spinoza's concept of multitude, Hardt and Negri appear to back off and come up with their own interpretation, leaving Spinoza behind. Hardt and Negri write:

> We insisted earlier that the multitude is not a social body for precisely this reason: that the multitude cannot be reduced to a unity and does not submit to the rule of one. The multitude cannot be sovereign. For this same reason, the democracy that Spinoza calls absolute cannot be considered a form of government in the traditional sense because it does not reduce the plurality of everyone to the unitary figure of sovereignty. From the strictly practical, functional point of view, the tradition tells us, multiplicities cannot make decisions for society and are thus not relevant for politics proper. (Hardt and Negri 2004, 330)

With the general acclaim that the trilogy has received, particularly *Empire*, and the instant international celebrity status conferred on Hardt and Negri by the corporate media and the academic establishment, one wonders if their work is supposed to provide a radical alternative, in any practical sense, to the existing imperial order that they describe. Despite Hardt's and Negri's reputation as intellectual activists, with Hardt ensconced in his position as professor of literature and Italian studies at Duke University, in Durham, North Carolina, United States, and Negri as an established figure in Italian politics, having personally suffered persecution and actual imprisonment in the aftermath of the murder of Italian Prime Minister Aldo Moro in March 1978 by the Red Brigades, the trilogy does not exhibit the sharp critical edge of a Marxist analyst. It does not even acknowledge historical materialism as the starting point of this analysis as though consciously shy about it. The multitude referred to in the work is not the working class that Marx alludes to as the progenitor of revolution. Hardt and Negri seem to fail in making a distinction between the high-profile protests in Seattle, Washington, against the WTO or in Genoa, Italy, against the G8 Ministerial Conference, on the one hand, and the down-to-earth resistance to neoliberal policies, e.g., water privatization in Cochabamba, Bolivia, land privatization in Chiapas, Mexico, and the diminution of food sovereignty in the Third World through food patenting by the heavily subsidized and globally verticalized biotech and food producing industry. More significantly, Hardt and Negri seem to ignore altogether the role of genuine anti-capitalist and anti-imperialist revolutionary movements in the peripheries of empire, the sort of movement led by Che Guevara, Ho Chi Minh, and Amilcar Cabral, movements that have borne the savage brunt of this empire but which have remained resilient in their resistance through revolutionary violence. By not identifying the United States as an empire in its own right, history, and motives, Hardt and Negri, in effect, absolve it of any culpability, and by identifying abstractly the network of global neoliberal institutions, e.g., the WTO and an assortment of regional trading schemes, the World Bank and the IMF and their regional surrogates like the Asian Development Bank, as "organisms," they also fail to assign proper blame to these reactionary institutions that have, in a concrete sense, performed well in propping up what should rightly be described as the American empire and have ignored the actual dynamics and mechanisms by which this empire has used these to its advantage. In invoking Spinoza, they have, in fact, blunted the edges of his critical philosophy against empire, even implying that, in the domestic scene, he was an advocate of conformity to the "universalistic" norms (or common culture in today's multiculturalist terminology) of a liberal state, based on his presumed experience as a member of a discriminated minority community in Holland, thus turning him, in effect, a defender of the status quo. In reality, Spinoza was anything but this. In the Preface to *Commonwealth*, Hardt and Negri rationalize this project as follows: "With the title of this book…, we mean to indicate a return to some of the themes of classic treatises of government, exploring the institutional structure and political constitution o f society" (Hardt and Negri 2009, xiii). Then i n Part 4 of the same book, in the chapter "Metropolis," Hardt and Negri develop the concept of the metropolis as "the skeleton and spinal cord of the multitude [a term they derive from Spinoza but which they use to mean simply "humanity"], that is, the built environment that supports its activity, and the social environment that constitutes a repository and skill set of affects, social relations, habits, desires, knowledges, and cultural circuits" (Hardt and Negri 2009, 149). They add: "The metropolis not only inscribes and reactivates the multitude's past – its subordinations, suffering and struggles – but also poses the conditions, positive and negative, for its future.... We understand the metropolis... as the inorganic body, that is, the body without organs of the multitude" (Hardt and Negri 2009, 149).

The essence of the above-quoted passages from Hardt's and Negri's series of books is not missed by San Juan who regards Spinoza's philosophy of freedom as an essential "intellectual weapon for the victims of imperial power, a resource of hope against nihilism and fatalistic commodification" (San Juan 2004, 344). San Juan further cites the "inalienability" of Spinoza's principle of human rights arguing that it "can renew the impulse for reaffirming the ideal of radical, popular democracy, and the self-determination of communities and nations" (San Juan 2004, 344–345). However, when San Juan turns his critical attention to Hardt's and Negri's application of Spinoza's notion of multitude as a vehicle for the "democracy for the multitude," and he discovers that Hardt's and Negri's democratic multitude requires "no external mediation by any organization or party" and that, San Juan continues, "the multitude's constituent power somehow will by itself actualize desire in action in a possible form of direct democracy as the absolute form of government" (San Juan 2004, 345). This flaw illustrates the vagueness and indeterminacy of Hardt's and Negri's proposed attempt at constructing an alternative "commonwealth," complementing the abstraction with which they define "empire" and the liberty they take in interpreting Spinoza's notion of "multitude."

The Present Task

Given the foregoing discussion, the remainder of this work seeks to critically identify the dual legacy of the Enlightenment as having brought progress to Europe and colonization to much of the rest of the world touched by colonialism. It seeks to draw the continuity between European dominance over the past four hundred years, on the one hand, and America's contemporary global hegemony, on the other. While the former was accomplished through direct control of the subject peoples, the latter is sustained through a series of semi-autonomous institutions operating under rules and principles that allow the United States a predominant voice and influence within them. More importantly, the present work seeks to understand historical and intellectual antecedents, particularly those that happened prior to the twentieth century as the young American republic ventured out into the

Caribbean and the Pacific in fulfillment of a role that was understood to be manifest, shaping how it emerged as the preeminent empire that it is today. It seeks to validate a belief on my part but which was articulated by Ince in an above quote, repeated here as follows: that the resort to force constitutes, as it has constituted, "*a dynamic internal to the historical emergence of global capitalist relations within the politico-legal framework of colonial empires*" (Ince 2018, 133–134) (italics added).

Along these lines, to be featured early in the discussion, is America's use of force in 1840 in the Fiji island group, herein taken as setting the pattern for the use of force against peoples of color outside what was considered the US proper, but paralleling the use of similar force against the indigenous peoples and the descendants of black slaves within the US mainland. But understanding the use of force accompanying the emergence of the United States as an empire would not be complete without the use of guile, ruse, and deception short of the use of force. One or the other of these means has been used, and historians have duly noted them as in the US pretense to aid and assist the Cuban revolutionaries in their effort to overthrow Spanish colonial rule in 1898, only to own Cuba motivated by the broader motive to assert hegemony over the Caribbean region and, in particular, to claim a stake in the future of the Panama Canal. Cuba would be "freed" only under the nefarious conditions laid down in the infamous Platt Amendment of 1903, crafted by then Secretary of War Elihu Root and introduced to the Senate by Connecticut Senator Orville Platt as a rider to the Army Appropriations Bill of 1901, adopted by the US Congress, and signed into law on May 22, 1903.[3] The amendment promised independence to Cuba only if, among others, Cuba would agree to allow the United States to intervene in Cuban affairs at any time the United States deemed necessary; if it agreed not to borrow money from foreign sources without the permission of the US Congress to defray its own expenses, including debts; and if it allowed the United States to establish a military base (subject to subsequent negotiations, resulting in the establishment of the Guantanamo base the agreement under which may be nullified only upon *mutual consent* of both parties, meaning, in practice, from the US standpoint, never). To an observant historian, this is typical of the unequal treaties imposed by European colonial powers on their hapless colonies wanting independence throughout much of the nineteenth century, lasting through the mid-twentieth century, and the American behavior in this particular case is in no way exceptional to that by its European competitors.

The overthrow of the Hawaiian monarchy in 1893 wherein the US Navy, in effect, outsourced the task of overthrowing the Hawaiian monarchy under conditions of plausible deniability to a private group of thirteen US citizens many of whom also happened to be descendants of God-fearing and Bible-thumping lay missionaries, Samuel Northrup Castle and Amos Starr Cooke, landed in Hawaii as part o f he American Board of Commissioners for Foreign Missions. In 1851, Castle and Cooke formed a business partnership, initially operating a department store. The partnership has since grown into one of the world's leading producer of fresh agricultural products.

Members of the above-named private group, organized into an Orwellian-type clandestine organization called the Citizen's Committee of Public Safety, were motivated by their desire to have Hawaiian land, at the time under communal ownership protected by the monarchy, declared open to privatization; they also envisioned ultimate annexation of Hawaii, under their leadership into the United States. For its part, the US Navy, influenced by Alfred Thayer Mahan's ideas about US Navy-led imperialism in the Pacific, began asserting its presence in the Pacific vis-à-vis European competitors. Essential to this program is the acquisition of a much-coveted deep water port, in a protective cove, in Hawaii which came to be known as Pearl Harbor. The coup against the Hawaiian monarchy made this acquisition a reality.

By the time the US acquired the Philippines in the aftermath of the Spanish-American War in 1898, the United States appeared to have the knack and appetite for more easy victories. The dynamics and speed with which the American Empire established itself as a Pacific power was a realization of the Tyler Doctrine promulgated by President John Tyler in a special message to the US Congress on December 30, 1842, barely two-and-a-half years after the Malolo Massacre, in which the United States sought to replicate in the Pacific the Monroe Doctrine designed for the Caribbean and the Americas in general.[4] The Tyler Doctrine invoked how the inhabitants of the Sandwich Islands (now Hawaii) needed US protection, but behind which was the desire to satisfy the need of US whaling vessels plying Pacific waters for a coaling station and the protection of the US navy from potential competitors, a guise for securing—albeit as a latecomer relative to European competitors—the broader economic and commercial interests of the United States around the Pacific rim, particularly China.

What will be described below will all sound very familiar to the Native Americans who have been subjected not only wanton violence but also to chicanery, false promises, deceptions, duplicities, and broken treaties throughout much of their history dealing with the US government. This commences with the arbitrary action by Spain in 1898 to cede—and the United States agreeing to purchase—the entirety of the Philippines, a territory over which it had little or no effective control by 1898, except for a fort in Manila (called Intramuros). In a manner that paralleled US actions in Cuba, under pretense of humanitarianism and military assistance against a colonial power, the United States, in effect, duped the leadership of the Philippine Revolution, again under conditions of plausible deniability, by appearing to provide small arms to the Filipino rebels and causing them to expect independence after the overthrow of Spain, only to be pursued in a vicious counterinsurgency campaign leading to the death of over a million Filipinos—both noncombatant civilians and rebels—in the immediate years that followed. The final act was the conquest and pacification of the Moroland over which Spain never exercised effective sovereignty in its more than three centuries of colonization of the Philippines but which Spain arbitrarily included in the sale to the United States. This process saw the duping of the Sultan of Sulu, yet again under conditions of plausible deniability, through a misleading translation of the Bates Treaty, by a German national hired as translator on a retainership by the US military and whose family maintained agricultural and commercial interests in Sulu, causing the latter (the Sultan of Sulu) to believe his sovereignty over the Sulu Sultanate would be respected by the United States. The US military's duplicity in Sulu was followed by the pacification of both the Maguindanao Sultanate in the heartland of Mindanao as well as the Maranao Sultanate, in the Lake Lanao region of northern Mindanao, through an assortment of tactics as cooptation, divide and rule, and, when peaceable means failed, scorched-earth methods against recalcitrant *datus* (chieftains) and their villages, invoking US conceptions of law and order held to be applicable in the southern Philippine setting as well as the rest of the country for that matter.

The pacification of the Philippines and of the Moroland, in particular, has been held up *ad nauseum* as models of counterinsurgency by US-based military historians, and the tactics and strategies developed, along with the experience gained, during the Philippine campaigns have been found to be instructive enough for inclusion in series of field manuals in most, if not all, of the services of the US military, e.g., army, marines, navy, and air force. Policing has also benefited from the experience particularly with the establishment of the Philippine Constabulary, later to influence the formation of the Moro Constabulary, both reactionary quasi-military police forces useful not only in pursuing rebels and bandits alike short of the full use of the military but also in gathering intelligence and for the monitoring of village population in the service of the foreign occupier. These studies, however, presume the moral ascendancy of the US colonial order, the inherent evil or misguided nature of the forces opposed to it, e.g., the anti-imperialist resistance, and the ahistorical manner in which they disseminate knowledge to generations of readers. Under these conditions, the US-led "war on terror," especially since 9/11 at the peak of American unilateralism, has been conducted in a manner that the United States has virtually been unchallenged in defining who the enemy is, and in not being held accountable for the innocent lives taken in the name of this "war." Moreover, this war on terror has spawned the growth of anti-terror-related industry producing new weaponry and surveillance equipment, strengthening the hand of the state but eroding civil liberties.

The academia has not been left unaffected as various institutions, often with funding from government agencies or in collaboration with them, have established anti-terrorism-related research institutes. Semi-independent and semi-private research institutes have also been founded for similar purpose, often making themselves available for commission, and for a fee, to conduct studies on the causes and nature of terrorism either in general or in specific cases. Many of these organizations conduct political forecasting studies or risk analyses in behalf of security-related government agencies or corporations wishing to make the best investment decisions under conditions of neoliberal globalization. What is common to all these institutions is their use of social science techniques, appearing to the both empirical and dispassionate about which the academicians and researchers feel good. What is not recognized, however, is the virtual weaponization of an entire discipline—social science—deployed at the service of institutions that serve as props for the neoliberal order and affirming, directly or indirectly, the central role that the American Empire plays in maintaining it.

This study seeks to highlight episodes in the rise of the American empire in the Pacific, particularly in the Philippines, that usually get ignored or papered over by mainstream historians. However, this goal is secondary to the broader purpose of drawing links between capitalism as a system of accumulation of value, the American empire as the preeminent state that ensures the persistence of this system amidst potential competing systems, and the contemporary neoliberal globalization, as a reincarnation of classical colonialism, and invested with all the *accoutrements* essential to conquer the commons for private profit, and, in the process, negate the meaning of "public" from daily vocabulary as institutions of the state are converted as conduit of public funds for private corporate welfare, all under the watchful guidance and supervision of the American empire.

By defining its goals as such, I seek to align this work with those by others who have labored to affirm the emancipatory purpose of knowledge production and to contrast it to those who seek to place it at the employ of the neoliberal global order. It is hoped that the reader gets the sense of what history means to San Juan who recognizes that history's teleology and trajectory, rather than unilinear, are dialectically characterized "by all kinds of cleavages, ruptures, discontinuities [to which humanity is subjected] inherited from the past and reproduced daily by the unequal division of international labor and distribution of resources" (San Juan 1995). San Juan agrees with Edward Said that much of these disruptions have emanated as a result of European colonial intervention. San Juan writes: "In *Orientalism* and *Culture and Imperialism*, Said has cogently shown how the Western epistemological construction of Other in the various disciplines serves the goal of asserting its own supremacy. The modalities of the West's representation of other peoples do not furnish objective knowledge; instead they fulfill the historical agenda of confirming the ascendant identity of the British, the French, the European in general, over against non-Western/non-Christian peoples" (San Juan 1995).

Put in another way, the dominant Western idea of history is premised on the Enlightenment concept of progress, with science playing a central role in the production of knowledge, in the mastery over nature, and in the art of governance. The logical culmination of this is the subordination of the individual to the state, and that of the Other to the Self, that Said was describing. To San Juan, history's teleological orientation connotes a dialectical struggle wherein the individual gains, in an immediate sense, liberation from Western colonial and imperial domination. San Juan writes: "'National liberation' is the phrase I used earlier to counterpoint transnational postmodernism. Why can we in the Third World not skip this stage since 'nation' and 'nationalism' have acquired dangerous, pejorative implications in the West? Because it sutures the fragments of colonized lives in popular-democratic mobilization and so creates the historic agency for change. Otherwise no collective transformation, only individual conversions. Its negativity possesses a positive side: it restores what [Mikhail] Bakhtin calls 'the dialogical principle' as the matrix of social practices" (San Juan 1995) (bracket added).

Notes

1. On the salience of the Third World as a specific place of origin for many artists and scholars who now find themselves in the "belly of the beast," San Juan offers the following reflections, writing in the last decade of the twentieth century: "Amid the ruins left by the whirlwinds of this century, we find writers from the 'Third World' (the term is itself a survival of the Cold War era) still writing/unwriting places, giving their habitations distinctive names and singular histories. From inside the 'belly of the beast' (to evoke the great Jose Marti's sense of displacement), I offer the following notes as homage to those kindred spirits, heirs of the rebellious Caliban, who are carrying on their struggle to map on the terrain of the imagination the space for the memoirs, sacrifices, and hopes of multitudes." This homage is Chapter 9, "Beyond Postmodernism; Notes on 'Third World' Discourse on Resistance," in *Hegemony and Strategies of Transgression: Essays in Cultural Studies and Comparative Literature* (Albany, NY: State University of New York Press, 1995), p. 193. Later in the same chapter, San Juan offers reassuring words as well as advice to the "kindred spirits" as follows: "For peoples who are victims of the 'modernist project' of mastery over nature and all 'the rest', it is less a matter of figuring out whether or not postmodernist styles can signify their lived experience as one of defining first their collective predicament as non-represented or unrepresentable in the present global hierarchy of power. Subalterns have to seize the means, the occasions, to invent their own strategy of resistance and self-presentations. The key lies in the nature of the modalities of representation and their geopolitical valence" (ibid., 201).
2. To these thoughts, San Juan adds: "*Beginning from the rise of merchant capital in the seventeenth and eighteenth cen*turies, the messianic impulse to genocide springs from the imperative of capital accumulation—the imperative to reduce humans to commodified labor-power, to saleable goods or services". See his *U.S. Imperialism and Revolution in the Philippines* (New York: Palgrave Macmillan, 2007), p. xv.
3. For facsimile of original copy, see: https://www.ourdocuments.gov/doc.php?flash=false&doc=55#.
4. For text of the Tyler Doctrine, see: https://loveman.sdsu.edu/docs/1842TylerDoctrine.pdf.

References

Bauzon, Kenneth E., *Liberalism and the Quest for Islamic Identity in the Philippines* (Durham, NC: Acorn Press in Association with Duke University Islamic and Arabian Development Studies, 1991), 219pp. Print.

———, "Themes from the History of Capitalism to the Rise of the US Empire in the Pacific, with Annotations from Selected Works of E. San Juan, Jr.", *Kritika Kultura*, 26 (2016): 408–443. In: https://www.researchgate.net/publication/301338166_THEMES_FROM_THE_HISTORY_OF_CAPITALISM_TO_THE_RISE_OF_THE_US_EMPIRE_IN_THE_PACIFIC_With_Annotations_from_Selected_Works_of_E.

Dirlik, Arif, "The Postcolonial Aura: Third World Criticism in the Age of Global Capitalism", *Critical Inquiry*, 20, 2 (Winter 1994): 328–356. In: http://jan.ucc.nau.edu/sj6/dirlikpocoaura.pdf.

Hardt, Michael and Antonio Negri, *Commonwealth* (Harvard University Press, 2009), 434pp. PDF version available in: http://www.thing.net/~rdom/ucsd/biopolitics/Commonwealth.pdf.

———, *Commonwealth* (Cambridge, MA: Belknap Press, 2010), 448pp. PDF version available in: http://www.thing.net/~rdom/ucsd/biopolitics/Commonwealth.pdf.

———, *Empire* (Cambridge, MA: Harvard University Press, 2000), 478pp. PDF version available in: http://www.angelfire.com/cantina/negri/HAREMI_printable.pdf.

———, (Cambridge, Mass: Harvard University Press, 2009), 434pp. PDF version available in:

———, *Multitude; War and Democracy in the Age of Empire* (New York: Penguin Books, 2004), 448pp. PDF version available in: http://rebels-library.org/files/multitude.pdf.

Ince, Onur Ulas, "Between Commerce and Empire: David Hume, Colonial Slavery and Commercial Incivility", *History of Political Thought*, 39, 1 (Spring 2018): 107–134. In: http://www.ulasince.com/wp-content/uploads/2018/02/Ince-2018-Between-Commerce-and-Empire.pdf.

San Juan, E., Jr., *Hegemony and Strategies of Transgression: Essays in Cultural Studies and Comparative Literature* (Albany, NY: State University of New York Press, 1995), 286pp.

———, *U.S. Imperialism and Revolution in the Philippines* (New York: Palgrave Macmillan, 2007), 265pp. Print.

———, *Working Through Contradictions: From Cultural Theory to Critical Practice* (Cranbury, NJ: Associated University Presses, 2004), 426pp. In: https://books.google.com/books?id=POQd0XbRsOQC&dq=San+Juan,+David+Fagen&source=gbs_navlinks_s.

CHAPTER 2

Background to Colonialism

Marxism begins with a grasp of the social totality in its historical development. The key concept is the mode of production consisting of productive forces and of relations of production.
  E. San Juan, *In the Wake of Terror* (2007)

Early Capitalism as Subject of Study

In exploring the subject of this chapter, salute is given to earlier, much more comprehensive efforts to understanding the origins and ramifications on the rest of the world of capitalism and its global expansion over the last five hundred years. The monumental, critically received two-volume work of French historian Fernand Braudel, entitled *Civilization & Capitalism 15th–18th Century* (1979), deserves special mention. While avoiding use of the historical materialist approach, Braudel nonetheless offers a wealth of information derived from his social historical approach which he pioneered. He influenced later scholars who proceeded to further investigate the nature of international political economy engendered by capitalism's spread worldwide. One of these scholars was Marxist-oriented Immanuel Wallerstein who, in 1974, began publication of a series, headlined *The Modern World-System*, the goal of which was to explore the history of the global capitalist-oriented economic system, expounding in the process on what has come to be known as world systems theory. Thus, the first volume was subtitled *Capitalist Agriculture and the Origins of the European World-Economy in the Sixteenth Century*; the second volume, *Mercantilism and the Consolidation of the European World-Economy, 1600–1750*; and the third, *The Second Era of Great Expansion of the Capitalist World Economy, 1730–1840*. Wallerstein's gratitude to Braudel was evidenced by his founding in 1976 of the Fernand Braudel Center for the Study of Economies, Historical Systems, and Civilizations, based at the State University of New York, Binghamton. Since its founding, the Braudel Center has hosted a long line of critical scholars, some of the Marxist persuasion and the majority, non-Marxists, most of whom have contributed to the publication series and gaining worldwide repute as a pioneering center of critical study.

Another notable book, less sweeping but no less profound book and influential to my study of the subject, is Michel Beaud's *A History of Capitalism 1500–2000* (2002). In this book, Beaud offers a survey of capitalism's five-hundred-year history, employing his expressly historical materialist approach to helping the reader make sense of the varied influences, e.g., social, political, cultural, religious, and economic, that have all contributed to the growth, spread, and persistence of capitalism to the present period albeit in its neoliberal form.

Colonialism and Racism

In the preceding chapter, I discussed some proponents of the Enlightenment legacy that saw Europe as the fountainhead of civilization, on the assumption that the Europeans were endowed with reason and industry, attributes that other peoples outside of Europe did not possess. As discussed, Locke's views on the matter were representative of those of the dominant sectors of European society, particularly those of the merchant class that reaped wealth through a state-induced and state-supported colonial project. The racial implication of attitudes such as those held by Locke is not hard to discern. For instance, Locke viewed indigenous peoples in the New World as inferior in their intelligence as well as in their capacity for industry, two measures that made Europeans distinct from other peoples outside of Europe. The accumulation of wealth arising out of colonialism, however, was also creating disparities in economic status so that classes were emergent, indicating that while the Enlightenment became a rationale for the economic progress of some in European society, not all were benefiting from it. This was especially true if one was poor in this society, or in settler colonies in the New World and elsewhere, but also if one's skin hue is other than European or, in the contemporary term, Caucasian. This was duly noted by Karl Marx and Friedrich Engels whose critique of the liberal ethos was substantiated by the type of racially loaded colonial policies that Europe had pursued to define its relationship with the rest of the world reinforced, later on, by Charles Darwin's biological theory of natural selection. Understanding European expansion and colonization particularly throughout much of the eighteenth and nineteenth centuries in this context is essential to understanding the race-based nationalism manifest in the behavior of the European state vis-à-vis its colonies.[1] This explains to a significant degree why, despite attempts to provide moral justification for the colonial project, e.g., the British sense of the "White Man's Burden" and the French conception of *"Mission civilisatrice"*, the sense of determinism about the superiority of European civilization over non-European societies has remained palpable, casting doubt as to whether or not the European colonial venture was, in the end, civilizing or ennobling.[2]

The implications of these racialized assumptions behind the European and, later, North American civilizing mission extend beyond merely treating the non-European race as inferior. Worse, they were treated as property as John Stuart Mill observed in his 1869 essay on the subjection of women.[3] In that essay that caught even Marx's admiration, Mill alluded to his concern not only about the subjection of women but also to what was referred to as common law that allowed "something of a free hand" to take slaves, more specifically, laws and statutes that had, in fact, been passed by the Parliament that defined slaves as property, secured the rights of owners, and facilitated the trade in slaves. Exemplifying this was when Britain allowed, in 1678, the sale of colonial subjects as though they were commodities. And, in 1713, under the terms of the Treaty of Utrecht that ended the War of the Spanish Succession, England was contractually bound to supply Spain's colonies with as much as four thousand slaves annually. For its part, the US Supreme Court decision in the Dred Scott case in 1857 affirmed the right of slave owners to pursue their fleeing slaves as property. Despite President Abraham Lincoln's emancipation proclamation in January 1863 and the subsequent reconstruction period following the Civil War, the former slaves and their descendants fared not much better, with the insult added to injury by the High Court's Plessy decision of 1896 affirming an apartheid system of race relations in the US.

Capitalism and the State

To say that the passage and enforcement of laws and decisions that normalized slavery on both sides of the Atlantic particularly prior to the US Civil War were an important foundation for capitalism is an understatement. Further, religion was part of the legitimating superstructure that allowed capitalism to flourish and grow. From the historical materialist perspective, racism and its manifestation through slavery were integral to the economic structure at the time. This was recognized as much by Du Bois in his 1891 essay, entitled "The Enforcement of Slave Trade Laws" wherein, as San Juan explains, "Du Bois analyzed the interface between ideology, politics, and economic structure. 'If slave labor was economic god, then the slave trade was its strong right arm; and with Southern planters recognizing this, and Northern capital unfettered by a conscience, it was almost like legislating against economic laws to attempt to abolish the slave trade by statutes....' Legal ideology and economic practice were so intricately meshed that one cannot privilege one category over the other" (San Juan 2010).

The distinct experience with the dialectical relationship between race and class in the United States, with its Civil War, and in Britain contending with Irish resistance, as observed and studied by Marx, has had an effect on the thinking of Marx, causing him to modify what would have been a unilinear view of history. San Juan explains this change of mind by Marx, citing a study by economic historian Kevin Anderson on Marx and the Third World, as follows:

> By 1853, and especially in his studies of Russia and non-western formations (from 1857 to his 1879–1882 notes on indigenous peoples), Marx formulated a multilinear and non-reductionist theory of social change that did not focus exclusively on economic relations of production. Anderson concludes that Marx's mature social theory "revolved around a concept of totality that not only offered considerable scope for particularity and difference but also on occasion made those particulars – race, ethnicity, or nationality – determinants for the totality".... In 1862, before the Emancipation Proclamation, Marx had already conceptualized the subjectivity or revolutionary agency of "free Negroes" as a crucial element in the victory of the Union forces. (San Juan 2010)

The implications of Anderson's and San Juan's assessment of Marx's belatedly-discovered multilinear view of history are profound. To begin with, by accepting the possibility of revolutions being led by non-workers outside of the proletarian class, e.g., peasants in agrarian societies, Marx consciously deviates from the prevailing Eurocentric interpretation of his earlier views that transition to socialism could only be brought about by workers in a maturing or mature industrialized society. Second, flowing from the first, transition to socialism need not require a prior stage of mature capitalism that creates exploited workers, e.g., the 1917 Bolshevik Revolution; it may also emerge from semifeudal and agrarian conditions from among the peasantry that have endured the ravages of colonialism. And, third, the fact that these conditions have prevailed in much of Asia, Africa, and Latin America—all continents of color—need not deviate also from the fact that the racism that these continents have endured for centuries, not dissimilar from the persistent racism endured by peoples of color within the United States and within each of the European states that have participated in the colonial enterprise, could not be detached from the exploitative economic system that largely regarded them as source of labor. This was pointed out by activist-scholar Angela Davis as she called out the discrepancy between the liberal idealism of these states, on the one hand, and the exploitation that has brought them affluence and progress, on the other, when she wrote: "While the lofty notions affirming liberty were being formulated by those who penned the United States Constitution, Afro-Americans lived and labored in chains. Not even the term 'slavery' was allowed to mar the sublime concepts articulated in the Constitution, which euphemistically refers to 'persons held to service of labor' as those exceptional human beings who did not merit the rights and guarantees otherwise extended to all."[4] San Juan adds his elucidation in clarifying and in recognizing the inseparability between racism as a construction, on the one hand, the emergence of classes as function of property relations, on the other, with the following analysis: "Our key heuristic axiom is this: the extraction of surplus labor always involves conflict and struggle. This process of class conflict in which identities are articulated with group formation, where race, gender, and ethnicity enter into the totality of contradictions between the social relations dominated by private property and the productive forces, is crucial."[5]

Notes

1. Here, San Juan elucidates on this important juncture of European history wherein the bourgeois class emerged from among "heterogeneous classes" and, from that position, proceeded to "resolve internal contradictions," and

to "restructure the state," in a "national form." This nationalized state then intervened "'in the very reproduction of the economy and particularly in the formation of individual' whereby individuals of all classes were subordinated 'to their status as citizens of the nation-state, to the fact of their being nationals'... The key term in this narrative of nationalization is 'hegemony,' in this instance capitalist hegemony (domination by consent) based on the formal nationalization of citizenship" (San Juan 2007).

2. At this juncture, it is significant to note, for purposes of clarity, that San Juan makes at least two critically important interventions: first, over suggestions that Marx, in his Capital, had intended for his mature capitalism in the European setting as rigid requisite for the creation of a proletarian class that would carry out revolution and that, therefore, this is a model appropriate to emulate everywhere else; and, second, over suggestions that Marx and Engels would have endorsed British imperialism particularly in India for its presumably progressive role in transforming the maligned "Asiatic mode of production," e.g., construction of a railway system throughout India, introduction of civil service, promotion of a free-wheeling media, and replacement of (or attempts to replace) ascriptive inequality, e.g., caste, with ethos of hard work and personal achievements. In a 2002 essay, entitled "Postcolonialism, Uneven Development & Imperialism: The Example of Amilcar Cabral" (a chapter in Crystal Bartolovich and Neil Lazarus, eds., *Marxism, Modernity, and Postcolonial Studies*, Cambridge University Press, 2002), San Juan explains that Marx, in a letter to a Russian journalist in 1878, clarified his thoughts on precisely this issue. Part of the letter reads: "[My critic] absolutely insists on transforming my historical sketch of the genesis of capitalism in Western Europe into a historico-philosophical theory of the general course fatally imposed on all peoples, whatever the historical circumstances in which they find themselves placed, in order to arrive ultimately at this economic formation that ensures, together with the greatest expansion of the productive powers of social labor, the most complete development of man. But I beg his pardon. (It does me both too much honor and too much discredit.) [Here follows the instance of the Roman plebeians.] Thus events that are strikingly analogous, but taking place in different historical milieu, lead to totally disparate results. By studying each of these developments separately, and then comparing them, one can easily discover the key to this phenomenon, but one will never arrive there with the master key of a historico-philosophical theory whose supreme virtue consists in being suprahistorical" (1982, 109–110).

On the second point, regarding Marx and Engels' alleged endorsement of British imperialism in India, San Juan quotes from a letter written by Marx himself to the *New York Tribune*, published on June 25, 1853, in which Marx intimated: "England, it is true, in causing a social revolution in Hindustan, was actuated only by the vilest interests, and was stupid in her manner of enforcing them. But that is not the question. The question is: Can mankind fulfill its destiny without a fundamental revolution in the social state of Asia? If not, whatever may have been the crimes of England, she was the unconscious tool of history in bringing about that revolution" (1959, 480–481). Thus, in shifting the question over to whether or not British imperialism is really the suitable instrument in bringing about a "fundamental revolution in the social state of Asia," Marx's answer is clearly in the negative, which is hardly an endorsement of it!

Three other significant points need to be made here. First, San Juan attributes to Cabral, as signified by this article as a tribute, in order to illustrate precisely that a Marxist-inspired revolution could occur—as indeed it has—in peasant and agrarian, non-capitalist, societies; second, to show disciples of postcolonialism, whose discipline thrives on, or in celebration of, the idea of "post-marxism," that Marxism is alive and well in the peripheries of the empire; and, three, Marxism, as an idea, transcends both spatial and temporal limitations imposed by its critics on the discredited assumption that it is eurocentric and that it has been defeated at the end of the Cold War. The fact that these revolutionary movements are greeted with fascistic state violence and propaganda attest to their potency in raising issues that only they have the courage to raise, e.g., "mode of production", "accumulation by dispossession", "surplus value," among others (San Juan 2002).

3. For text, see https://www.marxists.org/reference/archive/mill-john-stuart/1869/subjection-women/index.htm.
4. See Joy James, ed., *The Angela Y. Davis Reader* (Blackwell Publishing, 1998), p. 380.
5. See E. San Juan, "From Race to Class Struggle: Re-problematizing Critical Race Theory", *Michigan Journal of Race and Law*, 11, 1 (2005): 85. In: https://repository.law.umich.edu/mjrl/vol11/iss1/5. San Juan adds a salient point: "Given this emphasis on class struggle and class formation, on the totality of social relations that define the position of interacting collectivities in society, materialist critique locates the ground of institutional racism and racially-based inequality in the capitalist division of labor - primarily between the seller of labor-power as prime commodity and the employer who maximizes surplus value (unpaid labor) from the workers. The question of whose answer would explain the ideology and practice of racial segregation, subordination, exclusion, and variegated tactics of violence will maximize accumulation of profit and also maintain the condition for such stable and efficient maximization" (ibid., 86).

REFERENCES

Beaud, Michel, *A History of Capitalism 1500–2000*, 2nd Edition (New York: Monthly Review Press, 2002), 356pp.

Braudel, Fernand, *Civilization and Capitalism 15th–18th Century*, Volume I. *The Structures of Everyday Life—The Limits of the Possible*. Translation from the French, Revised by Sian Reynolds (New York: Harper & Row Publishers, 1979), 623pp.

San Juan, E., Jr., "African American Internationalism and Solidarity with the Philippine Revolution", *Socialism and Democracy*, 24, 2 (July 2010): 32–65. In: http://www.tandfonline.com/eprint/Jqxa3MbH6e8pXFCcAHb9/full#.VcjchPlUWUF.

———, *In the Wake of Terror: Class, Race, Nation, Ethnicity in the Postmodern World* (Lanham, MD: Lexington Books, 2007), 232pp.

———, "Nation-State, Postcolonial Theory, and Global Violence", *Social Analysis: The International Journal of Social and Cultural Practice*, 46, 2 (Summer 2002): 11–32.

CHAPTER 3

The American Empire in the Pacific

...This racial genealogy of the empire followed the logic of capital accumulation by expanding the market for industrial goods and securing sources of raw materials and, in particular, the prime commodity for exchange and maximizing of surplus value: cheap labor power. This confirms the enduring relevance of Oliver Cromwell Cox's proposition that 'racial exploitation is merely one aspect of the problem of the proletarianization of labor, regardless of the color of the laborer. Hence racial antagonism is essentially political-class conflict' (1948, 485).
    E. San Juan, *In the Wake of Terror* (2007a)

JUSTIFICATIONS AND RATIONALIZATIONS

The modern state system emerged as a consequence of the Treaty of Westphalia of October 1648, which ended the Thirty Years' War among warring European principalities and forces, some wanting to establish religious rule while others insisting on maintaining a secular order. In a way, this new order signaled the end of the dominance of the church as the sole determinant of order, and with the decline of the church, so did the concept of universal ecclesiastical authority. This modern state that ensued was vested with such attributes as sovereignty and territoriality, and it claimed juridical authority not only over this territory but also over the resources therein and the population that resided within this territory, conferring upon them the status of citizens and as members of a duly formed nation-state. Significantly, this state also claimed monopoly to the use of force, forbidding anyone from using force without its sanction or approval. It maintained a government that, while it claims to represent the will of its people, more accurately reflects the will and interests of the class that controls it. It thus makes laws consonant with these interests, and the enforcement thereof is designed to extract compliance from among the citizens who are also compelled, at one time or another, to serve in its military force. As described by sociologist Giovanni Arrighi, reflecting a consensus among many social scientists, the Treaty of Westphalia represented "the reorganization of political space in the interest of capital accumulation" and, further, signaled "the birth, not just of the modern inter-state system but also of capitalism as a world-system" (as quoted in San Juan 2007a). This description echoed the thinking of a Russian revolutionary theoretician Nikolai Bukharin who described the power of the modern state as sucking "in almost all branches of production; it not only maintains the general conditions of the exploitative process; the state more and more becomes a direct exploiter, organizing and directing production as a collective capitalist" (as quoted in San Juan 2007a).

The inter-colonial competition and rivalry, characterized by wars, during much of the seventeenth and the eighteenth centuries, as described in the introductory chapter of this work, illustrates this exploitative process referred to by Bukharin in the above-quote. Motivated by the desire to accumulate wealth, the mercantile powers of Europe raced across the globe, competed against each other, and tried to control as much of the world's resources, including labor and market, as possible. The slave trade was an essential component. San Juan quotes Marx as having described this trade as ushering in capitalism's "rosy dawn"[1] (San Juan 1995). The inter-colonial warfare is illustrated by the cases of the British-French wars over Canada, between the 1680s and the 1760s with each side using and manipulating indigenous Indians as allies; the Opium Wars, fought in various stages during the late 1830s through the early 1860s, mainly by Britain against China but also involving France as a secondary player,[2] and the Boer Wars fought mainly between the British, on one side, and the Afrikaners, of Dutch descent and who have migrated to and claimed dominion over much of South Africa during much of the 1890s up until the early 1900s, on the other. Attempts were made to diplomatically resolve inter-colonial disputes and minimize conflicts as in the Berlin Conference of 1884–1885, convened with the precise goal of partitioning Africa. Nonetheless, wars and skirmishes along predetermined colonial borders were commonplace. And, in the late 1890s, among the European powers, the Permanent Court of Arbitration, headquartered at The Hague, was set up in the hope of "seeking the most objective means of ensuring to all peoples the benefits of a real and lasting peace, and above all, of limiting the progressive development of existing armaments"; however, this did not prevent the onset of World War I, which was a result of inter-colonial and inter-imperialist rivalry. These legal frameworks established proved to be feeble attempts at curbing the economic aggrandizement and territorial expansion for the maximization of profit through war, lending credence to the assertions made by V. I. Lenin, in his 1916 extended essay "Imperialism, the Highest Stage of Capitalism," as well as by Nikolai Bukharin, in his 1915 book, *Imperialism and World Economy*. As will be shown in the following discussion, the belated entry into the colonial fray by the United States was undergirded by the same motives as those held by its European counterparts.

Exploration of the Pacific, and the Pathology of Violence: The Case of the Malolo Massacre

US leaders pinned their claimed exceptionalism—to be discussed further below—to their supposed disinterest in acquiring and conquering new territories, and that their soon-to-be-manifest westward attention, at least until the Spanish–American War of 1898, described in another section below, across the Pacific was claimed to be benign, motivated by nothing other than participation in the heightening inter-European competition in commerce and trade in the region. Laying this as a foundation for the claim to exceptionalism, in apparent contrast with European powers at that time, historian Nathaniel Philbrick writes: "European powers had served the cause of both science and empire, providing new lands with which to augment their countries' already far-flung possessions around the world. The United States, on the other hand, had more than enough unexplored territory within its own borders. Commerce, not colonies, was what the U.S. was after" (Philbrick, xviii).

It was with this explanation, at least initially and at the surface, that the United States sought to establish a stronger diplomatic and, eventually, a military presence throughout the Pacific by the middle of the 1800s. Paving the way was the commissioning by the US Navy of an exploring expedition in order to gather intelligence and knowledge about the Pacific, supposedly from top to bottom, through charts that would be of use to American whalers, sealers, and China traders. It is interesting, as Philbrick notes, that "[d]ecades before America surveyed and mapped its own interior, this government-sponsored voyage of discovery would enable a young, determined nation to take its first tentative steps toward becoming an economic world power" (Philbrick, xviii).

Thus was the declared intention of the US government when the US Navy was commissioned, in 1838, to undertake and commence a four-year scientific exploratory expedition of the Pacific that would lead to the discovery of the Antarctic land- and ice-masses; the Columbia River outlet to the ocean, following up on the Lewis and Clark Expedition that commenced from the inland between 1804 and 1806; and the charting of the scores of islands that would constitute what would broadly be referred to as the Fiji Island Group, all recounted in Philbrick's much-acclaimed book, *Sea of Glory: America's Voyage of Discovery—The U.S. Exploring Expedition* (2003). The US Ex. Ex., as it has come to be known, was commanded by one egotistical Commodore Charles Wilkes who, at the time of his appointment to head the expedition, has been running the US Navy's Department of Charts and Instruments for about five years. Wilkes was also to be immortalized as the inspiration of Herman Melville's Captain Ahab in his novel *Moby Dick* (1851). As an avid reader of maritime history, Melville studied and was inspired by the exploits of the Ex. Ex. whose many characters and experiences would be used as models i n his novel. In fact, to anyone familiar enough with the journey of the Ex. Ex. as well as with Melville's novel, one could find justifiable comparison between real-life Commodore Wilkes and fictional Captain Ahab in terms of their character but particularly with their obsession to control and to conquer, at the cost of sanity and reason, their respective objectives: in the case of Ahab, the white whale and, in the case of Wilkes, the white continent at the bottom of the world. But the Ex. Ex. which Wilkes commanded may also be understood as a metaphor for something else: the America's irrepressible, underlying quest to be a dominant, preeminent player in the world of international politics, then as now, commencing with the Pacific and at the cost of its image as being benign and exceptional, for right within the recorded history of the Ex. Ex. would one find contradictions which in the end would belie and negate any claim to benignity or exceptionalism.

It was as though the first massacre in the Pacific to be committed by the US military was foreordained against a people of color, the Fijians, an image about whom has been constructed from impressions gathered from tales from earlier contacts by other European explorers, e.g., the Swedes, the

British, and the French. In contrast to the sightings by the crew of *Peacock* and *Vincennes*, and to be joined later by the *Flying Fish* and the *Porpoise*, four of five ships commanded by Wilkes in the expedition, anchored, in early July 1840, near the village of Levuka, of "many little villages peeping amidst the trees and scattered huts clinging to the projecting ridges of rocks..." which were, in turn, "hailed with joy our return to the ever green Isles of the Tropics" following their Antarctic voyage, a more foreboding, racialized image was forming about the inhabitants themselves that lived in these villages. Philbrick offers a composite of this image, ultimately proving prejudicial and detrimental, among members of the crew in the following passage: "If the landscape was reminiscent of many of the islands they had already seen, the inhabitants were something altogether different. It wasn't just that the Fijians were bigger and more muscular, with darker skin and curlier hair than the Polynesians; it was the way they presented themselves to this already nervous group of *Papalangi*, the Fijian word for the white people. With a huge club resting on his shoulder, a Fijian warrior made a most intimidating sight" (Philbrick, 196). In another passage, Philbrick writes: "Whether it was due to the arrival of a new, more aggressive people or the result of a rise in population that led to increasing competition for natural resources, life on Fiji became decidedly more violent. In fact, warfare appears to have become a way of life. Circular forts were built just about everywhere, and cannibalism became one of the fundamental institutions of the islands. In the words of one archaeologist, 'man was the most popular of the vertebrate animals used for food'" (Philbrick, 197).

This image of the natives of Fiji was not exceptional. In fact, it was complemented by an image offered to Wilkes in his encounter with Wesleyan Methodist missionaries from England, who have arrived in the islands in 1837, particularly in the island of Somosomo, to conduct evangelical proselytization among the natives. In the opening chapter of a memoir by two of these missionaries, Thomas Williams and James Calvert, they write:

> The worst deformities, the foulest stains, disfiguring and blackening all the rest, are the very parts of Fijian nature which, while the most strongly characteristic, are such as may only be hurriedly mentioned, dimly hinted at, or passed by altogether in silence. The truth is just this, that within the many shores of this secluded group [of islands], every evil passion had grown up unchecked, and run riot in unheard-of abominations. Sinking lower and lower in moral degradation, the people had never fallen physically or intellectually to the level of certain stunted and brutalized races fast failing,

through mere exhaustion, from the mass of mankind. Constitutional vigour and mental force aided and fostered the development of every crime; until crime became inwrought into the very soul of the people, polluted every hearth, gave form to every social and political institution, and turned religious worship into orgies of surpassing horror. The savage of Fiji broke beyond the common limits of rapine and bloodshed, and, violating the elementary instincts of humanity, stood unrivalled as a disgrace to mankind. (Williams and Calvert, 1-2)

It was with this kind of image that Wilkes and the crew of his ships carried with them when they arrived in the Fiji Island Group. It was also the image that they had during the whole time that they conducted their survey of the islands and in their encounters with the inhabitants o fthese islands, the same image which also informed them of how they should behave toward these inhabitants, a behavior intended to impress upon these inhabitants the superiority of the white man and his law. An earlier indication of this was provided by an earlier series of events wherein Wilkes, diverging from his original mission of conducting a purely scientific expedition, had sought to extend US law upon an inhabitant, now Chief Veidovi, who had been accused of having led a massacre a few years earlier—in 1834—against crew members of the US private merchant ship, *Charles Doggett*. This incident was described to Wilkes by an adventurer named Paddy O'Connell, originally from Ireland but who has accordingly lived in these islands for the past forty years. O'Connell claimed to have witnessed this massacre and, based on his word, "Wilkes resolved to bring the perpetrator... to justice" (Philbrick, 201).

Wilkes resolved to bring Veidovi into custody through a sealed set of instructions that he issued to Captain Hudson of the *Peacock*. Hudson's subsequent actions later revealed what those instructions were, and they included, among others, a scheme with which to bring Veidovi into custody. B y bday's standards of international norm and behavior, the scheme would most likely fall under the category of entrapment, kidnapping, or hostage-taking, or a combination thereof, for it involved enticing Veidovi's brothers to a party onboard, one of them being a current chief, and then declaring that none of them would be allowed to leave until Veidovi turned himself in. The scheme worked but at the expense of alienating and mobilizing the whole populace against the *papalangi*, Fijian term for the white man, in possible retaliation. The contemplated punishment for Veidovi, at Hudson's discretion, was neither execution nor imprisonment but, rather, a trip to the United States where he would live in forced exile for several years following which "he would be returned to Fiji, having become a 'better man, and with the Knowledge, that to kill a white person was the very worst thing a Feegee man could do'" (Philbrick, 202).

Making matters worse, at this time, one of the ships under Wilkes' overall command, the *Vincennes*, captained by a Lieutenant Oliver Hazard Perry, assisted by second-in-command, a Passed Midshipman Samuel Knox, then tasked to survey and chart Solevu Bay, was blown ashore by strong gale, and stranded. Perry and Knox decided to abandon ship on a launch, hoping to return to Wilkes', but satisfied only by the safety offered by the open water from the natives in canoes chasing them. This gave an opportunity for the excited Fijians to essentially get aboard and loot the contents of the cutter that the natives thought to be of value. Upon hearing of this development a few days later, Wilkes had determined to retrieve the boat and all the looted contents back and teach the natives a lesson in the process. Philbrick describes Wilkes' preparations to accomplish this as follows: "Upon hearing Perry's report, Wilkes announced that they were going to get the boat back. He and Hudson would be leading a fleet of eleven boats, eighty men, plus the schooner, in an assault on Solevu" (Philbrick, 210). As Wilkes and his expeditionary force arrived at Solevu, he declared to the natives, through a Hawaiian interpreter, Oahu Jack, that "the natives hand over the boat and all the articles that had been left in it." Not having previously encountered such a "large body of white men [appearing] in arms, offering fight, upon their very shores," the native chief agreed to surrender the boat (Philbrick, 211).

But after Wilkes' officers had inspected the boat and reported to him that "the men's personal effects" were missing, Wilkes found a pretext to display his military might. Philbrick describes what happened next as follows:

> That afternoon, the fleet moved in for the attack. The boats grounded in about two feet of water, and the men, all of them armed with muskets, waded the rest of the way to shore under the leadership of Hudson. Wilkes elected to remain in his gig, which had been equipped with a Congreve war rocket.
>
> The village had been left deserted, and the natives, loaded with their possessions, could be seen climbing up a nearby hill, where they paused to watch the ensuing scene. In only a matter of minutes, the entire village was in flames. The popping of burning bamboo sounded so much like the report of a musket, that it was briefly believed that natives were fighting back, but such

was not the case. This did not prevent Wilkes from firing a few of his rockets at the natives up on the hill. Part-way between a skyrocket and a modern-day missile, the rocket left a smoky contrail before bursting into flame, and the Fijians could be heard shouting out "*Curlew! Curlew!*", or "Spirits! Spirits!" (Philbrick, 211)

Following the operation, Wilkes and Hudson congratulated each other for "having punished the insolence of these cannibals without any loss on our side." But the burning of this Fijian coastal village, unprecedented as it was in its fury by the US military against a colored people in the Pacific in this century, was a mere prelude to another unmitigated display of brute force. Philbrick offers a premonition to this next episode with the final sentence in his chapter entitled "The Cannibal Isles" with the following: "Just eleven days after the burning of Solevu, Wilkes would do as Dana [James Dana, the expedition's geologist, in a previous conversation] suggested. In addition to reducing yet another beautiful Fijian village to a smoking ruin, he would drench its sands in blood" (Philbrick, 212).

In a roundabout way, Philbrick describes, in the following honestly titled chapter, "Massacre at Malolo," how this came about. Without belaboring the point, this started during the last leg of the Fijian survey of the island group's westernmost constellation of tiny islands, by the second half of July 1840. Anticipating exhaustion of food supplies for the crew in the *Leopard* and the *Flying Fish*, officered by James Alden and Joseph Underwood, respectively, the officers decided to barter, say, some items of interest like muskets for food with the natives, as fate would have it, in the tiny island of Malolo. This then led to a chain of events in which the encounter with the inhabitants did not go very well. In hindsight, contact with the natives was conditioned by racially tinged arrogance and mistrust by the Americans, on the one hand, and a combination of naivete and eventual fear by the natives, on the other, complicated by the ebb and flow of the tide causing at some point the *Leopard* to run aground, an event that would prove pivotal later in the episode. Illustration of this contrasting demeanor was when, one day, the food search party led by Alden encountered a native who offered a piece of information about some hogs (four, in fact) that the Americans might have, in a barter, but which were located in the southern part of the island requiring a small boat to go fetch them. But Underwood took an unexpected and, perhaps, unnecessarily provocative decision before Alden embarked on his mission. As Philbrick describes: "Underwood insisted that one of the natives, who claimed to be the chief's son serve as a hostage to ensure his men's own safety [as they went to get the hogs]" (Philbrick, 215).

Here alone could one see the contrast in the demeanor between the Americans and the Fijians: The Americans taking ironically as "hostage" (Philbrick's term) one of the natives who have graciously offered hospitality so as the Americans will not go hungry, on the one hand, and the natives naively agreeing to allow one of them to be held as "hostage" and apparently thinking nothing of it and showing no malice in providing information about the hogs being quite a ways from where they were, on the other. In fact, the natives even helped push the *Leopard* into deeper waters, some in their canoes, when it was in danger of running aground in shallow waters despite fears on the part of the Americans that the Fijians would "claim the boat in accordance with Fijian salvage customs" and that the Fijians "had marked us as their victims," especially so that some of them, perhaps out of curiosity, had tried to clamber aboard during the process.

The deterioration of the situation came when the food search party led by Alden took a little too long to return, making Underwood anxious especially so as the *Leopard* had once again grounded. At that point, Underwood decided to walk to a nearby village, accompanied by seven of his crew, and, with the help of Oahu Jack, the interpreter, took a chance of chatting with the villagers, congregated in the shade of nearby trees; he also inquired as to the whereabouts of the hogs. After a while, Underwood met the village chief, who also happened to be the father of the hostage, with whom he (Underwood) tried to negotiate directly for the transfer of the hogs. In exchange for the hogs, the chief had, at that point, asked "for a musket, powder, and ball," and, later, as an afterthought, a hatchet (Philbrick, 217).

Meanwhile, in the course of these negotiations, the tide had once again risen for the *Leopard* to return to deeper waters to where Underwood had noticed Alden and his team had just returned. At around that point, a group of natives had also ventured, uninvited, into the *Leopard* in a canoe. The natives had presumably tried to make contact with the hostage and, as inferred from what transpired next, had apparently encouraged the hostage to break free, which he did. As the hostage jumped into the shallow waters and waded in about two feet of water toward dry land, Alden and Midshipman William Clark aimed their muskets at him but then decided, at the last second, not to shoot the fleeing native thinking that "a dead hostage would provide them with little leverage with the natives" (Philbrick, 218),

Alden lowered his musket and instructed Clark to fire only into the air but in the general direction of the fleeing hostage.

Upon hearing of the musket fire, villagers started pouring from their mangrove shades most of whom held some kind of a weapon. The village chief was almost certain that Alden and Clark had tried to kill his son. The villagers then ran after Underwood and his teammates, as they tried to scamper toward their boat, who tried to fire their muskets in self-defense but had no chance to reload. Midshipman Wilkes Henry tried to assist Underwood "but was struck in the back of the head by a short club and fell face-first into the water" and was quickly surrounded by the natives who began stripping him of his clothes (Philbrick, 218–219). Underwood himself was hardly able to flee and was struck by a club to the head and shoulder before dropping to his knees and then to the water, face first. Alden, who was in the *Leopard* the whole time, tried to maneuver the cutter closer to the shore in the rising waters. He also jumped ashore, though belatedly, to try to give aid to Underwood whom he found to be "stripped of most of his clothing, lying on his back on the shore" (Philbrick, 220). He then looked around and saw Henry's body "almost completely naked" (Philbrick, 220).

It was not long after this incident that Wilkes, who had just returned with his team of surveyors, onboard his cutter, the *Flying Fish*, from Linthicum Island, another part of the island group, had learned that something was not right, first, through the *Leopard*'s ensigns pulled at half-mast, then the Union flag "down" after which he concluded "something must have happened" (Philbrick, 221). He maneuvered his vessel close to shore, then on a small boat, then joined Alden in his cutter, the *Leopard,* where he viewed the lifeless bodies of Underwood and Henry. Wilkes was reported to have wept inconsolably, and his men were "excited to fury." There were suggestions of hot pursuit of the natives to their village to exact revenge, but Underwood, believing that if they had done so at that moment, it would have been foolhardy to do for there were "hundreds of [native] warriors…, and that there were less than two dozens of them [at the time]" (Philbrick, 221).

Following a burial for Underwood and Henry in the middle of a beautiful islet, in a grove of banyan trees, and away from Malolo where Wilkes had determined that there was no risk of exhumation by the natives, Wilkes now had to contend with his officers' demand that "immediate and crushing action be taken against the natives of Malolo" (Philbrick, 222). Philbrick explains that "[a]lthough no one had been more personally attached to the victims than Wilkes, it was now his responsibility to, in his words, 'prevent a just and salutary punishment from becoming a vindictive and indiscriminate massacre'" (Philbrick, 222). However, as subsequent events would show, it was doubtful whether Wilkes had really intended to prevent vindictiveness or indiscriminate massacre, or both. As everyone anticipated a revenge action, "the men were already cleaning their muskets and pistols, filling their cartridges with gunpowder, and making other preparations for the impending conflict" (Philbrick, 223). "Although Wilkes would later claim," Philbrick writes, "that he attempted to exercise due restraint in his actions against the natives, the journals of his officers tell a different story. '[W]ar was now declared against the Island,' [George] Emmons wrote, '& orders issued by Capt. Wilkes to spare only the women & children'" (Philbrick, 223).

The night of the burial, the *Flying Fish*, *Porpoise*, and the *Leopard*, patrolled the shores of Malolo. Wilkes and his officers had assumed that the natives were anticipating an attack and, hence, were also assumed to be preparing to defend themselves. The following morning, as Philbrick writes, "three divisions of about seventy officers and men," commanded by Lieutenant Cadwalader Ringgold, were landed on the southern shore of Malolo. They were under instructions by Wilkes to "march across the island to Sualib, the village where the murders had occurred" and, upon arrival there, "to kill as many warriors as possible and burn the village" (Philbrick, 223–224). Meanwhile, on the northern part of the island, a fleet of boats commanded jointly by Alden, George Emmons, and Midshipman Clark but still under the overall command of Wilkes, landed with the objective of burning down the village of Arro. The *Flying Fish* and *Porpoise* were also instructed to watch out for fleeing canoes and to pursue and destroy them.

As the land expeditionary force bound for Sualib waded ashore, it encountered a group of natives who had just boarded three canoes apparently bound for the nearby island of Malololailai. Through the interpreter, Oahu Jack, the natives were asked where they were from, and when they replied "Malolo," Philbrick writes: "Emmons unleashed his blunderbuss, immediately killing six natives as the rest dove into the water" (Philbrick, 24). The survivors were then segregated: The warriors were put in chains, while the women and children were put ashore in an exceptional observance of Wilkes' initial instruction. Emmons also took credit, as captain of the *Porpoise*, for pursuing five other fleeing canoes, each bearing eight warriors, as they attempted to escape to Malololailai. As Philbrick narrates,

Emmons spotted the canoes at around 4:00 p.m. that afternoon, emerging from the mangrove swamps. "Emmons had half his normal crew – just seven men. 'I thought the odds were too great to allow [the Fijians] any more advantages than they already possessed,' he wrote. Emmons raised the cutter's sails, which enabled the men who had been pulling oars to take up their muskets, and sailed for the nearest canoe. Once they were within range, Emmons opened fire with his blunderbuss. 'Many were killed at the first discharge,' he wrote, 'and others were thrown in so much confusion that but little resistance was made.' One native, however, was able to throw three spears at Emmons. After successfully dodging all of them, Emmons could see that the native was reaching for yet another spear. '[H]aving discharged my last pistol,' he wrote, 'I jumped into the canoe and jerked [the] spear out of his hands while Oahu Jack [the Hawaiian interpreter] dispatched him with a hatchet'" (Philbrick, 228). While one of the canoes managed to escape to safety, those in the water tried to swim in "various directions." Philbrick adds: "After shooting at a group of four natives who had reached the shallows (killing one and wounding two), Emmons and his men set to work butchering those still in the water. He later told Sinclair that the Fijians' "heads were so hard that they turned the edges of the cutlasses and our men had in some cases to finish them off with their boat axes" (Philbrick, 228). That night, Philbrick tells of a large group of sharks swimming about the schooner and quotes Sinclair who wrote in his diary: "[The sharks] must have had their fill of Fiji meat as they refused even to taste a piece of fat pork that was put over for them" (Philbrick, 228).

Later, the same expedition, a division consisting of about seventy men led by one of Wilkes' trusted officers, Lieutenant Robert Johnson, had approached the village of Sualib, which they found to have been converted into a fortress. It was surrounded by a twelve-foot deep ditch behind which was "a ten-foot high palisade built of large coconut tree trunks knitted together by a dense wicker-work. Inside this imposing wall of wood was another ditch, probably dug the night before, with the dirt piled up in front to form a four-foot wide parapet. Natives were already standing in the ditch, with only their heads exposed, prepared to fire their muskets and shoot their arrows through narrow openings in the palisade" (Philbrick, 224). Just as the native chiefs, distinguished by their white headdresses, stood just outside the fort and appeared to taunt the approaching sailors, and, upon Ringgold's order, the first in a series of Congreve war rockets was fired aimed at the fort with the intention of setting the village on fire. This was followed by a volley of gunfire from the sailors led by Sinclair as they rushed to the first ditch. Upon seeing the ditch, Sinclair saw the natives "thick as pigs" as bullets from his men poured through the stockade "thick as hail" (Philbrick, 225). About fifteen minutes into the slaughter, another Congreve rocket, launched from a portable launcher with bipods, was fired hitting the grass roof of one of the houses and then burst into flames. Congreve rockets were not known for their accuracy but could do their job if the object is in the general direction of flammable target which, in this case, wooden houses with thatched roofing. "If the fire should spread," wrote Philbrick, "the village would soon become an inferno. A warrior climbed up onto the roof and attempted to dislodge the rocket, but more than a dozen guns were quickly trained on him, and he fell, his body riddled with musket shells" (Philbrick, 226). As the flames spread, the native warriors abandoned the inner ditch and as they ran, they were "exposed to unrelenting fire from the sailors' muskets. Sinclair's double-barrel gun became so hot that he couldn't touch the barrel" (Philbrick, 226). Philbrick quotes from Sinclair's diary as follows: "The scene was grand, and beautiful and at the same time horrible what with the volleys of musketry, the crackling of the flames, the squealing of the Pigs..., the shouting of men and women and the crying of the children. The noise was deafening, above which you could hear rising now and then, the loud cheers of our men with 'There they go', 'Down with them,' 'Shoot that fellow,' etc. etc." (Philbrick, 226).

As the flames have exhausted their fury, the sailors attempted to enter the village. Philbrick then describes their experience as they inspected what remained of it as follows: "About an hour, some of the men attempted to enter the village. The heat was still so intense that Sinclair feared his cartridge might explode. They found calabashes of water, hampers of yams and many pigs, all burned to death; the villagers had clearly anticipated a long siege. They found spears, clubs, and muskets that had been abandoned by the natives in the ditch. In one of the houses, they found Underwood's cloth cap—'all mashed up by the blows which had felled him.' Most of the dead had been burned to cinders in the fire, with only four or five bodies, including that of the young girl, found lying amid the ashes. One of the victims was identified as the chief whom Sinclair had dispatched with his pistol. '[T]o satiate their revenge', several of the sailors threw the body into one of the smoldering houses 'and roasted him'" (Philbrick, 227).

Philbrick notes that the sailors agreed that the natives have put up a stiff but vain resistance; they were also satisfied that none of their fellows suffered any fatality. One sailor, though, suffered a "bad gash in the leg from an arrow," but other than this, everyone emerged from the battle unscathed. Following their complete and total destruction of Sualib, they then decided to join their comrades in a march to Arro. As Sinclair wrote in his diary, Philbrick notes, "We continued as we had commenced to destroy every house and plantation that we came across, and we marched in three lines, I do not think that one escaped us" (Philbrick, 227). As they arrived in Arro, by around sunset, Sinclair wrote in his diary that he was impressed that the village "must have been the most beautiful place situated as it was beneath the shade of a grove of lofty trees" though it has been turned into a wasteland, abandoned even before Alden, whose task it was to raze this village to the ground, which he did. Sinclair wrote further, and with a sigh: "Thank God we have taught these villains a lesson. [A] load has been taken off my conscience. I hope, however, we have not yet done with them" (Philbrick, 227).

One would think at this point that the thirst for vengeance has been satiated what with the complete razing to the ground of two villages, the massacre of much of the adult male population there, and the displacement and dispersal of untold women and children into nearby mountains. But as Sinclair had intimated in his diary, they were not yet done. As it turns out, the full and complete satisfaction of Wilkes and his men would come only if and when the physical and material destruction of Malolo and its population would be complemented by a total emotional and spiritual humiliation of what remains of the island's population, as the next and final episode in this drama would show. But it would also reveal the psyche among Wilkes and his men that would give historians an invaluable insight into the thinking and behavior of men in the US military as a tool of US foreign policy.

The following morning, Wilkes and his men, from their schooner anchored not far from the beach, noticed a group of natives who appeared to want to communicate something. So, Wilkes, accompanied by the interpreter, got on a small boat and approached the shore. As Wilkes walked toward the group, the rest of the members of the native entourage withdrew, leaving behind a woman bearing white chicken as a peace offering, along with several pieces of items that were taken from Underwood's and Henry's bodies. From his limited knowledge of Fijian customs, Wilkes understood that it was a customary practice among the natives "for a defeated people to sue for mercy before 'the whole of the attacking party, in order that all might be witnesses.'" Philbrick explains that Wilkes felt that if he did not insist on this custom to be observed, "the people of Malolo would 'never acknowledge themselves conquered'" (Philbrick, 229). So,

Wilkes, took the articles belonging to Underwood and Henry, but rejected the chicken and told the woman, through his interpreter, that if the natives agreed, he (Wilkes) would assemble all his men up on a hill in the southern part on the island later that morning for a ceremony to accept the chicken. He also issued a warning that if the natives and their chiefs did not show up for this event at the appointed time later that day, he would resume an attack against them. By noon, Wilkes and close to a hundred of his men were up on the hill. He wrote in his diary, "The day was perfectly serene, and the island, which but a few hours before, had been one of the loveliest spots in creation, was now entirely laid to waste, showing the place of the massacre, the ruined town, and the devastated plantations" (Philbrick, 229). The noontime passed but Wilkes appeared to manage to hold his patience until about four in the afternoon, when he saw, from a short distance, a long procession of natives "wailing" and "moaning." The line stopped at the foot of the hill, and Wilkes then issued a warning that if they did not climb up the hill "to do obeisance," he would "destroy them with his war rockets." Fearing further destruction, the natives conformed. Philbrick describes the scene as follows: "Falling to their hands and knees, with their faces toward the ground, the natives crawled up the hill to within thirty feet of Wilkes and his officers. As the natives behind him uttered 'piteous moans', an old man stood and begged Wilkes for mercy, 'pledging that they would never do the like to a white man. Offering Wilkes two young girls, which were quickly refused, the old man said that they had lost close to eighty men, and that they had considered themselves a conquered people" (Philbrick, 229–230).

Wilkes' response to all these shows of penance and humiliation, and Wilkes, through his interpreter, proceeded to give a lecture to the natives "about the power of the white man, insisting that if anything like this should ever occur again, he would return to the island and exterminate them." And, anticipating their departure for the next leg of their journey, i.e., a survey of Columbia River from its mouth in the Pacific northwest, with a planned stop in Hawaii, he instructed the natives that, by the next day, the natives must all come to the town of Arro "with all the provisions they could gather and that they would spend the entire day filling casks of water for his ships" (Philbrick, 230).

The following morning, the natives were in compliance, as seventy of them had been waiting and tasked by their chiefs to provide, taking all day, the provisions that had been demanded. As Philbrick describes, "Three thousand gallons of water…, along with twelve pigs and about three thousand coconuts. The natives also produced Underwood's pocket watch, which had been melted in the fire at Sualib, and Henry's eyeglasses" (Philbrick, 230). Wilkes would later rationalize, according to Philbrick, that "this was according to their customs, that the conquered should do work for the victors" (Philbrick, 230). With the demand for provisions having been fulfilled by the natives, Philbrick adds, not without a grain of irony: "Wilkes was left with nothing but the enormity of his loss. For the next few days he would be, by his own admission, 'unfit for further duty'" (Philbrick, 230). The loss, of course, that Philbrick was referring to was the loss of Underwood and Henry to both of whom Wilkes was particularly endeared, and not that of the natives who had just endured a whirlwind of a vengeance resulting in a massacre of their own, not to mention the destruction of their villages and plantations. Further, Wilkes nurtured lingering ill-feelings toward Alden whom he blamed for the deaths of Underwood and Henry, feelings which would boil over into accusations and counter-accusations between him and his officers and men about how the entire expedition was led and conducted, culminating in a court-martial in Norfolk, Virginia with a decision unfavorable to Wilkes. But this was still way into the future. As the expeditionary fleet departed the Fiji Island Group by mid-August, 1940, just had to vent his anger at one more object: Veidovi, the native chief who had been under detention for having incriminated himself with an admission to playing a leading role in the 1834 massacre of the crew members of the private merchant vessel *Charles Doggett*, was on board the *Vincennes* bound for the United States as part of his planned punishment. As a native chief, Veidovi was sporting an immense hair extending as long as eight inches over his shoulders. Before being taken captive, Philbrick narrates, Chief Veidovi "had more than a dozen barbers to attend to him; instead of a pillow, he had slept on a finely-crafted neck-stand that prevented his hair from being crushed at night" (Philbrick, 231–232). But Wilkes had other ideas. He decided to get rid of the symbolism, the "last vestige of his former life," he thought. Wilkes thus ordered that Chief Veidovi's hair be trimmed. "A close crop was made of his head by our ship's barber," Wilkes wrote in his diary, "who was much elated by the job and retained locks for presentation" (Philbrick, 232). Chief Veidovi, on the other hand, was devastated, and Wilkes seemed to savor the satisfaction of writing down in his diary: "[I]t was sometime before he [Veidovi] became reconciled to his new costume, and the mortification he experienced in having his huge head of hair [chopped] off" (Philbrick, 232).

The significance of the episode just narrated above, involving the US Navy, on the one hand, and the inhabitants of Fiji, on the other, goes far beyond the scientific mission which the exploring expedition was tasked to do, which it accomplished. To any critical observer, there are discernible and mutually reinforcing implications instructive enough to help understand the pattern and conduct of US colonialism and imperialism during the remainder of this century and beyond, either in the Pacific or elsewhere. First and foremost of these, the US economic system, based on a state-backed system of private accumulation and profit, was held at a status of preeminence. In fact, the exploring expedition was based on the premise that it would produce more reliable charts and maps that would assist US-based private merchants and whalers perform better, and identify locations of resources which the United States might covet and, thus, would later return to. This also assisted, no doubt, Commodore Matthew Perry in his expedition to forcibly open up Japan for trade with the United States in 1853. Thus, anyone interfering with these activities, such as what Chief Veidovi was charged as committing, would not be tolerated and, instead, be dealt with seriously and severely. The second implication grows out of the first: the application of US law outside the US proper. The capture of Chief Veidovi to be brought to the US for trial and punishment, based on US law, signifies an early stage of the internationalization of US law and its enforcement; it predates and precedes the kind of enforcement of US law seen especially since the so-called war on terror after 9/11.

Beyond the mere enforcement of US law abroad, however, we also see in this episode the *ad hoc* creation and application of new rules or laws applicable abroad and applied on non-US subjects or citizens on the premise that these enhance and/or protect US interests. As an illustration, in April 1840, a few months before the Malolo massacre, Wilkes paid a call to English Wesleyan Methodist missionary, John Hunt and his wife, Hannah, who had arrived at the island of Rewa in December 1838, where they stayed until July 1839 when they moved to another island, Somosomo, where they remained until August 1842. The Hunts formed part of a dedicated core of Wesleyan Methodist missionaries that have established missionary outposts in the South Pacific, particularly in Australia, New Zealand, Tonga, Samoa, and, now, Fiji, since 1815. Under a comity agreement, missionaries affiliated with the London Missionary Society, under the direction of John Williams, would direct their efforts in Samoa, while the Methodists, under the banner of the Wesleyan Methodist Missionary Society, would concentrate in the Fiji Island Group. The arrival of the Hunts in Fiji was originally to relieve two missionary couples and their children that have been nurturing a Methodist congregation and schools there, consisting of several hundred native converts scattered along several villages. The goal was eventually to set up at least ten mission stations in this island and in each of the adjoining great island of Vanua Levu and the greater island of Viti Levu over the coming years. Their arrival further placed them in an uncomfortable position of having not only to get acquainted with the native customs, much of which they found objectionable if not repulsive, but also learn at least a language to bridge the communication barrier. Above all these, however, is the challenge to secure their physical safety from any one of the tribes or members thereof who have been found to be quarrelsome among each other for one reason or another. These inter-tribal or inter-island conflicts often became a source of concern to the Hunts especially so as several of the chiefs forbade their members from becoming Christians. Hunt expressed this concern when Wilkes paid him a visit in early August 1840 while in Somosomo during which time Wilkes placed at the missionaries' disposal one of his ships should they ever wish to relocate to another island for greater safety. Wilkes wrote in his diary, as quoted by James Calvert in his narrative history of the Fijian Christian missions with which Wilkes was in "great sympathy," unaware or unconcerned, perhaps, of the ensuing implications of his entanglement with religious work in Fiji, as follows:

> It is not to be supposed, under this state of things, that the success of the Missionaries will be satisfactory, or adequate to their exertions, or a sufficient recompense for the hardships, deprivations, and struggles which they and their families have to encounter. There are few situations in which so much physical and moral courage is required, as those in which these devoted and pious individuals are placed; and nothing but a deep sense of duty, and a strong determination to perform it, could induce civilized persons to subject themselves to the sight of such horrid scenes as they are called upon almost daily to witness. I know of no situation so trying as this for ladies to live in, particularly when pleasing and well-informed, as we found these at Somosomo. (Williams and Calvert, 39)

Wilkes' "great sympathy" for the missionaries, however, went well beyond his generous offer to them for transportation. It also went into inserting himself into the inter-tribal/inter-island conflict by issuing the warning, directed in particular to Somosomo Chief Tui Cakau who, at the time, was at war with the chief of the island of Vuna, that if any of the tribes harmed the missionaries or threatened their security in any way, he would unleash his fury upon them like he did in Malolo Island during the previous month. As described by church historian Andrew Thornley,

> In an audience with Tui Cakau..., Wilkes sought greater care of the missionaries and protection of their property, warning of reprisals if they were harmed. With the intent to impress his chiefly audience, Wilkes told of two clashes between ships of his expedition and Fijians. At Solevu, on Vanualevu, the village was burnt to the ground, with the loss of at least five Fijians after one of the squadron's boats was dragged onto the shore. More seriously, at Malolo in western Fiji, following the murder of two of the expedition's sailors, while on a trading venture, the Americans destroyed all the villages on the island, canoes and yams; the people resisted and between 70 and 150 were killed. The news of the Malolo massacre had spread through Fiji. (Thornley, 143)

Thornley concluded in his narration that "[t]he visit of Wilkes, and a subsequent one from Captain Ringgold, commander of *Porpoise*, had its desired effect" (Thornley, 143). One of the missionaries, Richard Lith, a doctor, wrote in his diary: "[S]ince the American Squadron was in Feejee and punished two villages in different parts of Feejee, as well as took away a great chief [in reference to Chief Veidovi]..., the Feejeean chiefs generally have been made thoroughly afraid" (Thornley, 144). Indeed, not only did the rest of the chiefs get the message, Chief Tui Cakau too had a change of heart from being obstinate in his objection to the Western religion and to the missionaries' rejection of what they regarded as detestable native customs, e.g., cannibalism, polygamy, among others. Despite knowing and believing that every European sailor that came ashore his island has turned every Fijian woman into a prostitute, Chief Tui Cakau still placed himself at the service of the missionaries assuring them that they were free to choose a site for their school and church, and a temporary dwelling until a more suitable time and place were found, after the missionaries explained rather lamely that they were not in control of, or had any influence over, the behavior of the sailors or what they did.

To acknowledge that the missionaries were grateful to Wilkes for the benefits that they derived from his visit would be an understatement. Not only did Wilkes blur the line between religion and the state, he demonstrated the symbiotic relationship between colonialism and the missionary enterprise in which one reinforced the other. Wilkes recognized, even at the subliminal level, that religion was, in the words of San Juan in an important interview with cultural scholar Michael Pozo, an important "means of exacting consent" useful to the Western civilizing mission. In none of the accounts by the missionaries was there any expression of moral disapproval or outrage of the ruthless suppression by Wilkes of the inhabitants of Solevu and Malolo. To the contrary, the missionaries took comfort in these events having transpired so that they (these events) would serve as a reminder and a warning to the inhabitants of the islands, especially to their respective chiefs, and send quivers through their spine and, thus, make the inhabitants to be more amenable to the presence of the missionaries and their work. This was significant in one particular area: the subject of property. When Wilkes was talking about securing the life and property of the missionaries, he was, in effect, securing the English conception of property, anchored on private ownership, as opposed to the native Fijian custom of *kerekere*, or common ownership. Without them realizing it, the Fijians were gradually being introduced to the concepts of individualism and private ownership of property as their way of life was gradually being subverted. On the other hand, the rules that Wilkes promulgated, met with enthusiastic approval and endorsement by Hunt with whom Wilkes privately discussed before announcing them, were tantamount to state-drawn rules and regulations "relating to the protection of American whale shipping as well as oversight of Europeans in general" (Thornley, 36). In effect, the state, represented by Wilkes, serving as guardian of the flourishing privately based inter-oceanic trading system consonant with the still Euro-centered global market system requiring the institution of rationalized tariff and customs practices and complementary to the rise of nascent industries both in Europe and in North America at the time. But more than just securing the freedom for commercial whaling, Wilkes was ensuring that American whalers were able to secure and procure what at the time was a most important commodity: whale oil essential to industry and the military of a rising nation-state, e.g., lubrication for locomotives and ammunition. Thus, having been arbitrarily imposed on Somosomo's Chief Tui Cakau for his ratification under conditions resembling duress, the rules were interpreted as being for the benefit and betterment of the Fijians, and that these rules were symbolic of the benignity and rationality of European civilization which the missionaries felt duty-bound to spread. As Hunt wrote in his diary and quoted by Thornley in his narrative history:

> Law and justice are things which are but little known among the people but the measures now taken are calculated to give them some idea of both. It is much more honourable to a Christian Nation to improve the Natives by giving them regulations of this kind than to colonize their country and destroy the independence and lives of the natives. I am persuaded the American government has no idea of anything in these regulations but the protection of their shipping etc., and every nation ought to do this. (Thornley, 137)

It is with no doubt, based on the above-account, that religion facilitated colonialism particularly on the part of the British Empire that was at the time consolidating its dominance over the South Pacific region, dominance which the United States was not ready to challenge at that point but from which it was eager to benefit commercially.[3] In the case of Fiji, the Christian missionaries sought to transform and subvert the customs, habits, and beliefs of the natives through their church services, and educational instructions that they set up, creating ambiguity if not a crisis in identity on the part of these natives in an effort to get them to adopt a new one despite their belief that they were safeguarding "the independence and lives of the natives." In some parts of the colonized areas of the world, children of indigenous natives were taken away to boarding schools while in some parts, those who resisted were driven into banishment, often in flight from the application of force on them.[4] In one sense, this was a form of cultural genocide common throughout the colonized world despite the belief that such a practice was for their own good. It is likewise with no doubt that, in the case of the Fiji episode, the display and application of violence on the part of the US Navy in the incidents described herein were not an aberration but were, rather, inherent or, more precisely, pathologically inherent, in the modern nation-state exemplified by the United States, at the time just over sixty-years in age following its independence from Britain, and testing and flexing its masculine prowess in the Pacific.[5]

While apologists for empire and/or well-meaninged missionaries may look at their respective roles differently, from the vantage point of cultural theory, there is no denying that the ventures exemplified by the missionaries as described herein had contributed to the colonial project by reinforcing the cultural, political, and economic perceptions and practices that distinguished them, as representatives of a colonizing civilization, on the one hand, and the natives of Fiji as recipient subjects to this colonizing enterprise, on the other. In the words of cultural theorist John R. Eperjesi, in his important book *The Imperialist Imaginary: Visions of Asia and the Pacific in American Culture* (2005), the distinctions in perceptions, to a critical observer, are discernible through

> the binary oppositions that separate us from them, same from other, domestic from foreign, civilized from savage, developed from undeveloped, center from periphery, West from East, progress from stagnation, science from superstition, and so on. (Eperjesi, 3)

In this book, Eperjesi introduces the term "imperialist imaginary" as a useful conceptual tool with which to understand how the US empire, through its representatives, such as Wilkes in the story at hand, help define, represent or, for that matter, misrepresent and/or misrecognize, geography not so much in a physical sense but, rather, in a cultural sense as being potentially if not already an actual part of an integral whole, and which support or legitimize colonial expansion. As Eperjesi explains: "The imperialist imaginary names those practices of representation that project the vast, dispersed area of Asia and the Pacific as a unified region" (Eperjesi, 2). Further, these practices of representation are culled from

> a wide range of cultural materials – novels, poems, essays, advertisements, films, business, journals – in terms of the mapping functions that they perform. All cultural materials project, either explicitly or implicitly, conceptions and practices of space. That is, they offer historically specific ways of seeing distances and proximities, boundaries and limits, centers and peripheries, insides and outsides, and the big and the small, the symmetrical and the sublime, the open and the closed, origins and destinations, not to mention all of the ambiguous, uncertain, or unfixed areas in between. We tend to think that our knowledge of geography comes from maps used in geography class, the news, or the random copy of National Geographic lying around the waiting room at the dentist's office. One assumption that connects the various readings brought together here is that people derive their geographic sensibilities from all sorts of cultural texts. (Eperjesi, 2)

With this conception of mapping, surely Wilkes was engaged in the process twice over although he may not have been conscious of it: Once, through the official "objective" survey that he has been tasked to perform; and, twice, through the accumulated conceptions constructed in his head, such as the premise that the whole Pacific region—the American Pacific—would sooner or later fall, and be more clearly defined, within the United States realm of responsibility, including China as being already the ultimate goal or destination articulated by merchants, whalers, and fiction writers like Melville[6] albeit in a contrarian role as well as by the advocates of manifest destiny at the time, and drawn informally from an assortment of cultural, religious, and political artifacts that have formed part of his pool of knowledge and experience, including from the missionaries he (Wilkes) has encountered in Fiji and affirmed by his treatment of the Fijian natives who had the misfortune of crossing paths with him.

The Claim to Exceptionalism, Pretext to Imperialism

In a review of the rise of the modern-state system and its association with violence, San Juan offers his insight as follows:

> Typically described in normative terms, as a vital necessity of modern life, the modern-state has employed violence to accomplish questionable ends. Its disciplinary apparatus is indicted for committing unprecedented barbarism. Examples of disasters brought about by the nation-state are the extermination of indigenous peoples in colonized territories by "civilizing" nations…. (San Juan 2001)

San Juan also critiques post-modernist commentators on the Eurocentric conception of the nation-state by focusing largely on its ideologized nature and which defines identity as based on secular categories of citizenship as well as the "positivist logic of representation" presuming to supplant kinship or tribal affiliations but ignore the fact that, as San Juan explains, "the nation is a creation of the modern capitalist state, that is, a historical artifice or invention" (San Juan 2001). That commonality in language and culture may characterize a nation, but that is not a final determining factor. For while this commonality may be expedient and useful to the administration of a state, it is the fact of "commodity-centered economy" conditioned by a class-based distribution of wealth and control of labor that matters above all. This is what many commentators on the subject either miss or ignore, particularly among post-colonial scholars. They also miss this fact as the central and essential basis for understanding the state's intimate relationship with violence or state-sanctioned force, employed particularly and often in the fulfillment of its role in the "extraction of surplus value (profit)" and in the maintenance of a global "'free' exchange of commodities" (San Juan 2001). But more significantly, they miss the fact of manipulation of nationalism to suit the interests of the class in control of the state and its instruments of violence. As San Juan explains, "The doctrine of formal pluralism underwrites an acquisitive, entrepreneurial individualism that fits perfectly with mass consumerism and the gospel of unregulated market.... It is within this framework that we can comprehend how ruling bourgeoisie of each sovereign state... utilizes nationalist sentiment and the violence of the state apparatuses to impose their will" (San Juan 2007a, 116).

On the part of the United States, it was not so much the territorial aggrandizement of the European powers that had led the Americans to see themselves as morally aloof from the Europeans; it was, rather, their (i.e., the Europeans') apparent violence and brutality toward their respective subject peoples particularly toward those that advocated resistance to their rule. Specific illustrations of these were the Belgian practice of chopping off of the hands of captured escaped slaves in the so-called Congo Free State commencing in the 1880s; the British practice of beheadings of captured slave rebels, with their heads impaled in poles planted alongside roads in Jamaica during the 1820s and 1830s; the French violence toward the Tuaregs and other indigenous inhabitants of Algerian Sahara during the so-called *pénétration pacifique* ("peaceful conquest") of north Africa during much of the second half of the 1800s; the viciousness of Portuguese colonialism creating what has been described as "a management culture of violent domination and abuse" over its colonial possessions particularly of Brazil, Guinea, and Cape Verde, and the violent Dutch "civilizing" expeditions in West Papua during the 1880s, again involving beheadings, among various examples all throughout the colonial period.

Knowing this, any claim by the United States to exceptionalism falls flat on its face. There is no difference between it and its European colonial counterparts. Their respective economic systems, along with the concomitant claim to the monopoly of the use of force, are acquisitive in nature and inherently expansionist and exploitative. Further, in this context, it is easy to understand the inter-European wars and brutal pacification campaigns of their native subjects during much of the eighteenth and the nineteenth centuries, including the practice of *reconcentrado* deployed by the Spaniards against native Cubans prior to the US intervention in 1898, later to be popularly known as strategic hamleting replicated by the US military during the Philippine pacification campaign but with dismal consequences during its counterinsurgency operations in Vietnam. These were recounted in Gillo Pontecorvo's classic 1969 film, *Burn*, set in the section of the Caribbean region known as Lesser Antilles in a fictional Portuguese island of Quemada during the 1840s.[7] In that film, we also see recounted the British manipulation of domestic politics in Quemada, maneuvering the second-generation Portuguese elites (or *creoles*) to declare their independence from Portugal; by instilling the illusion of Western civilization's blessings which might someday be theirs to enjoy, Britain—though its agent Sir William Walker (played by Marlon Brando)—managed to manipulate the native population, i.e., descendants of African slaves, to rebel against the Portuguese elites and then, managed to persuade these elites to accept British assistance to quell this rebellion and, in the end, overthrow the same Portuguese elites that allowed them into the island to begin with. The character of Brando, William Walker, who was not so much an agent of the British Crown (although he felt loyalty to and affinity with it) but, rather, by the British West Indies Company, chartered by the Crown, that sought to establish sugar monopoly. Walker's role is a variant of what may generally be referred to as an economic jackal, a very important background feature if one wishes to understand the dark side of contemporary neoliberal globalization described in John Perkins' book, *Confessions of an Economic Hitman* (2005).

Upon the conclusion of the Spanish–American War, under terms of the Treaty of Paris of 1898, and the proclamation of the defeat of the Filipino revolutionary forces in the Philippines on July 4, 1901, the shift in US colonial administration from military to civilian rule was put into motion. It should be noted that this fairly expeditious shift to civilian rule has been one of the bases for exceptionalist claim that distinguished the United States from its European counterparts. Thus, from the onset of the Philippine–US War on February 2, 1898, until January 20, 1899, the US President, under war powers, ruled the new colony through the military governor. Beginning January 20, 1899, the colony was ruled through a succession of so-called Philippine Commissions headed by a Commissioner appointed by the US President. The First Commission, headed by Jacob Schurman, issued a report expressing the view that "Should our power by any fatality be withdrawn, the commission believed that the government of the Philippines would speedily lapse into anarchy, which would excuse, if it did not necessitate, the intervention of other powers and the eventual division of the islands among them."

On March 16, 1900, McKinley appointed the Second Philippine Commission headed by William Howard Taft. This body practically served as the colony's virtual government headed by a Governor-General, later to be subsumed under the Philippine Organic Act of 1902. The Second Philippine Commission was granted limited executive, legislative, and judicial powers enabling it to issue laws, draw up a penal code, and establish a judicial system, including a supreme court. It was also under Taft's governorship that a highly centralized public school system was established, in 1901. With English as its medium of instruction, the Taft Commission authorized the recruitment of teachers from the United States.[8] Under this program, some five hundred teachers boarded the US transport vessel *Thomas* in what Dinah Roma-Sianturi would later describe as a "pedagogic invasion" (Roma-Sianturi). After just under two decades of US colonial rule in the Philippines, Charles Burke Elliott, a former member of the (Second) Philippine Commission, expressed quite unabashedly a gendered and racialized representation of the US empire, in his 1917 report detailing the accomplishments of the Commission and using these with which to compare, with a sense of pride and confidence, the US empire with the European powers. Recalling Admiral George Dewey's victory over the Spanish armada at the Battle of Manila Bay in May 1898, and using the affectionate and genderized term "Columbia" to refer to the United States, Elliott wrote that Columbia "was then full grown, and Dewey's battle in Manila Bay was regarded as a sort of national coming out party. Henceforth she was to be considered in society." As such, the debutante apparently lost any inhibitions with regard to taking up any responsibility for expansion. In another breadth, Elliott justified this expansion because "virile nations are and have always been colonizing nations" (as quoted in Opisso). Elliott also took pains to elaborate albeit with flair and exaggeration on US exceptionalism, and why the United States was different from the European powers, in the following passage:

> America has controlled the Philippines for seventeen years, nearly a third of which were years of war and organization. In the short time, she has demonstrated not only that her people possess the Englishman's capacity for governing dependencies, but that they have a certain quality of enthusiasm for high ideals which British colonial history has not always disclosed and to the lack of which friendly foreign critics attribute her present difficulties in India and Egypt. Law, order, and justice prevail in the Philippines as in all the British colonies. The Filipinos have their national aspirations, their agitators, sedition mongers, irresponsible politicos and objectionable newspapers. They are as eager for self-government as the Indians and the Egyptians, but it is a noticeable fact that these conquered, irritable, and excitable people have not thrown a bomb or attempted to murder an American official. America's policy has not been repressive; it has not been presented a stone wall of opposition

to native aspirations, and it gives every indication of being successful. (as quoted in Opisso)

The claim to the exceptional nature of US imperialism, based on patently less than truthful description of Filipino resistance to US rule, particularly as distinguished from the European variety, is reinforced—uncritically as it is—by mainstream scholarship particularly on the part of US-based writers and academicians imbued with the functionalist framework. San Juan cites as a matter of example, the 1982 work of David Joel Steinberg, entitled *The Philippines: A Singular and a Plural Place*. In this book, San Juan observes that Steinberg gives credit to Filipinos at "both the elite and peasant levels," having presumably undergone a growth and maturation process as in an organism and for behaving in such a manner as to positively influence US policy and cause US colonialism to be a "self-liquidating" one, a feat hardly matched by any European colonial counterpart. San Juan goes on to explain:

> The trope of tutelage, the notion of American "exceptionalism," the evolutionary metaphor of "maturation," people of color as infantile wards, and so on-all these inform a whole corpus of texts formulating the legitimacy of U.S. occupation of the Philippines, from those of LeRoy, Worcester and Forbes to Hayden, Taylor, Stanley, Friend, May, and Karnow. Hence, Steinberg argues that mass education leading to functional literacy provided the technocrats, bureaucrats and functionaries of Taft's "Filipinization" campaign. This in turn "diffused the tight control of an interlocked and interrelated class" by the proliferation of subelites. (San Juan 1998)

San Juan elaborates on the theme of Filipino maturation, particularly on the part of the oligarchic elites whose appetite for power has apparently been restrained by education and inculcation of democratic values, for having presumably won the confidence of the US colonial administrators to be worthy enough to be awarded independence, as follows:

> Accompanying this apology for U.S. colonization is a view that has become hegemonic in U.S. scholarship, namely, the Filipino elite's success in forcing *"the American reformers [such as the Schurman and Taft commissions] to accept them and their world view."* In short, responsibility for the failure to radically transform the unequal power and property-relations does not lie with the American colonial administrators or with U.S. federal policies; it lies with the Filipino elite. Steinberg invokes the notion of "compadre colonialism,"

the policy of attraction and accommodation in which both sides, rulers and ruled, recognized the mutual advantages in their collaboration. Steinberg concludes his summary of the U.S. colonial period: *"The Americans surrendered to the* ilustrados *the means to achieve that goal [of making the Philippines the U.S. "showcase of democracy"]. The result was an odd mixture of theory and expediency, a perpetual compromise, a modern variant of indirect rule."* (San Juan 1998)

Another US-based writer whom San Juan trains his critical eye on is Stanley Karnow, author of the popular book, *In Our Image: America's Empire in the Philippines* (1989). San Juan describes this book as "probably the most effective tool of persuasion for what I would call the apologetic mode of Filipinology sustained by the insidious epistemological paradigm of structural-functionalism of the Cold War era" (San Juan 1998). San Juan is particularly critical of the deployment by Karnow of the functionalist mode of analysis used to explain presumed Filipino cultural values as *pakikisama* (tendency to get along), *utang na loob* (debt of gratitude), *hiya* (sense of shame), *amor propio* (self-esteem), and the *compadrazgo* system (extended non-blood family ties through baptismal and wedding sponsorships, etc.). These are used as a double-edged sword by self-anointed Filipinologists like Karnow to explain, on the one hand, the apparent resilience of the Filipinos in the face of colonialism and, on the other, as cultural impediments to progress, leading Karnow to conclude, as San Juan explains, that the US failure "to transform the Philippines into an authentic democratic society" was essentially due to these. In Karnow's words, Filipinos were "trapped in a tangle of contradictions ... History is responsible" leaving the US policy little or no room but to accommodate "Filipino traditions", including the "baffling web of real and ritual kinship ties" (San Juan 1998).

This clever sleight-of-hand on the part of apologists like Karnow to essentially exculpate the United States from any responsibility for the conduct of the military conquest and the brutal conduct of the pacification campaign throughout the Philippines to the exclusion of material factors. Further, little do Karnow and his fellow self-appointed Filipinologists acknowledge the conscious and deliberate design of the architects of colonial rule to utilize the collaborationist local elites or native aristocracy, facilitated by the teaching and the imposition of the English language, and the *pensionado* program, commencing in 1903, of enticing eager and ambitious Filipinos to travel to and study in the United States, and learn about the American culture and inculcate in them individualistic values with which to gauge success. By the year 1912, more than two hundred young Filipinos had been sent "stateside' under this program (Duka). As San Juan writes, citing the case of writers as point of reference: "While the U.S. imperial power preserved the tributary order via the institutionalization of patronage in all levels of society, the use of English by apprentice writers fostered individualism through the modality of aesthetic vanguardism. Personal liberation displaced the dream of national sovereignty" (San Juan 2000a).

1898—The Nexus of Global Events: The Spanish–American War of May 1898, the Philippine Revolution of June 1898, and the Expansion of the US Empire

As alluded to above, global events in 1898 seemed to offer the United States a fortuitous opportunity to demonstrate its exceptionalism from the Europeans. In February 1898, the US battleship, *USS Maine*, was on a visit to and docked at the harbor in Havana, Cuba, then a Spanish colony exploded killing over two hundred and fifty naval personnel. The following month, a US Naval Court of Inquiry had concluded that an "underwater mine" had caused the incident, without saying who planted the mine. It clearly implied that Spain or its agents were responsible. Under the pretext of punishing the Spaniards the influential media at that time, led by William Randolph Hearst and Joseph Pulitzer, proprietors of the news dailies *New York Journal* and the *New York World*, respectively, had whipped up a frenzy and inflaming public sentiments against Spain, and at the same time generating public support for US military intervention in Cuba presumably in behalf of the Cuban revolutionaries fighting against Spanish colonial rule. The Cuban revolutionaries had issued an appeal to the US government for military assistance, consisting of small arms with which to fight. They also requested US naval blockade of the island to prevent Spanish vessels both from entering and leaving the island nation. They never asked to be taken over. The United States did indeed intervene militarily but, as history bears, for its own purposes, a point well-made by moral philosopher Michael Walzer in critiquing US humanitarian interventionism in Cuba (Walzer, 101–104). In April 1898, the US Congress declared war on Spain, followed by the deployment of about seventeen thousand marines that were initially landed in June i n Santiago de Cuba on the east end of the island, quickly capturing Guantanamo Bay within days; in July, US troops mounted an assault on San Juan Hill featuring the so-called Rough Riders of which would-be Secretary of the Navy and President, Theodore Roosevelt, was a celebrated member.

Meanwhile, in late April, the US Asiatic Squadron, with its six fighting ships then plying between Hong Kong and Singapore under the command of Admiral George Dewey, received a direct order from then Secretary of the Navy, Roosevelt, to sail to Manila Bay with the expressed order of destroying the Spanish fleet. At Manila Bay, on May 1, the Spanish armada, officially called the Spanish South Pacific Squadron, was supposedly engaged—to be explained more below—by Dewey's fleet resulting in the complete destruction of the Spanish fleet, and the silencing of coastal defensive batteries, including the siege guns of Corregidor Island at the entrance to the Bay, while suffering not a single fatality and only eight wounded, a fact to be explored more below in relation to arrangements between US and Spanish authorities leading up to this so-called battle. As is well-known, this brief war ended with Spanish capitulation and the signing of the Treaty of Paris in December of that year. Under the treaty, control over the Spanish possessions of Cuba, Puerto Rico, and Guam was transferred to the United States. It was also stipulated that for the sum of twenty million US dollars, the Philippines would be turned over to and subsequently be ruled under US sovereignty.

It is well to note that simultaneous to the Cuban revolution against Spain was also the Philippine revolution against the same European colonial power. By this time, Spain had been the longest reigning European colonial power in Asia and, for the hundred years or so prior to this point, other European powers, including the United States, had been gradually overtaking Spain in terms of technology, economic power, and military might. Spain had become moribund. Motivated by their own desires for geographic expansion and appetite for economic gain, they were eager to challenge Spain's hegemony. Thus, in this context, it would be naïve to assume that the United States was motivated simply by altruism in helping the Cuban revolutionaries in their fight against Spain. The Monroe Doctrine had been in place since 1823 intended to discourage European powers out of hemispheric affairs, and the United States had been gradually consolidating its military strength, and eyeing eventual control and influence in the Caribbean region, particularly over the Panama Canal; it finally gained control and took over its construction from France in 1904 as apparent reward for supporting the secession of Panama from Colombia in 1903.

As for the Pacific region, the US military presence had been officially legitimated by a counterpart doctrine to the Monroe Doctrine, which was designed mainly for the Caribbean region. The Pacific doctrine was called the Tyler Doctrine named after US President John Tyler who promulgated it on December 30, 1842—two and half years following the Malolo Massacre—ostensibly for the so-called protection of the Hawaiian Islands from anticipated predations by European rivals. Again, for one to assume that US imperialism was motivated simply by its desire to benefit and protect the inhabitants of the Hawaiian archipelago would be naïve at best. The US Navy had for some time coveted the deepwater port which came to be known as Pearl Harbor. When a private coup plot against the indigenous Hawaiian monarchy was successfully carried out in January 1893 by descendants of godly American missionaries and their allies with such last names as Thurston, Dole, Castle, and Cooke, all united by the common desire to control the Kingdom's political future under conditions that would bring them and their respective family businesses economic profits (mainly from sugar, pineapple, and other tropical fruit production), and organizing themselves into the treacherous "Committee of Safety," with the tacit support of the US Navy and the conspiracy of US diplomat John L. Stevens, it was a matter of time that the Hawaiian Kingdom would be absorbed to be part of the burgeoning US empire, as in fact it did when it was annexed as an appurtenant territory in July 1898, and eventually as the fiftieth state of the Union in 1959. At the time that the coup plotters were lobbying the US Congress for annexation, they found an ardent advocate by the name of Theodore Roosevelt. In 1897, reports historian Thomas Dyer, "Roosevelt cast the proposed annexation of Hawaii in a sharply racial light. If Hawaii were not taken, he told Alfred T. Mahan, 'it will show that we either have lost, or else wholly lack, the masterful instinct which alone can make a race great,' an unthinkable circumstance for an individual who thought of the great races as possessing vigorous expansionist tendencies" (Dyer). It is not an unfair statement to say that, under the circumstances in which events took place, the Hawaiian monarchy was overthrown in an illegal coup, and the Hawaiian Islands and the resources therein were, in plain language, stolen, a historic wrong for which the native Hawaiians still have to receive justice, and a shameful deed which the US government, despite US President Bill Clinton's signing of Public Law 103–150, popularly referred to in the media as the "Apology Resolution," in November 1993, still has to, at the very least, translate any apology into deed.[9]

It is worth noting that during much of the second half of the 1800s leading up to the Spanish–American War of 1898, there has been cantankerous agitation for the westward expansion of the so-called American frontier. Among these agitators was Jane McManus Storm Cazneau (also known as "Cora Montgomery") who is claimed to be the first to use the phrase "Manifest Destiny" particularly in regard to her 1845 advocacy of the annexation of Texas from Mexico through her numerous newspaper columns and journal articles. Imperialism in the Pacific later gained more support particularly from among those with a platform in which to broadcast their views. Among these was Alfred Thayer Mahan, a Captain in the US Navy and President of the US Naval War College. In 1890, Mahan published his highly influential and widely read book, entitled *The Influence of Sea Power Upon History, 1660–1783*. An original copy of this book sits in a glass case at the Theodore Roosevelt Estate Museum in Sagamore Hill, Long Island, New York as a testament to the mutual admiration that Roosevelt and Mahan had for each other, and whose views complemented each other. Roosevelt believed that victory, augmented by Mahan's notion of naval imperialism, over the "aboriginal savages" of the world is foundational to securing the "heritage of the dominant world races" (Morris, 477). In Mahan's book, taking a cue from the British success in building an empire with the help of its navy, Mahan urged adoption of a series of forward-looking, and "vigorous foreign policy" on the part of the United States by building and procuring: a. merchant fleet to transport US goods to and from foreign markets; b. a "battleship navy" to secure these markets and deter potential rivals; and c. a network of naval ports for storing fuel and supplies, not to mention, as would later be realized, forward basing for interventionary forces particularly in the western Pacific. These suggestions are in line with the assessment—in the passage that follows—of the Office of the Historian of the US Department of State about Mahan's influential views at the time, views which were later vindicated:

> Mahan believed that the U.S. economy would soon be unable to absorb the massive amounts of industrial and commercial goods being produced domestically, and he argued that the United States should seek new markets abroad. What concerned Mahan most was ensuring that the U.S. Government could guarantee access to these new international markets. (US Department of State)

On the religious front, thanks to the work of one particular preacher, Josiah Strong, also a good friend to Roosevelt, who, through his preachings and polemical writings, including one entitled *Our Country: Its Possible Future and Its Present Crisis* (Strong 1885), argued for imperialism unabashedly in behalf of the Anglo-Saxon race based on religion subsumed under what he called the doctrine of world mission arguing, in his book: "The Anglo-Saxon is the representative of two great ideas, which are closely related. One of them is that of civil liberty. Nearly all of the civil liberty of the world is enjoyed by Anglo-Saxons: the English, the British colonists, and the people of the United States....The other great idea of which the Anglo-Saxon is the exponent is that of a pure spiritual Christianity." He adds: "It follows, then, that the Anglo-Saxon, as… the depository of these two greatest blessings, … is divinely commissioned to be, in a peculiar sense, his brother's keeper."

William H. Berge, a scholar on the subject and the period, assesses some of the implications of Strong's views in a 1973 academic article as follows, in part:

> Strong said that God was everywhere at war with greed and selfishness. Christian people should combat selfishness in nations as well as in individuals, and force should be used if necessary. The motive behind the use of force was the criterion with which to judge the action. There was little doubt in the minds of the pro-war clergymen; the war against "Spanish tyranny" was a judicious use of force. The religious sanction for the war with Spain, which came from the Protestant clergy, was in part the result of intense anti-Catholic feeling. (Berge)

Berge also explains that while Strong was not an advocate for imperialism for commercial reasons, he recognized the conjunction because, as Strong is quoted, "Whether or not the constitution follows the flag, opportunity does." Further, Berge explains of Strong's views as follows:

> The final appeal expressed, from what appeared to be a practical and rational point of view, was a call for the recognition of imperialism as the climax of a continuing movement. Strong felt that the United States had been destined to be the great imperial power. Had not the idea of "empire" been traveling westward for centuries? Another explanation flavored with Darwinism was presented in the October 1900 *Westminster Review*, where the author held that the imperial tendencies of any country were but one step in a process that has been in action since the first social organization.

It should be remembered, however, that the motivating force and ideological basis for Strong's support of expansion did not lie in a desire to make the United States politically and commercially powerful. It went much deeper than this. Strong was motivated by an intense sense of mission and divine destiny. The ideology of this mission and destiny was a combination of racism, religion, and nationalism. (Berge)

The likes of Strong from evangelical Protestant church denominations have shared similar views and fervor. As one illustration, Horace B. Silliman, a successful New York-based businessman, reportedly showed up unexpectedly at the Office of the Presbyterian Board of Foreign Mission, one day in 1899, within months of the news of Dewey's claimed victory in Manila Bay, bearing a gift of ten thousand US dollars. According to author Arthur Carson, Silliman possessed a "strong resolve to help shape Philippine education" and believed that the Filipinos needed "a new kind of education" in any case. Because the Board of Foreign Mission itself had been considering establishing a "mission in the Philippine Islands," the Mission Board was not hard to persuade and the fund was accepted to be used as Silliman had wished, i.e., the founding of a vocational institute but whose effect, through its extensive network with religious and cultural agents, was the endorsement of and collaboration with colonialism. This institute evolved to become a full-fledged, church-based institution of higher learning known as Silliman University, situated in the island of Negros, today an outpost of unquestioning fealty to neoliberal education, and offering its constituents, mainly alumni that have fanned across the globe, with an emotional sedative referred to as "Silliman Spirit" emphasizing personal bond with the institution but dulling any criticism of empire ("History of Silliman").

Notes

1. San Juan offers further assessment of the implications of the Europe-based mercantile trading, including the trafficking of slaves, the colonization of much of the rest of the world, and the crushing of resistance to this colonization, and the phenomenon of diaspora, in the following passage: "After about four centuries of the worldwide circulation of commodities—including the hugely profitable trade in slaves from Africa that inaugurated, for Marx, the 'rosy dawn' of capitalism—the stage was set for more intense capital accumulation based no longer on commercial exchange and the regional discrepancies in the price of goods but on the process of production itself.

'Place' gave way to space; lived time divided into necessary, surplus, and 'free' segments. Linked by relations of exchange governed by the logic of accumulation centered in Europe and later in North America, the trajectories of peoples of color, the 'people without history' in Eric Wolf's reckoning, entered the global labor market with the expansion of industrial capitalism, the commercialization of agriculture, urbanization, and the concomitant dislocation and displacement of populations from their traditional homelands" (San Juan 1995).

2. Here, San Juan interjects a point that during much of the 1700s and the 1800s at least up until the Opium Wars, movement of labor, referring to the so-called free workers, has been taking place, and that this diaspora of workers—bearers of labor power, according to San Juan, had been an essential component in the building of the industrial and commercial bases of modern capitalism. San Juan describes the process as follows: "In the nineteenth and early twentieth centuries, the movement of the bearers of labor power, 'free workers', at first involved mainly peasants pushed toward the industrial enters of the European peninsula; later, 50 million people left Europe between 1800 and 1924, 32 million of them bound for the factories and mines of the industrializing United States. (Of the 200 million migrants between 1500 and 1980, 42 million were from the continent of Asia.)" (San Juan 2000a).

Following the British humiliation of China at the conclusion of the Opium Wars, which gave Britain possession of Hong Kong as trophy, the United States became a beneficiary. San Juan explains how the migration of labor during this period has made a contribution to the consolidation of the US industrial and commercial base, essential to turning the United States as the preeminent capitalist bastion in the succeeding century: "Meanwhile, the victory of imperialism in China with the Opium War of 1839-1842 allowed foreign entrepreneurs or brokers to establish the apparatus for the 'coolie' trade that eventually facilitated the transport of 200,000 Chinese to the United States between 1852 and 1875.... In the 1860s, about 14,000 Chinese laborers were hired to build the transcontinental Central Pacific Railroad. Unlike the Chinese 'pariah capitalism' in other regions..., the Chinese exodus to North America could only mediate between an exploitative host society and a moribund tributary formation already subjugated by Western powers" (San Juan 2000a).

3. The combination of religion and violence has undoubtedly been a potent mix in achieving Western colonial aims under the guise of a civilizing mission. The clarity of this mix is contrasted with or compounded by the apparent lack or absence of official recognition [of this mix], perhaps as means of avoiding culpability and responsibility, among state leaders, on the one hand, and maintaining the ambiguity indefinitely and preserve a free hand for future action that might opportunistically be for the benefit of one or the other,

or both (church and state), as in the case of the Malolo massacre, on the other. In a 2005 article, San Juan cites US Permanent Representative to the United Nations, Samantha Power, from her 2002 essay, in which she cites apparent coincidental set of ambiguities confronted supposedly by US officials with regard to the nature of violence that has characterized recent and contemporary international relations. Much of this violence, of course, has been inflicted by the United States itself. However, that is not what matters. Rather, as Power notes and quoted by San Juan, it is the supposed "genuine" dilemma of US officials in "distinguishing the deliberate massacre of civilians from the casualties incurred in conventional conflict" (San Juan 2007b xv). With the Malolo massacre as a starting reference point, San Juan's reaction to the above-quote from Power somewhat apologizing for the ambiguity makes crystal clear the self-serving nature of this ambiguity, which allows for indefinite serial repetition of violence without accountability to the state or anyone acting in its name in the future. As in the current so-called war on terror being waged by the United States, the practical expediency of this deliberate ambiguity is illustrated by the support for an assortment of terrorist formations variously defined as "moderate" or "democratic" forces, such as those fighting in Syria manipulated to serve not so much their respective political or religious ends but, rather, to pursue broader US agenda in the Middle East region. As San Juan writes: "It is precisely the blurring of this distinction in colonial wars through racializing discourses and practices that proves how genocide cannot be fully grasped without analyzing the way the victimizer (the colonizing state power) categorizes the victims (target populations) in totalizing and naturalizing modes unique perhaps to the civilizational drives of modernity" (San Juan 2007b xv).

4. San Juan again offers an important historical insight on this important subject tantamount to cultural genocide as follows: "As with the American Indians, US colonization involved, among other things, the destruction of the specific character of a persecuted group by forced transfer of children, forced exile, prohibition of the use of the national language, destruction of books, documents, monuments, and objects of historical, artistic or religious value. The goal of all colonialism is the cultural and social death of the conquered natives, in effect, genocide" (San Juan 2005).

5. In hindsight, the episode described above turned out to be predictive of the US military demeanor, both domestically and, more so, internationally. Domestically, it was exemplified by the brutality with which the US Civil War was fought and won, exemplified by the infamous burning of the City of Atlanta in July 1864 and the subsequent march to the sea from there ordered by Union General William T. Sherman, happening during November and December, same year, wherein the soldiers engaged in a scorch-earth policy of burning, looting, and destroying civilian property that they could lay their

hands on with the ostensible purpose of terrifying the enemy civilian population throughout the Confederate South into withdrawing their support for the Confederacy and its army. And, during the American–Indian Wars, motivated essentially by the desire to eradicate Indian resistance to Federal forces, two examples come to mind: first, the Battle of Little Big Horn, in June 1876, where the destruction of the US Cavalry, led by Lieutenant Colonel George A. Custer, was not so much what was important but, rather, the intention to stamp out the Lakota Indians, including resort to the questionable tactic of holding noncombatant women and children as hostages, and second, the Massacre at Wounded Knee, in December 1890, where a band of Lakota Indians were mercilessly massacred at an encampment, including several fleeing Indians ritually shot in the back following which surviving participating officers were later awarded the Congressional Medal of Honor for "gallantry in action and soldierly qualities." Internationally, this pattern would be manifested in several notable cases including: (a) the suppression of the Philippine Revolution in brutal counterinsurgency campaign by the US Army from 1899 until 1913 featuring the use of "water cure" and several instances of massacres, among others; (b) the conduct of the Vietnam War, commencing with the use of so-called non-combat advisors in 1958 to the massive deployment of troops by 1968 involving the use of surrogate troops from South Korea, the Philippines, Australia, and New Zealand, and the shift to the Vietnamization program from 1971 until the end of this war in April 1975. During this war, we saw the adoption of an assassination program called Operation Phoenix tasked with eliminating civilians suspected of being part of the Viet Cong political structure, and the use of tactics such as Operation Rolling Thunder involving massive carpet bombing of Vietnam's countryside, and the use and deployment of prohibited and morally reprehensible weapons like Agent Orange, a chemical weapon used to defoliate forest vegetation but also to contaminate rivers, streams, and lakes, not to mention the soil which eventually gets into human reproductive system causing deformities in newborn babies, among other side effects; (c) throughout much of the Global South, support to prop up right-wing authoritarian regimes with all kinds of assistance including military, police, and para-military training and equipment geared particularly against domestic armed insurgency as well as for quelling above-ground non-violent opposition such as those directed against street protests, and union organizing; (d) likewise, throughout much of the Global South and the post-Cold War Eastern Europe, and complementary to (c) above, support for subversive activities, including sponsorship, training, and management of armed terrorist formations to terrorize civilian population, destroy civilian infrastructure, outright assassination of undesirable political leaders, including intervention in the electoral process and coups d'etat, all designed to subvert the duly established constitutional order and carry out a regime-change program, and install a regime more compliant to the liking of the United States; and, (d) in coordination with global financial institutions controlled by the United States, the deployment of "economic hit men" directed against borrowing countries, most of which are located in the Global South to ensnare them to accept large sums of low-interest loans collateralized by the borrowing countries' natural resources, and the privatization of public services including vital utilities, all designed to essentially transfer economic sovereignty to external supranational entities acting in conformity with the US neoliberal agenda, rejection of which would result in drastic consequences, including assassinations and coups.

6. While Melville's classic work Moby Dick is highly popular today especially among young readers, it was heavily criticized by literary critics of his time perhaps on account of it being misunderstood, or because in this novel he crystallized his views on the subjects of imperialism by the US and the European powers more broadly as well as on self-rule or independence on the part of Polynesian and African subjects. But even outside of this novel, Melville never tried to conceal his disdain for missionaries and their evangelizing work such as those he encountered in the Marquesan Islands in 1835 for perpetuating the image of the native islanders as "savage and bloodthirsty cannibals" (Blumenthal, 2). Also, in the second in a series of three lectures he gave commencing in 1857, entitled "The South Seas", Melville "indicts not only America's imperialist presumptions in the Pacific Islands, but her own self-conceived identity as a 'superior' and 'civilized' country" (Blumenthal, 3). Interestingly, San Juan offers a passing mention of Melville in the context of his (San Juan's) discussion of the radicalization of CLR James' thinking on British imperialism and the growth of Caribbean emancipatory consciousness. San Juan writes: "I should qualify this, however, by interpolating here the subsequent catalyzing role of the militant socialist tradition: it was the influence of Marxism, particularly American Trotskyism, along with radical French historiography, Herman Melville's fiction, and U.S. popular culture filtered through the mass media, that served as midwife to the anti-imperialist rebirth of cricket as an allegory of the West Indian quest for national recognition and self-determination" (San Juan 2000b).

7. This is a pertinent point to raise because the period in which this movie was set was one in which European powers were squabbling over influence and territory not only in the Caribbean region but also throughout the New World. The United States partook in the slave trade and benefited in its growth and development from the unpaid labor of slaves, a fact that it still has to reconcile itself with today. But at that period, the issue of slavery was resolved in two ways, according to San Juan. He writes: "The apparent incongruity of the 'unfree' (slave) inhabiting the terrain of the 'free' (laissez-faire market) disappears if we apply two analytic concepts: social formation and mode of production.

While the U.S. then may be defined as chiefly an emergent capitalist social formation from the time of its independence to the Civil War, one can discern in it two discordant modes of production: the slave mode in the South and the mercantile-industrial one in the North. The triumph of the juridical framework of capitalism (based on Lockean principles of alienable labor, etc.) and its state machinery led to the legal abolition of slavery in 1865. This is a clear sign that New World slavery was not similar to that in Graeco-Roman societies where slavery was not abolished by a legal act but by a long period of evolution when it was eventually superseded by another kind of dependent labor (serfdom) which became dominant, even though chattel slaves continued to exist up the late Middle Ages. What is clear, however, is that the elite in the U.S. South was mainly parasitic on coerced labor for its wealth and reproduction. Reconstruction eliminated the practice of coercion, the aristocratic habitus..., only to replace it with that of the market legitimized by Constitutional amendments, and (after 1877) by wholesale fraud, Jim Crow laws, and vigilante violence" (San Juan 2007a).
8. In 2001, San Juan received the prestigious Gustavus Myers Center for Human Rights Outstanding Book Award for Human Rights, for his book, *After Post-colonialism; Remapping Philippines-United States Confrontations*. In this book, San Juan comments on the "ideological maneuvers" employed by the United States in carrying out its self-appointed role as tutor to the ignorant and uneducated Filipinos as part of its "civilizing mission." He writes: "In 1898, the Philippines then became U.S. territory open for the 'tutelage' of its civilizing mission. Among other ideological maneuvers, the English language and American literary texts, as well as the pedagogical agencies for propagating and teaching them, were mobilized to constitute the natives of the Philippine archipelago as subjects of the U.S. nation-state. In sum, then, American English was used by the colonial authorities when the U.S. military suppressed the Filipino revolutionary forces and its Republic while waging war against the moribund Spanish Empire. Language became an adjunct of the imperial machinery of conquest and subjugation.... The 'otherness' of Filipinos comprised of multiple speech genres and semantic worlds eventually yielded to a unitary medium of communication enforced in government, business, media, and the public sphere. American English became the language of prestige and aspiration" (San Juan 2000a).
9. Both in collective memory and in popular literature today, the history of Hawaii just narrated here is remarkably blank. In pretty much the entire contemporary media and standard texts, Hawaii is presented as an exotic paradise, a vacation destination, with expensive urban living standards, and a source of high-value tropical fruits and other agricultural products. The natives are presented as curiosities welcoming visitors with garlands of beautiful tropical

flowers and relegated to providing entertainment with their dances and costumes at hotels and other cultural events. Not surprisingly, attempts on the part of native Hawaiians and their sympathetic supporters to remind visitors—and the world—about this portion of Hawaii's history, about the overthrow of Hawaii's constitutional monarchy in 1893, and about the current movement for the restoration of Hawaii's sovereignty are invariably discouraged, banned, or outrightly declared illegal by state and US federal authorities. Such is the case, for example, with the State of the Nation of Hawaii whose members, invoking the United Nations Charter as well as the US Public Law 103–150 condemning the United States for illegally overthrowing the sovereign government of Hawaii have engaged in acts of resistance including non-payment of taxes, land occupation, and the establishment of its own militia and security force to assist in the claim to restore Hawaii's lost sovereignty.

Other forms of resistance have taken an anti-neoliberal character and tone. One such movement is represented by the Land Defenders known largely in Hawaii as the Mauna Kea Hui dedicated to opposing what supporters say is the desecration of a sacred mountain and its surroundings as a result of the construction of a Canadian-funded eighteen-story telescope, popularly known as the Thirty Meter Telescope, purportedly the most powerful telescope for use by astronomers to peek at the solar system particularly the Milky Way and the galaxies nearby; this facility would also include a large office complex and a parking lot built over protected conservation land at the mountain's summit in addition to the construction of a new road leading to and from the summit. Another movement of this type is the loose anti-Genetically Modified Organisms (GMO) movement taking the parliamentary route of enacting legislation through local, county, and state institutions banning—or attempting to ban—GMO seed and plants from Hawaiian farms. Along these lines, legislators in the island—and county—of Kauai, in October 2013, enacted a legislation restricting the use of pesticides and the breeding and planting of GMOs by such biotech giants as DuPont, Pioneer, Syngenta, Monsanto, and BASF in the island. The legislation prohibits these companies from using pesticides in no-spray zones especially around schools, hospitals, homes, roads, and water systems. Even though the same bill would have included prohibition on the use of GMOs, the provision on this was removed during deliberations under threat from these companies that they would leave the island altogether if the bill passed containing these restrictions. Nonetheless, a group of these companies sued the island for its legislation and, in August 2014, a federal judge at the US District Court for the District of Hawaii overturned Kauai's law. On another front, on election day in November of 2014, voters in Maui County, which includes the islands of Maui, Lanai, and Molokai, persisted in their anti-GMO movement, defied the threats and intimidation by the biotech industry, and took the decisive step of approving a moratorium on the experimentation and planting of GMO plant products anywhere in the county. If this law stands, as it is once again being challenged in court by the biotech industry, one observer opines that this law would have "broken a crucial link in the biotech business model," especially so that, as one Monsanto representative admitted, "The majority of corn seed we sell to farmers in Argentina, Brazil and the U.S. has originated from Monsanto's Maui operations" and that, if the law is allowed to stand, Monsanto and other biotech companies would have to "scramble" in search of new places wherein to develop these seeds (Johnson).

The activist-oriented native Hawaiians, including members and supporters of Mauna Kea Hui, have also affiliated themselves with the Canadian-based Idle No More (INM) Movement, consisting of mainly Canadian indigenous groups. In INM's Web site, it calls on peoples everywhere "to join in a peaceful revolution, to honour indigenous sovereignty, and to protect land and water." In its Manifesto, the INM recalls the sad and shameful history of treaty violations on the part of the British Crown, not just the Canadian government. It affirms the sanctity of treaty agreements, asserting that these can neither be altered nor broken unilaterally. It declares, in part: "The spirit and intent of the Treaty agreements meant that First Nations peoples would share the land, but retain their inherent rights to lands and resources. Instead, First Nations have experienced a history of colonization which has resulted in outstanding land claims, lack of resource and unequal funding for services such as education and housing" (Idle No More).

Taking the reviews and commentaries of Kiana Davenport's novel *Shark Dialogues* as a jumping-off board for the reason that, in this case, "[t]he seductiveness of a hegemonic reading and interpretive approach persists in the institution of book reviewing," and taking the opportunity as well to comment on the significance of this novel on the saga of seven generations of a Hawaiian family that encompasses the events described here, San Juan, in a remarkable essay entitled "Cultural Studies Amongst the Sharks: The Struggle Over Hawaii" (2002), comments on the virtual whitewashing of Hawaii's past. San Juan writes: "By force of inertia, the sporadic reviews of Shark Dialogues veer toward a formalist aestheticism that politically occludes, if not totally expunges, what Edward Said would call the worldliness or circumstantial resonance of the work. The pretext of recuperating or reinstating pleasure that subtends the putative return to aesthetics affords an ingenuous justification for reaffirming the way things are: for Hawaiians, the unconscionable colonial domination of their homelands and continued cultural genocide. From this neo-conservative optic, art (for the formalists) helps us to transcend the reality of degradation and colonial occupation" (San Juan 2002).

To cite an example, San Juan points to the apparent default assumption by reviewers, particularly of the book in question, that Hawaii is a multicultural showcase where one can point to the success of assimilation without so much wondering whether or not the author, Davenport, agrees. San Juan writes: "[A] reviewer for the Library Journal praises the book as 'entertaining and educational', avoiding 'didacticism' as Davenport provides us much information about politics, leprosy and 'the racial melting pot that is Hawaiian society'. On the banal impression of Hawaii as a melting pot, which the novelist indirectly critiques as another ideology, the reviewer does no better than an academic scholar like Andrew Lind, author of Hawaii's People, who argues that the statistics on intermarriage in Hawaii testify to the advance of assimilationism. Can a reading of Shark Dialogues correct this misleading doxa?" San Juan's answer to this rhetorical question is, of course, obvious.

San Juan takes the opportunity, in this case of Hawaii, as a perfect historical specimen and the misreading of it as evidenced by the reviews of Davenport's novel, to clarify the nature and purpose of cultural studies as a sub-discipline or a field of study. San Juan advances many thoughtful arguments, but the following passage is particularly significant: "Cultural Studies is an attempt to situate these formalist approaches to literary texts—the search for verisimilitude, for commonsensical truth—in the sociohistorical context of hegemonic culture. Its concern is to demonstrate how social divisions pivoting around the categories of class, gender, race, nationality, location, etc. are invested with meaning and legitimized. Culture (including literary and critical practice) becomes the site in which social/political inequalities are represented and naturalised. Thus Cultural Studies rejects the empiricist fallacy that events and personalities by themselves embody singular meanings as though they were natural phenomena, givens that transcend experience and consciousness. Culture is conceived not as equivalent to the realm of aesthetics replete with transcendent moral values, but as a terrain of struggle for hegemony, a historical and discursive terrain where dominant and subordinate forces interact." And, San Juan adds: "The Cultural Studies project thus engages directly with the dialectic of social agencies and structures."

Further, San Juan offers a prescient advice in looking at and integrating into cultural analysis the sovereignty movement as well as the emergent indigenous-oriented anti-neoliberal empowerment in Hawaii today such as the examples cited earlier. San Juan writes: "The emphasis on the local against the abstract or formalist universalism of mainstream literary study is healthy. But when the localists stress geography or place as distilling history separate from the imperial world-system, they lapse into an empiricist fixation that is no improvement over the Eurocentric pluralism they bewail. What is more significant is the indigenous motivation of ho'oponopono (the 'setting to right of wrongs') that passionately informs the warring interests and motives of the various communities in Shark Dialogues."

Further, San Juan elaborates: "I see Cultural Studies as an intervention in re-conceptualising culture as the field where literary texts like Shark Dialogues can be rescued from the realm of apologetics and appreciated for its pedagogical and conscientising (to use Freire's over-used term) qualities. Following Jameson's suggestions, cultural studies can be more effective when culture is viewed more as the site par excellence of ideological struggle. In this arena of discursive practice, group antagonisms are represented and fought through, with the reading experience itself posing ethical questions to the reader/audience and, more urgently, political imperatives. Culture dramatises the idea of the Other, the forms of relations among groups characterised by envy and loathing. Cultural Studies allows us to interpret prestige as an emanation of group solidarity, the object of collective envy and struggle, which underlies racism and ethnic conflict."

With this conception of cultural studies, San Juan believes that the field is a step closer to reclaiming its "original revolutionary impetus", and it can do so "by center-staging the radical project of diverse indigenous forms of life. It can help preserve these singular forms as long as this field continues to expose and critique the complicity of disciplinary practices with hegemonic political power." As a matter of praxis, San Juan also believes: "With the tide of globalised capitalism sweeping over national boundaries, partisans of revolutionary hope need to lend support to the indigenous peoples of Hawaii and elsewhere in their struggle for sovereignty. Reason dictates the priority of self-determined locations for unique aboriginal cultures to flourish. Their singular forms of life remain the touchstones for realising visions of popular, egalitarian democracy sustainable for constructing a global ecumene. They also provide viable weapons to resist commodification and global business's crusade of 'civilizing' rogue nations and subjugating terrorist Others – IMF/WB (International Monetary Fund/World Bank) deterritorialisation by transnational violence."

REFERENCES

Eperjesi, John R., *The Imperialist Imaginary: Visions of Asia and the Pacific in American Culture*. Foreword by Donald E. Pease (Lebanon, NH: University Press of New England, 2005), 211pp. Print.

Morris, Edmund, *The Rise of Theodore Roosevelt*, The Modern Library Edition (New York: Random House, 2001), 920pp. Print.

Perkins, John, *Confessions of an Economic Hit Man* (New York: Plume, 2005), 303pp. Print.

Philbrick, Nathaniel, *Sea of Glory: America's Voyage of Discovery—The U.S. Exploring Expedition, 1834–1842* (New York: The Penguin Group, 2003), 452pp. Print.

San Juan, E., Jr., *After Postcolonialism: Remapping Philippines-United States Confrontations* (Lanham, MD: Rowman & Littlefield, 2000a), 272pp. Recipient, The Gustavus Myers Center for the Study of Human Rights in the United States Outstanding Book on Human Rights for 2001. Recipient, The Association of Asian American Studies Book Award for 2001.

———, "Antonio Gramsci on Surrealism and the Avantgarde". Originally published as International Gramsci Society Online article, January 2005a. In: http://www.internationalgramscisociety.org/resources/online_articles/articles/san_juan_01.shtml.

———, "Cultural Studies Amongst the Sharks: The Struggle Over Hawaii", *Third Text*, 16, 1 (2002): 71–78. In: http://www.tandfonline.com/doi/abs/10.1080/09528820110120731#.VeuOC5dUWUE.

———, "The Filipino-American War of 1899–1902 and Its Contemporary Resonance", Remarks prepared for delivery at the Bryn Mawr College, Pennsylvania, March 18, 1998, on the occasion of the program, "The Spanish-American-Cuban-Filipino War of 1898 and Its Legacy", *Austrian-Philippine Homepage* (1998). In: http://www.univie.ac.at/voelkerkunde/apsis/aufi/history/sonny3.htm.

———, "From Race to Class Struggle: Re-problematizing Critical Race Theory", *Michigan Journal of Race and Law*, 11, 1 (2005b): 75–98. Available in: https://repository.law.umich.edu/mjrl/vol11/iss1/5.

———, *Hegemony and Strategies of Transgression: Essays in Cultural Studies and Comparative Literature* (Albany, NY: State University of New York Press, 1995), 286pp.

———, *In the Wake of Terror; Class, Race, Nation, Ethnicity in the Postmodern World* (Lanham, MD: Lexington Books, 2007a), 232pp.

———, *U.S. Imperialism and Revolution in the Philippines* (New York: Palgrave Macmillan, 2007b), 264pp.

———, "The Multiculturalist Problematic in the Age of Globalized Capitalism", *Social Justice*, 27, 1 (2000b): 61–75. In: http://www.socialjusticejournal.org/archive/79_27_1/79_05SanJuan.pdf.

———, "Problems in the Marxist Project of Theorizing Race", in *Racism: Essential Readings*, edited by Ellis Cashmore and James Jennings (London: Sage, 2001), 422pp. In: https://books.google.com/books?id=Mms33VopsQQC&pg=PA225&lpg=PA225&dq=E.+San+Juan,+Jr.,+Marxism&source=bl&ots=bvkqbUURvu&sig=L1riVtuSHcfX_QXuzoDWgYC4WHo&hl=en&sa=X&ei=bVGHVcPvIoaXyQTU2YCQAw&ved=0CCgQ6AEwAjgK#v=onepage&q=E.%20San%20Juan%2C%20Jr.%2C%20Marxism&f=false.

Strong, Josiah, *Our Country: Its Possible Future and Its Present Crisis* (Charlotte, NC: Baker & Taylor for the American Home, 1885), 229pp.

Thornley, Andrew, *The Inheritance of Hope: John Hunt, Apostle of Fiji*. Translated into Fijian by Tauga Vulaono (Suva, Fiji: Institute of Pacific Studies, The University of the South Pacific, 2000), 531pp. Print.

Walzer, Michael, *Just and Unjust Wars: A Moral Argument with Historical Illustrations*, 4th Edition (New York: Basic Books, 1977), 361pp. Print.

Williams, Thomas and James Calvert, *Fiji and the Fijians: Mission History*, Volume 2. Edited by George Stringer Rowe (London, UK: William Nichols, 1858), 435pp. Print.

CHAPTER 4

Denials and Betrayals, Conquest and Capitulation

> Beginning from the rise of merchant capital in the seventeenth and eighteenth centuries, the messianic impulse to genocide springs from the imperative of capital accumulation—the imperative to reduce humans to commodified labor-power, to saleable goods or services. U.S. "primitive accumulation" began with the early colonies in New England and the slave plantations in the South. It culminated in the nineteenth century with the conquest and annexation of Puerto Rico, Cuba, Guam, Hawaii, and the Philippines. With the historical background of the U.S. extermination drives against the American Indians in particular, and the brutalization of African slaves and Mexicans in general, there is a need for progressive scholars and researchers to concretize this idea of genocide (immanent in the logic of imperial expansion) by pedagogical references to the U.S. colonial pillage and plunder of the Philippines.
>
> San Juan, *U.S. Imperialism and Revolution...* (2007)

THE STATE OF THE PHILIPPINE REVOLUTION AT THE POINT OF US INTERVENTION

At the time of the outbreak of the Spanish-American War, with the consequent US entry of the US Navy into Philippine territory, Filipino revolutionaries had already been, during much of the decade of the 1890s, engaged in organization and propaganda work.[1] In July 1892, the secret armed revolutionary movement that called itself *Kataas-taasang Kagalang-galang na Katipunan ng mga Anak ng Bayan* (roughly, meaning "Highly Esteemed, Most Respected Association of the Children of the Nation," or *Katipunan*, in short) was founded and led by a self-educated proletarian and erstwhile warehouse clerk, Andres Bonifacio, who also held the title Supremo, or otherwise President of *Katipunan*'s Supreme Council.[2] In August, that year, the armed rebellion against Spain was officially proclaimed in the village of Balintawak, a suburb of what is now Manila.[3] Independent of any foreign assistance, much less US intervention in their behalf, Filipino revolutionaries had been scoring important military victories over Spanish forces and their mercenary Filipino soldiers.

In March 1897, in the town of Tejeros, in the province of Cavite, south of Manila, local elites sympathetic to the revolution organized themselves into a faction of the provincial chapter of *Katipunan* called *Magdalo*, led by Emilio Aguinaldo, who came from a local land-owning class, and a general in the revolutionary army. At what came to be known as the Tejeros Convention, the question of overall leadership of the revolution was at stake, with *Magdalo* partisans arguing that Aguinaldo should lead the revolution because much of the military successes of the revolutionaries thus far had been attributed to him. Furthermore, the *Magdalo* partisans wanted to already transform the *Katipunan* into a revolutionary government but one headed by Aguinaldo. On the other hand, Bonifacio's supporters, identified with the faction called *Magdiwang*, insisted that Bonifacio was—and had been—the legitimate and unwavering leader all along since the time of *Katipunan*'s founding, and this was demonstrated once again by his leadership at the time of the official declaration of armed rebellion on August 29, 1896, realizing that any other course of action toward the Spanish authorities would be futile. This Convention showed the stark contrast between the *ilustrado* (petty land-owning) class wanting to seize control of the revolution, on one hand, and the mass base of this revolution, including Bonifacio who was clearly the leader and guiding inspiration for the movement, except that he was not from the *ilustrado* class. At this Convention, packed by Aguinaldo supporters, Aguinaldo was elected. Bonifacio was not even elected Vice President. For the position which he was elected—as Director of the Interior—his qualifications were questioned by a close Aguinaldo ally, Daniel Tirona, for the reason that he (Bonifacio) did not supposedly have the requisite education to hold the office.

The Assassination of Bonifacio, the Pact of Biak-na-Bato, and Exile

In the end, Aguinaldo's followers prevailed. Bonifacio and his supporters left, refusing in the end to recognize Aguinaldo's leadership. Following a flawed court-martial proceeding, Bonifacio and his followers were found guilty and convicted with sedition against the Aguinaldo-led revolutionary government. Aguinaldo's men were dispatched to pursue Bonifacio, his family, and supporters. Following a firefight, one of Bonifacio's brothers, Ciriaco, was fatally shot. Bonifacio, his wife, another brother Procopio, and surviving followers were subsequently captured and taken prisoners. On May 10, that same year, they were executed in front of a firing squad.[4] From this point on, the fate of the Philippine Revolution and its future, or so it seemed, laid squarely at the hands of Aguinaldo.

The same week as Bonifacio's execution, the Spanish colonial army launched operations to search and destroy Aguinaldo's forces. Aguinaldo fled Cavite and established temporary headquarters at a redoubt in an isolated location in the town of San Miguel, province of Bulacan north of Manila. There, between July and October, Aguinaldo consulted with his advisers following which a general assembly was called to draw up a republican constitution. The draft that was drawn up was reportedly patterned after the Cuban Constitution, with the legal advice of Isabelo Artacho and Felix Ferrer, among others. This Constitution provided for a Supreme Council consisting of the offices of a President, a Vice President, a Secretary of War, and a Secretary of the Treasury. Aguinaldo retained the office of President.

Following the assembly, Aguinaldo proclaimed the Constitution of *Biak-na-Bato* (literally, split rock), named after his hideout in the province of Bulacan, just north of Manila. Leaving the issue of Bonifacio's execution behind, several revolutionary leaders from around the country threw their support, albeit reluctantly, behind Aguinaldo's constitution which, among others, called for the representation of the Philippines in the Spanish *Cortes* (Parliament), press freedom, return of so-called friar lands to Filipinos, compensation for the *peninsular* (Spanish-born) and *insular* (native-born) civil servants, and equality for all Filipino inhabitants before the law. None of these would call for the liquidation of Spanish colonial rule. However, in December of that year, feeling exhausted from an apparently unwinnable fight, Aguinaldo, the poor and inept military leader and tactician that he turned out to be, and the *ilustrado* (native elite) that he was, and, further, apparently haunted by the memory of his power-driven betrayal of Bonifacio, accepted the offer from Spanish Governor-General Primo de Rivera, in behalf of the Spanish colonial government, in a compromise agreement called the Pact of *Biak-na-Bato*, negotiated between August and December of the same year. In this agreement, with a Philippine-born Spaniard named Pedro Paterno serving as the go-between between Aguinaldo, on one hand, and Spanish Governor Primo de Rivera, on the other, Aguinaldo would cease hostile acts against the colonial government, lay down their weapons, and agree to go on exile to Hong Kong. The colonial government, on the other, feeling compelled to make momentary peace with—and ease the military pressure from—the Filipino rebels so Spain could concentrate on quelling the rebellion in Cuba, agreed to deliver to the rebels, in incremental amounts, the total sum—tantamount to bribe—of eight hundred thousand Mexican pesos, half of which would be given, through the Chartered Bank, a Hong Kong bank, to Aguinaldo, another two hundred thousand to his officers (including Mariano Trias, Vice President; Antonio Montenegro, Secretary; Baldomero Aguinaldo, Treasurer; and advisers General Emilio Riego de Dios and Marciano Llanera), and the remaining two hundred thousand to be remitted at a later but unspecified time, if they all agreed to go on exile and basically affirm the continuation of colonial rule, and for Aguinaldo to order the rest of his soldiers to lay down their arms and cease hostile actions against the colonial government. There is no record that this final sum was ever delivered. Further, Primo de Rivera agreed to grant "self-rule" within a period of three years and to institute reforms that Aguinaldo had demanded. These broad terms, catering essentially to *ilustrado* interests, apparently met with agreement among the principals, and, on December 23, 1897, the Pact was signed and Aguinaldo and his fellow officers boarded the Spanish steamer *Uranus* bound for Hong Kong, arriving there on the thirty-first of December to commence their residence in exile.

Historians are generally of the consensus that neither side of this agreement intended to fulfill the terms. Aguinaldo had intimated that he accepted the money so that he could purchase weapons and presumably resume the fighting. And, in any case, many Filipino revolutionaries in the provinces never laid down their weapons, skeptical of the sincerity and ability of Aguinaldo to continue waging the fight, on one hand, and distrusting of any promises and assurances by the Spaniards, on the other. On the part of the Spanish colonial government, as is now well-documented, despite its inability to defeat the Filipino insurgents, it never had any intention to surrender to them. Following a brief lull in fighting, and by March of

1898, the Filipino revolutionaries resumed their series of attacks on Spanish positions. And, in a debunking of the conventional narrative that the Americans had defeated the Spaniards in the Philippines despite Dewey's apparent decisive victory in the Battle of Manila Bay on May the first; at that point in time, Dewey had no troops to land and take control of territory. The first wave of US Expeditionary Force, officially known as the Eighth Army Corps commanded by Brigadier General Thomas MacArthur Anderson, was still en route from Guam, after having taken that territory without firing a shot, arriving in Manila only on the first of June. In late July, reinforcements numbering 5000 troops under the command of General Wesley Merritt arrived from San Francisco, as did Anderson's troops earlier, following which preparations for the siege of Manila by the Americans intensified. Manila fell to the Americans on August 15 or so it seemed. Dewey stuck to his promise to keep the "*Injuns*" (referring to the Filipino insurgents) out of Manila.

The extent of the Filipino insurgents' control over the Islands was described as part of Aguinaldo's subsequent Declaration of Independence, on June 12. Thus, this so-called victory was, in fact, pre-arranged to give a pretext for Spanish surrender to the Americans rather than to the "inferior" subaltern native rebels who had, in any case at that time, essentially defeated Spanish forces in the provinces and have surrounded the last remaining outpost of Spanish power—the Intramuros—otherwise known as Old Manila, with about 15,000 Spanish soldiers still garrisoned inside, for the final siege until, as fate would have it, the Americans had intervened. The Spaniards had yielded Manila to the Americans, also without a fight.

THE MANIPULATION AND BETRAYAL OF AGUINALDO

The circumstances surrounding Aguinaldo's return from exile in Hong Kong back to the Philippines has been subject to disputation and varying account. A US-based historian, Kenneth E. Hendrickson, in a relatively recent book, *The Spanish-American War* (2003), gives the account, without much detail, that while in Hong Kong, Aguinaldo had made initial contacts with the Americans, with not much results despite the potential of cooperation with US forces. Hendrickson offers the following narrative:

> Aguinaldo later claimed that Colonel Leonard Wood, one of Dewey's officers, tried *to induce him to return to the Philippines and lead a new revolt with American aid*. There is no evidence to support this claim, but in any event,

Aguinaldo left Hong Kong in April bound not for home but for Europe. En route he stopped at Singapore, where he met the U.S. consul general, E. Spencer Pratt, who urged him to return to Hong Kong and discuss matters with Commodore Dewey. Aguinaldo agreed to go back *if Dewey invited him, and Pratt urged Dewey to do so. Dewey agreed*, and Aguinaldo departed on April 27. He later claimed that he returned to Hong Kong with *a clear understanding that the United States was now committed to Filipino independence*. E. Spencer Pratt had no authority to make such a guarantee and always claimed that he had not done so. There is no persuasive evidence upon which to base a conclusion either way. (Hendrickson) (italics added)

However, as cited in a piece by Bryan Anthony C. Paraiso, Shrine Curator at the Philippine National Historical Commission, a French journalist, in a book, *Aguinaldo et les Philippines* (Paris, 1900), testifies that:

A number of persons found the following role of the Commander of the Petrel, one of the vessels in the squadron of Admiral Dewey, to solicit the interview. This interview, followed by many others, was held on March 16: the Commander of Petrel urged strongly Aguinaldo to return to the Philippines and to resume hostilities against the Spaniards promising the assistance of the United States if war broke out against Spain. (*Plusieurs personnes vinrent trouver celui-ci de la part du commandant du Pétrel, un des navires de l'escadre de l'amiral Dewey, pour solliciter une entrevue. Cette entrevue, suivie de plusieurs autres, eut lieu le 16 mars: le commandant du Pétrel engagea vivement Aguinaldo à retourner aux Philippines et à reprendre les hostilités contre les Espagnols, promettant l'assistance des Etats-Unis si la guerre éclatait contre l'Espagne...*) (Paraiso) (italics added)

Another account—by the Philippine History Site of the University of Hawaii—claims that "[b]ack in Hong Kong, Aguinaldo was told by U.S. Consul Rounsenville Wildman that Dewey wanted him to return to the Philippines to resume the Filipino resistance." According to this same site, "Aguinaldo claimed that the American officials prodded him t*o establish a Philippine government similar to the United States, and that they pledged to honor and support the Filipino aspirations for independence.*" (The Philippine History Site) (italics added).

Nonetheless, Aguinaldo proceeded with his plan to travel to Europe on April 8, 1898, arriving in Singapore on the twenty-first. While on a stopover in Singapore, however, fate intervened. Through an interpreter, an English civil servant who worked in India named "Bray" (no first name given in the translated insurgent documents in the possession of US Major

4 DENIALS AND BETRAYALS, CONQUEST AND CAPITULATION   83

J. R. M. Taylor, quoted by Worcester), a meeting was evidently sought by US Consul to Singapore, E. Spencer Pratt. Based on Pratt's series of cable communication with Dewey, it was evident that the Americans were of the consensus about the utility of Aguinaldo, in behalf of the Americans—whether Aguinaldo realized it or not—in pursuing the US objective of conquering the Philippines, and that Aguinaldo could be induced to cooperate with the Americans by exploiting his discontent with the Spaniards in their non-fulfillment of the terms of the Pact of *Biak-na-Bato* and with the potential of US arms delivery for use by the insurgents. Following a series of meetings with Aguinaldo, Pratt reported, in a cable dated April 28, his delight to the Secretary of State that he was able to persuade Aguinaldo to return to Hong Kong, that he informed Dewey to the effect, and that Dewey responded to Pratt to: "Tell Aguinaldo come soon as possible." Pratt added:

> Just previous to his [Aguinaldo's] departure, I had a second and last interview with General Aguinaldo, the particulars of which I shall give you by next mail.
>
> The general impressed me as a man of intelligence, ability, and courage, and worthy the confidence that had been placed in him.
>
> I think that in arranging for his direct cooperation with the commander of our forces, I have prevented possible conflict of action and facilitated the work of occupying and administering the Philippines.
>
> If this course of mine meets with the Government's approval, as I trust it may, I shall be fully satisfied; to Mr. Bray, however, I consider there is due some special recognition for most valuable services rendered.
>
> How that recognition can best be made I leave to you to decide. (Worcester)

Whatever the veracity of either of the above account, Aguinaldo had decided to return, leaving Hong Kong on board the vessel *USS McCulloch*, courtesy of Dewey, on May sixteen and arriving in his home province of Cavite, on the nineteenth of May. Aguinaldo's decision to return was, as he has always claimed, and just as the above-quoted historian Hendrickson would concede, based on the firm conviction that "the Americans had promised to fight for Philippine independence" (Hendrickson). But Dean C. Worcester, in his own account, claimed that Aguinaldo left Hong Kong for the Philippines with "eyes wide open" on the knowledge that there was no commitment in one way or the other from either Dewey or Pratt, to Philippine independence, and that during a meeting between Aguinaldo and Dewey at the latter's flagship, *USS Olympia*, Philippine independence was never discussed nor was there a concession on Dewey's part to offer the Philippines a disinterested protectorate (Worcester).

Pratt's observation that Aguinaldo was intelligent, able, and courageous contradicts any suggestion that Aguinaldo was naïve. It is possible, in diplospeak, that Aguinaldo was made to understand one thing and Pratt's reporting to his superiors another. The same may be said of Aguinaldo's conversations with Dewey, from which Aguinaldo went away satisfied with Dewey's pronouncements, as he testified in his *Reseña Verídica* (1900) to the effect that:

> The Admiral received me in a salon, and after greetings of courtesy I asked him 'if all the telegrams relative to myself which he had addressed to the Consul at Singapore, Mr. Pratt, were true.' He replied in the affirmative, and added, 'that the United States had come to the Philippines to protect its natives and free them from the yoke of Spain.
>
> He said, moreover, that "America was rich in territory and money, and needed no colonies," concluding by assuring me, "to have no doubt whatever about the recognition of Philippine independence by the United States." Thereupon he asked me if I could get the people to arise against the Spaniards and carry on a rapid campaign. (as quoted in Worcester)

Further, Aguinaldo expressed satisfaction at the responses of Dewey to issues he raised particularly over his concern that the United States might not recognize Philippine independence after the Spaniards had been defeated about which Aguinaldo wrote, further:

> The Admiral replied that he "was delighted at my sincerity, and believed that both Filipinos and Americans should treat each other as allies and friends, clearly explaining all doubts for the better understanding between both parties," and added that, "so he had been informed, the United States would recognize the independence of the Filipino people, guaranteed by the word of honor of the Americans,—more binding than documents which may remain unfulfilled when it is desired to fail in them as happened with the compacts signed by the Spaniards, advising me to form at once a Filipino national flag, offering in virtue thereof to recognize and protect it before the other nations, which were represented by the various squadrons then in the Bay; although he said we should conquer the power from the Spaniards before floating said flag, so that the act should be more honourable in the sight of the whole world, and, above all, before the United States, in order that when the Filipino ships with their national flag would pass before the foreign squadrons they should inspire respect and esteem." (as quoted in Worcester)

Aguinaldo Returns from Exile, Proclaims Philippine Independence

News of Aguinaldo's arrival and the apparent prospect of the resumption of the struggle to put an end once and for all to over three centuries of Spanish colonial rule was greeted with much expression of enthusiasm and support all throughout the country. The Philippine History Site, cited above, describes the atmosphere as follows: "The resumption of the revolution brought an electrifying response throughout the country. From Ilocos in the north down to Mindanao in the south, there was a simultaneous and collective struggle to oust the Spaniards."

After arrival, it took a few days for Aguinaldo to organize (or reorganize as the case may be) his would-be government and team of advisers. Finally, in the afternoon of the twelfth of June, and despite the sentiment of his close, trusted adviser, Apolinario Mabini, to delay proclamation until a fully functional government has been established, Aguinaldo issued the proclamation of Philippine independence from Spain to an eager crowd gathered in front of his house in the town of Kawit. The proclamation was actually read in his behalf by Ambrosio Rianzares Bautista, in his official designation as War Counselor and Special Delegate, and who is also generally acknowledged to have composed the document patterned after the US Declaration of Independence from England. Among its salient provisions are as follows, based on translation by historian Sulpicio Guevara, herein quoted at length:

> Before me, Ambrosio Rianzares Bautista, War Counsellor and Special Delegate designated to proclaim and solemnize this Declaration of Independence by the Dictatorial Government of the Philippines, pursuant to, and by virtue of, a Decree issued by the Engregious [sic] Dictator Don Emilio Aguinaldo y Famy
>
> Taking into account the fact that the people of this country are already tired of bearing the ominous yoke of Spanish domination,
>
> Because of arbitrary arrests and abuses of the Civil Guards who cause deaths in connivance with and even under the express orders of their superior officers...
>
> Had resolved to start a revolution in August 1896 in order to regain the independence and sovereignty of which the people had been deprived....
>
> [T]hat by reason of the non-fulfillment of some of the terms, after the destruction of the plaza of Cavite, Don Emilio Aguinaldo returned in order to initiate a new revolution and no sooner had he given the order to rise on

the 31st of last month when several towns anticipating the revolution, rose in revolt on the 28th, such that a Spanish contingent of 178 men, between Imus Cavite-Viejo, under the command of major of the Marine Infantry capitulated, the revolutionary movement spreading like wild fire to other towns of Cavite and the other provinces of Bataan, Pampanga, Batangas, Bulacan, Laguna, and Morong, some of them with seaports and such was the success of the victory of our arms, truly marvelous and without equal in the history of colonial revolutions that in the first mentioned province only the Detachments in Naic and Indang remained to surrender; in the second all Detachments had been wiped out; in the third the resistance of the Spanish forces was localized in the town of San Fernando where the greater part of them are concentrated, the remainder in Macabebe, Sexmoan, and Guagua; in the fourth, in the town of Lipa; in the fifth, in the capital and in Calumpit; and in last two remaining provinces, only in their respective capitals, and the City of Manila will soon be besieged by our forces as well as the provinces of Nueva Ecija, Tarlac, Pangasinan, La Union, Zambales, and some others in the Visayas where the revolution at the time of the pacification and others even before, so that the independence of our country and the revindication of our sovereignty is assured.

And having as witness to the rectitude of our intentions the Supreme Judge of the Universe, and under the protection of our Powerful and Humanitarian Nation, The United States of America, we do hereby proclaim and declare solemnly in the name by authority of the people of these Philippine Islands,

That they are and have the right to be free and independent; that they have ceased to have allegiance to the Crown of Spain; that all political ties between them are should be completely severed and annulled; and *that, like other free and independent States, they enjoy the full power to make War and Peace, conclude commercial treaties, enter into alliances, regulate commerce, and do all other acts and things which an Independent State Has right to do,*

We recognize, approve, and ratify, with all the orders emanating from the same, the Dictatorship established by Don Emilio Aguinaldo...Head of this Nation, which today begins to have a life of its own, in the conviction that he has been the instrument chosen by God, inspite of his humble origin, to effectuate the redemption of this unfortunate country as foretold by Dr. Don Jose Rizal in his magnificent verses which he composed in his prison cell prior to his execution, liberating it from the Yoke of Spanish domination, and in punishment for the impunity with which the Government sanctioned the commission of abuses by its officials, and for the unjust execution of Rizal and others who were sacrificed in order to please the insatiable friars....

Moreover, we confer upon our famous Dictator Don Emilio Aguinaldo all the powers necessary to enable him to discharge the duties of Government, including the prerogatives of granting pardon and amnesty, ... (italics added)

To Aguinaldo and members of his revolutionary government as well as to the huge crowd in attendance coming from around the country, the significance of the event could not be emphasized enough. The Philippine flag, embroidered in Hong Kong by Marcela Agoncillo with the assistance of Lorenza Agoncillo and Delfina Herboza while still in exile, was hoisted for the first time. Played also for the first time, by a band, was the Philippine National Anthem. The declaration was signed by ninety-eight persons, who also served as witnesses including one American, by the name of L. M. Johnson, supposedly a Colonel of Artillery in the US Army. Standard history texts by Filipino authors including Agoncillo, Zaide, and Constantino either do not mention Johnson or, if they do (e.g., Zaide and Constantino), they do not elaborate on the significance. One American author, however, makes a special effort to describe Johnson disparagingly which, in the long term, offers critical readers some needed insight into Aguinaldo's possible motives, e.g., as a shred of symbolism, for inviting him, and those of Dewey, for declining the invitation and snubbing the ceremonies. This author is Dean C. Worcester, a professional zoologist by training and appointed by McKinley to serve in both the Schurman and the Taft Commissions, the only person holding the distinction of serving in both commissions, ironic because, as a top-level official in the colonial bureaucracy, he helped fashion and normalize policies based on the assumptions that the Filipinos were "uncivilized" and "savages" which he sought to demonstrate, under the guise of science, through his so-called ethnographic studies including what would be regarded today as sexual exploitation. Asian American literature and cultural studies scholar Nerissa Balce describes this in her series of studies, and writes that "Worcester even manipulated or coerced his young female subjects to disrobe their traditional clothes, and pose suggestively for his 'ethnographic' portraits. And these thousands of photographs were, [and here, Balce quotes US historian and former colonial military officer in the Philippines, James H. Blount], were widely advertised in America than anything else connected to the Islands" (Balce 2014). While serving in the Taft Commission, commencing i n 1900, he was concurrently appointed to the influential position as Secretary of the Interior, where he served until 1913. In his book, *The Philippines: Past and Present* (1914), he writes of the event:

> Invitations to the ceremony of the declaration of independence were sent to Admiral Dewey; but neither he nor any of his officers were present. It was, however, important to Aguinaldo that some American should be there

whom the assembled people would consider a representative of the United States. "Colonel" Johnson, ex-hotel keeper of Shanghai, who was in the Philippines exhibiting a cinematograph, kindly consented to appear on this occasion as Aguinaldo's Chief of Artillery and the representative of the North American nation. His name does not appear subsequently among the papers of Aguinaldo. It is possible that his position as colonel and chief of artillery was a merely temporary one which enabled him to appear in a uniform which would befit the character of the representative of a great people upon so solemn an occasion! (Worcester)

Worcester's intention in diminishing the significance of an American presence at Aguinaldo's inauguration was in conformity with his entire portrayal of Filipinos as incapable of self-government.

Dewey's Plausible Deniability

In his testimony before a US congressional inquiry on the Philippines established in 1899, Dewey affirmed, and repeatedly so, when questioned by Tennessee Senator Edward Ward Carmack as to whether he sought the help of the Filipino insurgents led by Aguinaldo, in the following manner:

Senator Carmack: You did want a man there who could organize and rouse the people?
Admiral Dewey: I didn't want anybody. I would like to say now that Aguinaldo and his people were forced on me by Consul Pratt and Consul Wildman; I didn't do anything—
Senator Carmack: Did they have any power to force him upon you?
Admiral Dewey: Yes; they had in a way. They had not the official power, but one will yield after a while to constant pressure. I did not expect anything of them; I did not think they would do anything. I would not have taken them; I did not want them; I did not believe in them; because, when I left Hongkong, I was led to suppose that the country was in a state of insurrection, and that at my first gun, as Mr. Williams put it, there would be a general uprising, and I thought these half dozen or dozen refugees at Hongkong would play a very small part in it. (as quoted in Worcester)

In other words, based on Dewey's testimony, Aguinaldo made a fool of himself for believing what he did about what he thought was the benevolence and generosity of the United States. Especially so that he made special mention, in his declaration of independence, which "followed the advice of the American consul-general of Hong Kong, Rounsenville Wildman, and contained the following statement: '....*as the great and powerful*

North American nation has offered its disinterested protection to secure the liberty of this country, I again assume command of all the troops in the struggle....', based on Aguinaldo's ardent expectation that the word of the US, or its representatives with whom he has dealt, was worth trusting." (The Philippine History Site)

Thus was laid the foundation for US occupation of the Philippines and its future policy toward this new colony. The US decision to acquire and keep the Philippines from Spain along with Cuba, Puerto Rico, and Guam by virtue of the Treaty of Paris of December 1898 and ratified by the US Senate in February 1899 appeared to confirm America's belief about its own "Manifest Destiny"; it also offered an opportunity to showcase the difference with the America's European counterparts by enunciating its policy of benevolent assimilation, at least toward the Filipinos.[5] No doubt, there was abundant evidence that many leading American opinion-makers and opinion-shapers at the time were convinced of US moral superiority or, for that matter, the need to assert "manhood." In retrospect, however, and in the view of this author, the said Treaty of Paris was based on a lie and, despite the moralizing about America's "Manifest Destiny" and its civilizing mission as a moral duty, this lie could not obfuscate the fact that, at the end of the day, neither the Cubans nor the Filipinos had asked to be taken over and be occupied by another foreign power. They had asked (in the case of Cuba) or hoped (in the case of the Philippines) for assistance, but not to be taken into bondage. What the Filipinos and the Cubans had both encountered in common, instead, was a glib and manipulative North American power which has, at least for decades until then, been gradually growing and expanding—through stealth or outright theft—to whet its appetite for resources and power in consonance with the economic needs and requirements of a system based on capital accumulation and labor extraction. This is perhaps most candidly and unabashedly articulated by Halstead, with the previous US annexation of Hawaii in mind and the more recent victory over Spain particularly in Guam and the Philippines, in the following words: "With Guam as part of the territory of the United States, we have a direct line of possessions across the Pacific, in the order of Hawaii, Guam and the Philippines; while in the northwesterly direction from our Pacific coast we have the islands forming a part of Alaska. By holding all these islands we will be prepared to control practically the commerce of the Pacific, the future great commercial highway of the world" (Halstead). With Spain as a moribund, spent power and, having lost effective control over the colony, this author is of the view that it had no right to cede to the US what it no longer owned.[6] The United States, on the other, had no moral right to purchase the same based on a lie that it helped spin, both knowingly and deliberately simply because it wanted to own. As described in a now-standard Philippine history reader, so that the episode would no longer be dismissed as a mere conspiracy theory, historian and political scientist Boone D. Schirmer and Stephen Rosskamm Shalom, in their introduction to the section on the Philippine–American War in their outstanding anthology, *The Philippines Reader: A History of Colonialism, Neocolonialism, Dictatorship and Resistance* (1987), offer the following summary:

> In August 1898 the Spanish command in Manila and U.S. officers representing Admiral Dewey conferred behind the backs of Aguinaldo and his men in their positions outside Manila. An agreement was reached that, after a sham battle, the Spanish would surrender to the U.S. military, on the condition that the Philippine nationalists be excluded from Manila. To this condition U.S. officials readily agreed. After the mock battle took place as planned the U.S. military took over Manila from the Spanish and came into direct confrontation with the Filipinos. In February 1899 U.S. troops were ordered to move through the Philippine lines, and the war began. (Schirmer and Shalom)

Major General Merritt, Commander-in-Chief of US forces in the Philippines, and who received the prearranged instrument of capitulation from Fermin Jaudenes, General-in-Chief of the Spanish Army in the Philippines, admitted as much in the following account, as quoted by journalist Murat Halstead, embedded among Dewey's forces, in his chapter on the capture of Manila, as follows:

> For these reasons the preparations for the attack on the city were pressed, and military operations conducted without reference to the situation of the insurgent forces. The wisdom of this course was subsequently fully established by the fact that *when the troops of my command carried the Spanish intrenchments, extending from the sea to the Pasay road on the extreme Spanish right, we were under no obligations, by prearranged plan of mutual attack, to turn to the right and clear the front still held against the insurgents, but were able to move forward at once and occupy the city and suburbs.* (Halstead) (italics added)

General Merritt also confirmed, in the same account, that the said prearranged plan took no consideration of the wishes of the Filipino revolutionaries, that they were considered essentially a nuisance, and that he issued instructions to "brush aside" the Filipino insurgents if they were getting in the way of the US military operations, even as they (i.e., the Filipino insurgents) were also ready and waiting in their trenches to assault or enter Manila, as the case may be, and to plant the Philippine flag atop the Spanish fortification on the thirteenth of August and upon the Spanish surrender. On the Filipino revolutionaries, General Merritt added, three days after the mock battle but before leaving for Paris for the peace negotiations, the following statement:

> Doubtless much dissatisfaction is felt by the rank and file of the insurgents that they have not been permitted to enjoy the occupancy of Manila, and there i s some ground for trouble with them owing to that fact, but notwithstanding many rumors to the contrary, I am of the opinion that the leaders will be able to prevent serious disturbances, as they are sufficiently intelligent and educated to know that for them to antagonize the United States would be to destroy their only chance of future political improvement. (Halstead)

Thus, if its purpose was to defeat Spain in the Spanish-American War, it had done that. The next step—the moral step—would have been to respect the wishes of the inhabitants to be free of any foreign domination and free to chart their own course. And, there was no honor for the United States to connive with Spain over the surrender of Manila. As San Juan explains: "Dewey held Aguinaldo at bay with false promises of U.S. support. The Spaniards, after a mock battle already agreed upon, decided to surrender to General Merritt on August 13" (San Juan 2009), coming in the wake of what is now revealed as a prior understanding to provide the Spanish colonial authorities a face-saving device to hand over sovereignty to the Americans so as not to surrender to the insurgents; this paved the way for the signing of the Treaty of Paris in December of that year, and ratification by the US Senate on February 6 of the following year. However, morality had no binding force at this point, and the consequences of this colonial takeover have been dire to the Filipinos. As payment for this lie, more than four thousand American soldiers would die, and more than a million Filipinos—combatants and civilians alike—would perish. On this sorry and shameful episode, a Filipino textbook offers his candid assessment as follows: "Thus, the Philippines formally came under the rule of the United

States just a change from one colonial master to another. In fine, the Americans through deceit and stealth had stolen the freedom that Filipinos had fought for with their life, blood, sweat, and tears" (Duka).

It is the study of these consequences that critical scholars like San Juan wish to explore and want students of history to critically examine as an antidote to mainstream scholars, historiographers, and popular media that would otherwise whitewash—wittingly or unwittingly—this sorry episode in Philippine history or relegate it to the dark recesses of memory. To ensure this does not happen, San Juan writes:

> What I want to call attention to is the resonance of this event in the hermeneutic discourse and historiography of U.S. scholars on Philippine affairs, the way it established the framework of intelligibility for constructing what became the accepted knowledge of Philippine society, Filipino character and psychology, and Filipino culture. In short, the interpretations and judgments expressed about this episode afford us a symptomatic reading of the theoretical grid of interests and motives - in short, the ideological apparatus - through which commonplace truths and received notions about the Philippines and Filipinos have been filtered and shaped. (San Juan 1998)

One could begin, for instance, in critically examining the process and the presuppositions by which US President William McKinley took in deciding to annex the Philippines as an appurtenant part of US territory. As San Juan describes:

> McKinley justified the forcible annexation of the Philippines to a delegation of Methodist Church leaders in 1899 with these words: Since the natives were "unfit for self-government," McKinley intoned, "...there was nothing left for [the United States] to do but to take them all, ... and uplift and civilize and Christianize them." (San Juan 2013)

But many Americans were not persuaded by expressions of benevolence by McKinley, particularly on his assurances that that the Americans were not coming to the Philippines as "invaders" or as "conquerors" but, rather, as "friends." Mark Twain, for example, expressing the sentiment of the Anti-Imperialist League of which he was an ardent supporter, wrote, in a letter to the *New York Herald* on October 15, 1900, that "I have seen that we do not intend to free, but to subjugate the people of the Philippines. We have gone to conquer, not to redeem.... and so I am an anti-imperialist. I am opposed to having the [American] eagle put its talons on any other land."

In 1901, Twain followed this sentiment up with the publication of a highly acclaimed satirical essay, entitled "To the Person Sitting in Darkness." In this essay, Twain asks, quite rhetorically:

> Shall we? That is, shall we go on conferring our Civilization upon the peoples that sit in darkness, or shall we give those poor things a rest? Shall we bang right ahead in our old-time, loud, pious way, and commit the new century to the game; or shall we sober up and sit down and think it over first? Would it not be prudent to get our Civilization tools together and see how much stock is left on hand in the way of Glass Beads and Theology, and Maxim Guns and Hymn Books, and Trade Gin and Torches of Progress and Enlightenment (patent adjustable ones, good to fire villages with, upon occasion), and balance the books and arrive at the profit and loss, so that we may intelligently decide whether to continue the business or sell out the property and start a new Civilization Scheme on the proceeds? (Twain 1901)

NOTES

1. In San Juan's award-winning book *After Postcolonialism* (2000), cited earlier, testifies that, by the time the Americans had interrupted the Philippine Revolution against Spain, "a Filipino nation had already been germinating with over 200 revolts against Spanish colonialism. Filipino intellectuals of the Propaganda Movement (1872-1896) had already implanted the Enlightenment principles of rationality, civic humanism, and autonomy (sovereignty of all citizens) in the program of the revolutionary forces of the Katipunan and the first Philippine Republic. At the outset, the Propagandistas – Jose Rizal, Marcelo H. Del Pilar, Graciano Lopez Jaena, and so on – used the Spanish language to appeal to an enlightened local and European audience in demanding reforms" (San Juan 2000).

   San Juan pays particular attention to the role of Dr. Jose P. Rizal in the Propaganda Movement and in the Revolution overall. Rizal, today, is revered as the country's foremost hero. He authored two very important novels, namely *Noli Me Tangere* (1887) and *El Filibusterismo* (1891), works which, according to San Juan, "incorporated all the resources of irony, satire, heteroglossia (inspired by Cervantes and Rabelais), and the conventions of European realism to criticize the abuses of the Church and arouse the spirit of self-reliance and sense of dignity in the subjugated natives. For his subversive and heretical imagination, Rizal was executed – a sacrifice that serves as the foundational event for all Filipino writing" (San Juan 2000).

   In another essay, entitled "Jose Rizal: Rediscovering the Filipino Hero in the Age of Terrorism," composed as an Afterword to the revised edition of San Juan's book, *Rizal in Our Time* (2011a), San Juan takes the time to critically review some popular biographical works that had been written on Rizal. In the process, San Juan takes the opportunity to clarify and locate Rizal's position as an individual actor, in particular, his own personal agency, in light of the social, political, cultural, and economic milieu that he lived in, and without falling into the tendency of hero worship. Looking over the biographical works on Rizal by such varied authors as Austin Coates, Rafael Palma, Leon Ma. Guerrero, and Nick Joaquin, among others, San Juan then offers the general assessment that these writers have "all attempted to triangulate the ideas of the hero with his varying positions in his family, in the circle of his friends and colleagues in Europe, and in relation to the colonial Establishment. Their main concern is to find out the origin of the hero's thoughts and their impact on the local environment." San Juan contends that these authors are inherently flawed by the very nature of their approach which suffers from "the twin errors of contemplative objectivism and individualist bias" permeating their accounts. "They ignored," San Juan explains, "the historical-materialist axiom that the changing circumstances and of personal sensibility/minds, as Marx advised, 'can be conceived and rationally understood only as revolutionary practice' – that is, sensuous collective praxis in material life" (San Juan 2011a).

In this approach that San Juan suggests as a means of avoiding the common trap to which many historians fall when they merely describe, in a narrative form, the sequential series of events surrounding a hero's life, and erroneously assuming that they have done their job, San Juan invokes what Marx has written, one in "Critique of Hegel's Doctrine of the State," and the other in *The German Ideology*, wherein individual protagonists are considered in the context of the political economy that they inhabit. San Juan explains further that "[i]n the 'Theses on Feuerbach,' Marx posited that the 'human essence is no abstraction inherent in each single individual. In its reality it is the ensemble of the social relations.'... In the ultimate analysis, the individual subject may be viewed as a microcosm on the whole social fabric that generates his potential and his actuality, without which this monadic figure has no meaning or consequence. Reciprocally, the opaque density of the social background is illumined and concretely defined by individual acts of intervention, such as Rizal's novels, without which society and the physical world remain indifferent." San Juan concludes: "We need this dialectical approach to comprehend in a more all-encompassing way Rizal's vexed and vexing situation, together with his painstakingly calculated responses – all cunning ruses of Reason in history (for Hegel). Such ruses actually register the contradictions of social forces in real life, reflected in the crises of lives in each generation" (San Juan 2011a).

2. San Juan has paid homage to Bonifacio through various venues and outlets. In a recent lecture before the faculty, students, and staff of the University of the Philippines–Visayas, in February 2014, San Juan reiterates his esteem for Bonifacio the revolutionary and explains through the historical-materialist perspective, an approach shunned by mainstream historians and biographers of Bonifacio. San Juan explains: "From a historical-materialist perspective, Bonifacio is less than an individual than an embodiment of collective forces that were stirred up by the Propagandists, mainly by Rizal's novels and his failed *Liga*. The Katipunan is not just a collection of disgruntled individuals but an organized assemblage of conscious mind mobilized for directed, planned action. It laid the ground for constructing the counter hegemonic vision of future national-democratic struggles: the Sakdalista, Huk, NPA/NDF, etc." (San Juan 2014b).

San Juan also clarifies the ideological orientation of the *Katipunan* and distinguishes it from the dominant orientations of Spain and the United States and, for that matter, that of Emilio Aguinaldo and his coterie of petty elites. San Juan writes: "Unlike the hero-worshipping habits imposed by aristocratic Spain and the utilitarian U.S., the ideology of the Katipunan emphasized cooperation, mutual aid, and the welfare of the community. National solidarity, not individualism. The revolution initiated by Bonifacio's Katipunan contradicted the cacique mentality of the Aguinaldo circle, petty holding proprietors, titled ilustrados, the Westernized intelligentsia. While Bonifacio and his circle were themselves products of the European Enlightenment, especially the radical philosophes, they also functioned as organic intellectuals of the workers and peasants. Not the pasyon but the habitus of indyo artisans and urban workers (Manila then was a collection of neighborhoods) shaped their everyday conduct, a life-form whose virtue inhered in spontaneous feelings, rituals of sharing, emotive gestures and clandestine agitation rather than detached inquiry" (San Juan 2014b).

Finally, San Juan reminds us that knowledge and beliefs are not detached from social consequences, such as any attempt to deny—such as what many historians have tried to do—the agency of Bonifacio, the *Katipunan*, and the collective social forces that sustained both. San Juan writes: "In sum, the narrative of Philippine modernity based on the rational autonomy of each individual talent harnessed for the common good begins with Bonifacio and the Katipunan. Incredulity toward this master-narrative can only sustain the abuses of dynastic warlord families, proprietors of semi-feudal estates, as well as their comprador-bureaucratic networks in government. Consumerist individualism and lumpen criminality are morbid byproducts of this interregnum between the old dying system and the new one still convulsed by birth pangs" (San Juan 2014a).

3. San Juan gives his readers a glimpse of the sociopolitical conditions prevailing during the generation of, and context to, the revolutionaries, including that of Rizal, as well as the impact of international events such as the opening of the Suez Canal in the following passage: "By the time Rizal was born in 1861, the predominantly feudal/tributary mode of production was already moribund and an obstacle to further socioeconomic development. Trade and commerce expanded when the country was opened to foreign shipping in 1834–1865, especially after the completion of the Suez Canal in 1869 (Arcilla). Vestiges of courtly love and chivalric ways dissolved in the triumph of the cash-nexus warranted by merchant and circulation of capital, further validating profitable marital exchanges to expand or consolidate property. A national market arose. While the islands for the most part remained tribal and rural under the grip of the rent-collecting frailocracy and its subaltern principalia, land-tilling families such as those of Rizal flourished within the limits of the colonial order. The family household organization enabled the socially constructed gender asymmetry based on biological difference to segregate daughters from sons (women assigned to procreation and child nurturance, men to public affairs) and adversely affect their potential to develop as creative human beings and morally responsible citizens." (San Juan 2011b)

"Political power continued to be monopolized by the peninsulares in the bureaucracy and military, together with the religious orders. They controlled large estates and appropriated the social wealth (surplus value or profit) produced by the majority population of workers and peasants most of whom were coerced under law (for example, the polo servicios) and reduced to slavish penury. Ruthless pauperization also doomed indigenous folk deprived of access to public lands, animals, craft tools, and so on. Only a tiny minority of Creoles and children of mixed marriages (mestizos of Chinese descent) were allowed to prosper under precarious, serf-like, and often humiliating conditions that eventually drove them to covert or open rebellion. Rizal was one of these children sprung from the conjuncture of contradictory modes of production and reproduction of social relations, a child responding to the sharpening crisis of the moribund, decadent Spanish empire" (San Juan 2011b).

4. On Bonifacio's execution and the legacy he left behind, San Juan reflects on the lessons learned: "Bonifacio's execution by the Aguinaldo clique reminds us that unless class divisions, and their attendant ideology of narrow class or familial interests (both of which are maintained by US hegemony) are overcome, we cannot progress as an independent nation and a people with dignity and singular identity. This unity is something to be theorized in consonance with practical organized movements… Bonifacio is being resurrected everyday in the numerous efforts of our countrymen to oppose imperialist diktat and the subserviency to their imperialist patrons of our politicians. Compradors,

and landlords – the oligarchic elite – whose lives have been molded to maintain a violent system whose grant of 'impunity' for torturers and killers is a clear sign of its moral and political bankruptcy" (San Juan 2014a).
5. Here, San Juan, along with others, contests this presumed civilizing claim by the US and that, as also shown in this essay, there is, in fact, no difference between the US style and ferocity of colonialism, on one hand, and the European style, on the other, in terms of motives, interests, means, and outcome. To begin with, San Juan regards the victory of the United States over Spain in their "splendid little war" (a phrase attributed to then US Ambassador to Great Britain John Hay, in a letter he wrote to then Secretary of the Navy Theodore Roosevelt) as "[t]he foundational event in the chronicle of the expansion of U.S. coercive sovereignty…" (San Juan 1996). He recalls Mark Twain's famous satirical essay, "To the Person Sitting in Darkness," from which he quotes: "We have pacified some thousands of the islanders and burned them, destroyed their fields, burned their villages, and turned their widows and orphans out-of-doors, furnished heartbreak by exile to some dozens of disagreeable patriots; subjugating the remaining ten millions by Benevolent Assimilation, which is the pious new name of the musket; we have acquired property in the three hundred concubines and other slaves of our business partner, the Sultan of Sulu and hoisted our protecting flag over that swag. And so, by these Providences of God – and the phrase is the government's, not mine – we are a World Power" (as quoted in San Juan 1996).
6. A nugget of a quote from San Juan's essay, "Dialectics and History: Power, Knowledge, Agency in Rizal's Discourse" (2006) is here helpful to give context to Spain's weakened status in international politics at this point in time vis-à-vis other powers, particularly the United States, as follows: "Spain was unable to remedy the paralysis and lethargy induced by the Empire's accumulation of loot from the American continent." In this essay, San Juan was trying to explain Rizal's clarification about the subject of indolence being imputed upon Filipinos as being a product of climate or nature. A central thesis by Rizal, San Juan explains, is that indolence is universal and that "natural laws alone cannot account for human behavior within the totality of the social relations of production."

REFERENCES

Balce, Nerissa, "The American Vampire and the Filipino Journalists: Philippine Libel Laws Then and Now", *Interaksyon*, February 22, 2014. In: http://www.interaksyon.com/lifestyle/essay-the-american-vampire-and-the-filipino-journalists-philippine-libel-laws-then-and-now.

Henrickson, Kenneth E., Jr., *The Spanish-American War* (Westport, CT: Greenwood Press, 2003), 178pp. In: https://books.google.com/books?id=Qv5srwHj4XsC&pg=PA73&lpg=PA73&dq=spanish+american+war,+Hendrickson&source=bl&ots=DnB2Tu_mBs&sig=2EB5RVdL5NY8pEyz1U-Uk8g_1cI&hl=en&sa=X&ved=0CEEQ6AEwBmoVChMI77H5xcWsxwIVS1s-Ch26HAD9#v=onepage&q=spanish%20american%20war%2C%20Hendrickson&f=false.

San Juan, E., Jr., *After Postcolonialism: Remapping Philippines-United States Confrontations* (Lanham, MD: Rowman & Littlefield, 2000), 272pp. Recipient, The Gustavus Myers Center for the Study of Human Rights in the United States Outstanding Book on Human Rights for 2001. Recipient, The Association of Asian American Studies Book Award for 2001.

———, "An African American Soldier in the Philippine Revolution: An Homage to David Fagen", *Cultural Logic* (2009). In: http://clogic.eserver.org/2009/SanJuan.pdf.

———, "Dialectics and History: Power, Knowledge, Agency in Rizal's Discourse", *The E. San Juan, Jr. Archive*, August 9, 2006. In: http://rizalarchive.blogspot.com/2006/08/rizals-discourse.html.

———, "The Filipino-American War of 1899–1902 and Its Contemporary Resonance", Remarks prepared for delivery at the Bryn Mawr College, Pennsylvania, March 18, 1998, on the occasion of the program, "The Spanish-American-Cuban-Filipino War of 1898 and Its Legacy", *Austrian-Philippine Homepage* (1998). In: http://www.univie.ac.at/voelkerkunde/apsis/aufi/history/sonny3.htm.

———, "History, Literature, and the Politics of Time". Presentation delivered at the University of the Philippines, Visaya, on February 4, 2014 (2014a). In: http://rizalarchive.blogspot.com/2014/01/lualhati-bautistas-desaparecidos-andres.html.

———, "Jose Rizal: Re-discovering the Revolutionary Filipino Hero in the Age of Terrorism", Afterword (Modified, 2011a) to *Rizal in Our Time: Essays in Interpretation* (Pasig City, Philippines: Anvil Publishing, 1997), 144pp. In: https://www.univie.ac.at/ksa/apsis/aufi/rizal/RediscoveringRIZAL.pdf.

———, "Kafka & Torture: Deconstructing the Writing Apparatus of 'In the Penal Colony'". Posted January 2014b. In: https://www.academia.edu/11779952/KAFKA_AND_TORTURE.

———, "Notes on U.S. Genocide in the Philippines", *The Philippines Matrix Project*. Posted June 16, 2013. In: https://philcsc.wordpress.com/2013/06/16/notes-on-u-s-genocide-in-the-philippines/.

———, *The Philippine Temptation: Dialectics of Philippines-U.S. Literary Relations* (Philadelphia, PA: Temple University Press, 1996).

———, "Sisa's Vengeance: Rizal and the Mother of All Insurgencies", *Kritika Kultura*, 17 (2011b): 23–56. In: http://kritikakultura.ateneo.net/images/pdf/kk17/sisa.pdf.

———, *U.S. Imperialism and Revolution in the Philippines* (New York: Palgrave Macmillan, 2007), 265pp. Print.

Schirmer, Daniel B. and Stephen Rosskamm Shalom, eds., "The Philippine-American War" (Editors' Introduction), in *The Philippine Reader: A History of Colonialism, Neocolonialism, Dictatorship, and Resistance* (Boston, MA: South End Press, 1987), pp. 8–19. In: https://books.google.com/books?id=TXE73VWcsEEC&pg=PA9&lpg=PA9&dq=mock+battle+for+Manila,+Spain,+United+States&source=bl&ots=9855VslcAG&sig=DByMdbBDVSWMv676gLi57_lnQ8Q&hl=en&sa=X&ved=0CB0Q6AEwADgKahUKEwiM5uyV07HHAhVIbj4KHR0iA40#v=onepage&q=mock%20battle%20for%20Manila%2C%20Spain%2C%20United%20States&f=false.

Twain, Mark, *To the Person Sitting in Darkness* (New York: Anti-Imperialist League of New York, 1901). In: http://xroads.virginia.edu/~drbr/sitting.html.

Worcester, Dean C., *The Philippines: Past and Present*, Volumes 1–2 (New York: Macmillan, 1914). In: http://www.gutenberg.org/files/12077/12077-h/12077-h.htm.

CHAPTER 5

The Philippine–American War, 1899–1913, and the US Counterinsurgency and Pacification Campaign

[War] is thus not an end in itself but an instrument or tool to advance ends associated with will, purposes, designs beyond individual passions or whims. In the literary archive, war manifests itself customarily in the conflict of individual wills or passions. But, in the process of unfolding, the human telos becomes perverted by the means, by its instrumentalization.
San Juan, *War in the Filipino Imagination*… (2011)

Pacification of a People "Sitting in Darkness"

For much of the rest of 1898, Aguinaldo busied himself organizing his provisional government particularly at the local government level. He heeded the advice of his close advisor, Apolinario Mabini, a lawyer despite his paralytic condition, to transform his government from a provisional dictatorship to a provisional revolutionary one. Mabini argued that the declaration of independence that he issued on June 12, 1898, was much too fawning towards the Americans. Commencing on the 15th of September, that same year, a constitutional convention called by Aguinaldo convened in the town of Malolos. After much deliberation particularly over the three drafts proposed by Pedro Paterno, Apolinario Mabini, and Felipe Calderon, the draft closest to Calderon's proposal was adopted providing for a republican, representative system of government, with separate branches of government with a judiciary free and independent from either legislative or executive control. It also provided for freedoms of association, the press, and of religion, due process and privacy rights, among other liberal ideas. In December of the same year, Aguinaldo finally gave approval to the draft submitted to him and, pending ratification by the Malolos Congress, he issued an order that both its letter and spirit, meanwhile, be complied with because it represents the "sovereign will of the Filipino people." On January 20, 1899, the Malolos Congress gave its ratification and, the following day, Aguinaldo promulgated it. In his inaugural speech, after congratulating the convenors, Aguinaldo expressed optimism that the Philippines, henceforth, "will have a fundamental law which will unite our people with the other nations by the strongest of solidarities, that is the solidarity of justice, of law and right, eternal truths which were the basis of human dignity." Of the conviction that the struggle against Spanish colonial rule was over and that there would be no need for further struggle, declared:

> *We are no longer insurgents, we are no longer revolutionists, that is to say armed men desirous of destroying and annihilating the enemy. We are from now on, Republicans, that is to say, men of law, able to fraternize with all other nations, with mutual respect and affection.* There is nothing lacking, therefore, in order for us to be recognized and admitted as a free and independent nation. (Aguinaldo 1899) (italics added)

Aguinaldo's new constitution, however, no matter how optimistic he was, was never implemented. As though paying a eulogy over the demise of this constitution, George A. Malcolm, former Associate Justice of the colonial-era Supreme Court of the Philippines, in a 1924 article, wrote: "[I]n order to do the constitution justice, it should also be recalled that many provisions which to the American observer seem strange, to the Filipino were natural and fitting. After all, the constitution did conform to many of the tests of a good constitution, and it is to be presumed that it did faithfully portray the aspirations and political ideals of a people" (Malcolm).

As to Aguinaldo's statement that he and his fellow revolutionaries were no longer "insurgents," this turned out to be rather premature. In view of the changed situation which would see his revolutionary forces collide with the American forces, the latter would now see themselves as overseers of a new-found property, and that Aguinaldo and his soldiers were now to be considered as insurgents, in effect, interlopers in their own country. Although Aguinaldo neither desired nor planned it, the war with the Americans was imposed upon him by circumstances as when an incident at the San Juan Bridge temporarily demarcating the line separating the American forces from the Filipino fighters, on February 4, 1899, an American sentry shot and killed a Filipino soldier. The preceding circumstances and the events that took place are described in a now-standard Philippine history text quoted at length as follows:

> On January 24, 1899, the War Department announced that General Otis who was then in charge of the American forces in the Philippines could now conduct hostilities against the Filipinos whom the Americans considered as mere insurgents and bandits. In line with his new orders, Otis requested Admiral Dewey to place his ships in a position to give U.S. troops supportive fire, which the latter obliged. On February 2, a U.S. officer regimental commander gave secret orders to their officers and men to bring about a conflict if possible. On the same day Nebraskan troops, still under orders to withhold fire, went into the territory beyond Manila's city limits, on which the Filipinos held their lines and regarded as their own. After a harsh dispute, the Philippine troops withdrew under orders from their high command.
>
> On February 4, General Otis took the decisive step. He ordered the Nebraskans to open fire on further nationalist "intruders." That evening Private William Grayson and friend, of the 54th Nebraska Regiment, were ordered to patrol even further into the territory held by the nationalists. In language reflecting the racist attitude then found in the US forces from top to bottom, Private Grayson narrated what happened:
>
> About eight o'clock something rose slowly up not twenty feet in front of me was a Filipino. I yelled "Halt!"… He immediately shouted "Halto" at me. Well, I thought the best thing to do was to shoot him. He dropped… Then two Filipinos sprang out of a gateway about fifteen feet from us. I called "Halt!," and Miller fired and got one. I saw that another was left. Well, I think I got my second Filipino that time. *We retreated to where our six other fellows were, and I said, "Line up, fellows, the niggers are in here all through these yards."* The Filipinos in the immediate area returned fire and the war began (Duka). (italics added)

The war that followed—officially lasting about three years up to Aguinaldo's capture—with all its gore and violence has been described by numerous historians. It suffices for now to quote passages from the concise essay by historian Luzviminda Francisco clarifying to contemporary students that the Philippine–American War commencing in 1899 was "America's First

Vietnam." On this first battle of this war, Francisco reports that thousands of Filipino soldiers, armed mostly with *bolos* (long, single-edged native knife), and Remington rifles and Mausers captured from the Spaniards, were killed and that hundreds more were later to die from their wounds, battling US soldiers no less than twenty-one thousand in number armed with much more superior weaponry and assisted by Dewey's battleships that steamed up the Pasig River, lobbing 500-pound shells "with pulverizing effectiveness" (Francisco).

Having realized that the Filipino revolutionaries could not be successful "by fighting on American terms of fixed position, set-piece battles in the classical military tradition," they soon resorted to "mobile warfare" more suited to their "superior knowledge of the terrain and the universal support they enjoyed among the people…" (Francisco). They also realized that they were fighting a new enemy "which gave no quarter and which was prepared to disregard the fundamental rules of warfare" (Francisco). Further, they also realized that "[t]he Americans were contemptuous of Filipinos generally and they had little respect for [their] fighting ability" (Francisco).

By October of 1899, the Filipino revolutionaries had been scoring victories, mostly in small skirmishes but also in rare large encounters. One of these large encounters occurred on June 10, 1899, when a Filipino force of three thousand men, commanded by Generals Ricarte and Noriel, encountered in an ambush a division of US forces numbering four thousand in the province of Laguna, south of Manila that were subsequently "cut to pieces" (Francisco).

Beginning in November of the same year, the US military command began establishing garrisons all throughout the country. With this action came the policy that "Filipino guerrillas were no longer treated as soldiers of an opposing army but were considered to be bandits and common criminals (ladrones). When captured they were treated as such" (Francisco).

By early 1900, the garrison network appeared to work in favor of the Americans, as the occupation of towns appeared to go unimpeded by any significant guerrilla resistance. However, while the garrison network may have extended the US military's reach to much of the country, it also overstretched them, at least until further reinforcements arrived. As Francisco explains that the garrison network:

> seriously thinned the U.S. troop strength and the Americans were continually being counterattacked and ambushed. It was becoming clear that the entire

Islands would have to be "pacified." Moreover, guerrilla activity was both increasing and becoming increasingly effective. Being incessantly ambushed, boloed and betrayed was nerve-wracking and the Americans began to exercise their mounting frustration on the population at large. All the "niggers" were enemies, whether or not they bore arms. Patrols sent to fight the guerrillas usually had difficulty locating the enemy and often simply resorted to burning barrios in their path. Village officials were often forced at bayonet point to lead American patrols, and non-combatants began to be held responsible for the actions of the guerrillas. Any form of resistance to American objectives subjected the perpetrator to a charge of treason. (Francisco)

Nonetheless, the setting up of garrisons all through the country seemed to favor, overall, the US military's counterinsurgency campaign, particularly in its effort to capture the elusive revolutionary leader, Aguinaldo, hoping that in so doing, the insurgency would finally come to an end. General Frederick Funston, the officer that, in fact, led in the capture of Aguinaldo on March 23, 1901, through a combination of ruse and use of informers and double-agents, including former allies and confidants of Aguinaldo himself, described in his memoirs such garrisoning policy as follows:

> Scattered all over the Philippines we had more than seventy thousand troops, counting native auxiliaries, and these in detachments varying in size from a regiment to less than a company garrisoned every town of importance and many places that were mere villages. Through the country everywhere were the enemy's guerrilla bands, made up not only of the survivors of the forces that had fought us earlier in the war, but of men who had been recruited or conscripted since. We had almost worn ourselves out chasing these marauders, and it was only occasionally by effecting a surprise or through some streak of good fortune that we were able to inflict any punishment on them, and such successes were only local and had little effect on the general conditions. These guerrillas persistently violated all the rules that are supposed to govern the conduct of civilized people engaged in war, while the fact that they passed rapidly from the status of peaceful non-combatants living in our garrisoned towns to that of men in arms against us made it especially difficult for us to deal with them. (Funston)

By the middle of 1900, the Filipino fighters were still undefeated despite their obvious disadvantages in arms, a fact causing embarrassment to General Otis and to President McKinley who was facing an electoral challenge in the upcoming November elections. Accordingly, General Otis was replaced by General Arthur MacArthur as commander of the military expeditionary forces in the Philippines. Very shortly, he conducted counterinsurgency operations against the Filipino forces, guided by his extensive experience combating against the Indians during the Indian wars. Also, by late September, McKinley had sent a federal judge, William Howard Taft, to head the Second Philippine Commission, succeeding the first one headed by Schurman. The Taft Commission, as the Second Commission came to be popularly referred to, was tasked with establishing a civil government. To form this government, Taft recruited former members of the Aguinaldo government who have since turned-coat including individuals with such last names as Buencamino, Legarda, Luzuriaga, Paterno, and among others. These individuals were united by their common background as *ilustrados* or petty local, landowning elites who invariably supported some form of autonomy under, if not outright collaboration with, US rule.

With MacArthur's designation as the new commander of the US forces in the Philippines, one may discern a shift both in US military attitude and in tactics. As explained by Francisco:

> Tired of being chronically harassed and boloed by the Filipinos and finding it difficult to pin the guerrillas down in the kind of conventional firefight they so urgently desired, the Americans began to resort to revanchist attitudes and policies. If the American command had ever believed they enjoyed any popular support in the Philippines (apart from the handful of wealthy puppets serving in the Taft regime), a year and a half of war certainly dispelled any continued illusions on the matter. If the people supported the guerrillas then the people must also be classified as the enemy. (Francisco)

One does not need to think hard to understand the implications of this. The pacification campaign under MacArthur commenced with the declaration of martial law in December 1900. It further commenced with the assumption that, because of the popular nature of the resistance to US rule, the people were to be treated as suspect and, therefore, as enemy. "Everyone was now considered an active guerrilla or a guerrilla supporter," Francisco explained. Under this pretext, coastal villages in the Visayas were shelled freely by the US Navy before the landing of troops. During the January–February 1901 period, Francisco writes that the whole island of Marinduque, with a population of 51,000, were herded into five strategic hamlets much like the *reconcentrados* used by Spain in Cuba prior to the Spanish–American War of 1898. Hamleting was used as well in northern Luzon. On numerous occasions, this turned into outright depopulation campaigns against populated towns and villages. No distinction was made between guerrillas, guerrilla sympathizers, or just plain civilians. Francisco quotes a US Congressman, who preferred to be anonymous, and who candidly spoke about this campaign with the following words:

> You never hear of any disturbance in northern Luzon because there isn't anybody there to rebel.... The good Lord in heaven only knows the number of Filipinos that were put under the ground. Our soldiers took no prisoners, they kept no records, they simply swept the country and wherever and whenever they could get hold of a Filipino they killed him. (Francisco)

Keeping no record of US military atrocities during the pacification campaign was obviously self-serving. It kept an air of deniability. It also often freed the soldiers and their officers from any sense of accountability or guilt that might otherwise hinder or curtail their discretion in pursuing military operations. Variably referred to as "scorched earth policy" or, more euphemistically, "protective retribution," it gained expressions in the actual words of officers such as General William Shafter who told the *Chicago News* quite candidly and unapologetically, "it may be necessary to kill half the Filipinos in order that the remaining half of the population may be advanced to a higher plane of life than their present semi-barbarous state affords." Or, those by General "Howlin' Jake" Smith, a participant in the Wounded Knee Massacre, who instructed his men, during a pacification campaign in Samar in late September 1901, to "kill and burn, kill and burn [anyone above the age of ten]. I want no prisoners. The more you kill and burn, the more you please me." About three months later, this atrocity was replicated in Batangas when, Major General J. Franklin Bell set out to render the province uninhabitable. Consequent to this scorched-earth policy, at least a hundred thousand residents of the province had been killed.

Atrocities like the examples cited here were often justified by the assumption or rationalization that the Filipinos were "savages," uncivilized or, as Rudyard Kipling described them in his poem, "Half-devil and half-child." Elihu Root, Secretary of War under Theodore Roosevelt, thought so too. William Howard Taft, the new Civil Governor of the Islands, held the opinion that Filipinos were inferior "to the most ignorant negro." Roosevelt himself was reported as telling Kipling that "in dealing with the Philippines I have first [to deal with] the jack-fools who seriously think that any group of pirates and head-hunters needs nothing but independence in order that it may be turned forth with into a dark-hued New England town meeting" (Dyer).

To a discerning observer, one would note that in McKinley's assimilation proclamation, the true motive of the US takeover of the Philippines is repeated a number of times within the same declaration, not noticed as being sinister or malevolent by the general public, or by mainstream historians for that matter, perhaps because the entire declaration was couched in benign, benevolent tone but definitely setting the economic path—decidedly capitalist—from which the colony cannot go astray and which it must now take. Thus, under this declaration: (a) the authority of the US government over the Islands was for the "confirmation of all their private rights and relations" as basic, fundamental pattern of relations guaranteed to secure capital accumulation and labor extraction for private profit, with the state committing to be the guarantor; (b) pending legislation paving the transition to civilian rule, the military, meanwhile, must ensure the enforcement of "the municipal laws of the territory in respect to private rights and property" patterned after property laws in the United States; (c) while government must maintain public services, assets, and property, "private property, whether belonging to individuals or corporations, is to be respected," a provision evidently designed for the benefit of US-based corporations and the wealthy class and their *ilustrado* surrogates in the Philippine colony; and, finally, (d) in what could be interpreted as precursor not only the invocation of eminent domain based on military necessity but also of what has become common today as the privatization of military functions through use of contractors: "If private property be taken for military use, it shall be paid for…," as the flexible term "private property" may also extend to the services provided by whoever or whichever happens to own this property, e.g., a private mercenary or arms manufacturing corporation, with which or with whom the government enters into a contractual obligation.[1]

The manifestly economic content of McKinley's Benevolent Assimilation Proclamation confirmed or complemented the material and economic motives that were concealed behind the aura of benevolence. As San Juan explains:

> Material interests were indubitably paramount in the turn-of-the-century discourse on progress and civilization. U.S. policy decisions and consequent practices were framed in a "regime of truth" based on the now-well-known politics of colonial representation. Roxanne Lynn Doty (1996) describes this

discursive economy that has since framed North-South relations, in Foucaultian terms, as the denial of the transcendental international signifier, sovereignty, to Filipinos and other newly conquered indigenes; that is, the denial of the capacity to exercise agency. Force is justified because the annexed or colonized are unruly, undisciplined, rebellious, disposed to resist the laws established by the civilizing missionaries. What stood out in the cry or colonial possession is the need for a naval port and springboard for penetrating the China market and demonstrating American power in the Asia/Pacific region. This ideological legitimacy for the occupation was voiced by Senator Alfred Beveridge, among others. After rehearsing the profits to be gained from trade and natural resources, he repeated a familiar refrain from past conquests of the Native Americans, the Mexicans, and other indigenes: "They [natives of the Philippines] are a barbarous race, modified by three centuries of contact with a decadent race. The Filipino is the South Sea Malay, put through a process of three hundred years of superstition in religion, dishonesty in dealing, disorder in habits of industry, and cruelty, caprice, and corruption in government. It is barely possible that 1,000 men in all the archipelago are capable of self-government in the Anglo-Saxon sense". (San Juan 2009, as quoted from Schirmer and Shalom 1987, 25)

This was echoed by General Arthur McArthur who thought the natives needed "bayonet treatment for at least a decade," while Theodore Roosevelt felt that the Filipinos needed a good beating so they could become "good Injuns" (cited in Ignacio 2004). The "barbarous" natives, however, resisted for a time longer than anticipated, offering lessons that still have to be learned, even after Korea and Vietnam, and the quagmires in Iraq and Afghanistan. Despite neoconservative revisionists that the U.S. "savage war of peace" in the Philippines was humane, humanitarian, and honorable under the circumstances, U.S. intervention to annex the Philippines continues to haunt the conscience of some humanists and historians of international relations. (San Juan 2009)

With the exception of a small percentage of the population, most Americans were not aware of the realities on the ground in the Philippines: the deception and betrayal of the Philippine revolutionaries, the militant resistance to the imposition of American rule, the million-and-a-half Filipino deaths sacrificed resulting from counterinsurgency campaigns, including countless massacres perpetrated either in retribution against the *insurectos* in Luzon and the Visayas, or as part of the pacification campaign against the *Moros* in Mindanao and Sulu, e.g., infamous massacres at *Bud Dajo* in March 1906, and at *Bud Bagsak* in June 1913.[2] Thankfully, the late historian Howard Zinn, unique among US-based historians, recalled these incidents in his classic book, *A People's History of the United States: 1492–Present*, not allowing incidents like these to be erased from memory.

RACIAL DIMENSION OF PACIFICATION

Not much attention has been devoted until recently by mainstream historians to the US pacification campaign's racial dimension, in particular, the participation of Black American soldiers, also referred to as "Buffalo Soldiers," in what would be a racist war of subjugation against a people wishing to be free of foreign domination and control. Even the assumption behind why they were recruited to serve in the US military. According to the War Department, the Black soldiers were "naturally adapted t o survive the tropical climate" (San Juan 2010). These soldiers were dispatched to the Philippines following the Battle of Manila, to assist with the capture of Manila and, subsequently, to quell and defeat the Philippine revolutionary forces during the Philippine–American War that followed. The attention focused by San Juan on this dimension is, therefore, a rarity among scholars especially in that it re-focuses critical attention on certain realities: (a) the relations experienced by the Black American soldiers that fought in the Philippines reflected their experience in the broader society back in the United States; (b) the identity between the Philippine revolutionary struggle, on the one hand, and the struggle for black emancipation in the United States, on the other; and (c) the significance of the common anti-imperialist solidarity movement.

As a backgrounder, soon after the eruption of the Philippine–American War in February 1899, four regiments of Black American soldiers were dispatched to the Philippines. The 24th and the 25th infantry regiments were sent from San Francisco in February, and the 9th and the 10th Cavalry were sent as reinforcements by summer of that same year. These Black regiments were sent in the midst of vocal opposition to the war of intervention, as expressed in numerous newspaper articles and public pronouncements by Black leaders in opposition to this war. Among these was W. E. B. DuBois who condemned the war as an "unjust imperialist aggression and that "the slaughter of Filipinos a 'needless horror'" (San Juan 2009). The Anti-Imperialist League, founded in October 1899 and of which DuBois was a founding member, invoked the sentiment of Frederick Douglass who, some six decades earlier, expressed the view that the struggle of the "Negro people were identical with that of the struggling colonial peoples" (San Juan 2009).

Indeed, opposition within the Black American community appeared to be borne out by the continuing Jim Crow treatment against the blacks particularly in the American South. With the Supreme Court decision on the *Plessy* case in 1896, segregation became law, and racism continued to symbolize not only absence of social opportunities but also persistent economic disparity and inequality. Many Black American soldiers who have returned from the war in Cuba and who thought that they would be welcomed back as heroes, in fact, were welcomed back and praised from many quarters as heroes even by their superior military officers. This did not negate the experience of many others, however, who, upon, return, were hurled with insults, and many white soldiers who also were in Cuba with them, along with many white residents in their communities, participated in hurling these insults. Historian Robert B. Edgerton tells of the experience of a Black resident of Georgia, upon returning from that war, that the storied valor of Black soldiers "has intensified prejudice against him." Black heroism was seen simply too much as a threat to white supremacy. Roosevelt appeared to stoke the fires of hatred towards the blacks when, in his memoirs published in *Scribner's Magazine* in 1899, famously entitled "The Rough Riders," he falsely interpreted some black soldiers from the 10th Cavalry running to the rear as cowards during a raging battle. After it was clarified later by a black soldier, Sergeant Preston Holliday, from the same regiment who witnessed the incident, that those soldiers that Roosevelt saw were, in fact, ordered to get needed supplies, Roosevelt then acknowledged that his assumption was wrong but that, according to historian Edgerton, "he refused to repudiate his published accusation of cowardice" (Edgerton).

But just as many Black American soldiers who returned from Cuba were being vilified and insulted, ironically, there were also many black voices in support of the idea that black soldiers should go fight in the Philippines. An example of this was exemplified by an editorial by the *Indianapolis Freeman* which, on July 1, 1899, expressed the following: "It is now said that colored troops are to be sent to the Philippines. The sooner the better. The Negroes must be taught that the enemy of the country is a common enemy and that the color of the face has nothing to do with it." Yet another view was expressed, quoted in a book by George P. Marks, III, entitled *The Black Press Views American Imperialism (1898–1900)* (1971), in which the writer expressed the view that should Black American soldiers are sent to fight in the Philippines, they should not view the conflict in racial terms. "It pays to be a little thoughtful," the writer was quoted as saying, "The strife [against the Philippines] is no race war. It is quite time for the Negroes to quit claiming kindred with every black face from Hannibal down. Hannibal was no Negro, nor was Aguinaldo [the Filipino nationalist leader]. We are to share in the glories or defeats of our country's war; that is patriotism pure and simple" (as quoted in "The Philippine War"). A third sample is not an expressed endorsement of the war but takes a presumably neutral stance that it was not for the individual soldier to decide whether to oppress a people or not but it is this soldier's duty simply to obey. And fulfill one's oath. This type of rationalization is expressed in one quoted passage from a book by Stan Cohen, entitled *Images of the Spanish-American War, April-August, 1898* (1997), as follows: "The sentiments of most Black soldiers in the Philippines would be summed up by Commissary Sergeant Middleton W. Saddler of the 25th Infantry, who wrote, "We are now arrayed to meet a common foe, men of our own hue and color. Whether it is right to reduce these people to submission is not a question for soldiers to decide. Our oaths of allegiance know neither race, color, nor nation" (as quoted in "The Philippine War").

In an essay by San Juan on the participation of the Black American soldiers to which they were thrust, a picture of the war is presented, an important context to consider in trying to understand the varying responses by these soldiers. To recapitulate, the year of 1899 began with the inauguration of Aguinaldo's Malolos Republic in January. In February, the very young republic was forced into a war when it became evident that the Americans were simply not content with defeating the Spaniards but also in taking over the country entirely, and preventing Aguinaldo's republic from ever coming into fruition. The revolutionary forces of Aguinaldo at first tried to engage the American forces frontally in traditional formations. Due to a combination of inferior and inadequate weaponry, the Filipino forces suffered very heavy casualties, numbering in the hundreds of casualties almost per encounter. Subsequently, the leadership of Aguinaldo decided to resort to mobile warfare. As San Juan explains: "[The Filipino revolutionaries] were forced to resort to mobile warfare, utilizing their knowledge of the countryside and universal support from the populace in the face of vastly superior US firepower" (San Juan 2010). This was significant in that this also inaugurated what is later described as anti-colonial "people's war" as well as the ruthless response to it, "low-intensity warfare" (San Juan 2010).

During the April–May period, there was bickering within the Aguinaldo revolutionary government resulting in a cabinet shuffle, with Pedro Paterno replacing Mabini in his post, and Felipe Buencamino appointed as Secretary of Foreign Affairs, two individuals that would later defect to the Americans. According to historian Edgerton, four regular army black regiments that had served in Cuba and been re-deployed to the southwest to guard against anticipated Mexican incursions, were dispatched to the Philippines during spring, 1899. These were followed, accordingly, by two additional all-black volunteer regiments in July to be part of a total (at that point) of a 70,000-man US contingent to battle with the Philippine revolutionaries.

In the southern Luzon and the Visayan region, Filipino resistance was meeting with some success, but that the responses by the US military have also become more brutal if not genocidal. This was true in such provinces as Panay and Samar. As San Juan notes,

> Mobile tactics and eventually guerrilla strategy reduced the US garrisons to easy targets, with the US troops finding themselves ill-suited and ill-equipped to confront their enemies who lacked adequate firearms, often fighting with bolos – long-bladed knives – and spears. The Filipino insurgents resembled the proverbial fish swimming in the ocean of their sympathizers so that by subterfuge and hand-to-hand combat, the rebels overcame the odds against them. After protracted fighting with unconscionable losses, the US army began to treat all the "niggers" as enemies, whether armed or not; it resorted to destroying villages and killing civilians. In the second year of fighting, 75,000 troops escalated the war against the Filipino masses, not just the sporadic guerrillas in the "boondocks" (the term adopted from the Filipino word *bundok*, contested mountainous terrain). (San Juan 2010)

The US military forces responded with more gruesome tactics including treating all civilians as suspects, and outright torture through such means as "water boarding" or "water cure," *reconcentrado* or hamleting, and outright depopulation all of which have become notorious with their inhumanity, exemplified by the violent depopulation of Samar.

In the midst of the gruesome brutality of the US pacification campaign, the Filipino revolutionaries tried to appeal to the humanity especially of the Black American soldiers in the hope that not only would they refuse to fight in behalf of a colonial army but that they would defect to the revolutionary cause. One such appeal was contained in a pamphlet clandestinely distributed by the revolutionaries among the Black soldiers. San Juan quotes at length from a book by Willard Gatewood Jr., entitled, *"Smoked*

Yankees" and the Struggle for Empire: Letter from Negro Soldiers, 1898–1902 (University of Arkansas Press, 1987), as follows: one of these handbills as follows:

> It is without honor that you are spilling your costly blood. Your masters have thrown you into the most iniquitous fight with double purpose – to make you the instrument of their ambition and also your hard work will soon make the extinction of your race. Your friends, the Filipinos, give you this good warning. You must consider your situation and your history; and take charge that the blood of…Sam Hose proclaims vengeance. (as quoted in San Juan 2010)

With knowledge on the part of the Black American soldiers of many atrocities committed by the US forces, many of which these soldiers also participated in, and exposed to the pamphlets from the Filipino revolutionaries appealing to their humanity, many white officers frankly expected many Black soldiers to defect to the Filipino revolutionaries' side. Historian Edgerton describes this initial anxiety on the part of the white officers and offers as well a brief discussion of the circumstances surrounding the defection of David Fagen, as follows:

> Faced by the evidence of this open racial antagonism, along with a flood of Filipino insurgent propaganda leaflets urging the black troops to join them in their fight against white tyranny, many white officers expected black soldiers to desert in large numbers. To their surprise, throughout the three-year campaign, only five black soldiers deserted to the Filipino insurgents, many fewer than the numbers of white soldiers who deserted. The most notorious of these by far was Corporal David Fagen who did not desert for political reasons but because he felt harassed by his sargeant (sic). Fagen fought with the rebels for two years, rising to the rank of captain before a bounty hunter brought his head to the Americans to claim the reward that had been offered. (Edgerton)

Edgerton, here, seems to diminish the number of Black African soldiers, led by David Fagen, a captain in Company 1 of the US 24th Infantry, that defected over to the revolutionary cause. He negates as well the political significance of Fagen's defection, reducing it to petty personal differences between Fagen, on the one hand, and his sargeant, on the other. Thus, Edgerton fails to appreciate the importance of the atmosphere generated by white supremacy; and, he fails to appreciate the significance of the anticolonial struggle or, for that matter, any struggle for self-determination on the part of any colonized people as signified by his clinging on to the term "insurgent," a preferred term by the counterinsurgency planners designed precisely to excise any legitimacy to the revolutionary cause. San Juan offers a much-needed antidote to the otherwise numbing effect of conventional scholarships like that of Edgerton's such as in the following passage on the critical symbolisms of recognition and denial in history:

> Fagen was one among fifteen to thirty deserters from four regiments of "Buffalo Soldiers" dispatched to the Philippines in July and August 1899. Seven thousand African Americans were involved in the war. After fighting the Native Americans as "Buffalo Soldiers," these four regiments were mobilized for the Spanish American War. As the New York State Military Museum reminds us, the use of black soldiers by the War Department conformed to the belief that black soldiers were "naturally adapted to survive the tropical climate" (New York State Military Museum 2006). In fact, the 7th, 8th, 9th and 10th US Volunteer Infantry were later formed in response to the government need for soldiers "immune to tropical diseases." Incidentally, it was members of the 10th Cavalry that used their "Indian fighting skills" to save Theodore Roosevelt and his "Rough Riders" from certain extermination. But they never received recognition equal to Roosevelt's. When the Philippine resistance proved tougher than the officials estimated, the War Department recruited two regiments of black volunteers, the 48th and 49th Infantry and sent them to the Philippines in early 1900 to stay until the official end of the war. (San Juan 2010)

Finally, San Juan discerns the multi-faceted significance of the David Fagen story in the way that hardly anyone in mainstream scholarship has. First, San Juan draws attention to the anti-colonial character of the Philippine revolutionary resistance to US occupation and control, although it was bourgeois (elite-led) rather than socialist, something that might be understood in the contemporary language of self-determination; second, San Juan draws attention to the genocidal character of the US military response, during both the conventional and unconventional stages of the war, a fact still to be acknowledged because of the conscious and deliberate policy of not maintaining official record of the atrocities; third, San Juan draws the significance of this period as the germinal or foundational stage of the modern development of surveillance and what has been described in military literature as "low intensity warfare" affirming the violent foundation of the US state; and, fourth, San Juan appreciates the exemplary nature of Fagen's story for cross-national solidarity between and among anti-colonial/anti-imperialist movements, armed or through the essential complement of propaganda work, as exemplified by expressions of solidarity with contemporary anti-colonial/anti-imperialist struggles in Vietnam, southern Africa, Central America, and elsewhere.

Pacification of Moroland
Deluding the Sulu Sultanate

Although Mindanao and Sulu had never been under effective Spanish colonial rule, Spanish authorities had nonetheless taken the liberty of including it in the cession, along with the rest of their Philippine territorial possessions, to the United States following their defeat in the US–Spanish War of 1898. This cession was sealed in the Treaty of Paris, dated December 10, 1898, which provided, among other provisions, for Spain to receive the sum of $20 million from the United States for the Philippine territory alone, and for the relinquishing of Spanish sovereignty over Cuba, Puerto Rico, and Guam to the United States. This gave the United States the legal basis to claim sovereignty and impose control over the whole of Mindanao and Sulu region.

Not long after the Treaty of Paris of 1898 took effect, the United States took steps to assert its ownership and control over the Mindanao and Sulu region, traditional home of Muslim Filipinos. In April 1899, overall commander of US forces in the Philippines, Major General Elwell Otis, designated Brigadier General John C. Bates, a veteran of the Indian wars as well as in the Cuba campaign, as field commander for Mindanao and Sulu, such region having just been converted into a distinct Military District. General Bates would be the first of three veterans of the Indian wars to command this region, the two others being Brigadier General William Kobbe, appointed March 20, 1900, and Brigadier General George Whitfield Davis, appointed August 31, 1901.

On May 9, 1899, troops from the US 23rd Infantry Battalion, under the command of Captain Edward B. Pratt, took over the walled garrison of Jolo, in the Sulu Archipelago, from the departing Spanish soldiers following a brief ceremony. Interestingly, the Spaniards had turned over to the Sultan of Sulu a garrison they had under their control in the island of Siasi rather than to US authorities, with the Sultan having made the trip from his seat in Maimbung to Siasi to oversee the transfer (Kho).

The following day, the Spanish fort in Zamboanga—named Fort Pilar—was also evacuated of Spanish troops although it was reported that "no American troops could be spared to occupy the city and Zamboanga was abandoned to a well-armed Christian Filipino militia aligned with Aguinaldo..." (Fulton). A token number of troops were also landed in other parts of the Visayas, e.g., Palawan, as well as in Cotabato, Polloc, Parang, and Banganga, all in Mindanao, that same year. Because the US troops were preoccupied with the suppression of the Filipino resistance in Luzon and parts of the Visayan region, it was acknowledged that not much more troops could momentarily be spared towards the effective control of the entirety of Mindanao and Sulu, especially if there was a sustained popular resistance. It was in recognition of this fact that General Otis gave a specific set of tasks for General Bates to accomplish as follows: (a) to dissuade the Moros from joining the rebellion in other parts of the country; (b) to prevent a Moro front from developing while pacification of the rest of the country was in progress; (c) to induce the Moro leadership to acknowledge US sovereignty; and (d) to create the foundation for a more enduring relationship between the Moros and the United States.

The problem of integrating—and legitimizing—the Mindanao-Sulu region within the orbit of US control appeared to be daunting from the outset. To begin with, Spanish authorities, including the colonial administrators in the Philippines, had committed an arbitrary act by exceeding their prerogative in including this region in their cession to the United States. One source of explanation for this action may have been the differing interpretation of the 1878 treaty that the Sulu Sultan had entered into with Spain. Historian Madge Kho writes: "Scholars fluent in both Spanish and Arabic found the treaty to have translation flaws, which would have implications in the 1898 cession of the Philippine Islands to the United States The Spanish version states that Spain had sovereignty over Sulu, whereas the Tausug version describes a protectorate relationship rather than a dependency of Spain" (Kho). Thus, in the description of the territory they were ceding to the United States, as described with technical precision in Article III of the Treaty of Paris, the Spanish authorities had acted as though Sulu, and the entirety of Mindanao—was under the effective sovereignty and legal jurisdiction of Spain, and the US negotiators had readily assented to this travesty as a matter of expediency and opportunity.

No doubt, Moro leaders were morally, legally, and historically correct, even to this day, in claiming their independence from Spain at the time the Treaty of Paris was negotiated and ratified. For one thing, for centuries the sultanates of Sulu and of Maguindanao have had a series of treaties of friendship and commerce as well as diplomatic intercourse with foreign powers including China, the United States, Spain, Britain, Germany, and the Netherlands.[3] A notable example of these was a "most favored nation" treaty of 1417 between the Ming Dynasty of China and Sultan Paduka Batara of Sulu. Then, Spain had a series of treaties with Sulu and Maguindanao leaders, namely the Sultan Kudarat-Lopez Treaty of 1645 and 1648, and the Rajah Bungso-Lopez Treaty of 1646 all of which define and demarcate "the respective dominions of the sultanates of Maguindanao-Buayan and Sulu and the colonial possessions of Spain over the Visayas and Luzon. Even the United States has entered into a treaty of trade and commerce, entered into in 1842 with then-reigning Sultan of Sulu and Sabah Mohammad Jamalul Kiram I.[4] Further, on July 22, 1878, Spanish monarch, King Alfonso XIII, entered into a Treaty of Peace and Amity with the Sulu Sultanate which "allowed Spain to set up a small garrison, covering about 15 acres, in the town of Jolo. Outside the wall, the Sultan still ruled" (Kho). This was followed by a Treaty of Conciliation, ten years later, with the Sultan of Maguindanao and Rajah Buayan as an attempt to end long-running hostilities between the two parties. Filipino historian Cesar Adib Majul, in his classic work *Muslims in the Philippines* (1973), has described these treaties as conferring effective recognition of the sovereignty and authority of the Sulu and Maguindanao sultanates, and in possession of the requisite elements of what would today be regarded as a nation-state, on the part of the foreign powers involved even though one or the other had offered a form of protectorate status to—but not sovereignty over—these sultanates. Contrary to what some historians may believe, these treaties, which were honored by Spain until the last days of its colonial rule over the Visayas and Luzon, never indicated surrender nor capitulation on the part of the indigenous leaders of Maguindanao and Sulu.

Reinforcing Spain's recognition of the distinct sovereignty of the sultanates of Sulu and Maguindanao was a series of Royal decrees, promulgated over a consistent period of time, all of which clearly indicated the extent of territory to which the Spanish colonial authorities consciously exercised their authority. Historian Musib M. Buat enumerates and describes these decrees as follows: "The Royal Decree of July 30, 1860 decreed by Queen Isabella II of Spain and the Royal Decree of July 15,

1896 and the Maura Law of 1893 that provided organization of municipal governments excluded the Moro territories of Mindanao, Sulu and Palawan. The latter Spanish decrees merely proposed for the establishment of politico-military governments in occupied territories of Mindanao, Sulu and Palawan, excepting the territorial dominions of the Sultanates of Mindanao and Sulu" (Buat).

It is interesting to note that even US President William McKinley had misgivings about the actual extent of Spanish sovereignty and territorial control in the Philippines. Nonetheless, he accepted the reality brought about by the US victory over Spain and the emergence of the United States as an imperial power with designs—ostensibly to keep doors to free trade open—in East Asia and the Western Pacific, and for which the Philippines would play an important part. Justifying US conquest of the Philippines, therefore, was an important task when it had gone out of its way, as integral to its claim to exceptionalism, in arguing that it differed from its European counterparts in exploiting lands they had conquered. On December 28, 1898, McKinley issued a statement to the US Congress with that task in mind, and his statement came to be known as the Benevolent Assimilation Proclamation. In that Proclamation, he assured the Filipinos and his audience in the US Congress, that, among others, "the authority of the United States is to be exerted in securing [their] persons and property," that the Americans were coming "not as invaders or conquerors, but as friends," and that, further, "the mission of the United States is one of benevolent assimilation substituting the mild sway of justice and right for arbitrary rule" (McKinley).

It was in this intellectual frame that McKinley treads carefully when he instructed General Bates to contact and negotiate with the Sultan of Sulu based on—if not patterned after—this sultanate's treaty with Spain of 1878. Bates wasted no time in contacting and negotiating a treaty with Sultan Kiram and his advisers. The Sultan was amenable to negotiations with Bates to whom he presented a 16-point draft treaty which proposed, among others, a protectorate but not sovereignty over the sultanate on the part of the United States. The Sultan had envisioned that the flags of the United States and the sultanate would fly alongside each other and not one higher than the other. The Sultan's proposal would forbid the United States from interfering with the customs and religion of the inhabitants within the sultanate and would further require the United States to continue the Spanish practice of remitting specified monthly stipends to the Sultan and his datus. More significantly, the Sultan would retain sovereignty and authority over the whole of the sultanate, and the United States was neither to occupy any part of it without the Sultan's expressed permission, nor dispose of, sell or transfer ownership and control of the sultanate or any part thereof to any third party whatsoever.

Without explicitly expressing his rejection of the Sultan's proposals, Bates instead offered a set of counterproposals—15 in total—which contained the essential elements of what he had been instructed to accomplish at the time of his appointment the most important of which was the acceptance (or, rather, the appearance of acceptance) of—and acquiescence to—US sovereignty by the Sultan in his capacity as the supreme authority of the sultanate. Appearance is hereby asserted in that, of the two drafts that were signed, one in Tausug (the predominant dialect among inhabitants of the Sulu Archipelago including the Sultan, his family, and his cabinet), and the other, in English, the Tausug version never alluded to the word "sovereignty" much less implied that the Sultan was acceding to US sovereignty. As historian Kho writes: "Article I of the Treaty in the Tausug version states 'The support, aid, and protection of the Jolo Island and Archipelago are in the American nation,' whereas the English version read 'The sovereignty of the United States over the whole Archipelago of Jolo and its dependencies is declared and acknowledged.'" Kho further mentions that US Army physician of Lebanese descent Najeeb Saleeby, who was deployed at the time in Mindanao and Sulu, had "caught the translation flaws and charged Charlie Schuck, son of a German businessman, for deliberately mistranslating the treaty" (Kho).

This episode has been noted by several historians including the late eminent theologian and historian Peter Gowing who, in his pioneering work, *Mandate in Moroland: The American Government of Muslim Filipinos 1899–1920* (1983), professes that the word "sovereignty" was nowhere found in the Tausug version (Gowing, 122). However, a gentleman-historian (surprisingly not an academic), Robert A. Fulton, offers fresh insights in his relatively recent and arguably the most important book on the subject albeit admittedly written with the US perspective in mind, entitled *Moroland 1898–1906; America's First Attempt to Transform an Islamic Society* (2007). Culled from Fulton's account, (Charlie) Schuck was one of four sons of a German national, Herman William Frederick Schuck, who was a merchant ship captain and trader between Singapore and Sulu since the mid-1860s. While providing scant information about the elder Schuck's first wife, Fulton narrates that Schuck married a Tausug woman related to the Sultan, Jamalul Alam. With his Tausug spouse, Schuck also had an adult son (named Julius) who was, at the time of the arrival of US forces in Sulu, in North Borneo studying English. Due to family connections and his competence in the Tausug dialect, Schuck became a trusted advisor to the Sultan. In fact, one of his accomplishments was his inter-mediation, mainly as an interpreter and translator, in the negotiation between the Spanish authorities and the Sulu Sultan of the Treaty of 1878; this treaty apparently gave Spain "nominal" though not necessarily effective authority over the Sulu Sultanate.

The first batch of US forces from the 23rd Infantry arrived in Jolo, the capital of the Sultanate, on May 19, 1899. This batch was commanded by Capt. Edward B. Pratt, and it consisted of two battalions comprising 733 foot soldiers, 19 line officers, 2 surgeons, and a chaplain (Fulton, 20). The first-ever US soldier to assume a guard's post at the Jolo fort, which had just been taken over from the departing Spanish soldiers, was Pvt. Needhom N. Freeman, who described his impressions and capturing the mood of the final day, the 22nd of May, that the Spaniards were in Jolo, as follows:

> ...the Spanish flag on the blockhouse was hauled down by the Spanish soldiers and the Americans unfurled to the breeze the Stars and Stripes. The Spanish seemed to be very much grieved, the officers wept, the Americans were jubilant. Everything passed into our hands, and the various responsibilities of the place with all its dangers also passed to us. The natives who belong to the Morro (sic) tribe are treacherous. We know nothing about them and their intentions. Guards were put on duty at once.... (as quoted in Fulton, 22)

According to Fulton, Capt. Pratt wasted little time in familiarizing himself with the terrain, the customs, and the personalities of Sulu at large. One of his fortunate moments was when he learned about the Schuck family particularly the first four sons of the elder Schuck, namely Edward (Eddy), Charles, Herman, and William. All were apparently proficient not only in German but also in Tausug and Spanish, and all offered to serve as interpreters and translators on "as needed" basis. Of the four, however, Eddy stood out for his proficiency in English, Spanish, Tausug, and Samal. Capt. Pratt, apparently impressed by the language skills of the four children, decided to put them all on retainership, assuring them of steady income, and "used their knowledge to collect as much information as possible about the peoples and the islands. The relationship established with the Schuck family would prove invaluable to the Americans for the next twenty-one years" (Fulton, 24). All of them, either singly or collectively, have been particularly useful to the US military, often accompanying no less than Gen. Bates himself and other military officials in their jaunts around the Sulu Archipelago, sanctioned by Dewey under the guise of pursuing pirates and slave traders, and in their meetings with the Sultan.

The presence of Saleeby as part of the US military structure of Sulu was soon to make a critical difference in the future of the Sulu Sultanate in view of his critical voice. Fulton acknowledges that Saleeby, who has studied Moro culture, language, and history, particularly that of the Tausugs, and upon careful study of the two versions of the Bates Treaty, had "found a critical difference between the two [versions]" and had no personal or political motive to be contrarian in this case. However, he (Fulton) also acknowledges that the English version was apparently one which Gen. Bates had "intended to use... to resolve the ambiguous ownership question over Moroland that had been presented by the Treaty of Paris. By implication, the Tausug version was not expedient for the same purpose. This sentence was the bedrock of the legal position Taft had crafted..." (Fulton, 241). Thus, given the motive revealed by Fulton to align claimed US sovereignty over the Moroland, on the one hand, and the text of the Treaty of Paris, on the other, and given the fact that the translator Schuck derived his pay from the US Government, and with him in possession of both the means and the motive, it is hardly surprising that the "mistranslation" might have been deliberate, taking advantage of the ignorance and naivete of the Sultan and his retinue—despite some disagreement among some members of his cabinet—on matters of global power politics, a fact which provided another rationale for the misdeed.

A side effect of this whole matter was that Saleeby, despite his having been appointed as a member of the Moro Province Legislative Council, became less trusted by some of the most powerful personalities in the colonial administration not the least of whom was Gen. Leonard Wood, as Commander of the Philippine Department, who was uncomfortable towards and irritable with Saleeby. As Fulton notes, as a means of degrading his importance, Wood wrote disparagingly about Saleeby in his diary for September 3, 1899; "Saleeby is an unknown quantity, has a good deal of the Oriental about his way of doing business," and, further, in a letter to his wife several months later Wood alluded to Saleeby as "about as poor [a specimen] as you often run across among presumably decent people" (Fulton, 240–241). Saleeby became even less trusted as he tried to elevate what he must have regarded as malicious on the part of Schuck for his suspected deliberate mistranslation of the official texts of the Bates Treaty. In a private letter to Major Hugh L. Scott, who was part of Wood's entourage in the Philippines for his experience in ethnographic work among the Crow Indians in the US upper midwest, learning Indian sign languages and culture in the process, and heretofore as an associate of Saleeby in learning about Moro culture, Wood expressed hope that Scott would tell on Saleeby, as follows: "If you find that Saleeby is mixing up in Jolo intrigue I wish you would let me know. I regret very much to say that I do not feel entirely easy about him. I may be exceedingly unjust with him in feeling this way but it is an uncontrollable antipathy; I am rather inclined to trust intuition and first impression" (Fulton, 240).

Many US postcolonial scholars on Moro culture and history, including the present one, have come to regard Saleeby's scholarly contributions as generally fair, even sympathetic to the Moros in the Philippines. Because he was at the employ of the US military, the policies that might have emanated from his studies might have provided an alternative pathway to the manner in which the whole of Moroland may eventually have been integrated into the US colonial architecture of pacification and rule, then under Taft's care, which, as it was, was founded much on trickery, opportunism, force, and violence. Underlying these were racist and racialized assumptions resulting in antipathy towards the Moros, and the non-Moro Filipino wards as a whole. These were all evident in the motivations behind negotiations for the Bates Treaty, which were to buy time until the resistance in central and northern parts of the colony had been quelled. These motivations included why Saleeby's charges against Schuck could not be allowed to move forward, because of the political embarrassment it would bring, first, to the McKinley Administration that negotiated the Treaty of Paris and in accepting the Bates Treaty, then, to the Roosevelt Administration that came after McKinley's assassination.

Rationalizations for the abrogation of the Bates Treaty ranged from legalistic to moralistic. As Fulton explains: "The Taft legal argument for abrogation, based entirely on the English version, was that upon signing, the Sultan and datus had clearly ceded their ownership claims to the island, and the subsequent provisions simply described the new relationships of the Sultan and datus as subjects of the U.S" (Fulton, 241). Taft was head of the Philippine Commission originally created by McKinley to serve as the US President's surrogate executive in the Philippines. Taft served in that capacity until December of 1903 when he was appointed Secretary of War by the Roosevelt Administration. Before Taft departed for Washington,

DC, to assume his new duties, Wood met with Taft earlier that month to exchange farewells but also to present Taft a document containing his own recommendations—eight altogether—for the abrogation of the Bates Treaty. Aside from reinforcing Taft's legalistic argument cited earlier, Wood also cited several moralistic and pragmatic reasons including the following:

> a. The agreement stands in the way of the establishment of a good government, inasmuch as it recognizes the authority of a class of men whose authority... is exercised not through laws, but through the power of slavery and peonage.
> b. ...the oft-repeated offense of sending juramentados into Jolo.
> c. The persistent refusal of the Moros to observe the general instructions given them concerning slavery at the time of the signing of the Bates agreement and often afterwards...
> d. They have frequently stolen properly belonging to the United States.
> e. The character of the Sulu laws alone considered is sufficient reason why we should have no agreement with them. And,
> f. ...acts of treachery and rebellion... (Fulton, 237–238)

Fulton notes that the Sultan was neither informed ahead of time of the US intention to abrogate the agreement, nor was there any explanation offered afterwards especially concerning the cessation of the monthly stipends. Fulton then offers a fair assessment of Wood's report to Taft, writing: "Wood took advantage of prevailing myths, exaggerations, and religious bigotry in demonizing the Moros, emphasizing 'religious fanaticism' and claiming and ascribing to the datus an 'oft-repeated offense of sending *juramentados* into Jolo' [even though only one of such offense was reported by Scott in four years]." On the matter at hand, Fulton concludes that Wood's report "was not written as an argument to obtain a decision from the policy makers up the line, Taft and Roosevelt. They had made up their minds well in advance, and Taft had been complicit in writing the document. The real purpose was to justify a unilateral abrogation to the American public and to posterity. In doing so, Wood indicted the Moros, their culture, and Islam" (Fulton, 238–239).

On March 2, 1904, the US finally unilaterally abrogated the Bates Treaty. Two years later, the Massacre of Bud Dajo happened, and in 1913, the Massacre at Bud Bagsak, marking the final collapse of the Sulu Sultanate both as a political community and as basis for organized resistance. For all practical purposes, the Sulu Archipelago has become an integral part of the Philippine colony.

Dividing and Conquering the Maguindanao and Lanao Sultanates

The conquest and pacification of Maguindanao and the Lanao Lake region took a different path. Even though the arrival of US forces in Mindanao and Sulu were near-simultaneous following the defeat of Spain and the signing of the Treaty of Paris, the pattern of the early US attempts at establishing its authority in the Maguindanao and Lanao region has been somewhat different from that employed in the Sulu region. For one thing, the nature of Moro social and political organization Lanao has been of a markedly different nature. The sultanate system here, unlike the Sulu Sultanate and, to a certain extent, the Maguindanao Sultanate, has been decentralized into four distinct but confederated principalities, namely Unayan, Masiu, Bayabao, and Baloi. The decentralization of power, shared among royal houses—numbering sixteen—is almost as old as its founding by Sharif Kabungsuwan of the Maguindanao Sultanate in 1520 and whose influence was later adopted by the Lanao royal houses following Kabungsuwan's missionary visits to the Lanao Lake region, located some 70 kilometers from the settlement where he (Kabungsuwan) had originally landed and settled in following his journey from Johore, in present-day Malaysia. That settlement came to be known as Malabang, facing what is today as the Ilana Bay, and traces its name from the Maranao word "mala" (big) and "bang" (call to prayer), reminiscent of Kabungsuwan's distinctively loud call to prayer. Interestingly, Malabang also became the headquarters of the great warrior Sultan Kudarat during much of his resistance fight against the Spaniards and where he was buried upon his death. Each of the aforementioned principalities, whose confederation dates back to 1640, was tasked with the responsibility of securing not only the territory that has been recognized within the confederation falling within its jurisdiction, but also to serve as guardian of their respective cultural and religious traditions.

When the US occupation forces began arriving in the Philippines in June 1898 following Spain's surrender, President McKinley, in line with his policy of benevolent assimilation, issued a general set of instructions to Major General Wesley Merritt, commander of the US Expeditionary Force, that included the following: (1) "to respect local customs, laws, and governmental routines as far as possible…; (2) "to impress on the inhabitant of the islands that the United States Army had not come to make war on the Philippine people but to protect them…; (3) "Private property was to be strictly respected…; and, (4) "the U.S. occupation was to be as free from severity as possible" (Beede, 332). Further, pertaining to dealing with the

Moros, McKinley crafted an Executive Order, with the advice and assistance of his Secretary of War Elihu Root, issued on September 7, 1900, which served as basis for policy guideline for the Philippine Commission which served as his surrogate executive in the Philippines under the leadership of William Howard Taft as its Commissioner. The Executive Order stated, in part:

> In dealing with the uncivilized tribes of the Islands the Commission should adopt the same course followed by Congress in permitting the tribes of our North American Indians to maintain their tribal organization and government, and under which many of those tribes are now living in peace and contentment, surrounded by a civilization to which they are unable or unwilling to conform. Such tribal governments should, however, be subjected to wise and firm regulation, and without undue or petty interference constant and active effort should be exercised to prevent barbarous practices and to introduce civilized customs. (Fulton, 111)

Behind these seemingly benign intentions, however, the underlying goal of the US occupation forces was to engage in a "civilizing mission" whose very nature entailed the ultimate imposition of US authority and sovereignty over the newly-acquired Philippine colony, as spelled out in the Treaty of Paris.[5] As one might expect, this would inevitably subordinate Merritt's instructions the practical implementation of which, through a military government, would rest on the shoulder of Merritt's successor, Maj. Gen. Otis, commencing in August 1898. Thus, the nature of policies, tactics, and practices employed at various times, geographic conditions, and prevailing local customs and political practices, both by military and civilian officials, necessarily have to be measured by this yardstick. Accounting for variations in specific conditions among the Moros of Sulu from those of Maguindanao and the Lake Lanao regions, McKinley designated Brig. Gen. George Whitfield Davis, a veteran of the Indian Wars and up to that point Provost Martial for Manila, as field commander for the Mindanao and Sulu Military District. Within six weeks of his assumption of duties on October 24, 1901, Davis submitted a set of recommendations addressed to his immediate superior, Maj. Gen. Adna R. Chaffee, commanding general and military governor of Mindanao and Sulu, with copy furnished to Taft. The recommendations, contained in a 12-page document entitled "General Davis' Report on Moro Affairs," were undoubtedly meant to represent

Davis' views on how to resolve the "Moro Problem" as he saw it. In his prefatory statement, Davis wrote:

> The student of history knows that the transition from patriarchal forms and medieval feudalism to a government of law, was slow in the extreme even with the Caucasian race... [T]he worst misfortune that could befall a Moro community and the nation responsible for good order among the Moros, would be to upset and destroy the patriarchal despotism of their chiefs, for it is all they have and all they are capable of misunderstanding. (Fulton, 106)

Near the end of his report, in which he compared the Moros to the Indians in the US Great Plains, including the military solution required to subdue them, Davis laid down five specific recommendations, namely (1) the setting aside of the Bates Treaty which he believed should never have been negotiated to begin with; (2) the bypassing of sultans in favor of the local datus; (3) recognition of hereditary datus as paid public servants; (4) establishment of a military, not civilian, government in all of Moroland; and, (5) free trade for up to ten years between the Moroland and the rest of the country (Fulton, 109). With all its presuppositions about Anglo-Saxon supremacy, the backward character of Moro society, and primary role of the military in the civilizing process, the report was accepted by Gov. Taft and who, with Gen. Chaffee's concurrence, endorsed it to Sec. Root and President Roosevelt for adoption, and laying the basis for much of what is to come.

It is in this context that one might begin to see a different approach by the colonial authorities in the Maguindanao and Lanao regions from that which was concurrently employed in the Sulu region. In Maguindanao, particularly in the Rio Grande and Pulangi River in the central and northern sections of Cotabato, the presence of the US military since the departure of token number of Spanish troops in June of 1898 has been rather unchallenged until 1903 when the so-called Ali rebellion erupted. Datu Ali, son of Datu Uttu of Buayan, had sought to emulate his father's heroic successful resistance against the Spaniards in forming his own resistance movement against the US occupation forces. The US military quelled this rebellion through a combination of diplomacy and force or, as it was, divide and conquer. The US military had successfully sought to coopt Datu Piang, Datu Ali's father-in-law, thereby weakening Datu Ali's base of support. At that time, Datu Piang was reputed to be the most influential among colonial datus of Cotabato even though he did not descend from royal blood.

Born in 1850 to a Chinese trader from Amoy named Tuya Tan and one of the unnamed concubines of Datu Uttu, the Sultan of Buayan, Piang nonetheless grew up as a protege of Datu Uttu who conferred on him the title "Minister of Lands." When Datu Uttu fell out of grace with the Spaniards, Datu Piang stepped in to fill the void, built an alliance with Datu Uttu's former allies, and sought the goodwill and friendship of the Spaniards. It was this political agility, though others may see as verging on opportunism and susceptible to cooptation, which made him useful to the US occupation forces at the time when they needed someone like him to help them suppress other recalcitrant members of the native population. By the time the Spaniards had abandoned Cotabato in 1899, he was the recognized Sultan of Mindanao among the natives not out of royal lineage but out of effective control. He relished that title just for a few months, however, when the US forces arrived later that same year, taking away any semblance of power that he had. With his subservience to the new foreign masters, along with his willingness to collaborate with them in the suppression of his competitors in the interest of "law and order," his reputation has come to be known as "America's Great Friend" (McKenna, 91–93).

The US military planners had sought to employ a similar approach for the Lanao Lake region, not wanting to take what would appear as a direct heavy-handed military approach to pacification. Perhaps as an unintended beneficiary to the Bates Treaty, though intended for the Sulu Archipelago, both the Maguindanao and the Lanao Lake regions saw relative peace during the brief life of that treaty in a sense that there was no (or, not yet any) active, organized resistance to the US military presence there. As in Maguindanao, US military operations were few and focused mainly on enforcing laws against banditry, cattle-rustling, or interceding in quarrels among clans (Beede, 346). Fulton explains this particular period of relative calm in the following fashion: "The capture of Emilio Aguinaldo in April [1901] and the surrender of many of the commanders on the island of Luzon had led to the mistaken belief among the Americans, including the army, that the long and violent insurgency in the north was almost over. Moroland had been among the most pacified and 'peaceful' regions of the Philippines in the sense that no one had been shooting at American soldiers nor in open rebellion against the United States. In two-and-a-half years, fewer than a dozen soldiers had been killed or wounded in all of Mindanao and Sulu, and those incidents were considered isolated and criminal acts" (Fulton, 103).

But as things would turn out, it was precisely from the posture of law and order enforcement that the nature of US involvement would gradually evolve from police action to military operations in the Lanao Lake region. It would also feature the kind of inter-clan conflict that the US military inevitably found itself drawn to. The most serious of these is described by historian Benjamin Beede as follows:

> In April 1900, Datu Udasan of Malabang raided the town of Callalanuan and carried away captives and loot. A detachment of 25 troopers from Parang [Cotabato] under Lt. Col. Lloyd M. Brett, aided by Datu Piang's 100 men was sent to look into the incident. The result was an armed clash between Piang's men and Udasan's followers, two Moro groups traditionally in conflict. The death of Datu Amirul Umbra and fourteen of Udasan's men intensified the feud between the Malabang Maranaos and the Maguindanaos. U.S. officials were blamed by the Maranaos for taking sides with the Maguindanaos, a violation of the terms of the Bates Agreement even though it was primarily for the Sulu region. The Maranao attacks on a U.S. exploring party in 1902 and the killing of a U.S. soldier in Parang [Cotabato] were traced to Maranao resentment for the killing of Datu Umbra and two kinsmen of Datu Dacula, Umbra's father. (Beede, 346)

But a fact not mentioned by Beede in his account is the fact that a month earlier, in March, Gen. Davis had ordered Lt. William D. Forsyth to lead some of his cavalry soldiers of the 15th Cavalry to blaze a trail from Parang to the Lanao Lake region, unmistakably a move in behalf of the United States to assert control and impose US authority over this recalcitrant and yet uncontrolled region. But sensing that the foreign invaders were unduly intruding into their territory, the Maranaos reacted by engaging in a harassing move against the intruders resulting in the death of two soldiers on two separate occasions, three weeks apart in March and April, namely Pvt. Lewis and Pvt. Mooris, both of the 27th Infantry Regiment, then encamped in Malabang at an old Spanish fort named *Corcuera*, commanded by Col. Frank D. Baldwin. Aside from the killing of Pvts. Lewis and Mooris, the Moros had reportedly ridden away with some 18 cavalry horses along with the *krag* rifles belonging to the dead soldiers. The Maranao raiders then retreated to Buldon but not before suffering five casualties among themselves. It was later determined that the Maranao bandits as they were referred to, belonged to the clan of the Sultan of Bayang to whom they were believed to be loyal followers.

To the US military authorities, this act on the part of the Moros was not simply an act of banditry; it was an act of brazen defiance to US authority which could not be allowed to go unpunished. No less than Gen. Chaffee himself realized the importance of impressing upon the Moros the gravity of the situation that he decided to personally visit the town of Malabang, in the southeastern corner of the Lanao province, in early April [1902], "inviting the Sultans and Datos of the Lake region to come in and hold a 'friendly' conference with him," assuring them that he did not come as an occupying force (Allen and Reidy, 15). He also conveyed the demand that the killers of the soldiers be surrendered to US authorities, and was stern in giving April 27 as the deadline for such surrender. The Moro leaders, however, spurned the call to this meeting and, instead, "defied the Americans to come and fight" following which Chaffee realized the futility of any further peaceful means. Consequently, he cabled Washington and requested permission, "reluctantly" granted, "to proceed to the Lake region and administer a lesson to the recalcitrant Sultans and Dattos," but not after Col. Baldwin took a precipitate action that seemed intended to limit his options (Allen and Reidy, 16). By the third week of April but before Chaffee's ultimatum to the datus arrived, Col. Baldwin decided to "force the issue" and, without seeking the approval of his superiors Gen. Davis and Gen. Chaffee, decided to form an punitive expeditionary force henceforth to be known as the Lake Lanao Expedition, and began marching on April 17. Despite the apparent show of insubordination, which should have been punishable under the military code of discipline, both Gen. Davis and Gen. Chaffee instead reluctantly decided to go along with Baldwin's bold move, who claimed to know the names of the accused murderers of the US soldiers, and from which *rancherias* (settlements) these and their fellow ambushers came; these *rancherias*, accordingly, included Bacolod, Bayang, Butig, Maciu, and Taraca. Gen. Davis, in particular, assured Sec. Root, who had demanded that Baldwin return to the fort in Malabang, arguing that a withdrawal by Col. Baldwin's forces at this time "would weaken tenuous U.S. authority on the island" (Maggioni). Faced with an apparent *fait accompli*, Gen. Chaffee instructed Gen. Davis, Commander of the Seventh Separate Brigade, to personally accompany Col. Baldwin. In more ways than one, Gen. Davis appeared more than eager to comply as he saw an opportunity to actualize the recommendations he had outlined in his report as discussed previously. The expedition also gave him a chance to personally encounter the Moros for whom he had envisioned a benign, civilized future not unlike the reservations for the Native Americans intended ostensibly to preserve Native American culture and way of life.

Based on the account of Allen, an embedded journalist, and Reidy, a participant-soldier, the expeditionary force consisted of 6 companies of the 27th Infantry, 2 troops of the 15th Cavalry, and the 25th Battery of Field Artillery. On the 17th of April, the expedition began its trek into the interior of Mindanao "which had, as yet, never been explored by white men" (Allen and Reidy, 17). For several days the column passed through a mountain range which ran parallel to the coast, engaging in minor skirmishes on at least a couple of occasions with small Moro bands, then progressed deeper inland and closer to the seemingly more impregnable complex of fortifications, four in total, which consisted the settlement of Bayang (or Bayan), the expedition's main objective, arriving there on the 1st of May. Upon settling at a temporary encampment some distance from Bayan, Gen. Davis then proceeded to compose a message, reportedly in Arabic script, for immediate delivery to the Sultan of Bayan. The message contained a demand for the Sultan's surrender by noon of the following day, May 2, or "suffer the consequences" for failure to comply. In their account, Allen and Reidy testify that the message had been delivered and received but that it was not responded to. What was taken as an indirect response, instead, were the number of shots presumably by the Moros that night directed at the expedition's encampment but that a decision was made not to return fire until the noon deadline of the following day, May 2. By daylight of May 2, the camp broke and the expeditionary force moved closer to Bayan and, in fact, about a thousand yards from the entrance to the first of four forts, called the Binidayan fort, Allen and Reidy wrote that "several natives appeared there, firing a few shots and flourishing their weapons, all the time yelling like mad. It was now plainly seen that the Moros were determined to have war" (Allen and Reidy, 21). But as it was not yet twelve noon, the artillery was positioned and trained on Fort Binidayan situated on a crest but well within reach of the artillery shells. As the twelve o'clock deadline came, Gen Davis stepped forward and "took one long, lingering look in the direction of Fort Binidayan, and then, not seeing any signs of a peace envoy, but, on the contrary, every indication of hostility, he turned slowly to Captain W.S. McNair, of the 25th Battery, and gave the signal to 'let it go'" (Allen and Reidy, 22). Thus began the Battle of Bayan!

As the artillery bombardment continued, the infantry swung into action. Allen and Reidy described this moment as follows: "The work of demolishing the Binidayan Fort had now begun in earnest, companies 'F' and

'G' of the 27th Infantry advanced in line of skirmishes, while the Artillery continued a slow fire on the Fort, company 'H' and 'F', and crossed the intervening ridge and then through the little valley, while 'G' went off to the right, to flank Binidayan and at the same time to make a demonstration against Fort Pandapatan, which was to the right and rear of Binidayan" (Allen and Reidy, 23–24).

As if to stress the discipline and professional training of the infantry soldiers, Allen and Reidy wrote that as the soldiers started to assault the fort, with "determination written on their faces," and with "every head... erect, [and with] every man in his place.... There was not a bit of confusion, simply and orderly line of men counting up to do battle.... They laid down prone on the ground then and poured a withering fire into the fort and trenches, which quickly routed the enemy" (Allen and Reidy, 24–25).

At that point, the Moro warriors holding Fort Binidayan decided to give it up and fled to the momentary safety of Fort Pandapatan, situated "to the right and rear of Binidayan." Infantry soldiers quickly took control of Binidayan and unfurled "Old glory" to the breeze atop Binidayan's shattered walls, signifying victory with no losses to the US forces at this stage of the fight. But the Moros were not so fortunate because "here and there a mangled body of a dusky warrior dotted nature's carpet, some already dead, others breathing their last, but stubbornly defying the Americans to do their worst" (Allen and Reidy, 26).

A brief lull ensued during which the artillery was re-positioned and trained on Fort Pandapatan, where everyone anticipated would be where the real battle would be fought. The infantry from Companies "E", "F", "B" had moved down Binidayan Hill and closer to the Fort. From their new position, they could see no less than 20 red flags flying atop Pandapatan's walls which signified to them Moro defiance. The time was 2 o'clock, and without waiting much longer, the artillery opened up "and the big fight was on" (Allen and Reidy, 28). The infantrymen advanced "smothering other unseen trenches on their way, until by nightfall there was not a rifle but could shove its muzzle into the very face of the trench behind which the Moro warriors laid in waiting, peering down the slope between the explosions for something they feared more than the whistling fragments of Krupp shells—the blue-shirted form of the silent American soldier, with whom the Moros knew the ultimate issue rested" (Allen and Reidy, 28–29). As the soldiers continued their assault on the fort's walls, "the mountain guns howled and roared over them, the walls grew troubles and shaky, falling in and falling out, dimly seen between the curtain of smoke and sheet of flame whirling about the leaping stones" (Allen and Reidy, 29). The Moro warriors, however, showed some stubborn, if not ultimately vain, resistance because as the "[a]rtillery roared in anger and anguish..., long streams of fire continued to pour from the fort with regular intervals, and more blue-shirted figures went tumbling down the hill" (Allen and Reidy, 30). However, this show of Moro resistance was answered by even more vigorous bombardment as the "[a]rtillery turned loose all its little dogs of war and they barked fiercely and hurled death projectiles into the fort and trenches with renewed vigor" (Allen and Reidy, 30–31). But still the Moro fighters refused to surrender. Allen and Reidy described this heroic moment of the Moros that even they could not help but admire, as follows: "But the fanatical Moros would not give up; there they stood in the very midst of that hurricane of death, calm, immovable, and indifferent to it all. Their resistance could not help but be admired as they stood there calm and defiant, against that advancing, enveloping thunderstorm of musketry. But it must not be imagined that they were idle; far from it. If one can imagine taking a handful of pebbles and hurling them with a strong force against a pane of glass, then, and then only, can one imagine the whirlwind of bullets which the Moros were pouring into that little army of Americans out there in the open" (Allen and Reidy, 31–32). Allen and Reidy admit that nothing like the fierceness of this battle currently being waged "had ever been seen before and nothing like it will be seen again" (Allen and Reidy, 32). As the infantry drew closer to the walls, "they were very near the dangerous zone of the exploding shrapnel and were compelled to halt to keep from being struck by their own men.... [T]he air was filled with flying projectiles which went screaming and screeching across the open and striking the walls of the fort with a mighty impact..." (Allen and Reidy, 33–34). In describing the approaching climax of the day's battle, Allen and Reidy made sure to highlight the dramatic role the artillery played as it "let itself go" again and again in support of the unrelenting advance of the infantry. "'Boom', 'boom', 'boom', in quick succession, and then the wall crumbled, vanished in parts, and lo! Behold! The flags were down! The crimson colors were dangling in mid air for an instant, then were caught in the shower of bursting shrapnel and hurled to the ground" (Allen and Reidy, 35–36). The Moros fought with "fanatical frenzy" but all in vain. As the troops reached the top but just outside the walls, the artillery stopped, the Moros fell back and their position seemed practically abandoned, although not quite really. Sporadic shooting came from the direction of the fort throughout much of the night as torrential rain fell. Col. Baldwin's men tended the wounded and accounted for any dead, and he readied his men for a renewed assault by daybreak the following day.

But as the awaited daybreak came, to the soldiers' surprise, the fighting they were anticipating to resume did not materialize. They saw white flags fluttering above the fort's walls signifying surrender and fall of the fort. Allen and Reidy explained this moment as follows: "At last the big fight was over. After nearly twenty-four hours of continual firing the Americans had conquered. It had been a splendid battle, and what manner of death the vanquished had suffered only those who looked into the fort and trenches after the battle, can say" (Allen and Reidy, 39). Allen and Reidy describe the sight of the fallen Moro warriors in gruesome detail, as follows: "The mangled bodies of the Moro dead were piled up eight and ten deep in places, and only those acquainted with the technicalities of a slaughter house can imagine the sight as it appeared the next morning after the battle. But these people would have war, and war they got, in all its glory. Just eighty-three survivors remained out of the hundreds that resisted the Americans" (Allen and Reidy, 39–40). Among the notable dead on the Moro side were the Sultan of Pandapatan, the Sultan of Bayan, and his heir, Rajah Muda (Fulton, 133). As for casualties on the US side, while providing no precise figure, Allen and Reidy wrote: "But it must not be imagined that this great victory had been achieved without loss to the Americans. Their casualties were far greater than those of an ordinary battle, numbering close to a hundred" (Allen and Reidy, 40).

News of this victory prompted profuse messages of congratulations from the highest officials of the US government to the officers and men of the Lanao Expeditionary Force. From Gen. Chaffee to Gen. Davis came the following message, dated May 4, 1902: "Please accept my congratulations for yourself, and express to Col. Baldwin and all the officers and men engaged in the Battle of May 2, my high appreciation of their bravery, gallantry and soldiery conduct. My congratulations to both officers and men. I sincerely regret the death of some and the wounding of others. Let no comfort be withheld from the latter that can be supplied them" (Allen and Reidy, 44). And, from Pres. Roosevelt to Gen. Chaffee, dated May 5, is the following: "Accept for the Army under your command, and express to General Davis and Colonel Baldwin especially, my congratulations and thanks for the splendid courage and fidelity which has again carried our flag to victory. Your fellow countrymen at home will ever reverence the memory of the fallen, and be faithful to the survivors, who have themselves been faithful unto death for their country's sake" (Allen and Reidy, 43–44). Finally, an excerpt from the message of Gen. Davis to his soldiers, reflecting his civilizing impulse and paternalism towards the Moros, as follows:

> Soldiers: Words at my command fail to convey an adequate expression of admiration for the gallantry and self-sacrifice which I saw displayed by the assaulting lines and investing cordon on the 2nd of May. The memory of this sanguinary action will be treasured by all participants and observers as long as they live.... At this moment of exaltation and triumph do not forget the vanquished foe, whose persistent gallantry commanded the admiration of all who saw the magnificent defense of their stronghold. A race of men who have been able to make such a fight, and who have turned this wilderness into a garden, have many qualities which if guided right will make them and their posterity valuable citizens. None can doubt who have seen what they have accomplished without the aid which civilized people enjoy. Let no word or act be brought home to the American soldier that discredits or disparages these Moros. Let it be the unremitting effort of every officer and soldier to assist and elevate them, a sacred duty which is devolved upon the Army, an added burden which must be borne; and every American relies upon their troops to execute this sacred trust.... Our flag is an emblem of freedom and honor, and it remains with you that it shall become such an emblem to the Moros, and ever so remain. (Allen and Reidy, 45)

Worth citing are no less than some personal thoughts of Allen and Reidy themselves. In the Preface of their book, Allen and Reidy wrote: "It has been the aim of the authors to give an *unbiased* description of the Battles, just as they occurred, and it is expressly desired that the public as well may derive some satisfaction from a perusal of the following pages" (Allen and Reidy, 9) (italics added). Reidy too wrote an ode to the fallen soldier in a nine-stanza poem excerpts of which are as follows:

> The battle commences, loud crashes the bolos
> And the gleam of the bayonets shine forth like the stars of the sea,
> Colonel Baldwin's command is now heard by the brave and the bold,
> As onward they charge like lions leaping mad at a fold.
>
> The meet in hot conflict, they bleed in the midst of the strife,
> *For their country's freedom, for their glory, their honor and life,*
> The battle is over amid cheers from the victors of war,
> But alas, one brave hero has fallen with many a scar. (Allen and Reidy, 8) (italics added)

It is not known whether Reidy referred to any specific soldier or to those killed in general, metaphorically in this poem. But one casualty on the US side, Lieutenant Thomas A. Vicars, who led Company F, was killed "when a cannon [*lantaca*, or small brass cannon used by the Moros] literally blew off his head" (Fulton, 132) was notable enough for a new camp, set up the next day on the same site where the demolished Bayan forts once stood, to be named Camp Vicars, with Captain John J. Pershing designated as its commander. Another noteworthy piece of document is a sermon delivered by the Chaplain of the 27th Infantry, the Rev. George D. Rice, on the Sunday following the battle. The sermon was rather lengthy but suffice it to excerpt his commendation of the troops, and his thoughts as to which side God was on, and comparing the courage displayed by the US soldiers and by those of the Moros, as follows:

> I am going to speak to you to-day on courage, and how I saw it displayed on May 2d, while you were engaged in open combat with the Moros. There was a time when I thought that true courage was the absence of fear. But after witnessing the battle of this week I have seen that which has caused me to think differently now, because you demonstrated to me on that day that true courage was not the absence of fear, but the conquest of it. Surely, yours was the highest order of courage.... It was surely a high order of courage that caused Sgt. Graves to swing himself over the out stockade of Binidayan when the fanatic Moro and his knife could be seen above. It was courage of the most godly type that took Corporal McGovern down into the trenches to prop up the hands of wounded men and give them water.... It was courage of the Christian soldier that inspired Sergt. Major Ingold and Sergt. McCarthy, both wounded, to speak words of hope to their comrades". (Allen and Reidy, 51–52)

Then, Rev. Rice takes time to talk of the kind of Moro courage that he saw, as follows: "The courage displayed by the Moros is very different. The Moros were caught in a trap. They knew it, and they fought the desperate fight of their lives. You can drive a mouse into a corner like this, and he, too, will turn. Bravery through necessity is not the true courage which comes of Christ" (Allen and Reidy, 52).

The messages of praise and congratulations sampled above may signify the climax to this story, but there is a denouement consisting of a series of further conflicts. These episodes, although not as dramatic as the Battle of Bayan, nonetheless, showed lingering signs of resistance which impelled the US authorities to take further suppressive actions combined with some tact and diplomacy in the pacification of the rest of the region surrounding Lake Lanao, an approach that would be associated—rather prematurely or erroneously—with Capt. Pershing.

Within about a week of the Battle of Bayan, Gen. Chaffee arrived in Bayan to inspect the troops and hear accounts from the officers and men about their experiences in the expedition thus far. One of the accounts he heard was from Capt. Pershing who, for weeks prior to the commencement of the Lake Lanao Expedition led by Col. Baldwin, had been on his own trying to get to know some datus whom he had met during his weekly discreet intelligence gathering venture at a marketplace, which met once a week, in Iligan, at that time considered a Muslim enclave in a predominantly Christianized northern Mindanao. Accessible to Lake Lanao's entrypoint at Marawui (now, Marawi) through an old trail used by the Spaniards, Capt. Pershing had appreciated the geographic significance of Iligan just as it could serve as a preferable alternative to Malabang for purposes of bringing in supply from Manila.

The valuable personal contacts Capt. Pershing has made paved his visit with these datus, coming mainly from the eastern side of the lake, often unarmed to show trust and earn the confidence of his hosts with whom he also exchange gifts. One of these datus was the former Sultan of Madaya, Ahmai-Manabilang, who has abdicated his nominal position in favor of his nephew, whom he had sent as an intermediary with Capt. Pershing. Historian Fulton describes Capt. Pershing's approach to Manabilang as follows: "Pershing took pains to accord all the honors to Manabilang, putting him and his retinue up for the night in the officers' quarters and giving special instructions to his men on showing respect" (Fulton, 121). In his numerous visits with Manabilang, Capt. Pershing, who had attained a level of conversational proficiency in the Maranao dialect, had endeavored to "explain at length the principles of American policy, stressing the respect of Islam and its customs that had been accorded elsewhere, and American good intentions" (Fulton, 121).

On account of the friendship that he has been able to build that he could later claim that the formation of a potential coalition of datus was averted from joining the fight in Bayan on May 2, suggesting that the victory was not necessary all due to the leadership of Col. Baldwin who was viewed by his superior, including Gens. Davis and Chaffee, as having a rather impetuous tendency. It was because of Capt. Pershing's approach that earned him the confidence of Gens. Davis and Chaffee when he was designated commander of Camp Vicars, bypassing Col. Baldwin, who was nonetheless promoted to Brigadier General, then soon reassigned to command the Visayan Department. Gen. Davis himself would be promoted to Major General and designated to replace Gen. Chaffee who would shortly be promoted to Lieutenant General and, later, appointed as Second Army Chief of Staff in Washington. In line to fill Gen. Davis' soon-to-be-vacant position was Brig. Gen. Samuel S. Sumner, a veteran of the Indian campaigns, then assigned as commander of the District of Southern Luzon during which time he notably was not in good terms with Gen. Chaffee for refusing the latter's order to implement a "population concentration program" reminiscent of the infamous practice of *reconcentrado* employed in Cuba by the Spaniards to suppress the Cuban insurgency. Gen. Sumner would be Capt. Pershing's immediate superior.

Another characteristic strategy associated with Capt. Pershing, which some historians have described as "divide and conquer" was his focus on finding who among the datus were susceptible to friendship and who, among them, tended to be hostile, realizing that "the Moros, by the very nature of their societal institutions, were already divided" (Fulton, 145). Fulton explains: "[Pershing] sensed that at some point he would have to fight some of the most recalcitrant datus, but unlike Baldwin, he knew he could not fight everyone, and it would be most unwise to fight someone he did not have to and unnecessarily add more enemies as a result" (Fulton, 145).

The opportunity would come before too long for Capt. Pershing to demonstrate in practice his patented brand of what would today be called counterinsurgency. As mentioned earlier, when Gen. Chaffee arrived at Camp Vicars after the Battle of Bayan, he issued an invitation, in the words of Allen and Reidy, "to the principal sultans and datos, who were then commanding tribes of savage bolomen along the most impassable regions of the lake shores. The subject matter of his messages were authoritative invitations to come into the camp and hold a friendly conference with him" (Allen and Reidy, 60–61). Many responded affirmatively, and terms for peace had been agreed upon but, unfortunately, not for long. Allen and Reidy explain why, as follows: "Their terms of peace were, to say the least, short lived, for in the early part of the month of July a detachment of men was brutally and unexpectedly attacked by a band of bolomen on the trail. They were outnumbered by the enemy, and consequently many of the Americans were wounded and some three or four killed outright" (Allen and Reidy, 61–62). A further evidence to the deteriorating peace conditions and spirit of rebellion in the lake region was when the Sultan of

Bacolod sent a defiant message to Capt. Pershing a translation of which is as follows:

> We ask you to return to the sea because you should not be here among civilized Moros, for you are not religious. If you stay here we will fight you this month, and in no event will be your friends, because you eat pork. We say to you that if you do not leave this region, come here and the sultan will sacrifice you, and if you do not wish to come, we will come to you and fight. (Allen and Reidy, 63)

Within a few days, the Sultan of Maciu also sent Capt. Pershing a similarly toned defiant message. Allen and Reidy described the resulting mood at Camp Vicars as follows: "Circumstances now began to look grave at Camp Vicars. The Americans had endeavored by every means in their power to prevent further hostilities and trouble, but had failed in all their efforts to bring about peace between themselves and the dark-skinned natives of the trackless plains of Mindanao" (Allen and Reidy, 63).

Actual acts of violent resistance against the Americans by the Moros did not resume until the evening of August 12 when, as narrated by Allen and Reidy, "the most appalling and most ghastly murder that has ever been witnessed took place about two hundred yards from the camp. The moon had disappeared temporarily behind a dark cloud, the men had all retired for the night, and everything seemed tranquil, when suddenly the camp was aroused by the firing of shots in rapid succession by the members of the outpost" (Allen and Reidy, 64). As it turned out, the sentries assigned to guard outpost No. 4 had been attacked by about 20 Moro raiders, and the soldiers soon found themselves "fighting desperately for their lives." Reinforcement arrived but to no avail as it arrived

> too late to prevent the massacre and death of their fallen comrades, for the savages had by this time made well their escape, after performing one of the most savage, most treacherous and most blood-curdling deeds, that has ever hitherto been recorded in the pages of bloody history. Not content with killing their victims, they had cut them with their bolos and long spears, until their bodies were beyond recognition". (Allen and Reidy, 65)

This attack was followed two nights later by another raid by a party of about 30 Moro warriors who fired wildly at the camp.

Following a brief investigation, it was determined that the attackers belonged to the tribes loyal to the sultans of Bacolod and Maciu, respectively. It was decided that an attempt be made to send messages to the datus of the lake region, particularly to the sultans of Bacolod and Maciu, "demanding, rigidly, an explanation regarding the recent attacks… as well as the immediate surrender of the murderers in their tribes who were guilty of committing various acts of injustice and cruelty since the historical battle of May 2" (Allen and Reidy, 67). There being no response other than the usual "defiant, insolent, and sullen nature" (Allen and Reidy, 67) and seeing that no "restoration of peace in the island of Mindanao could not be brought about by fair and honourable means," it was decided that a lesson needed to be administered, one that "they would not very readily forget" (Allen and Reidy, 67–68). Such action would mollify the soldiers who were craving for revenge at the same time it would satisfy the suggestion of some friendly datus that the Americans had to do something if they "were not to lose their credibility" (Fulton, 147).

Historian Fulton gives the account that, at this juncture, Capt. Pershing went to Gen. Sumner who, in turn, went to Gen. Chaffee who, for his part, sent a cable to the War Department detailing the incidents and suggesting that something forceful needed to be taken. The War Department sent back a reply essentially giving a green light to a military action, but with some caution, in the following words: "The President hopes every effort will be made to keep peace with the Moros but leaves decision as to what is necessary to military authorities on the ground." (Fulton, 147).

Shortly thereafter, Gen. Chaffee ordered Gen. Sumner to organize an expedition specifically directed against Sultan Uali of Butig, and Sultan Cabugatan of Maciu, settlements which were situated a few miles apart on the eastern side of the lake (Fulton, 147). Gen. Sumner wasted no time putting together a combined force from Malabang and Vicars, consisting of about 1800 soldiers, and to simultaneously attack Maciu, Butig, and Bacolod, settlements considered to be the most bothersome, comparatively speaking. However, this was disapproved by Gen. Chaffee in favor of a smaller but cautious attacking party to be organized and commanded by Capt. Pershing, who ended up planning and executing a series of punitive campaigns around the lake region in the form of an expedition that would bear his name, the Pershing Lake Lanao Expedition. The objectives of the expedition, as explained by Fulton, are as follows: (1) "to demonstrate that Americans could capture and destroy the cottas, which the Moros still believed to be impregnable, and that it could be done swiftly, efficiently, and with minimal damage to the Americans"; and, (2) "to demonstrate restraint, killing no more Moros than was absolutely necessary and rigorously avoiding damage to their civilian, as opposed to their 'war' property" (Fulton, 148). These objectives were consistent with Capt. Pershing's overall counterinsurgency doctrine, in modern parlance, aimed towards pacification of the restive Moroland, at least at this very early stage of his campaign. Based on his perusal of transcripts of Capt. Pershing's voluminous papers, historian Fulton was able to cull his (Capt. Pershing's) approach towards pacification in the following description:

> He [Pershing] demonstrated intimate knowledge of correct Maranao protocol, but was blunt in the messages he conveyed. He made plain what was open for discussion or negotiation and what lines could not be crossed, such as theft or the killing of a soldier, he would first give an opportunity for redress, holding the datu of the offending party responsible. If redress did not occur, Pershing would arrest the datu and hold him, albeit with dignity and without privation (sometimes even in his own quarters), while rigorously avoiding any insult or humiliation. (Fulton, 145)

The first stage of Capt. Pershing's campaign is sometimes referred to as the Butig-Maciu expedition in that it called for dealing with the incidents in early August, as described above, whose perpetrators were suspected as followers of the sultans of these settlements and were to be arrested. But in view of the inclement weather and the outbreak of cholera, the expedition to the settlement of Bacolod was postponed until the spring of the following year in what would be the third of four stages. The plan originally included Bacolod whose defiant datu threatened war instead in response to Gen. Sumner's written message that "the chance was now given to him and his people to make friends with the Americans before it was too late" (Fulton, 154). As quoted by Fulton, the Sultan (of Bacolod) "declares war at once as we wish to retain the religion of Mohammed. Cease sending us letters" (Fulton, 154).

The Butig-Maciu expedition, according to Fulton, consisted of "one troop of the 15th Cavalry, four companies of the 27th Infantry, the 25th Artillery Battery with two small Maxim-Nordenfeldt mountain guns and one 3.6-inch field mortar (all transportable by pack mule), a surgeon and small detachment of the Hospital Corps, an officer of the engineers, and a quartermaster. Some 643 officers and men would be supplied by a sixty-mule pack train. While quite adequate for the mission, it did not by any stretch constitute overwhelming force" (Fulton, 148).

The expedition left Camp Vicars on the 18th of September, encamped at Pantauan, a small town on the approach to a secondary objective: the small settlement of Gauan along Lake Butig, a small satellite lake to Lake Lanao about four miles away. The following day, the party advanced towards Gauan, guarded by a complex of three fortifications. The operation against Gauan and its defenders proved to be relatively easy. A combination of mountain guns and sniper shots carried much of the day, showing Capt. Pershing's patient but deliberate tactic that set the pattern for the succeeding objectives. Fulton explains:

> Unlike Bayan, there would be no direct assaults or attempts to storm the forts until the defensive works had been greatly reduced. Small assaulting parties might rush the walls, but only to set fires and quickly retreat. Reckless heroics were discouraged. The advance against the cotta's defenses was slow and paced, keeping up continual, but well-aimed, rifle and artillery fire, with the intention of pressuring the Moro defenders to abandon the cottas. There was no attempt to cut off escapes. The only prisoners Pershing wanted were those who surrendered voluntarily, not because they were trapped. (Fulton, 149)

After this successful foray into Gauan, the expedition would have proceeded to Maciu as planned had it not been for unanticipated impassable swamps brought about by the rainy season. Without much choice, Capt. Pershing decided that the expedition return to Camp Vicars and have the troops rest for a few days. On September 28, the expedition resumed its journey, marching across a semi-reconstructed trail to Maciu, thanks to the hard work over two days by the engineers and their crew. On the 30th, Maciu was within sight, most especially the red flags of defiance that fluttered above its forts. But because it was dusk, the expedition encamped for the night giving the soldiers a much needed rest.

At this juncture, Allen and Reidy described the defiant mood they found at Maciu and acknowledged that it was unsurprisingly characteristic of the Sultan Cabugatan of Maciu whom they described as "defiant, haughty, and semi-savage" (Allen and Reidy, 82), and one "who had hitherto held his stronghold and expansive territories with creditable success for centuries against even the haughty Spanish soldiers. But his day of gloom was fast approaching, when he and his clan of bolomen would be compelled to submit to the sons of America..." (Allen and Reidy, 75).

As dawn broke the next day, the soldiers shared a "hurried breakfast" then on they marched against "Maciu's tribe." At the summit of a nearby hill, they positioned the Battery about 400 yards in distance from a fort, formidable in appearance, that stood in the way to Maciu. Allen and Reidy related what happened next:

> As soon as the first shot from the Artillery was fired the Moros began to abandon the fort.... The Infantry had formed a semi-circular skirmish line around the stronghold and now, the Battery having ceased firing, they began to move forward, closing around the fort. At last they reached it and after scaling its high walls, they found that the greater part of its inmates had fled in the direction of Maciu, taking their arms with them. The soldiers soon began to destroy the fort, and in a very few moments, it was reduced to ashes. (Allen and Reidy, 89–90)

Then, after having destroyed the fort, the soldiers, followed a trail in the direction of the lake "destroying, as they went, everything in the shape of forts or strongholds which they encountered, and from which they had been fired upon" (Allen and Reidy, 90). This seemed reminiscent of a scorched earth practiced by the US military in other parts of the country against the *insurrectos*, but Allen, the primary author, addressed the question with an air of authority as to whether or not this was of a "cruel nature," in the following words: "To this I can only state that having been amongst them since the origin of hostilities in the island of Mindanao, up to the present date, and having become rather familiar with their treachery and cruelties to American soldiers, wherever they could get a chance, I think as far as my judgment is concerned that they have been given a lesson which, to say the least, they richly deserve" (Allen and Reidy, 91). However, the main objective—Maciu—still laid ahead.

The next day, the camp broke and shortly after 7:00 in the morning, the march began realizing that that day was "designated for the capture of Maciu" (Allen and Reidy, 92). As the troops drew closer to Maciu's fort, the troops deployed in skirmish lines as they advanced towards the fort and "prevent, if possible, the escape of any of the blood-thirsty Moros whose wild cries we could now hear within" (Allen and Reidy, 93). The Battery, having been positioned infront of the fort, immediately went into action. Allen and Reidy narrate: "The Artillery had opened up on the left.

'Boom!, Boom!!' went the cannons, and a rain of solid shot and shrapnel was hurled at the fort, and for a space of a moment nothing could be seen but the flying fragments, and splinters of bamboo and debris high in the air" (Allen and Reidy, 93). The Moros responded with their *lantacas*, followed by a volley from their rifles. But then the Artillery, now aimed to the right of the fort, responded with a steady volley. By 2:00 p.m., however, it seemed as though the Maciu fort was impregnable. Consequently, the artillery was moved closer to the fort, some 50 yards away which Allen and Reidy note that "it never has been known in the history of battles where Artillery has engaged an enemy at so short a range" (Allen and Reidy, 96). Despite this, "the Moros remained obstinate to the last singing wildly their religious songs to their God 'Allah' in the very midst of the struggle" (Allen and Reidy, 96). However, by around midnight, when the Moros had realized that the Americans were determined to take the fort, including the use of scaling ladders when needed, it appeared that the Moro fighters tried to escape from the fort and make a dash to freedom, which was anticipated. But Allen and Reidy attest to something contrary to Capt. Pershing's principle of allowing for escape for those who wished to escape, as follows "In an instant every soldier was on the alert. They kept on coming, however, seemingly regardless of death or the rain of bullets. But few of them escaped or even lived to tell the tale, for as fast as they left the fort they were being shot down by a constant stream of fire from the Infantry, and when the morning dawned it was found that the Sultan of Maciu, with another leader and tribesman, had fallen, never to breath again" (Allen and Reidy, 98–99). No fatalities on the American side during the assault on Maciu were recorded, although two soldiers were severely wounded. To these wounded soldiers, Allen offered consoling words for, in any case, "their sufferings were doubly avenged, for many a hitherto unconquerable Moro has fallen upon the green and now deserted territories of the Sultan of Maciu, with the bones of his mortal composition bleeding on the green sward, under the tropical sun of his native skies" (Allen and Reidy, 100). For his part, soldier-poet Reidy composed a couple of stanzas to memorialize Maciu's now-deceased sultan not so much to honor him but, rather, to put him (the Sultan) where Reidy thought he belonged, and to elevate in esteem the soldiers he fought against and the civilization they represented:

> Where once in triumph on his trackless plains
> The haughty Moro sultan loved to reign,

With shacks proportioned to his native sky,
strength in his arm, and lightning in his eye,
He roamed with uncovered feet, his sun-illumined zone.

The dirk, the bolo, and the spear his own;
Or lead the combat wild without a plan
An artless savage, but a fearless man.
But his "sun" of triumph, has set to rise no more
O'er the quiet waters of Lake Lanao's shores. (Allen and Reidy, 101)

Allen and Reidy end their eyewitness narrative of the history of the US conquest of the Lake Lanao region by also paying tribute to the 27th Infantry established in Plattsburgh, New York, only in the early part of 1901 and then shipped to Mindanao via Manila in December of that year. To the soldiers of this infantry, who have served with gallantry a genderized (or, rather, sexualized) reference to their country ("Fair Columbia"), Allen and Reidy wrote: "It is with feelings of pride and national patriotism we have watched through many a stormy year the steady growth and accomplishments of our immortal Army, whose splendid display of true valor and military discipline has attracted the attention and well-deserved admiration of all nations through the universe, whether exhibited on the expansive parade ground..., on the far away 'Eastern Isles,' under the warm rays of the tropical sun, where many a true and stout-hearted son of 'Fair Columbia' has sacrificed his young life for his country's cause" (Allen and Reidy, 103). And, not to be ignored was the 25th Battery of Field Artillery, a mountain battery organized in the Philippines only in September 1901 from out of what used to be the Light Battery "C" of the 7th Artillery. To this Battery, Allen also tried his hand in poetry and composed a poem entitled "The Mountain Battery" to honor its members but specifically its commander, Capt. W. B. MacNair, excerpts of which are as follows:

The stout-hearted warriors who have fallen in battle
In defence of their country, its freedom to save,
Whose memory shall live and will ne'er be forgotten
Though long have they mouldered to dust in their graves,

Could they but look back from their graves of cold slumber,
Where in silence they are sleeping long ages away,
And see their successors, brave, bold, and undaunted,

Who have fought the proud Moros on Mindanao's plains.

For foremost in the ranks of victorious honor,
Are the heroes who founded the illustrious name

Of the 25th Battery, and one may well ponder,
On the name of the Commander, with world renown fame. (Allen and Reidy, 113)

Allen and Reidy note that Capt. Pershing's Moro campaign successfully concluded on January 1, 1903, in which "'Old Glory' of fair 'Columbia' is now unfurled to the gentle touch of the oriental zephyrs on the hill-tops of Mindanao, for all times to come" (Allen and Reidy, 101). The reference to "Columbia" is a reflection of the popularized notion, common since the second half of the 1700s, of a goddess of virtue and progress—and then of democracy—seen to represent the United States, famously depicted in John Gast's 1872 painting in which Columbia is seen floating in mid-air, dressed immaculately in white, holding a school book and telegraph wire, a clear attempt at linkage with the Enlightenment, guiding settlers in their westward expansion, and offering protection ostensibly including potential harm from the "savage" Indians.

In context, it is important to understand that Capt. Pershing's punitive expedition throughout the entire 1902–1903 period actually consisted of four distinct phases—two in the second half of 1902, and two in the first half of 1903—in which the phase described by Allen and Reidy involving the campaigns against the sultans of Gauan, Butig, and then Maciu, constituted just the first and the second of these, respectively. The conquest of Bacolod would have been included in the late 1902 campaign had it not been for the prevalence of cholera among its population. When the epidemic was deemed to have subsided by March of 1903, the campaign resumed on April 5, reaching the vicinity of Bacolod on the 7th. The following day, a frontal assault on the fort was made, after the sultan turned down an offer to surrender unconditionally. When the battle was over, over a hundred Moro warriors were dead, including the sultan, and the fort was razed completely to the ground. The next campaign began just two days after the Bacolod campaign. This involved the capture of the fort at Calahui, about three miles away from Bacolod, this time, however, easy by comparison. The night of the 9th, soldiers fired several rounds in the general direction of the fort with "the intent of impressing the Moros that their position was untenable," their fort being surrounded on three sides by water leaving no room for escape. The joint victory over Bacolod and Calahui came to be known by the combined name as the Battle of Bacolod. The next and final stage of the campaign, commencing on May 2, involved the capture of the cottas at Gata and Taraca, respectively. The first of these, happening on May 4, involved heavy firefight featuring prominently the artillery and vicious hand-to-hand combat between the infantrymen and the Moro defenders. The next day, the expedition proceeded to Taraca. Upon arrival, however, Capt. Pershing and his soldiers were pleasantly surprised to find white flags of surrender flying above the fort. Its leader, Datu Ampuan-Agaus, and his retinue of officers, came out to surrender and were taken prisoners. But while the fort was taken without any firefight, an escape attempt was made that night in which the escapees were fired upon, killing four of them. Datu Ampuan-Agaus managed to escape, and he remained a fugitive for the next twenty years (Fulton, 161).

The completion of the campaigns finally brought about the pacification of the entire Lanao Lake region. But Capt. Pershing's expeditions also had the combined task of mapping this region and circumnavigating it in the process. Following the campaign at Gata an Taraca, the expedition proceeded to Marahui at the north end of the lake and where Agus River, supplied with water from the lake, begins its turbulent flow to Iligan Bay via the majestic Maria Cristina falls. Upon reaching Marahui, on the 8th of May, Capt. Pershing and his party were met by Gen. Sumner. During their brief stay in Marahui, a reception was had wherein friendly datus from around the lake were invited, along with the Pandita of Nuzca who was, at that time, the "acknowledged religious leader of the Islamic faith for all of Lake Lanao" (Fulton, 161). Fulton assessed Capt. Pershing's feelings about the significance of the Pandita's visit, and wrote: "To Pershing, the visit of this particular holy man was of 'signal importance; it was more than evidence, it was an announcement of that at last the outpost stronghold of Islam in the east of Asia had capitulated'".[6] On the 10th of May, Capt. Pershing's expedition began its march back to Camp Vicars but, this time, on the other side of the lake so as to lay claim not only to the circumnavigation of the lake but also to serve as an announcement of the completion of the lake region's mapping and pacification and, more than a symbol, the unchallenged US sovereignty.

Touted by students of counterinsurgency today as a model for successful counterinsurgency operations, Capt. Pershing's campaigns involved a combination of patient intelligence-gathering, personal diplomacy, familiarity with the sociocultural terrain, recruitment of native allies, controlled and measured application of force, and clarity of objective—a model for current-day counterinsurgency requiring employment of experts from such disciplines as anthropology, sociology, and political science. While historian Fulton diverges from many historians in classifying Capt. Pershing's tactic as one of "divide and conquer" among the local chiefs, Fulton takes Capt. Pershing's word at face value and concludes: "But the Moros, by the very nature of their societal institutions, were already divided. Rather, Pershing focused on sorting out who were his friends, who were his enemies, and who were in between" (Fulton, 145). To this writer, however, it mattered less what approach or tactic Capt. Pershing used and that, further, he was being given credit more than he deserves for the above-mentioned components of his approach. To this writer, whether or not Moro society was "divided," an assumed—and much validated—approach always involves the transformation of the conquered society, either sooner or later, into something compliant or acquiescent to the wishes of the conqueror. Education is a fine example of this, and Gen. (Elwell). Otis realized the counterinsurgency significance of setting up schools, in fact, throughout the country in drawing the Filipino youth away from any insurrectionary thoughts or activities. But while persuasive elements to the approach are never taken for granted, so are the coercive ones. This involves search for friendly allies useful for intelligence-gathering purposes, as Capt. Pershing has done, but this also involves search for potential traitors by offering rewards or incentives to weaken the enemy, using natives against natives as was the intention in the case of the Moro Constabulary's establishment, followed, eventually by relentless pursuit through military means as he was widely recognized for doing around the Lanao lake region, but also, ignominiously, at Bud Bagsak in Sulu.

In his third campaign in April 1903, in what came to be known as the Battle of Bacolod, Capt. Pershing did allow his soldiers to employ a "scorched earth" policy in razing to the ground all structures that "seemed like a fort" (ostensibly a euphemism for huts or houses) and to shoot at will, even in the air, just to induce terror among the population as they marched to the lakeshore. This was hinted at in so many words by Allen and Reidy in their text in a manner reminiscent of Gen. William T. Sherman's "March to the Sea" after burning Atlanta during the US Civil War, albeit it in a much smaller scale. Capt. Pershing himself appear to have lost his charm when he commanded, now as a Brigadier General, having been promoted in 1906, over one of the most celebrated atrocities committed against the Moros at Bud Bagsak in the island of Jolo, in the Sulu Archipelago, in June 1913. This happened during his second tour of duty in the Philippines that lasted from November 1909 until December 1913 during which time he also served a Governor of the Moro Province. In his memoirs, Capt. Pershing rationalized the policies and actions of his office, e.g., "disarming and taming the Moros" (phrase taken from the title of Chapter 19 of his memoirs), that inevitably led to the massacre in the following words:

> It was in the possession of arms by the criminal elements that nullified the most earnest efforts toward civil rule and left the peaceably inclined inhabitants at their mercy. To my mind, although many Americans opposed it, there was but one solution – the disarming of the Moros and other non-Christians. The problem had been left to the discretion of the provincial governors and hitherto none had considered it wise to make such an attempt.... I did not decide to undertake it until convinced that there would be a continuance of the disorders until disarmament was accomplished and that it should be done even though the most drastic means might be necessary. I anticipated comparatively little trouble dealing with the scattered wild tribes but considerable with the Moros – who, though not fully united, had a bond of union in their religion. There were predictions made by both Americans and Moros that the attempt would bring about a Holy War – Muhammedan against the 'unbeliever' – a bloody thing to contemplate, but I did not believe it would have this effect. In fact many of the dattos and sultans themselves favored the project provided all, good and bad alike, could be disarmed.... We entered into it fully realizing that here and there force would have to be employed from the beginning but with the firm conviction that it was the only solution to the problem. (Pershing, 285–286)

Thus, here, Capt. Pershing ignored the counsel of previous governors against the project, but listened only to the words of friendly datus who had something to gain from their adversary or rival datus being disarmed or vanquished. Finally, he believed that there was no other solution except to use maximum force, and that, further, this would ignite some kind of a holy war in the minds of the Moros. Contrary to his own advice to respect the religious sensibilities of the Moros during his Lanao campaigns, here he was not reticent about igniting some kind of a religious warfare. Sadly, on both counts, his judgment proved erroneous although from the military standpoint, the subjugation was complete.[7] In his memoirs, he recounts the Batttle of Bud Bagsak as "the last and also the greatest battle against the

Moros," offers ritualistic and patronizing admiration to the Moros for making "a stand worthy of the best traditions of a warrior race" and describes the casualties on both sides as follows:

> Our total casualties in the five-day battle were one officer and fourteen men killed and twenty-five wounded. On the other hand the Moro loses, while not actually known, were probably between two and three hundred, as many had fled before the final assault was launched. With [the Moro leader] Amil's death and this defeat the opposition of the Jolo Moros en masse came finally to an end. (Pershing, 302)

What mattered in the end was that Capt. Pershing was laying the groundwork for the integration of Moroland into the colonial Philippine body politic, based on apparent paternalistic principles which, in fact, served to conceal aggressive system of private property and labor relations that would be integrated into—and foundational to—what would be more popularly referred to in the post-World War II era as neoliberal globalization. That the United States has been successful in establishing this global order, and seizing the initiative from the European colonial powers, has been due in large part to exhaustion of the latter from their wars with each other over colonies and, in part, from their wars against national liberation movements in their far-flung colonies. In point of fact, Capt. Pershing's pacification campaign around Lake Lanao may serve as a metaphor for—or certainly a precursor to—how the United States has, throughout much of the twentieth century to this day, gone around the world pacifying or, in some cases, disciplining peoples that were reticent to US leadership or its vision of the future characterized by a borderless world governed by neoliberal rules, e.g., privatization, deregulation, liberalization, the fundamental purpose of which is to commodify, monetize, and privatize chunks of the global commons for the gain of a few. Paving the way for these rules to be applied in Asia was the US foreign policy of "Open Door" enunciated in a series of notes sent from the office of US Secretary of State John Hay, commencing with the first of these dated September 6, 1899, and distributed to the diplomatic missions of Britain, France, Russia, and Japan, countries that seemed to the United States to be fast-carving up parts of China as their own respective spheres of influence, and corralling the Chinese market that has, up to that point, worked to the trading and investment detriment of the United States. The gist of this policy, which served as a cornerstone of US policy in East Asia up until the beginning of World War II in which the Philippines would play a key role as a stepping stone to China, was the preservation of the principle of free trade and equal privileges, particularly in investment opportunities and access to port facilities, among all countries that had trading interests in China.

Laying the Foundation for Racialized State Violence

Despite current efforts by revisionist, neoconservative-oriented US-based historians to whitewash US atrocities in the turn-of-the-last-century annexation of the Philippines, some even referring to it as the "savage war of peace," that US intervention, as San Juan observes, continues "to haunt the conscience of some humanist and historians of international relations," particularly over the question of Filipino casualties as a consequence of that war (San Juan 2009). San Juan explains:

> Current controversy among scholars surrounds the tally of Filipino victims of U.S. pacification. Journalist Bernard Fall cited the killing three million Filipinos in "the bloodiest colonial war (in proportion to population) ever fought by a white power in Asia," comparable to the carnage in Vietnam. Describing it as "among the cruelest conflicts in the annals of Western imperialism," Stanley Karnow, author of the award-winning *In Our Image*, counts 200,000 civilians and 20,000 soldiers ...., while others give 600,000. Filipina historian Luzviminda Francisco arrives at the figure of 1.4 million Filipinos sacrificed for Uplift and Christianization – in a country ruled by Christian Spain for three hundred years. Even Kipling at the outbreak of the war urged the U.S. to "take up the White Man's burden" and tame the "new-caught sullen peoples, half-devil and half-child," Mark Twain wrote some of his fiery pieces denouncing "Benevolent Assimilation" as the "new name of the musket" and acidly harped on the "collateral damage" of the U.S. "civilizing mission": "Thirty thousand [U.S. soldiers] killed a million [Filipinos]. It seems a pity that the historian let that get out; it is really a most embarrassing circumstance..." (San Juan 2009)

Alongside the fashioning of a compliant, elite-based political system that was expected to carry out the wishes and the interests of the US empire following an eventual granting of formal independence, the US colonial authorities created a Philippine army, a national police force, and an internal security apparatus the primary functions of which would not so much be for the protection of the country from external aggression but, rather, for counterinsurgency-related social control and the suppression of internal opposition to the US occupation and to the client regime. Recruitment of members for elements of the US colonial military and intelligence was inspired by the recruitment of so-called Macabebes of Pampanga Province, hailed as "instant success" as models of native collaborators, followed later by recruits from other regions like the Tagalogs, Ilokanos, Bisayans. The concept of recruiting native collaborationists is traceable to the Spanish period the legacy of which persists to this day under the neocolonial regime and with the disciplinary supervision of the US empire (Pobre, 75–76). During US colonial rule, many of these were used to supplement the US Army as members of the Philippine Scouts as tools of suppression, many of whose officers were trained at the Philippine Military Academy, authorized and established in 1908 so that, by 1912 Philippine Scouts, later to form the core of what would be the Philippine Army, numbered by as much as 5485 out of a total of 12462 US troops (Pobre, 78–79). This US occupation, after all, stood in opposition to the Filipinos' right to self-determination, being in violation of the wishes of the Filipino people to be left alone, having just successfully waged a war of independence against the Spanish colonial regime.

Much of the success of the US colonial regime in laying the institutional framework for state violence rested on the recruitment of natives to perform various functions, including serving as spies, scouts, police, or mercenary soldiers. In this context, the use of "water cure," a torture and interrogation technique that was a precursor to "water boarding" that gained notoriety at Abu Ghraib and Guantanamo especially during the early stages of George Bush's so-called war on terror declared following 9/11, became a normal component of the US counterinsurgency. Much of the practices used in the Philippine campaign were carried over, in any case, from the American Indian Wars, along with the racialized attitudes towards the natives.

Further, the 1935 Philippine Constitution had to be amended in 1947 to grant "parity" to Americans citizens (and corporations) enjoyed by Filipino citizens in the exploitation and development of Philippine natural resources, as demanded by the Bell Trade Act passed by the US Congress in 1946 and ratified by the Philippine Legislature as condition for independence, on July 2, precisely two days prior to the official independence proclamation, on July 4. This was followed by a series of spurious, one-sided so-called treaties, e.g., the Mutual Defense Treaty and the Military Bases Agreement, plus provisions for direct military-to-military collaboration and coordination through the Joint United States Military Advisory Group

(JUSMAG), misleading in that the term "joint" refers to the involvement of all the US armed services, and not to United States-Philippine consultations as equal partners, the US empire has continued to secure important basing facilities in the country and, therefore, to project its power and might in the East Asia-Pacific region for decades to come.

Laying the Foundation for Colonial Education

One of the greatest challenges that the US colonial administration faced was reorienting the Filipino mind from any nationalist tendency, including the erasure of any memory or support for the successful Philippine Revolution against Spain, or of the rude interruption of this revolution by US intervention, or the brief insurrection against the US occupation, and the defeat of this insurrection, followed by the process of cultivating support if not adoration for the colonial order under the United States and its promise for eventual "freedom" and "independence".[8] As it turned out, this was not much of a challenge at all as its educational program, including free public education especially at the grade level, was designed not so much to educate the Filipinos and prepare them for a sustainable economic life upon independence but, rather, to augment the counterinsurgency program of the US Army and to cultivate loyalty to the US flag, ensuring the Filipinos' disorientation as to their true identity (Bauzon 1992; Veric 2003). This was confirmed by one of the leading nationalist intellectuals and educators of his time, Renato Constantino, who wrote, in a highly praised and influential essay, entitled "The Miseducation of the Filipino," the following:

> The moulding of men's minds is the best means of conquest. Education, therefore, serves as a weapon in wars of colonial conquest. This singular fact was well appreciated by the American military commander in the Philippines during the Filipino-American War. According to the census of 1903: "....General Otis urged and furthered the reopening of schools, himself selecting and ordering the textbooks. Many officers, among them chaplains, were detailed as superintendent of schools, and many enlisted men, as teachers..."
>
> The American military authorities had a job to do. They had to employ all means to pacify a people whose hopes for independence were being frustrated by the presence of another conqueror. The primary reason for the rapid introduction, on a large scale, of the American public school system in the Philippines was the conviction of the military leaders that no measure

could so quickly promote the pacification of the islands as education. General Arthur MacArthur, in recommending a large appropriation for school purposes, said: "...This appropriation is recommended primarily and exclusively as an adjunct to military operations calculated to pacify the people and to procure and expedite the restoration of tranquility throughout the archipelago..." (Constantino)

Further, in this essay, Constantino criticized previous and the current generations of students and educators for having been uncritical to the colonial education that they have received. "They seem oblivious," he wrote, "to the fact that the educational system and philosophy of which they are proud inheritors were valid only within the framework of American colonialism. The educational system introduced by the Americans had to correspond and was designed to correspond to the economic and political reality of American conquest" (Constantino).

It is this education, inadequate and inappropriate as foundation for even an aspirant medium-sized prosperous industrial economy, that Filipinos would take with them in a diaspora as they join the ranks of Overseas Filipino Workers (OFWs) that would fan out into the four corners of the globe in search of jobs from whose remittances their loved ones back home hoped to benefit but, in fact, the parasitic Philippine oligarchs that control the country's political system also expect to share through the revenue they siphon off to their friends and families.[9] And the stories that a good many of them tell upon their return are quite different from the success stories one might expect otherwise. San Juan poignantly offers a summary narration of this story in his chapter on history, representation, and the advent of what San Juan refers to as "feminist praxis in Filipino writing" of and about the Filipino diasporic experience in his 1995 book, *Hegemony and Strategies of Transgressions*, as follows:

> The advent of a feminist praxis in Filipino writing ... in the 1970s and 1980s may be explained by the phenomenon of millions of Filipino contract laborers, mostly women, sojourning in the Middle East, Europe, Japan, Hong Kong, Singapore, and elsewhere. When these migrant workers return home, they construct stories of their heterogeneous experiences that assume a narrative form conflating the quest motif with the seduction/ordeal motif – a plot that violates all probabilities found in the schemas of semiotic narratology. When the female subaltern returns, the mimesis of her struggle for survival almost always implicates the diegesis of the world system as a metanarrative of the global circulation of commodified bodies and phallocentric

energies. Exchange of her labor power shortcircuits the time/space compression of the postmodern economy. Whether as a household servant in Kuwait or "hospitality girl" in Tokyo, she narrates the lived experience of victimage as a reversal of the "civilizing mission". She thus repeats the whole epic of colonization – but with a difference: her gendered subject-position or agency yields not surplus value but the hallucination of commodity fetishism when consumer goods and traumas become cargo myths for native consumption in the Philippines. In this sense, the migrant worker as 'speaking subject' destabilizes the regularities of the "New World Order" and the "free market" discourse of individual self-fulfillment. Her fabula decenters the *sjuzhet* of technocratic modernization. Overall, this new genre of migrant narrative explodes the traditional definitions of the gendered subject provided by the Symbolic Order of dependent capitalism while its transgressive allegory destroys the conventional plots of immigrant success and postcolonial hybridity. (San Juan 1995)

As an essential complement to the colonial educational process, colonial administrators also made sure that Filipino cultural habits and tastes are shaped in a manner that suited US colonial aims. This included the cooptation of the Masonic Movement, conduit of liberal ideas held among leading Filipino nationalist leaders—among whom were Andres Bonifacio and Jose Rizal—that fought against Spanish colonial rule, and influencing the structure and ritual of the anti-colonial resistance movement, *Katipunan*. Under US rule, however, the Masonic movement was reformed inevitably to suit the aims of the US occupation, turning it into a reactionary movement commencing with the establishment of the first lodge, a movable one, by members of volunteer regiment from North Dakota of the Third Expeditionary Force in July 1898. Subsequently, Filipino masons Ambrosio Flores and Gracio Gonzaga endeavored to restore Filipino-led Masonry leading to the establishment of Logia Modestia in 1899. Its leaders then sent an appeal, in November 1900, to Masonic lodges in the US beseeching their masonic brothers there "to use all your moral and material influence with the government at Washington to bring this dreadful war to an end." This comes in the wake o f he arrival earlier that year of US-based masons led by one Manly B. Curry who then set up the first fraternal organization called the Sojourner's Club, in April 1900 ("History of Masonry..."). Attracting both Filipino and Americans, especially those at the employ of the colonial regime, organizations like the masonry—along with their subsequent respective youth affiliates, e.g., the Order of De Molay for boys

(1930/1946), and the Order of Job's Daughters for girls, along with various other civic-oriented organizations with headquarters in the United States, e.g., the Rotary and Lions clubs, with Philippine branches founded in 1919 and 1949, respectively, became ladders for social acceptance and upward status; and, under the guise of fraternity and sorority, these organizations became training grounds for moulding personal character, civic engagement, respect for authority, compliance with laws, and good citizenship, lending significant degree of legitimacy to the US colonial regime as the common motto "Service to God, country, and fellowmen" became tacitly understood to be within and in support of—and not in resistance to—the colonial or, for that matter, the neo-colonial framework.

On another front and in a pioneering series of outstanding works including *Body Parts of Empire: Abjection, Filipino Images and the American Archive* (University of Michigan Press), Nerissa Balce calls attention to the portrayal by the European powers of non-European, non-white female bodies as means of justifying the superiority of the European civilization. In one essay, Balce writes:

> The black female body has long been part of the imperial archive of Europe informed by the politics of colonization, slavery, prostitution, and pornography. The sexualization of the black female body can be mapped in the canonical writings of nineteenth-century French writers such as [Honore de] Balzac, [Emile] Zola, [Charles Pierre] Baudelaire, and others. The figures of the mulatta, the prostitute, or the slave woman in nineteenth-century French novels and essays were what T. Denean Sharpley-Whiting refers to as icons of the 'Black Venus' or 'sexualized savages'. The lubricious images of black women, as sexual and dangerous bodies, are constructions of 'feminized darkness' and representations of French imperial power. (Balce 2006) (Brackets added)

Even before the Americans took possession of the Philippines from Spain, they have already gained significant experience in the portrayal of non-white, non-European women that they have encountered in the process of expanding the American frontier. Balce, in her account, explains:

> Drawings and photographs of breast-baring brown women from indigenous cultures... have long been part of American porno-tropic tradition. Island women...of the Pacific, have been part of an American Pacific fetish even before the arrival of Admiral George Dewey to Manila in 1898. (Balce 2006)

Balce adds that as far back as the last decade of the 1700s, American authors and artists have visualized the so-called South Seas as a place "inhabited by dark-skinned, cannibalistic savages or as a space for an interior voyage of the self-facilitated facilitated by the white author's or narrator's encounter with primitive cultures" (Balce 2006). Also playing role in the propagation of the Pacific Islanders as somewhat exotic but otherwise backward and uncivilized were traders, adventurers, and politicians creating the body of works, beliefs, attitudes, and policies that came to be what literary and cultural studies scholar Paul Lyon—and which Balce quotes—as "American Pacific Orientalism."

Once in possession of the Philippines, this Orientalist mindset became the template with which colonial policies were forged. As Balce explains, "Thus the histories of European conquest and American imperial expansion are the contexts of the representation of the Filipina savage. As sexual bodies.., the representations of native women in general are artifacts of empire" (Balce 2006).

More significantly, this orientalist template was not without military implications. As Balce notes: "At the turn of the twentieth century, photography made possible a recasting of imperial violence. By visualizing empire through the lens of domesticity, the bloodier and more disturbing aspects of U.S. imperial expansion were excised from the American nation's myths" (Balce 2006). Balce borrows a term from sociologist, Lanny Thompson, "imperial archipelago" or islands territories—including the Philippines—which have fallen under US domination, wherein one finds "a visual and textual archive created by writers, artists, journalists, soldiers, schoolteachers, academics, and politicians who wrote about the culture and peoples of the new 'U.S. colonies'" (Balce 2006).

During the early colonial era in the Philippines, the dissemination of popular images had the function of justifying not only the "civilizing mission" but also the harsh military treatment verging on genocide inflicted upon the fighters during the Filipino-American War and the subsequent counterinsurgency lasting for another decade or so. Singled out by Balce in her study is a highly popular book, entitled *Our Islands and their People, as Seen with Camera and Pencil* (1899), by journalist Jose de Olivares. In this book, Olivares writes, and Balce quotes, in part:

> they are a dark people – some are diminutively black – and our soldiers have fallen into the habit of calling them "niggers"... Many of the people resemble the negro in appearance, but that is as far as the similarity goes. For all the

practical purposes of civilization, the mirthful, easy-going African is superior to these treacherous and blood-thirsty hybrid Malays.... (as quoted in Balce 2006)

A critical discussion of the "American Pacific orientalism," as cited earlier, in the Philippines would be lacking if the contributions by one man were not discussed: Worcester, briefly mentioned earlier in reference to his disparagement of the Aguinaldo's inauguration on June 12, 1898. As mentioned earlier, Worcester served in both the First (Schurman) and the Second (Taft) Commissions. In 1900, he also served as Secretary of the Interior, a position which enabled him to shape policies impacting affairs outside of Manila, a position he held until 1913. One of his favorite hangout was Dumaguete, home to the colonial-era Silliman Institute (now Silliman University) which not only provided him an academic environment that legitimized his ethnographic work but also his counterinsurgency planning, illustrating the symbiosis between religious missionary work and colonial administration. Zoologist by training, Worcester had been referred to by historian Blount as a "reptile finder" although he found much more than reptiles. In his preoccupation as head of the intelligence section of the US military during the early phase of the Philippine–American War, recruited by General Otis for the position, he managed to build an extensive network of nationwide spies targeting insurgents. According to Balce, Worcester was

> a pioneer of counterinsurgency. A zoologist by training, he used his scientific skills and photography to gather data and classify information about the Philippine Islands and the Filipino people for the purpose less of science, however, than that of military surveillance, war, and the maintenance of U.S. military rule in the islands. (Balce 2014)

Balce describes further Worcester's *modus operandi* in the following words:

> Every morning Worcester would go over the local newspapers and type his notes on Filipinos (and some Americans) of interest to the American colonial government, such as Filipino nationalists, collaborators, elite Filipino families, etc. His data gathering became the foundation for an effective system of counter-intelligence that would prove helpful to counterinsurgency efforts once guerrilla war by Filipinos began. (Balce 2014)

If Worcester was not as well-known in his role as an intelligence officer, perhaps by the very nature of this function, he has certainly made a name, if not a notoriety, for himself in his other preoccupation: as a cultural agent of sort. As a zoologist, Balce notes that Worcester had a simplistic racial theory, i.e., that Filipinos that have not been Christianized were simply "savages," and that those that have been Christianized, whom he referred to as semi-civilized—were more often than not corrupt. It is in this context that we may understand his disparagement of the Aguinaldo regime, and the belief that Filipinos were simply incapable of self-government. It may also be said that much of his racial beliefs were an emanation from late nineteenth century thinking traceable to Social Darwinism. But it was because of the air of intellectualism that he projected that he was able to gain the confidence of McKinley, who appointed him to position in the two presidential commissions.

One of the tools of the trade that Worcester employed to much success was a relatively new piece of technology: the hand-held still camera. With this device, he went around the country taking photographs, e.g., of mountain-dwelling Igorots in their g-strings, of dog-eating villagers, and, according to historian and cultural studies scholar Mark Rice, whom Balce cites, Worcester even managed on various occasions to manipulate or coerce "his young female subjects to disrobe their traditional clothes, and pose suggestively for his 'ethnographic' portraits," all for the purpose of demonstrating the primitivism, the backwardness of the way of life of Filipinos justifying US colonialism (Balce 2014). Many of these photographs found their way into newspapers, magazines, and travelogues, particularly in the United States with the consequent effect that the civilizing spirit has been strengthened and, more significantly, displacing the images of otherwise brutal war against and pacification of the Filipinos. Balce's sobering assessment is worth quoting at length as follows:

> With the violence of the Philippine-American War in mind, it thus becomes possible to "picture the invisible," to imaginatively reconstruct the violence of American rule in the Philippines. The photographs of Filipinas… display docile bodies under imperial control. The notion of "docility"… was indeed an objective of U.S. colonial rule…. Filipinos needed to become meek and useful to be considered educated and civilized. Thus it was not enough to jail, deport, execute, or hang [them]. The next generation of Filipinos had to be disciplined through a U.S. system of education…. Travel cultures supported the project of docility….Echoing earlier travel texts…, many of the texts would emphasize how far removed the Philippine Islands were from the modern and civilized cultures of the West. (Balce 2006)

In retrospect, the foundation laid by Worcester and his associates has been indispensable to the US colonial rule, contributing to the conversion of a self-determined Filipino nationhood to one under colonial tutelage. This was not because of an unconscious, guiltless historical accident but because of a deliberate, conscious series of human decisions made by individuals claiming to represent an exceptional civilization and empowered by a military machine but which, by the nature of their acquisitive and expansionist economic system, were bound to subdue others to their will.

A feature of the US colonial regime, to which Worcester has contributed, has been the establishment of the most elaborate surveillance system as described by Alfred McCoy in his *Policing America's Empire; The United States, the Philippines, and the Rise of the Surveillance State* (2009). As context to the massive surveillance exposed by whistleblower Edward Snowden, McCoy's work is praised in the book's dust cover as follows: "Armed with cutting-edge technology from America's first information revolution, the U.S. colonial regime created the most modern police and intelligence units…. In *Policing America's Empire*, Alfred W. McCoy shows how this imperial panopticon slowly crushed the Filipino revolutionary movement with a lethal mix of firepower, surveillance, and incriminating information….. In trying to create a democracy in the Philippines, the United States unleashed profoundly undemocratic forces that persist to the present day".[10]

Notes

1. San Juan provides important context to US economic motives in gaining control over the Philippines with much-documented violence of genocidal proportions, despite invocation of moral duties implied in McKinley's proclamation. In another one of San Juan's highly-praised books *U.S. Imperialism and Revolution in the Philippines* (2007b), he explains: "Beginning from the rise of merchant capital in the seventeenth and eighteenth centuries, the messianic impulse to genocide springs from the imperative of capital accumulation—the imperative to reduce humans to commodified labor-power, to salable goods and services. U.S. 'primitive accumulation' began with the early colonies in New England and the slave plantations in the South. It culminated in the nineteenth century with the conquest and annexation of Puerto Rico, Cuba, Guam, Hawaii, and the Philippines," all of which has occurred in the historical backdrop of "the U.S. extermination drives against the American Indians in particular, and the brutalization of African slaves and Mexicans in general, events which San Juan rightfully

encourages progressive scholars and researchers to use as "pedagogical references [toward the concretization] of the U.S. colonial pillage and plunder in the Philippines".

2. The tradition of resistance has continued even after the granting of formal independence by the United States to its client government, the Government of the Republic of the Philippines (GRP) in July 1946. Immediately following World War II, this resistance was carried out under the banner of the *Hukbalahap* (acronym for *Hukbo ng Bayan Laban sa Hapon*, or People's Anti-Japanese Army, *Huk* for short) Movement. Clashes in personal styles of leadership, ideological differences, and disagreements over tactics among its leadership, combined with counterinsurgency campaign waged by the US-backed government through its US Army-trained and CIA-guided Philippine army and police, eventually led to the decline of this movement. In December 1969, the spirit of resistance was rekindled with the re-establishment of the Communist Party of the Philippines, along with its military arm, the New People's Army, under the intellectual inspiration of Jose Maria Sison. With this movement seen as the only active militant movement in resistance to the neocolonial order, San Juan offers his thoughts in a 2015 piece, entitled "Hypothesis Toward Synthesizing a Radical Critique on the Neocolonial Order in the Philippines (in Filipino)," with the view in mind of impressing upon the resistance movement the importance of acquiring the proper intellectual and historical tool with which to carry out this resistance. The article is summarized in its Abstract (translated into English) as follows: "In studying Philippine history, the tradition of anti-imperialist revolution (whether visible or deliberately erased) is what informs the analysis of every social occurrence. No telos or linear outline is posited because each event is determined by complex contradictions between social relations and material production whose effects cannot be precisely calculated. By virtue of attempts to comprehend the meaning of events and intervene at opportune moments, we can change the direction and tempo of historical transformations. We can elucidate neoliberal hegemony by analyzing the ideology that motivates acts, sentiments, and aspirations of mass consumers. We need to diagnose the norms of commodity fetishism and possessive individualism. In the process of critique, one can discern the dialectics of objective circumstances and subjective forces operative in class struggle. Thus the masses acquire a space of freedom to change institutions, modes of conduct, structures of personal interaction, etc. Philippine history and culture are fashioned by the collective effort of citizens to win sovereignty, authentic independence, and liberation from the dictates of global capitalism, in particular U.S. imperialism, foreign corporations, and the local oligarchy conniving with them." See https://www.academia.edu/12297524/HYPOTHESIS_

TOWARD_SYNTHESIZING_A_RADICAL_CRITIQUE_OF_THE_
NEOCOLONIAL_ORDER_IN_THE_PHILIPPINES_in_Filipino_.

3. At this point, San Juan interjects and explains the sociohistorical background of the Moro community as follows: "From the middle of the 15th century up to the military conquest of Mindanao and Sulu by American forces, the Moro sultanate (Sulu, Maguindanao) evolved as segmentary states, more precisely tributary formations in which lineage or kinship interfaced with more elaborate and partly centralized organizations for production and defense. By 'tributary formation' (following Samir Amin) is meant a stage of social development whose mode of production is characterized by extraction of the surplus product by the exploiting class by non-economic means, through the agency of the superstructure (religious ideology), and where the essential organization of production is based on use-value, not exchange value. With an economy comprised of primitive agriculture using slaves and other servile hands, minimal gathering and hunting/fishing activities, and a flourishing commerce, the datus (local chieftains) enforced their rule through the superstructure (kinship, personal attributes, religious ritual), and through violence operating within the parameters of consent" (San Juan 1986, 71).

4. The US representative in this diplomacy was no less than Commander Charles Wilkes of the US Navy Pacific Exploration Expedition, passing through the Sulu Archipelago following his blood-soaked mission in the Pacific on his return to the Norfolk Naval Base in the United States. This agreement, referred to by many historians as the Wilkes Treaty, turned out to be the first of many more treaties to come between the United States and the Philippines, this one through the Sulu Sultanate. For full text of this treaty, please see "Today in Philippine History, February 5, 1842, the Wilkes treaty was signed at Soung, Island of Sulu," *Kahimyang*, posted January 16, 2013, in https://kahimyang.com/kauswagan/articles/1421/today-in-philippine-history-february-5-1842-the-wilkes-treaty-was-signed-at-soung-island-of-sulu.

5. At this point, San Juan makes an important qualification about the presuppositions behind the US colonial pacification and subsequent administration of Moroland as context for explaining the current conflict in the southern Philippines. He writes: "While antagonism between Muslims and Christians dates back to the Spanish colonization from 1565 to 1898, and U.S. colonial domination from 1898 to 1946, the present conflict is not religious as usually construed, but fundamentally political and economic in terms of the division of social labor and its satisfaction of developing human needs. It was the Spaniards who, trying to establish theocratic rule over the islands by conquering and converting the indigenous communities, established the boundary between the 'infidels' (Muslims) and the 'civilized' (Christians). Ethnic

difference, of course, legitimated the violent exploitation of the natives and the theft of their lands and resources" (San Juan 2007b, 95).
6. Amidst the adulation following Capt. Pershing's success in pacifying the Lanao region, paving the way for the integration of the Moroland into the entire Philippine body politic under US rule, San Juan offers the following reflection: "There is no doubt the U.S. policy of integration and assimilation through mass education, jurisprudence, and 'free enterprise led to the obsolescence of the datu power and sultanate authority. But it was the government-sponsored migration of Christians, Chinese, and other settlers—accelerated by President Ramon Magsaysay's resettlement of former Huk rebels in the 1950s—that exacerbated the land disputes raging throughout the entire period of U.S. colonial rule. Unknown to most Moros, the Torrens land title registration system nullified the traditional communal land system, resulting in numerous protests, among them the 1926 Alangkat uprising led by Datu Maporo and the 1950 Kamlon insurrection in Jolo" (San Juan 2007b, 96).
7. On the brutalization of the Moros under the hands of the Americans, San Juan adds the following sobering rejoinder: "Arguably, the Moros have been one of the most brutalized victims of colonial domination and religious chauvinism in world history (Ahmad 1982). When the United States annexed the Philippines in 1898, it had to suppress open and covert native opposition up to 1915, at the cost of 1.4 million lives. The historians' consensus is that the fiercest resistance (or at least forty-one organized rebellions from 1900 to 1941) were mounted by the Moros in the battle of Mt. Bagsak, Jolo, on June 13, 1913, during which three thousand Moro men, women, and children were killed, and at Mt. Dajo, Jolo, on March 9, 1906, where U.S. troops ruthlessly massacred over six hundred men, women, and children (Tan 1987). Unable to subdue the Moros by violence alone, the United States negotiated tactical compromises with the local datus, coaxing their support with 'education trips' and other concessions (Majul 1988a). The U.S. 'policy of attraction' tied to coercive pacification accounts for the careers of Moro chieftains like Hadji Butu, Datu Piang, and others who preferred American tutelage over 'Filipinization' through the Philippine Commonwealth and the Republic (Asani 1980)" (San Juan 2007b, 97).
8. This period of American colonial rule was both challenging and stimulating enough to inspire San Juan to compose one of many of his outstanding and highly praised books, *The Philippine Temptation; Dialectics of Philippine-U.S. Literary Relations* (1996). That the violent and coercive nature of the US occupation and the subsequent imposition of civil—but still colonial—administration over the Philippines until 1946 were quite apparent. San Juan wrote: "Violence was... the midwife of Philippine dependency and underdevelopment." What disturbed San Juan was the apparent silence if

not complicity of United States, and US-based, literary personalities, particularly those of note, of "humane letters" towards the US colonial project in the Philippines, silence and complicity that would provide the condition toward "the erasure of its imperial history" and to the perpetuation of its hegemony. San Juan narrates his own personal account of applying for institutional support from prominent foundations and research institutions one of whose avowed functions is to grant support for precisely the kind of research project that San Juan had proposed. But, lo and behold, most were non-takers, which should not be much a surprise given the fact the questions he sought to investigate were designed to question the basic assumptions behind the imperial project to begin with, and to uncover the nature and role of literature (and those that wrote it) in validating such imperial enterprise and its outcomes. Among such essential questions that San Juan had proposed to investigate were as follows: (a) "How did U.S. canonical test propagate certain beliefs, attitudes, and dispositions that reconciled Filipinos to their subordination?"; (b) "How did Filipinos respond to subjectifying modes of U.S. ideological apparatuses, particularly schooling, and various instrumentalities that affected family life, sexuality, religious practices, and so on?"; (c) "How and why did U.S. literary values and ideals continue to exert a powerful influence on the Filipino intelligentsia throughout half a century, producing in some an acquiescent or adaptive response, yet in others a critical reaction?"; and (d) "After the grant of formal independence in 1946, what elements in U.S. cultural theory and practice continued to extract consent (backed by coercive suasion such as jobs, public recognition, and so forth) and collaboration from Filipino intellectual circles?" (San Juan 1996).

9. On the issue of Filipino diaspora, San Juan has a veritable library of contributions exploring various dimensions and aspects of the issue. Seen within the context of the international division of labor under the neoliberal order, the Filipino diaspora is seen as an outcome of the extractive nature of this system. He writes: "Within the framework of the global division of labor between metropolitan center and colonized periphery, a Marxist program of national liberation is meant to take into account the extraction of surplus value from colonized peoples through unequal exchange as well as through direct colonial exploitation in "Free Trade Zones," illegal traffic in prostitution, mail-order brides, and contractual domestics (the Philippines today supplies the bulk of the latter, about ten million). National oppression has a concrete reality not reducible totally to class exploitation; but it cannot be fully understood without the domination of the racialized peoples in the dependent formations by the colonizing/imperialist power" (San Juan 2007a).

In terms of the economic benefits of OFW remittances, San Juan summarizes them as follows: "OFW earnings suffice to keep the Philippine economy afloat and support the luxury and privileges of less than 1 percent of the people, the Filipino oligarchy. They heighten household consumerism, disintegrate families, and subsidize the wasteful spending of the corrupt patrimonial elite. They are not invested in industrial or agricultural development (IBON 2008). Clearly the Philippine bureaucracy has earned the distinction of being the most migrant- and remittance-dependent ruling apparatus in the world, by virtue of denying its citizens the right to decent employment at home. OFW remittances thus help reproduce a system of class inequality, sexism, racism, and national chauvinism across the international hierarchy of core and peripheral nation-states" (San Juan 2011).

Here, San Juan describes briefly the domestic factors, including policies, compelling citizens to work overseas: "Neoliberal policies known (the "Washington Consensus") maintained the cycle of crisis and systemic underdevelopment, rooted in the iniquitous class structure and the historical legacy of political, economic and military dependence on the U.S. These provide the framework for the increased foreign penetration and control over the national economy, the unremitting dependence on raw material exports and (since 1970s) of human resources (Fast 1973; IPE 2006), coupled with the deteriorating manufacturing and agricultural sectors caused by ruinous trade and investment policies. 'Free market' development schemes packaged with "trickle-down" reformist gimmicks implemented by successive regimes after Marcos have precipitated mass hunger (Lichauco 2005). As Pauline Eadie (2005) has cogently demonstrated, the role of the Philippine state in perpetuating poverty and aggravating the exploitation of Filipino citizens cannot be discounted, no matter how weak or 'failed' in its function as a mediator/receiver of supposedly neutral global market compulsion" (San Juan 2011).

San Juan also assesses the broader implications of the labor export policy of Global South countries like the Philippines on existing power relations between the rich countries of the Global North, on one hand, and the poor countries of the Global South, on the other. San Juan writes: " In effect, the Filipina domestic is what enables European/North American bourgeois society and, by extension, the relatively prosperous societies of the Middle East and Asia, to reproduce themselves within their nation-state domains and thus sustain capital accumulation with its horrendous consequences" (San Juan 2011).

Finally, as to what Filipinos can do as a step towards amelioration of their poor economic condition, San Juan offers some insight from his concluding reflections in this essay as follows: "This process of engagement would be historically contingent on the fluctuating crisis of global capitalism. Essentially, Filipino dislocation on both levels — as a people colonized by US imperial power, and as a quasi-nation subordinated to global capital, in the process of uneven development (Mandel 1983) — constitutes the horizon of its project of affirming its identity as a historic bloc of multisectoral progressive forces. This bloc will play its role as a revolutionary protagonist in the political terrain of a united front against disciplinary neoliberalism (Gill 2009), in an era when US hegemony (political + military) is yielding to a multipolar global arrangement. Filipino nationalism thereby acquires critical universality as part of a universal anti-capitalist trend with a long internationalist record of struggle (Lowy 1998). Perhaps the Filipino people, claiming their sovereign right to a historically specific position in the civilizational arena, would then become equal, active participants in a worldwide coalition of forces against monopoly finance capital and its local agents, be they labor recruiters, neocolonized bureaucratic states, financial consortiums, or transnational institutions like the IMF/WB, WTO, or even a supra-national entity like the UN controlled by wealthy industrialized elites. Only in this process of active solidarity with other subordinated or excluded peoples will OFWs, given their creative integrity and commitment to self-determination, be able to transcend their deterritorialized fate in a truly borderless world without classes, races, or nationalities. We envisage germinating from the combined ideas and practices of OFW struggles an alternative, feasible world without the blight of class exploitation and gendered racialized oppression— the concrete totality of an emancipated, commonly shared planet satisfying human needs and wants" (San Juan 2011).

10. San Juan provides an apt and concise summary of the fifty-years or so of direct US colonial rule over the Philippines, and its implication for the future, in one of his recent books, *Between Empire and Insurgency; The Philippines in the New Millennium* (2015), which also affirms McCoy's account, as follows: "One can summarize the fifty years of direct US colonial rule as an illustration of hegemony won initially through military power and stabilized through the twin methods of bureaucratic coercion and cooptation. When the Philippines was granted formal-nominal independence in 1946, the United States had set in place an Americanized privileged minority, an oligarchy of landlords, bureaucrat-capitalists, and compradors that would fulfill US economic needs and global foreign policy. Consensus on elite democracy and the formal trappings of representative government was obtained through decades of violence, cooptation, moral persuasion, and a whole range of pedagogical-disciplinary methods, with the active collaboration of the religious institutions (both Catholic and Protestant). Hence, the Philippines today is a nation, basically agricultural and dependent on foreign investments..., devoid of the full exercise of its sovereignty (the

United States has veto power over its military and foreign policy). Its political system is characterized by the presence of formalistic liberal-democratic institutions administered by a tiny group of oligarchic families, reinforced by the Church, and a vast military-police apparatus chiefly dependent on US aid... rationalized by the US-led 'war on terror' .... There is at present no national-popular will, only a subalternized elite whose ascendancy and survival depend on direct or mediated (via World Bank-IMF) US military and political patronage" (San Juan 2015, 16–17). Admittedly, this quote indicates the overall thrust of this book, which is the continuation of a critical interrogation of the nature of colonialism and neocolonialism, and the role of popular revolutionary movements and intellectuals in bringing about a radical democratic transformation in the Philippines and beyond.

References

Aguinaldo, Emilio, "Inaugural Address", *Official Gazette*, Government of the Philippines, January 23, 1899. In: http://www.gov.ph/1899/01/23/inaugural-address-of-president-aguinaldo-january-23-1899/.

Allen, James Edgar and John J. Reidy, *The Battle of Bayan and Other Battles, Being a History of the Moro Campaign from April 17 to Dec. 30, 1902: A Record of Events Occurring during a Period of Eight Months' Service in the Lake Region of Mindanao—Also Letters of Congratulation from His Excellency the President of the United State, Major General Adna R. Chaffee, and Others* (Manila: E. C. McCullough & Co., 1903). In: https://ia800202.us.archive.org/7/items/battleofbayanoth00alleiala/battleofbayanoth00alleiala.pdf.

Balce, Nerissa, "The American Vampire and the Filipino Journalists: Philippine Libel Laws Then and Now", *Interaksyon*, February 22, 2014. In: http://www.interaksyon.com/lifestyle/essay-the-american-vampire-and-the-filipino-journalists-philippine-libel-laws-then-and-now.

———, "The Filipina's Breast: Savagery, Docility and the Erotics of the American Empire", *Social Text*, 24, 2 (Summer 2006): 89–110. In: https://nerissabalce.files.wordpress.com/2008/11/balce_the-filipinas-breast.pdf.

Beede, Benjamin R., ed., *The War of 1898 and U.S. Interventions, 1898 to 1934: An Encyclopedia* (London, UK: Routledge, 1994), 778pp.

Fulton, Robert A., *Moroland: The History of Uncle Sam and the Moros 1899–1920* (Bend, OR: Tumalo Creek Press, 2016 ed.). In: http://www.morolandhistory.com/00.Text%20Document/a_brief_history_of_.htm; http://www.morolandhistory.com/00.Text%20Document/a_brief_history_of_.htm#_American_Troops_arrive.

McCoy, Alfred W., *Policing America's Empire—The United States, the Philippines, and the Rise of the Surveillance State* (Madison, WI: The University of Wisconsin Press, 2009), 659pp. Print.

McKenna, Thomas M., *Muslim Rulers and Rebels: Everyday Politics and Armed Separatism in the Southern Philippines* (Oakland, CA: University of California Press, 1998), 343pp.

Pershing, John J., *My Life Before the World War, 1860–1917: A Memoir* (Lexington, KY: University Press of Kentucky, 2013), 744pp. Preview in: https://books.google.com/books?id=aNfrnkW2AF4C&pg=RA1-PT371&lpg=RA1-PT371&dq=John+Pershing,+Lanao&source=bl&ots=sYTL48pIpS&sig=NRM03opHR349EwCFsGEwW91MEu4&hl=en&sa=X&ved=0ahUKEwiq4O2Og4XVAhXDHT4KHVEvDx4Q6AEIQjAE#v=onepage&q=John%20Pershing%2C%20Lanao&f=false.

San Juan, E., Jr., "African American Internationalism and Solidarity with the Philippine Revolution", *Socialism and Democracy*, 24, 2 (July 2010): 32–65. In: http://www.tandfonline.com/eprint/Jqxa3MbH6e8pXFCcAHb9/full#.VcjchPlUWUF.

———, "Afterword: From Development to Liberation—The Third World in the 'New World Order'", in *Development and Democratization in the Third World: Myths, Hopes and Realities*, edited by Kenneth E. Bauzon (Washington, DC: Crane Russak/Taylor & Francis, 1992), pp. 297–310.

———, "An African American Soldier in the Philippine Revolution: An Homage to David Fagen", *Cultural Logic* (2009). In: http://clogic.eserver.org/2009/SanJuan.pdf.

———, *Between Empire and Insurgency—The Philippines in the New Millenium: Essays in History, Comparative Literature, and Cultural Politics* (Quezon City, Philippines: University of the Philippines Press, 2015), 318pp.

———, *Crisis in the Philippines: The Making of a Revolution* (South Hadley, MA: Bergin & Garvey Publishers, 1986), 265pp. Print.

———, *Hegemony and Strategies of Transgression: Essays in Cultural Studies and Comparative Literature* (Albany, NY: State University of New York Press, 1995), 286pp.

———, *In the Wake of Terror; Class, Race, Nation, Ethnicity in the Postmodern World* (Lanham, MD: Lexington Books, 2007a), 232pp.

———, *The Philippine Temptation: Dialectics of Philippines-U.S. Literary Relations* (Philadelphia, PA: Temple University Press, 1996).

———, *U.S. Imperialism and Revolution in the Philippines* (New York: Palgrave Macmillan, 2007b), 265pp. Print.

———, "War in the Filipino Imagination: Filipino Writers in the United States Wrestling with the Minotaur", *The Philippines Matrix Project, Interventions Toward a National-Democratic Socialist Transformation*, December 13, 2011. In: https://philcsc.wordpress.com/2011/12/13/war-memories-in-filipino-writing-in-the-united-states/.

Schirmer, Daniel B. and Stephen Rosskamm Shalom, eds., "The Philippine-American War" (Editors' Introduction), in *The Philippine Reader:*

A History of Colonialism, Neocolonialism, Dictatorship, and Resistance (Boston, MA: South End Press, 1987), 8–19. In: https://books.google.com/books?id=TXE73VWcsEEC&pg=PA9&lpg=PA9&dq=mock+battle+for+Manila,+Spain,+United+States&source=bl&ots=9855VslcAG&sig=DByMdbBDVSWMv676gLi57_lnQ8Q&hl=en&sa=X&ved=0CB0Q6AEwADgKahUKEwiM5uyV07HHAhVIbj4KHR0iA40#v=onepage&q=mock%20battle%20for%20Manila%2C%20Spain%2C%20United%20States&f=false.

Veric, Charlie Samuya, "Culture from Imperialism: American Colonial Education in the Philippines", in *Back to the Future: Perspectives on the Thomasite Legacy to Philippine Education*, edited by Corazon D. Villareal (Manila, Philippines: American Studies Association of the Philippines in Cooperation with the Cultural Affairs Office, US Embassy, 2003), 417pp.

CHAPTER 6

The Cold War and the Post-Cold War Hegemony

> Citizenship in a liberal democratic order is necessarily premised on difference. The citizen is an abstraction, a formal product of a "thoroughgoing transubstantiation" of all the particular qualities, elements, and processes that are symbolized in the constitution of the modern liberal state. But this constitution is nothing else but the exaltation of private property, in short, the sanctification and legitimation of the basis of the disintegration of the state. Everything is turned upside down: the ideal of equality is praised in order to defend the cause of inequality, private property, as fundamental and absolute. Ultimately, the source of its permanent crisis, cannot be resolved except through a socialist/communist revolutionary transformation.
>
> E. San Juan, *Spinoza and the War on Racial Terrorism* (2004)

Electronic supplementary material The online version of this chapter (https://doi.org/10.1007/978-981-32-9080-8_6) contains supplementary material, which is available to authorized users.

© The Author(s) 2019
K. E. Bauzon, *Capitalism, The American Empire, and Neoliberal Globalization*, https://doi.org/10.1007/978-981-32-9080-8_6

Hegemony Based on Capital Accumulation and Labor Extraction

The United States emerged from World War II with barely a scratch. The European powers emerged exhausted, much of their colonial possessions stripped from them or have become independent, some through political negotiation while many, through revolution. The United States used its diplomatic influence to lay down the institutional framework for a postwar political, economic, and financial order with the establishment of the United Nations, the establishment of the Marshall Plan calling for the massive infusion of funds to ensure the economic and industrial recovery of Western Europe along capitalist lines, a similar funding scheme called the Colombo Plan supposedly to assist Third World countries develop along the "modernization model," and the establishment of the Bretton Woods institutions (i.e., the World Bank (WB) and the International Monetary Fund (IMF)) to ensure a financial order closely supervised or coordinated by the US Department of the Treasury.

The ensuing Cold War with the former Soviet Union further gave pretexts for the United States to intervene on numerous occasions in the internal affairs of countries around the globe. The Truman Doctrine, following the enactment of the Foreign Assistance Act of 1947, became the basis for US interventions in Greece and in Italy, respectively, preempting popular will by waging counterinsurgency against the Democratic Army of Greece, which fought to drive away and defeat the German Nazi and Italian fascist occupation forces, and installing a Nazi-sympathizing, British-imposed government in Greece following the end of the Civil War in 1948, culminating in the establishment of a right-wing military junta in 1967; whereas, in Italy, US intervention guaranteed the victory of the right-wing Christian Democrats, and preempting victory by the progressive coalition, in the much-compromised Italian elections in 1948.

In the Third World, US intervention is legion including support for the French in maintaining its colonial possession in Indochina; sponsorship of *coups d'etat* by military and security elements in such places as Iran, Guatemala, Indonesia, Chile, Pakistan, and the Philippines; sponsorship of assassination campaigns, through surrogate organizations, of leaders the United States considered "undesirable"; sponsorship of death squads and paramilitary organizations, along with the arming and funding of police, security, and intelligence agencies in countries where there are active left-oriented resistance to US-imposed/US-backed authoritarian governments, e.g., countries in Central America during the 1980s; long-standing support for despotic Arab monarchs throughout the Middle East; support for the apartheid regime in South Africa; and, support for right-wing guerrilla groups in rivalry to other guerrilla but anti-colonial organizations in Africa, e.g., in Angola, the Congo, Zimbabwe, and much more.

To contend that the United States has been a habitual or serial intervenor in the affairs of countries around the world throughout much of the Cold War, and driving the engines of the neoliberal brand of globalization, might not make much sense unless one makes the broader relationship with the very essence of the US capitalist system and its logic of accumulation and expansion. Here, San Juan makes a succinct statement, as follows:

> Founded on the logic of capital accumulation, globalization is a late-modern phenomenon of profit-centered industrialization. For the first time, finance capital is able to cross national boundaries and control erstwhile sovereign domains, facilitated by rapid leaps in the technology of electronic communication and transportation. Despite the sophisticated and insidious mode of extracting surplus value derived from the labor-power of millions, it is still centrally dependent on its ownership or control of the means of production, together with the forces of production needed to generate value: the masses of workers, including peasants and intelligentsia or middle strata of society in charge of the state and the ideological bureaucratic machinery of governance.
>
> Without the exploitation of labor-power and the private expropriation of surplus wealth, global capital would cease to exist. Class division and class inequality are necessary for profit accumulation, without which globalization powered by finance capital would be unthinkable. (San Juan 2007a)

Furthermore, just as class divisions were being obviated, racial hierarchization was intensifying as an organizing principle domestically under the theme of multiculturalism, on the one hand, and internationally as a basis for foreign policy, on the other, as recorded in the texts of emergent disciplinary tendencies subsumed under postmodernism. As San Juan explains, this was particularly evident during the decades of the 1970s and the 1980s, as he writes:

> Before the ascendancy of the global village of multinational corporations and its administered pluralist ethos in the 1970s, the US elite under Nixon reinforced the racial hierarchy through its attacks on radical trends among people of color; soon, covert and open repression encouraged religious separatism, national chauvinism, and the consolidation of the underclass (chiefly, African

Americans). At this conjuncture, East Asians on the West Coast in particular were instrumentalised to breathe new life into the assimilationist syndrome. Later on, with the return of finance capitalism in the Reagan-Bush years and the influx of Irish and Mexican immigrants after 1965, modernism as an ideological disciplinary complex and structuring habitus [As quoted in Bourdieu 1993] is displaced by postmodernist tendencies—subaltern studies, deconstruction, post-colonialism, Foucaultian modalities of suspicion, etc. Asian American cultural production, with its scholastic authorities and texts, finds its niche in this new tri-polar world (US, Europe, Japan as leaders in the G7 bloc) characterised by the rise of Japan as a peer partner in global hegemony, with Asians as "no longer 'second class citizens'" [As quoted in Gills 1993: 212]. (San Juan 2010)

Keen on developments particularly in foreign policy and international relations, San Juan is able to reflect on the reciprocating impact between the production of social knowledge, on the one hand, and the influence of society on how this knowledge is produced, on the other. Thus, it is not entirely a mere coincidence that the US entente with China and the rise of Japan as a US surrogate power in northeast Asia also happens to be the same period as the intensification of US propaganda against the "evil empire," as Reagan described the former Soviet Union. And as pressure is mounted the predominantly Black-led civil rights movement in the United States, the political class and the mainstream media anointed Asian Americans as the "model minority" to conveniently serve, as San Juan describes, as the "buffer race," holding them up as an example of a successful minority that the blacks might someday want to become!

State of Permanent Warfare

The rise of the United States as a superpower following the World War II and as a hyper-power following the end of the Cold War has also meant, in one respect, an unparalleled ability to impose its will and pursue its interests on pretty much the rest of the globe. In military terms, this means pursuit of "full spectrum dominance," a term described in the US Department of Defense document, "Joint Vision 2020," released in May 2015 and an updated version of the Joint Vision 2010, which serves as the blueprint for any military operations, current or future, in fighting America's wars of varying intensity, e.g., high, medium, and low, either in collaboration with surrogate allies or not, in order "to defeat any adversary and control the situation across the range of military operations" (Garamone). Any casual observer of US military operations and engagements since 9/11 need not look far and hard to find examples as the United States has internationalized its domestic law and declared a so-called war on terror that has served as a pretext for encroaching into every nook and cranny in the globe in search of the elusive terrorist, exacting an unprecedented number of deaths and casualties either directly by the United States or by its surrogate allies, e.g., the North Atlantic Treaty Organization (NATO), and warming the cockles of even the most lukewarm neoconservative advocate of the Project for a New American Century (PNAC) for permanent warfare toward unquestioned US global hegemony in the name of "national security".[1] This is affirmed in the latest in a series of official documents containing military doctrines including the 2015 National Military Strategy, a mere twenty-four page document which essentially states US commitment to global domination by force through the invocation of so-called security challenges that have to be met in order to "protect the homeland" and to "advance our national interests" (Whitney). This document further lists six objectives among which is "the security of the global economic system," making it clear that the US military is poised not merely for the defense of the homeland from any potential external aggression but also for the prosecution of resource wars. The division of the world into different military commands, the establishment of a string of military bases around the world, the covert if not blatant destabilization campaigns against independent-minded governments are just a few among many, many other devices that the United States has employed—and will employ—consistent with this objective. One thing certain, it will secure maintenance of the global order which it dominates by insisting on compliance on the part of countries around the globe (at least among signatories to neoliberal-oriented international treaties) much like what the British did during the mid-1800s in enforcing free trade on China through the Opium Wars. The implications of this on legitimate revolutionary, secessionist, and political movements all across the globe, are not hard to apprehend just as these implications are also foreboding on self-determining and self-respecting but non-ally sovereign states and nations around the globe that refuse to submit to the US imperial *diktat*, or which have not yet succumbed to thinly disguised "democracy programs" that often come under various color revolutions (Bauzon 2014).

Principles and Institutional Structures of Neoliberal Globalization

That the militarization of US foreign policy and neoliberal globalization have gone hand in hand—and will continue to be hand in hand in the foreseeable future—should not surprise anyone. For one thing, militarization is encoded in the Charter of the World Trade Organization (WTO), under the so-called security exceptions clauses in Chapter XXI. Despite formal prohibitions on state subsidies on domestic companies, these clauses provide an official loophole wherein states may subsidize domestic companies engaged in producing or providing security-related products and services. The obvious intent of these clauses has been—and continues to be—to allow the big arms-producing countries, rather than small, poor countries, to continue manufacturing and distributing their arms products, or to provide these products to their preferred destinations particularly in conflict zones around the globe, fueling these conflicts even more, allowing the arms manufacturers to make their profits, while enabling the arms-exporting country to gain military advantage or enhance its political influence over the outcome of the conflict[2] (WTO; Staples).

However, with or without sanction from the WTO, the United States has simply used its ability to defy common rules of the neoliberalism if it suits its purpose while preaching to others to obey the same. Under the principle of protectionism, the United States has codified these violations into domestic law, thus making them legal. Again, as in the security exception clauses pertaining to arms subsidies, the United States has provided—and continues to provide—subsidies to domestic-based corporations, turning them into virtual missionaries of US-led globalization and economic hegemony, through the mechanism of the Overseas Private Investment Corporation (OPIC) which serves, in practice, as a conduit for public funds to provide subsidized, low-premium insurance to US-based companies for purposes of insuring their assets in case of destruction or damage owing to political unrest, or even protection from unanticipated taxation demanded by the host-country and problems associated with convertibility of currency, among other potential problems. Created by the US Congress in 1969 at the behest of then US President Richard Nixon, the OPIC's functions and authority are derived from the Foreign Assistance Act of that same year. According to this law, the OPIC's overall purpose was "to mobilize and facilitate the participation of US private capital and skills in the economic and social progress of less developed friendly countries and areas, thereby complementing the development assistance objectives of the United States" (Bauzon 2000).

It is common among commentators to attribute the principles of privatization, trade liberalization, and deregulation as being at the core of the neoliberal ideology, but something they omit, either purposely or inadvertently, is right under their noses as a daily reality, as already highlighted earlier in this section: militarization. Famed *New York Times* and Pulitzer Prize-winning columnist Thomas L. Friedman, an avid proponent of neoliberal globalization and cheerleader for regime change in such places as Iraq and Ukraine, once wrote quite confidently and with hubris: "The hidden hand of the market will never work without a hidden fist – McDonald's cannot flourish without McDonnell Douglas, the builder of the F-15. And the hidden fist that keeps the world safe for Silicon Valley's technologies is called the United States Army, Air Force, Navy and Marine Corps" (Friedman, a). In a later work, entitled *The World Is Flat—A Brief History of the Twenty-First Century* (2005), in its introductory pages, Friedman explains what it means to think of the world as "flat": "When you think of the world as flat, a lot of things make sense in ways they did not before. But I was also excited personally, because what the flattening of the world means is that we are now connecting all the knowledge centers on the planet together into a single global network, which – if politics and terrorism do not get in the way – could usher in an amazing era of prosperity and innovation"[3] (Friedman, b).

What Friedman chose to ignore is the fact that politics and terrorism are an integral part, or essential ingredients of, the neoliberal globalization that he wishes to miseducate his readers about. Through politics, institutional mechanisms and policies appropriate for their desires and interests have been put in place by the dominant forces, subverting the democratic institutions in their own respective countries. Notorious among these institutions, with a long, documented record of dragging hapless countries into a state of debt servitude are the WB and the IMF. During the 1960s and 1970s, when money was cheap, they made loans available to just about any country that expressed a desire to borrow, so long as they were ideologically vetted (in the way that Chile, before 1973, was not), and so long as they agreed with the conditionalities that were attached with the loan(s) which meant, in other words, agreeing with the prescriptions for structural adjustments in their domestic economy and economic decision-making, and allowing external, supranational organizations, like a Trojan Horse, to predetermine domestic policies.

Many of the countries that borrowed from these institutions were either civilian authoritarian governments or were outright military dictatorships. Within their respective societies, these governments served the interests of various constituencies variously described as plutocrats, oligarchs, or simply the wealthy class that maintained close ties with the government and the military and who, understandably, maintained influence in law- or policy-making even though all shared the common traits as being unelected, self-selected, and self-perpetuating, having succeeded in establishing an affinity of interests—through their dominant sway over cultural, educational, and informational institutions—between their interests and much of the rest of society. And, consequently, many of these government adopted repressive policies, deploying internal security agencies of various types and allowing the same to use intimidation or torture, toward any group or individual that appeared to oppose government and its policies, especially those with neoliberal orientation that facilitated the transfer of public assets and services to the private, profit-making sector often under highly dubious or questionable circumstances.[4]

Thus, to Friedman, "globalization" is normal; no need to prefix it with "neoliberal" because it is automatically assumed to be such. No alternative is considered, echoing one of the phrases made famous by former British Prime Minister Margaret Thatcher when she declared: "TINA, there is no alternative!" But Friedman's assumption about "knowledge centers" being now "flattened" implying shared equality in a sense that the planet is now being held technologically "together into a single global network," ignores the basic fact of contemporarily existing uneven development between the Global North and the Global South, and within each. It does not ask who owns the technology, what motivates the owners, what this technology is used for, who benefits from it, and what power relations results from this unevenness.

Further, Friedman ignores the growing global resistance to neoliberal globalization, e.g., the success of the non-Marxist *Ejercito Zapatista Liberacion Nacional* (EZLN) which has been at the forefront of militant resistance to land privatization in southern Mexico; the resistance by the indigenous community in Bolivia against water privatization particularly in the City of Cochabamba; the formation of farmers' cooperatives through South and Southeast Asia to store their own seeds and to conserve their own water table against the predatory practices of companies like Monsanto and Coca Cola; the success of the landless peasants and workers in Brazil, organizing themselves into *Movimento dos Trabalhadores Rurais*

Sem Terra (MST) against agrarian injustices; the ongoing street protests at ministerial conferences of such supranational neoliberal-oriented organizations as the WB and the IMF, the WTO, and the World Economic Forum (WEF) usually held in various cities around the globe such as those held in Seattle, Washington State, United States; Montreal, Quebec, Canada; Rome, Italy; Davos, Switzerland, among others. Equally if not more significantly, there are also the militant protracted anti-imperialist/anti-colonial as well as indigenous-based struggles for self-determination and which may or may not be guided by Marxist-Leninist revolutionary principles aimed at the root of global exploitation—capitalism itself in the form of armed resistance. These forms of resistance may manifest themselves in various ways and under various conditions and symbolisms, and that these varying conditions and particularities have to be taken into account when assessing them. As San Juan counsels:

> What remains to be carefully considered, above all, is the historical specificity or singularity of each of these projects of national liberation, their class composition, historical roots, programs, ideological tendencies, and political agendas within the context of colonial/imperial domination. It is not possible to pronounce summary judgments on the character and fate of nationalist movements in the peripheral formations without focusing on the complex manifold relations between colonizer and colonized, the dialectical interaction between their forces as well as others caught in the conflict. Otherwise, the result would be a disingenuous ethical utopianism such as that found in U.S. postnationalist and postcolonialist discourse which, in the final analysis, functions as an apology for the ascendancy of the transnational corporate powers embedded in the nation-states of the North, and for the hegemonic rule of the only remaining superpower claiming to act in the name of freedom and democracy. (San Juan 2003)

What these anti-imperialist and anti-neoliberal globalization movements teach people like Friedman and Thatcher (if she were still alive) is that, yes, there is an alternative to the existing system, that another world is possible, and that ordinary folks at various levels and in every corner of the globe are indeed rising up, taking matters into their own hands, and exerting their own agency in fashioning their future.

Uneven Development and Neoliberal Globalization

Despite Friedman's pretense about writing a sweeping history of the twenty-first century, in the same book cited above, he makes little or no critical note of uneven development between the metropolitan powers, on the one hand, and the peripheries, on the other, that was directly attributable to colonialism; no reference to Walter Rodney's brilliant book on how Europe underdeveloped Africa, and not even any reference to—indicating knowledge of or familiarity with—the variety of dynamic alternative propositions offered by dependency theory, the world systems theory, and the Marxist/neo-Marxist theory about the exploitative, acquisitive, and expansionist nature of capitalism; the international division of labor; the liberalized international trading rules that maintain and perpetuate dependency and inequality; and the institutional enforcement mechanisms that apply these rules.[5] No, he does not admit to the proposition that the neoliberal principles, as enumerated above, are a mere rationalization for the shrinking of the global commons represented by what amounts to as the corporate theft and exploitation of the globe's resources as in the days of classical colonialism, and that it represents a denial of the same from those that truly own them, through privatization schemes, causing the state to divest itself of its public service functions, and prying open the economies of so-called emerging markets through mandatory trade liberalization and deregulation that put corporate profits above people's welfare, the environment's well-being, public health, and workers' rights, and subverting democracy in the process. Indeed, these principles of neoliberalism are routinely incorporated in any trading organization be it the WTO or any of its regional counterparts be they in North America, around the Pacific rim, the North Atlantic region, or Western Europe, and Friedman thinks these are just fine![6]

Thus, Friedman and many more like him, assuming they have the interest and the inclination, would do well to learn from those who have a deeper understanding of history, including from those that Friedman may not agree with, such as San Juan who explains that one of the most valuable insights one can discern from Marxist historiography is that "capitalism as a world system has developed unevenly, with the operations of the 'free market' determined by unplanned but (after analysis) 'lawful' tendencies of accumulation of surplus value" (San Juan 1998). As San Juan elaborates:

> With the rise of merchant capitalism, diverse modes of production with varying temporalities and "superstructural" effects have since then reconfigured

the planet. In a new cartography, we find metropolitan centers subordinating peripheral territories and peoples. Colonialism and later finance-capitalism (imperialism) compressed time and space, sharply juxtaposing a variety of cultures linked to discrepant economies and polities, with the colonizing center dictating the measure of modernity. (San Juan 1998)

From the above-quote, any fair-minded, history-conscious, reasonably informed learner would know that San Juan confirms what many other historians have already written about, with much more ample documentation, and could discern, further, that history has not been kind to those in far-flung corners of the globe that have been ravaged by European colonialism even though the Europeans themselves may rest content of their virtues and accomplishments.

Those that bask in the glory of European colonialism and, now, the might of the US empire, should be reminded, nonetheless, that colonialism has left a painful if not ugly legacy that causes the descendants of old colonialism's victims to suffer indignities today when colonialism is said to be a thing of the past. These indignities are manifested in a variety of ways including the perpetuation of uneven development between what has been described as the metaphorical center, in reference to the developed economies of Western Europe and North America, on the one hand, and the poor, largely agrarian countries in what has also been referred to metaphorically as the peripheries, sharing the common experience of having been stripped and exploited of their natural wealth by foreigners, a process that continues to this day under the guise of neoliberal globalization. San Juan adds:

After World War II, the accelerated migration of former colonial subjects into the metropoles, together with the refinement of technologies of communication and foreign investment, heightened the spectacle of heterogeneous languages and mixed practices coexisting with the homogenizing scenarios of everyday life in both center and margin. (San Juan 1998)

The growth and rise of the US empire—a point emphasized in this work— did not happen by chance. Neither did its economic system based on private property, capital accumulation, and labor extraction, happen naturally in accordance with the guidance of the "Invisible Hand." Otherwise, the system of slavery, the genocidal policy toward the native Americans, and the continuing wars against nations of color across the globe under the pretext of the war on terror, contemporary versions of the pacification campaigns waged in the olden days of Indian Wars and the wars of subjugation in the Cuba and the Philippines, all of these would have meant nothing, and nothing at all. The next section intends to shed more light as to the racial nature of this empire and why it has been so difficult, for so long, to admit such particularly among members of the political class and the intelligentsia.

Notes

1. Here, San Juan reveals a paradox about the contemporary "state": On the one hand, it is argued that under (neoliberal) globalization, it is becoming—if it has not already become—obsolete because national borders are presumably coming down, giving way to (a) "borderless" world; and, (b) the convergence between the "state" and the "nation" has been seen as a "malignant paradox" because of their association and linkage with malevolent phenomena as World War II-era genocide perpetrated by the Nazis against the Jews, the "ethnic cleansing" seen in the Balkan region in the wake of the end of the Cold War, and the kind of "terrorism" inflicted on the United States on 9/11. In response, the US "nation-state," seeing itself besieged especially since 9/11, has felt justified and necessary in invoking "national security" to protect itself and to wage its "war on terror." Among those adhering to this line of argument, San Juan singles out proponents of postmodernism who see the ideological nature of the modern state, particularly as identity-conferring, as essentially "evil," and generating the kind of nationalism that led to the kinds of destructiveness cited but do not see that this identity may precisely be articulated and manipulated by the dominant class in order to "reinforce the prevailing ownership/allocation of economic and symbolic capital." San Juan chastises these postmodernist critiques of the nation-state for missing the point. He writes: "But these critiques seem to forget that the nation is chiefly a creation of the modern capitalist state, that is, a historical artifice or invention." San Juan quotes an Italian scholar, Giovanni Arrighi who observed that the Treaty of Westphalia, which settled the Thirty Years War, signified the "'reorganization of political space in the interest of capital accumulation' and signalled 'the birth, not just of the modern inter-state system but also of capitalism as a world-system'" (1993, 162). Under this prevailing world system characterized by inter-imperialist rivalry, San Juan likewise quotes Russian revolutionary, Nikolai Bukharin, who wrote: "[T]he state power sucks in almost all branches of production; it not only maintains the general conditions of the exploitative process; the state more and more becomes a direct exploiter, organizing and directing production as a collective capitalist. (Callinicos, 1982, 205)" (San Juan 2007a).

San Juan pursues further the subject of the state and its relationship with violence, or the use of force, and the dynamics of conferring legitimacy to state violence, or violence sanctioned by it. This is key to understanding—in order to "demystify" if not condemn—the extraordinary claim to and exercise of force that the United States has exhibited to this day thus far. As a step in this direction, San Juan recalls and endorses the work of French writer Pierre Bourdieu who reformulated the Weberian thesis that the state was a juridical entity with the monopoly to the use of legitimate force. Thus, Bourdieu is quoted as follows: "The state is the *culmination of a process of concentration of different species of capital*; capital of physical force or instrument of coercion (army, police), economic capital, cultural or (better) informational capital, and symbolic capital. It is this concentration as such which constitutes the state as the holder of a sort of metacapital granting power over other species of capital and over their holders... It follows that the construction of the state proceeds apace with the construction of a *field of power*, defined as the space of play within which the holders of capital (of different species) struggle i*n particular* for power over the state, that is, over the statist capital granting power over the different species of capital and over their reproduction (particularly through the school system). (1998, 41-42)" (San Juan 2007a).

The state that Bourdieu speaks of may very well be that of the US nation-state. Contrary to the experience of most other countries around the globe to the effect that their respective claims to sovereignty are disappearing, being undermined by forces of neoliberal globalization, San Juan allays any uncertainties. He writes: "Contemporary cultural studies posit the demise of the nation as an unquestioned assumption, almost a doctrinal point of departure for speculations on the nature of the globalization process. Are concepts such as the nation-state, national sovereignty, or nationalities, and their referents obsolete and useless? Whatever the rumors about the demise of the nation-state, or the obsolescence of nationalism in the wake of September 11, 2001, agencies that assume its healthy existence are busy: not only the members of the United Nations, but also the metropolitan powers, with the United States as its military spearhead, have all reaffirmed their civilizing nationalism with a vengeance.... With WTO and finance capital in the saddle, the buying and selling of labor-power moves center stage once more" (San Juan 2012).

2. US support to the government of the Republic of the Philippines (GRP), to the tune of millions of dollars in the form of direct military assistance, military arms sales, and line of credit over several decades, offers one such example by which the United States has tried to influence the outcome of the ongoing counterinsurgency campaign being waged against the Marxist-oriented Communist Party of the Philippines (CPP) and its military arm, the New People's Army (NPA). The NPA has been waging a legitimate, politically motivated insurgency campaign, has claimed a belligerent status under international law, and has proclaimed adherence to existing humanitarian law in areas of conflict. Due to its belligerent status, it has been recognized by the GRP for purposes of negotiating ceasefires, exchange of prisoners, and transport of

humanitarian supplies and personnel across territories. However, according to San Juan, "The U.S. government and the European Council have thus criminalized and repressed the revolutionary movement in the Philippines. Opposed to thousands of individuals and organizations in the Philippines calling for the resumption of peace talks, the Powell doctrine [named after former US Secretary of Defense Colin Powell, serving under then US President George W. Bush] effectively dismantled the ongoing negotiations between the National Democratic Front (which includes the CPP and NPA) and the Philippine government (GRP) that have been occurring since 1990. under the sponsorship of Holland, Belgium, and Norway, with the endorsement of the European Parliament in the 1997 and 1999 resolutions. ... It appears that the U.S. and European states, by classifying the CPP, NPA, and Sison [i.e., Jose Maria Sison, founder of the CPP in exile in the Netherlands] as terrorists, have rejected any logical or semantic criteria as well as international norms for distinguishing between terrorists who employ violence with criminal intent and organizations or individuals waging armed struggle for openly declared political goals, especially those involving national liberation, radical social reforms, and political democratization. Ignoring universally applied criteria and norms, the GRP demonizes political organizations and individuals critical of its policies and programs that serve narrow class interests and betray national sovereignty to imperialist powers" (San Juan 2007b).

3. San Juan responds to Friedman, albeit indirectly, by calling his apparent ignorance on the barbarity of the conditions that has been visited upon those at the receiving end of the labor exploitation attendant to the brand of globalization that he endorses, particularly caregivers and domestic workers from the Global South. San Juan writes: "Amid the tide of barbarization attendant on the putative benefits of global capitalism – celebrated by such pundits as Thomas Friedman and other neoconservative defenders of privatization, deregulation, and cutting of social services, we have witnessed a paradigm shift among scholars studying the phenomenon of the Filipino diaspora. Critical intelligence has been hijacked to serve vulgar apologetics. For example, the employment of Filipina women as domestics or nannies to care for children, old people, the chronically infirm or disabled, and so on, has been lauded as altruistic" (San Juan 2015, 138).

San Juan offers a very critical and important elaboration on the racialized global economic system, as exemplified in the export of women workers as "caregivers" and integrates research performed by other scholars on the subject, in the following extended passage: "Race, national, and class forces operate together in determining the exchange value (the price) of migrant labor. The reproduction of a homogeneous race (in Europe, North America, Japan, etc.) integral to the perpetuation of the unjust social order is connected with the historical development of nation-states, whether as imagined or as geopolitically defined locus. Historically, membership in the community was determined by race in its various modalities, a circumscription that is constantly being negotiated. It is in this racialized setting that European women's positioning as citizen acquires crucial significance. This is the site where Third World domestics play a major role, as Anderson acutely underscores: 'The fact that they are migrants is important: in order to participate like men; [white European] women must have workers who will provide the same flexibility as wives, in particular working long hours and combining caring and domestic chores.' (2000, 190) The distinction is fundamental and necessary in elucidating the axis of social reproduction rooted in socially productive praxis. Such a vital distinction speaks volumes about migrant domestic labor/care as the key sociopolitical factor that sustains the existing oppressive international division of labor. *This key distinction undermines all claims that globalized capitalism has brought, and is bringing freedom, prosperity, and egalitarian democracy to everyone*" (San Juan 2015, 140) (italics added).

4. At this point, San Juan recalls the work of writer Jean Franco who, in her essay entitled "Killing Priests, Nuns, Women, Children" (1985), created a postmodern nightmare characteristic of the so-called postmodern times. The article's title alludes to numerous acts of atrocious terrorism committed by US-backed, -trained, -funded, -directed paramilitary groups and death squads throughout Central America during the 1980s that invaded what should have been sacred or democratic spaces occupied by church workers, children, and the old and the infirm but which/who were nonetheless not spared in the name of counterinsurgency, such as the assassination of Archbishop Oscar Romero, the massacre at El Mozote, and the kidnapping and murder of four Maryknoll sisters perpetrated by cadets and officers trained at and graduated from the US Army's infamous School of the Americas, then located in Panama, subsequently relocated to Fort Benning, Georgia, United States. San Juan writes: "Jean Franco observes that with the rise of the internal security state funded by the West (IMF-World Bank), all hitherto immune spaces in the underdeveloped countries – Church, family as refuge and shelter – are gone, just as affect and depth have vanished in simulations and spectacles. She notes the unprecedented sacrilege committed by U.S.-sponsored 'low-intensity warfare' in the destruction of utopian space, specifically that associated with nuns, priests, women, and children. The 'disappeared' no longer occupy a space that can be put 'under erasure': 'the smell of the cadaver will not be dispelled by the commodity culture, a debt-ridden economy and the forms of restored political democracy'" (San Juan 1995).

On the current state of postmodernity, San Juan also recalls the work of Geographer David Harvey, *The Condition of Postmodernity* (1989) wherein Harvey offers the following describes postmodernism and what it all means, in this brief passage: "From what I think is the best account so far of this transition, David Harvey's *The Condition of Postmodernity*, we learn that postmodernism is a historical response to the recent crisis of accumulation, a crisis that manifests itself in the disorienting compressions of time-space which have periodically occurred since the decline of the Middle Ages. The symptoms of this crisis include *inter alia*: the disintegration of the sovereign subject; the loss of the referent; the collapse of the linkage between moral and scientific judgment; the predominance of images over narratives, aesthetic over ethics. Ephemerality and fragmentation have displaced eternal truths and unified, organic experience" (San Juan 1995).

5. In an earlier essay, entitled "Dependency: History, Theory, and a Reappraisal" (with colleague Charles Frederick Abel) (1986), I distinguished between the early and the late types of dependency theses, citing respective proponents of each. I wrote: "[V[ariations are discernible among scholars indigenous to Latin America and those to the West and among early and late. Early structuralists – bearing some ECLA-influenced ideas – held that the size of the country's market determined industrialization. In other words, structural dependence is traceable to the constraints imposed by the size of the economy. These constraints could be overcome, not through preferential treatment, foreign aid, and protection – as these would tend toward capital-intensive industries unable to compete in the world market – but rather through regional integration, of which the Latin America Free Trade Area (LAFTA) was an expression. Later structuralists have argued that integration would not solve but, on the contrary, would aggravate the problem of dependence. In their analyses, they have adopted a broader historical approach and have become more sophisticated in their investigation of the various dimensions of dependency" (Bauzon 1986).

6. The position of San Juan on the issue of uneven development has been clear, articulate, and well-publicized in various of his essays, in contra-distinction from the position of apologists for neoliberalism like Friedman. In a chapter to a compendium on development and democratization, entitled "Afterword: From Development to Liberation – The Third World in the 'New World Order,'" San Juan writes, in part: "We know from any historical standpoint that the uneven development of the Third World is the logical consequence of the international division of labor and the accumulation of capital by the colonial powers of the West and North from the sixteenth century to the present. But since then, the patterns of imperialist exploitation of the world's labor and resources have undergone a series of mutations. When the prescription of import substitution carried out in the post-war years failed to usher sustained, independent growth, the elite of the dependent countries resorted to export-oriented industrialization in the 1950s and 1960s. The result? A rich harvest of massive human rights violations by U.S. backed authoritarian regimes, systematic corruption of cultures, degradation of work through

'warm body exports' (migrant labor), and unrelenting pauperization of the masses. In the free trade zones where global assembly line generates superprofits out of cheap labor, total surveillance and draconian prohibitions prevail. Both empirical evidence and substantial testimony demonstrate that the cult of the gross national product (GNP) as institutionalized by the disciples of W. W. Rostow's *The Stages of Economic Growth*, among others, has brought with it only rampant unemployment, widespread poverty, cycles of repression and stagnation, cultures and environment destroyed for peoples of color whose underemployment is reproduced daily by such development formulas" (San Juan 1992).

San Juan has treated the subject of uneven development more thoroughly elsewhere, such as in: "Postcolonialism, Uneven Development, & Imperialism: The Example of Amilcar Cabral" (2002a); and Chapter 7, "Postcolonial Criticism and the Vicissitudes of Uneven Development." In: *Racism and Cultural Studies: Critiques of Multiculturalist Ideology and the Politics of Difference* (2002b), the simple point being that anyone claiming that we are now in a "postcolonial" stage in history is living in a different planet!

References

Bauzon, Kenneth E. (With Charles Frederick Abel), "Dependency: History, Theory, and a Reappraisal", in *Dependency Theory and the Return of High Politics*, edited by Marianne Tetreault and Charles Fredrick Abel (Westport, CT: Greenwood Press, 1986), 270pp. In: https://www.academia.edu/3382095/Dependency_History_Theory_and_a_Reappraisal.

———, "Political Forecasting and the Third World Economies: A Critical Assessment", *Kasarinlan: Philippine Journal of Third World Studies*, 15, 1 (2000): 23–64. In: https://www.academia.edu/3382032/Political_forecasting_and_the_Third_World_economies_a_critical_assessment.

———, "Secession in the Formal-Legalist Paradigm: Implications for Contemporary Revolutionary and Popular Movements in the Age of Neoliberal Globalization". Posted September 2014. In: https://www.academia.edu/8370651/Secession_in_the_Formal-Legalist_Paradigm_Implications_for_Contemporary_Revolutionary_and_Popular_Movements_in_the_Age_of_Neoliberal_Globalization.

Franco, Jean, "Killing Priests, Nuns, Women, Children", in *On Signs*, edited by Marshall Blonsky (Baltimore, MD: Johns Hopkins University Press, 1985).

Friedman, Thomas L., *The World Is Flat—A Brief History of the Twenty-First Century* (New York: Farrar, Straus and Giroux, 2005), 488pp.

San Juan, E., Jr., "Afterword: From Development to Liberation—The Third World in the 'New World Order'", in *Development and Democratization in the Third*

World: Myths, Hopes and Realities, edited by Kenneth E. Bauzon (Washington, DC: Crane Russak/Taylor & Francis, 1992), pp. 297–310.

———, *Between Empire and Insurgency—The Philippines in the New Millenium: Essays in History, Comparative Literature, and Cultural Politics* (Quezon City, Philippines: University of the Philippines Press, 2015), 318pp.

———, *Beyond Postcolonial Theory* (New York: St. Martin's Press, 1998), 325pp. Print.

———, "Filipino OFWs Versus the Neoliberal Ideology of Transnationalism: Interrogating Transnationalism: The Case of the Filipino Diaspora in the Age of Globalized Capitalism". Posted July 20, 2012. In: https://philcsc.wordpress.com/2012/07/20/filipino-ofws-versus-the-neoliberal-ideology-of-transnationalism/.

———, "From Genealogy to Inventory: The Situation of Asian American Studies in the Age of the Crisis of Global Finance Capital", *International Journal of Asia Pacific Studies*, 6, 1 (January 2010): 47–75. In: http://ijaps.usm.my/wp-content/uploads/2012/06/Genealogy.pdf.

———, *Hegemony and Strategies of Transgression: Essays in Cultural Studies and Comparative Literature* (Albany, NY: State University of New York Press, 1995), 286pp.

———, "Imperial Terror, Neo-Colonialism, and the Filipino Diaspora". A Lecture Delivered at the 2003 English Department Lecture Series at St. John's University. *St. John's University Humanities Review*, 2, 1 (Fall 2003). In: http://facpub.stjohns.edu/~ganterg/sjureview/vol2-1/diaspora.html.

———, *In the Wake of Terror; Class, Race, Nation, Ethnicity in the Postmodern World* (Lanham, MD: Lexington Books, 2007a), 232pp.

———, "Postcolonialism, Uneven Development, and Imperialism: The Example of Amilcar Cabral", in *Marxism, Modernity, and Postcolonial Studies*, edited by Crystal Bartolovich and Neil Lazarus (Cambridge, UK: Cambridge University Press, 2002a), pp. 221–239. In: https://www.academia.edu/10130036/POSTCOLONIALISM_UNEVEN_DEVELOPMENT_and_IMPERIALISM_The_Example_of_Amicar_Cabral—by_E_San_Juan_Jr.

———, *Racial Formations/Critical Transformations: Articulations of Power in Ethnic and Racial Studies in the United States* (Amherst, NY: Humanity Books/Prometheus Books, 1992c), 163pp. Recipient, 1993 National Book Award in Cultural Studies from the Association for Asian American Studies. Recipient, the Gustavus Myers Center for the Study of Human Rights in the United States Outstanding Book on Human Rights for 1992.

———, *Racism and Cultural Studies: Critiques of Multiculturalist Ideology and the Politics of Difference* (Durham, NC: Duke University Press, 2002b), 428pp. In: https://www.dukeupress.edu/Racism-and-Cultural-Studies/.

———, "Spinoza and the War of Racial Terrorism", Originally published in *Left Curve, No. 27, and as Chapter in Working Through the Contradictions: From Cultural Theory to Critical Practice* (Lewisburg, PA: Bucknell University Press, 2004). In: http://www.leftcurve.org/LC27WebPages/Spinoza.html. Also available in: https://philcsc.wordpress.com/2014/11/17/spinozas-philosophy-the-body-race-freedom-by-e-san-juan-jr/.

———, *U.S. Imperialism and Revolution in the Philippines* (New York: Palgrave Macmillan, 2007b), 265pp. Print.

CHAPTER 7

The Racialized State

A review of the geopolitical formation of the United States demonstrates a clear racial, not simply ethnic, pattern of constituting the national identity and the commonality it invokes. As oppositional historians have shown, the U.S. racial order sprang from a politics of exploitation and containment encompassing inter alia colonialism, apartheid, racial segregation, xenophobia, exploitation, marginalization, and genocide....
   This racial genealogy of the empire followed the logic of capital accumulation by expanding the market for industrial goods and securing sources of raw materials and, in particular, the prime commodity for exchange and maximizing of surplus value: cheap labor power.
   E. San Juan, "Post-9/11 Reflections..." (2004)

KNOWLEDGE PRODUCTION AND THE COLD WAR IN THE UNITED STATES

The onset and prevalence of the Cold War mood, for good or bad, depending on one's perspective, had an inevitable conditioning effect on the production of knowledge. Those justifying belief in the verity of the Western model of political and social organization, with their respective assumptions about Weberian-inspired rationality and the inevitability of progress modeled after the Darwinian proposition about biological growth or, alternately, the Newtonian presumption about the machine-like ordering of the universe, found themselves in preeminent positions in academic and research institutions setting the agenda for research, teaching, and development planning. The impact of the Cold War on the production of social knowledge may alternately be described as rather crass, crude, numbing as will be detailed below. San Juan has been candid with his own colorful description, elucidating in particular on the Cold War's displacement of class as an explanatory variable as follows:

> The implacably zombifying domination of the Cold War for almost half a century has made almost everyone allergic to the Marxian notion of class as a social category that can explain inequalities of power and wealth in the "free world." One symptom is the mantra of "class reductionism" or "economism" as a weapon to silence anyone who calls attention to the value of one's labor power, or one's capacity to work in order to survive, if not to become human. Another way of nullifying the concept of class as an epistemological tool for understanding the dynamics of capitalist society is to equate it with status, life-style, even an entire "habitus" or pattern of behavior removed from the totality of the social relations of production in any given historical formation. Often, class is reduced to income, or to voting preference within the strict limits of the bourgeois (that is, capitalist) electoral order. Some sociologists even play at being agnostic or nominalist by claiming that class displays countless meanings and designations relative to the ideological persuasion of the theorist/researcher, hence its general uselessness as an analytic tool. This has become the orthodox view of "class" in mainstream academic discourse. (San Juan 2003b)

The displacement of class saw the corresponding rise of non-threatening, even outrightly conservative, heuristic and/or explanatory paradigms. These include structural-functionalist and systems theory approaches, exhibiting traces of organismic and mechanistic principles drawn from Darwin and Newton, respectively, became dominant paradigms, with their status quo-affirming and conservative predispositions. These are exemplified by dominant functionalist theorists like Talcott Parsons and Bronislav Malinowski and their disciples in the disciplines of sociology and anthropology, respectively, who postulated that essentially society consists of different albeit unequal parts but with mutually reinforcing functions. Thus, a modern society like the United States is seen as consisting of a plurality of groups which, although they may have varying if not competing interests, all assume the basic validity and legitimacy of the social order within which they operate and, hence, contribute consciously or otherwise to its persistence. This view has, in fact, evolved into a coherent theory of society and politics of which Robert Dahl, with his series of works, e.g., *A Preface to Democratic Theory* (1956), *Who Governs?* (1961), and *Pluralist Democracy in the United States* (1967), became the gold standard of pluralist analysis among mainstream US-based sociologists and political scientists during much of the Cold War, and Dahl's influence persists to this day. Alternately and deriving in part from the assumptions of cybernetics, David Easton also popularized a mechanistic analysis of the US political system, and modern polities in general, with the publication of his series of studies including *The Political System: An Inquiry into the State of Political Science* (1953), and *A Systems Analysis of Political Life* (1965). These works, too, were part of the standard reading especially for graduate students—including this writer—during the 1970s and subsequent years.

While Dahl, Easton, and virtually the entirety of the social science establishment have proudly proclaimed their behavioral credentials, professing adherence to the tenets of empirical analysis, little acknowledgment is offered about the influence that society, in fact, exerts, through various sources including ideological, cultural, religious, and political, among others, in the process of producing social knowledge. In an earlier work, I pointed this out (Bauzon 1991), but in another work, I quoted a critic, Alvin W. Gouldner, emerging from the conflict theory sub-school of functionalism (otherwise known as neofunctionalism), who acknowledged that, among social scientists, there are (a) "world hypotheses," and (b) "domain assumptions" both of which provide needed assumptions and orientations that enable social scientists to navigate and render meaningful various types of circumstances which, in the end, serve the function of linking them with society. These are ingrained in the social scientists' private mood which ultimately bears on his public and political conduct. Domain assumptions in particular, according to Gouldner, "have implications about what is possible to do, to change in the world; the value they entail indicate what course of action are desirable and thus shape the conduct. *In this sense, every theory and every theorist ideologizes social reality*" (Bauzon 2014, italics added).

Even while rejecting Marx, neofunctionalists, cited above, have managed to co-opt the concept of conflict from its class context and assigned to it the label of "conflict theory"; this theory was then applied to the analysis of groups and turned it into something benign and non-threatening thus disarming and pacifying the Cold Warriors and ideological guardians of the state who might otherwise come knocking at their door. It is understandable that conflict theory had a great appeal to mainstream social scientists, particularly in the departments of sociology and political science, who wanted to bolster their progressive or maybe even radical credentials but who, in fact, were devoid of any solid grounding on class analysis much less any familiarity with the dynamic diversity that has accompanied the intellectual ferment taking place within the Marxist tradition during much of the last century. This ignorance is even more apparent since the end of World War II, during the Cold War period, with the advent of vigorous anti-imperialist liberation struggles taking place in the peripheral regions of the European and North American empires, and the guile and amoral nature by which these liberation struggles were being suppressed often with the blessing of and endorsement by mainstream academics in these metropolitan continents.[1]

Rise of the Neoliberal Pedagogy

To help make sense of the point being made here, i.e., producers and purveyors of supposedly value-free knowledge, in fact, promote their own preferred ideological presuppositions. No better illustration of this point could be found than Irving Louis Horowitz's pedagogical lament about what he refers to as *The Decomposition of Sociology*, which is the phrase he used to title his 1993 book. I n his book, Horowitz complains that "much contemporary sociological theory has degenerated into pure critique, strongly influenced by Marxist dogmatism," a charge which, as shown in the above-discussion, has no basis in fact, in apparent reference to the de-fanged and de-Marxified conflict theory. Horowitz nonetheless takes the occasion to "nationalize" the discipline by accusing these imaginary Marxist sociologists—and social scientists in general—for being "anti-American." The jacket reads: "Such thinking has a strong element of anti-American and anti-Western bias, in which all questions have one answer – the evil of capitalism – and all problems one solution – the good of socialism.... Indeed, in one area after another, Horowitz shows how this same formulaic thinking dominates the field, resulting in a crude reductionist view of contemporary social life." And to assure the readers of his presumed ideologically free-stance, the book jacket adds: "At a time when the world is moving closer to the free market and democratic norms..., such reductionist tendencies and ideological posturings are outmoded," here reflecting a triumphalist attitude in the wake of the end of the Cold War.

This period in history is apparently an opportune time for Horowitz to offer his vision of what social science ought to be. As the book jacket explains further:

> Horowitz offers an alternative, positive view of social research. He urges a larger vision of the social sciences, one in which universities, granting agencies, and research institutes provide an environment in which research may be untainted by partisan agendas – where policy choices will not be hindered by the prevailing cultural climate. He counsels sociologists to move away from blind advocacy, to meet the challenges of the twenty-first century by utilizing the knowledge of other times and places, and to take into account the shrinking globe – in short, to develop and maintain a new set of universal standards in this era of a world culture.[2] (Horowitz)

The case of Horowitz, discussed above, illustrates precisely the point being made here, i.e., advocates for neoliberalism assume a kind of hubris in assuming that their way of thinking is the normal way to which all others should conform. As in the case of Horowitz, there is the default assumption that liberal democracy and free trade are the standards to which the rest of the world should emulate, and that advocating for these is not being biased; only those that are critical of them or are against them are (biased). There is the further assumption that the principles of liberal democracy, as a political ideology, are compatible with the principles of free trade, as an economic system. The assumed normality of these systems of thought is reflected, for instance, in the teaching of "economics" as a course in any standard college curriculum. This course is assumed to be of the capitalist variety without so much admitting that there are other economic systems other than—if not better than—capitalism itself.

This system of thought ultimately oriented around lending credence to neoliberalism has caught the interest of progressive, non-Marxist public intellectual and educator, Henry A . Giroux who, among his voluminous works, interrogated the issue further in an essay entitled "Neoliberalism as a Form of Public Pedagogy: Making Political More Pedagogical" (2011). Setting aside momentarily the present author's difference with Giroux over the issues of multiculturalism and the value of historical materialism as an approach, Giroux, nonetheless, in this essay, makes an important suggestion that academic-based producers of knowledge, far from being objective and dispassionate, have, in fact, become—and remain—part of a much larger set of pedagogical forces whose main purpose is to reinforce the existing sociopolitical order—in the current case, neoliberalism—with which they maintain an opportunistic if not parasitic symbiotic relationship. He writes: "Within neoliberalism's market-driven discourse, corporate power marks the space of a new kind of public pedagogy, one in which the production, dissemination, and circulation of ideas emerges from the educational force of the larger culture. Public pedagogy in this sense refers to a powerful ensemble of ideological and institutional forces whose aim is to produce competitive, self-interested individuals vying for their own material and ideological gain" (Giroux 2011). Giroux further assesses the impact of this type of pedagogy on other issues or, for that matter, on alternative pedagogies. He writes:

> Corporate public pedagogy culture largely cancels out or devalues gender, class-specific, and racial injustices of the existing social order by absorbing the democratic impulses and practices of civil society within narrow economic relations. Corporate public pedagogy has become an all-encompassing cultural horizon for producing market identities, values, and practices. (Giroux 2011)

In no other contentious issue do we find the verity of Giroux's point—shared by many other committed scholars and public intellectuals of like mind sampled here—than over the racialization of the neoliberal state/empire, and the inequality that inheres in it. For example, legal scholar and professor of law, F. Michael Higginbotham, in a recent book, *Ghosts of Jim Crow: Ending Racism in Post-racial America* (2013), recounts how racism persists in the United States despite the election of Barack Obama to the highest political office in the land. Higginbotham recounts how, upon Obama's election, highly placed public figures let out a deluge of racist and derogatory remarks, including Congressman Doug Lambon who complained that being linked at all to Obama was "like touching a tar baby," or former Congressman Newt Gingrich characterizing Obama disparagingly as the "food stamp president," or, further, a federal judge, Richard Cebull, sending an e-mail chain designed to denigrate Obama's mother "by comparing blacks to animals in analogizing interracial marriage and sexuality to bestiality" (Higginbotham). Higginbotham reflects on the causes of this persistent racism in his book, which he synthesizes in the following passage:

I submit that there is a vicious cycle. The false notion of white superiority/black inferiority ingrained through slavery led to whites separating themselves from blacks through Jim Crow practices. This racial isolation permitted the false notion to reinforce itself and continue, thus making it easier for blacks to be victimized by race-based and race-neutral policies, and further contributing to false notions of a racial hierarchy today; and there is also the impact of black self-victimization. This process has existed for centuries and continues to benefit whites and disadvantage blacks. (Higginbotham)

On a more concrete level, Higginbotham cites a number of US Supreme Court (henceforth, High Court) decisions since the 1954 *Brown v. Board of Education* decision reinforcing the institutional and legal basis for racism. These include, among others: (a) *Milliken v. Bradley* (1974), invalidating a desegregation plan in Detroit, Michigan; (b) *Gratz v. Bollinger* (2003), invalidating an affirmative action admissions program by the University of Michigan taking into consideration race as a factor; and (c) *Parents Involved in Community Schools v. Seattle School District No. 1* (2007), invalidating as well the City of Seattle's desegregation plan. Several other High Court decisions rendered especially during the successive chief justiceships of Warren Burger (1969–1986), William Rehnquist (1986–2005); and John Roberts (2005–present) left no doubt about the rightward drift of the High Court in areas beyond school desegregation, particularly in the areas of due process, allowing more authority to law enforcement over Miranda rights protections; privacy rights, allowing little or no oversight over intelligence and security agencies of the government over privacy rights of citizens; and executive prerogative, allowing the executive branch to claim and extend executive powers with regard to the use of force overseas including outright invasion and occupation of sovereign countries, detention and enhanced interrogation (euphemism for what amounts to as torture) of so-called enemy combatants; and extra-judicial execution—without court approval—of suspected individuals through the use of unmanned aerial vehicles (UAVs), commonly known as drones, authorization of the funding of so-called pro-democracy groups, through such agencies as the US Agency for International Development (USAID), among various other conduits, for the purpose of influencing or predetermining the electoral and policy-making processes in certain target countries (Bauzon 2005), or otherwise influencing public opinion there in a direction favorable to US interests; and authorization of the funding, training, and arming, of terrorist groups and paramilitary formations for the purpose of engaging, either clandestinely or covertly, in terrorist acts designed to carry out regime change of undesirable regimes in target countries, or to get rid of certain officials associated with these regimes with "extreme prejudice," meaning arbitrarily, without any lawful basis, and through violence.

On issues that would have far-reaching implications both on the political economy and the political process of the country, the High Court has handed down such decisions as would grant corporations the right to patent life, to tear down neighborhoods to make way for real estate development through eminent domain, to now contribute unlimited and undisclosed campaign contributions as a matter of free speech, giving rise to the phenomenon of "Dark Money", and confer upon corporations the status of corporate personhood to enable them to enjoy the First Amenment right of free speech as "persons", among others. In overwhelming number of these decisions, which collectively consolidate neoliberalism from the constitutional standpoint, the US Congress has either been an acquiescent bystander and not getting in the way through exercise of its constitutional mandate of oversight to at least show a semblance of checks-and-balances among the branches of government, or, finally, has actively collaborated with the executive branch's overreaching activities with continued funding.

Another notable legal scholar whose work could not be ignored when discussing the racist nature of the US state is Michelle Alexander. In her much-praised 2011 book, entitled *The New Jim Crow: Mass Incarceration in the Age of Colorblindness*, Alexander notes the rise in prison population in the United States in the past three decades and compares it to that of earlier periods as context to the structural basis of what she refers to as New Jim Crow as a form of caste. She writes:

> What has changed since the collapse of Jim Crow has less to do with the basic structure of our society than the by language we use to justify it. In the era of color blindness it is no longer socially permissible to use race explicitly as a justification for discrimination, exclusion, and social contempt. So we don't. *Rather than rely on race, we use our criminal justice system to label people of color criminals and then engage in all the practices that we supposedly left behind. Today, it is perfectly legal to discriminate against criminals in nearly all the ways in which it was once legal to discriminate against African Americans.* Once you're labeled a felon, the old forms of discrimination— employment discrimination, housing discrimination, denial of the right to vote, exclusion from jury service—are suddenly legal. As a criminal, you have scarcely more rights, and arguably less respect, than a black man living in Alabama at the

height of Jim Crow. *We have not ended racial caste in America, we have merely redesigned it.* (Alexander, italics added)

And the whole point of this? Alexander comes to this sobering conclusion:

> Quite belatedly, I came to see that mass incarceration in the United States had, in fact, emerged as a stunningly comprehensive and well-disguised system of racialized social control that functions in a manner strikingly similar to Jim Crow. (Alexander)

THE FETISH OF MULTICULTURALISM

Both Higginbotham and Alexander express the sentiment of many well-meaninged reformers of liberal orientation, who express the view that racism and inequality may somehow be eradicated through incremental reforms, say, of the criminal justice system accompanied by civil society movement much like the previous civil rights movement. Further, through the dissemination of a unifying civic culture anchored on adherence to the secular and secularizing principles of the US Constitution, admonishing political leaders to perform their duties and safeguarding the pluralist nature of US society, the rest of the members of society would be inspired to both tolerate and appreciate each other group's cultural, ethnic, religious, and social status and background.[3] Further, the assumed pluralist nature of US politics presupposed that competing groups would eventually balance themselves out, with the government playing the role of a referee, that there is not one group that monopolizes power, that power changes hands periodically from one group to another, and that this is the best means by which the interests of the members of participating groups could be secured through such means as competitive elections, bargaining, and negotiations. This pluralist notion of US politics is an integral component of the broader approach to the problem of integration or assimilation in a society consisting of a multiplicity of ethnic and racial groups with all kinds of traditions. This has been called the multicultural approach or paradigm or, in short, multiculturalism.

One of the problems with the multiculturalist paradigm is shown in the irony noted by Ajamu Baraka with President Obama eulogizing, in May 2015, before a predominantly black audience the victims of Dylann Roof, a white supremacist who gunned down in cold blood nine black members of a predominantly black congregation in Charleston, South Carolina known for its tradition of opposing slavery. Baraka writes, in part:

> However, it was at the funeral of Rev Pinckney, the pastor of the Emanuel African Methodist Episcopal Church murdered by Dylann Roof, where the concluding act of the governments' obscene efforts to co-opt and deflect the pain of the attack played to a world-wide audience. *President Obama turned in one of his best performances of a life-time of performances for white supremacy. His eulogy was a masterful example of his special talent to embody an instrumentalist "blackness" while delivering up that blackness to the white supremacist, U.S. settler project. In his eulogy, he couched his narrative of "American exceptionalism" in the language of Christian religiosity that was indistinguishable from the proclamations of the religious right that sees the U.S. as a state bestowed with the grace of their God.*
>
> Obama sang "Amazing Grace" [a hymn composed by a white slave trader] and lulled into a stupefying silence black voices that should have demanded answers as to why the Charleston attack was not considered a terrorist attack, even though it fit the definition of domestic terrorism, or why the Obama Administration collaborated with suppressing the 2009 report from the Department of Homeland Security (DHS), which identified violent white supremacist groups as a threat to national security more lethal than the threat from Islamic "fundamentalists". (Baraka 2015b, italics added)

Thus, despite apparent efforts at promoting the fetish of multiculturalism, to borrow San Juan's phrase, one is at the same time presented with the paradox of being expected to adhere to a presumed "common culture," also expressed alternately as "civic culture," "general education," "civic nationalism," and "republicanism," among others. This paradox is expressed in a way that is either deceptive or sinister through the presumed respect which this fetish of multiculturalism is supposed to elicit from everyone. In the end, however, the opposite becomes true. Commenting on the slogan "One in many" engraved in US dollar coins symbolizing the presumed unity of many in a supposedly multicultural United States, San Juan writes that, the slogan, first of all, is misleading because it merely conceals a hegemonic ideology. "Officially," San Juan writes, "the consensual ideology of the U.S. is neoliberal 'democracy' founded on the normative utilitarian individualism with a neo-Social Darwinist orientation." San Juan adds:

It is within this framework that we can comprehend how the ruling bourgeoisie of each sovereign state utilizes nationalist sentiment and the violence of the state apparatuses to impose their will. Consequently, the belief that the nation-state simultaneously prohibits economic freedom and promotes multinational companies actually occludes the source of political and judicial violence.... One can then assert that the most likely source of political violence... is the competitive drive for accumulation in the world market system where the propertied class of each nation-state is the key actor mobilizing its symbolic capital made up primarily of ethnic loyalties and national imaginaries. (San Juan 2007)

In another essay, San Juan explains: "The multiculturalist respect for the Other's specificity, within the existing framework, is the very form of asserting one's own superiority. According to Slavoj Zizek, this paradox underlies multiculturalism as, in fact, the authentic 'cultural logic of multinational' or globalized capitalism" (San Juan 1999). As what San Juan regards as a "theoretical wedge" between and among various ethnic groups, already potentially conflictual among themselves as they are, the ideology of multiculturalism in actuality has the effect of displacing "the organising category of class, founded on the unequal division of social labour and therefore unequal power, as the ordering principle of US capitalism" (San Juan 2010a). In another essay, San Juan elaborates on the implication of multiculturalism within the existing framework with the following conclusion:

> The conclusion to be drawn is thus that the problematic of multiculturalism-the hybrid coexistence of diverse cultural life-worlds-which imposes itself today is the form of appearance of its opposite, of the massive presence of capitalism as universal world system: it bears witness to the unprecedented homogenization of the contemporary world. It is effectively as if, since the horizon of social imagination no longer allows us to entertain the idea of an eventual demise of capitalism-since, as we might put it, everybody silently accepts that capitalism is here to stay-critical energy has found a substitute outlet in fighting for cultural differences which leave the basic homogeneity of the capitalist world-system intact. (San Juan 2004)

This is precisely an important rationale—and context—to consider in weighing the comment by Baraka, cited earlier, in his criticism of Obama with regard to white supremacy and his role in promoting US imperialism abroad. In assessing the prevailing atmosphere under the Obama Administration, Baraka comments further as follows: "This is the mindset and the politics of this Administration and the political culture in the U.S., where the differential value placed on black life allows black life to be reduced to an instrumental calculation when considering issues of international public relations and domestic politics" (Baraka 2015b). This is what explains Obama's role, despite having been subjected himself to vile expressions of racism, could still stand before a multitude not as someone who pledges to meaningfully end racism during his presidency but as someone who will continue to legitimize and consolidate, in Baraka's estimation, the existing structure—particularly its violent component—of the white-led settler state, which is what the United States is. As Baraka explains in a separate piece, he writes, in part:

> No rational person exalts violence and the loss of life. But violence is structured into the everyday institutional practices of all oppressive societies. It is the deliberate de-humanization of the person in order to turn them into a 'thing' — a process Dr. King called "thing-afication." It is a necessary process for the oppressor in order to more effectively control and exploit. Resistance, informed by the conscious understanding of the equal humanity of all people, reverses this process of de-humanization. Struggle and resistance are the highest expressions of the collective demand for people-centered human rights – human rights defined and in the service of the people and not governments and middle-class lawyers. (Baraka 2015a)

In concurrence with Baraka, San Juan elaborates on the white supremacy theme extrapolated from Obama' eulogy by extending the analysis to America's claim to exceptionalism and the consequent displacement of the "Others" through their subsumption to a homogenizing ideology of the "liberal nation-state."[4] San Juan writes, in part:

> With this figure of subsumption or synecdochic linkage, *America reasserts a privileged role in the world— all the margins, the absent Others, are redeemed in an inclusive, homogenized space where cultural differences dissolve or are sorted out into their proper niches in the ranking of national values and priorities.* We thus have plural cultures or ethnicities coexisting peacefully, in a free play of monads in the best of all possible worlds — no longer the melting pot of earlier theory but now a salad bowl, a smorgasbord of cultures, the mass consumption of variegated and heterogeneous lifestyles.
> There is in this picture, of course, *a core or consensual culture to which we add any number of diverse particulars*, thus proving that our principles of

liberty and tolerance can accommodate those formerly excluded or ignored. In short, your particular is not as valuable or significant as mine.

On closer scrutiny, this liberal mechanism of inclusion—what Herbert Marcuse once called "repressive desublimation" — is a mode of appropriation: It fetishizes and commodifies Others.

The universal swallows the particulars. And the immigrant, or border-crosser like Guillermo Gomez Pena or Coco Fusco, our most provocative performance-artists, is always reminded that to gain full citizenship, unambiguous rules must be obeyed: Proficiency in English is mandatory, assimilation of certain procedures and rituals are assumed, and so on and so forth. (San Juan 1999, italics added)

Denial of Historical Materialism and the Postcolonial Retreat

To wrap-up of this subject of racialization in this segment of the work, this author wishes at this juncture to highlight insights from a scholar and public intellectual with a lifelong commitment beyond issues of social justice and toward the broader struggle for human emancipation from all forms of exploitation and oppression in the truest tradition of Marxist scholarship, E. San Juan Jr., referred to throughout this work as "San Juan." In this author's estimation, San Juan has distinguished himself for his dexterity in using his pen as weapon in the struggle against injustice particularly in the form of colonial and neocolonial exploitation in much of the Third World. Among his outstanding works have also been an eloquent statement against the scourge of racism and the inequality it breeds in the United States and elsewhere. As a scholar-activist described by cultural critic and philosopher Fredric Jameson as "a scholar of remarkable range and varied talents," accorded by political scientist Bertell Ollman his "[h]ighest recommendation," and lauded by the late historian Manning Marable for his "challenging perspective" and whose "analysis is absolutely vital for both scholars and activists," San Juan stands out among academicians from the Third World who, through the power of his intellect, the integrity of his position, and his command of the language of criticism, has been relentless and uncompromising in his challenge to conventional wisdom which, in the end, serves not only to accommodate itself with the hegemonic and exploitative imperial order but also serves to validate it. He has likewise been critical of disciplines of thought, e.g., cultural studies, which, while initially presuming to be progressive, has, in fact, "subverted the early promise of the field as a radical transformative force" (San Juan 2003a).

Such also is the case with postcolonialism, a sub-school of thought in literary and cultural studies emergent in the last thirty years much of it centering on the works of its presumed set of "founding fathers" including Edward Said, Homi Bhabha, and Gayatri Spivak. These writers have, in fact, provided much of the basis for postcolonialism evolving into a paradigm in its own right but whose presuppositions are even attributable, at least in large part, to the earlier works of Michel Foucault. The kernel of the postcolonialism's problematization of its task is summed up by San Juan as follows:

> [P]ostcolonial theory seeks to explain the ambivalent and hybrid nature of subjects, their thinking and behavior, in the former colonies of the Western imperial powers, mainly the British Commonwealth societies. It seeks to prove that the colonial enterprise was not just a one-way affair of oppression and exploitation, but a reciprocal or mutual co- or inter-determination of both metropolitan master and "third world" subaltern. Whatever the subtle differences among postcolonial critics, they all agree that colonialism, for all its terror and barbarism, presents a rhetorical and philosophical anomaly: the postcolonial subject as identical and different from the history textbook's portrayal of the submissive and silent victim of imperial conquest. It claims to be more sophisticated or "profound" than the usual left or even liberal explanation of colonialism. (Pozo)

Despite its purported sympathy for the dehumanized victims of imperialism and colonialism, postcolonialism as it evolved as a paradigm eventually revealed distinct tendencies which betrayed its purported original vision. San Juan identifies three reasons why, namely:

> [F]irst, post colonialists obscure or erase historical determination in favor of rhetorical and linguistic idealization of the colonial experience; second, the post colonialist mind refuses to be self-critical and assumes a self-righteous dogmatism that it is infallible and cannot be refuted; and third, the practical effect of post colonialist prejudice is the unwitting justification of, if not apology for, the continued neo-colonialist – 'globalizing' is the trendy epithet – depredation of non-Western peoples, in particular indigenous groups, women, and urban poor in Latin America, Asia and Africa.[5] (San Juan 2003a)

Having expressed as much about the basic contours of postcolonialism as reflected in the works of Bhabha and Spivak, noted mainly for their unreserved hostility to historical materialism as an approach to explaining the persistence of racism, poverty, violence, war, particularly the Zionist State's aggression in Palestine, and the very nature o f capitalism as a system of capital accumulation and labor exploitation. Exemplifying postcolonialism's rejection of historical materialism is Bhabha's egregious attempt to "obscure or erase historical determination" through some "rhetorical" as well as "linguistic idealization" alluded to in the quote above. San Juan takes one of Bhabha's essays, "Remembering Fanon: Self, Psyche, and the Colonial Condition" and subjects it to deconstruction. In Bhabha's mind, perhaps, there could not be a more appropriate target for a makeover than Fanon himself, known universally for his uncompromising analysis of racism as essential feature of European colonialism (and now, American imperialism), the convergence between colonialism and the exploitative character of capitalism, the violent nature of colonialism (and imperialism), and the "cleansing" effect of counter-violence used—without apology—by the victims of colonialism and imperialism as an instrument of emancipation.

San Juan uses the title "Immobilizing Fanon" in the subsection critiquing Bhabha for, indeed, that is what Bhabha has ended up doing through a series of steps including: (a) "[situating] Fanon in the topos of ambivalence" in the "uncertain interstices of historical change"; (b) Denial of a "master narrative or realist perspective that provides a background of social and historical facts against which emerge the problem of the individual or collective psyche"; and (c) the relegation o f he psyche "as a sociohistorical construction inserted into a web of cultural artifices and artificial boundaries [thus making Fanon] reject the Hegelian 'dream for a human reality in-itself-for-itself' for a nondialectical Manicheanism." To San Juan, Bhabha, on this last point, culminates his (Bhabha's) reification of the "Manichean colonial world that Fanon poignantly delineated in his [Frantz Fanon's] classic work, *The Wretched of the Earth* for the sake of freezing Fanon in that twilight zone of difference, the in-between of displacement, dispossession, and dislocation that Bhabha hypostatizes as the ineluctable essence of postcoloniality." Then, San Juan concludes: the "[r]eductive closure of Fanon is complete" (San Juan, *Beyond Postcolonial Theory*, Chapter 1, pp. 27–28).

Of Said's exceptional status among the originators of postcolonialism, San Juan offers exception to Said whose postcolonial approach is distinguished from the "scholastic and verbal magic" of Bhabha and Spivak. San Juan pays homage to Said by recognizing his body of works for

> its clarity of historical reference and political thrust. Its resonance is clear. Its critique of U.S. imperialist hegemony, especially in the Middle East, cannot be doubted.... It has provided weapons for oppositional "minority" intellectuals. It has been useful in "conscienticizing" (Paulo Freire's term) a larger audience than those addressed by [Jacques] Derrida or [Michel] Foucault. (Pozo, brackets added)

San Juan elaborates on his homage to Said in a 2003 interview with Michael Pozo, Editor of the *St. John's University Humanities Review*: "Although I have criticized his inadequate views on Marxism, I consider Edward Said's commitment on behalf of Palestinian self-determination – a 'nationalism' different from Arafat and the bourgeois elements – a s a progressive one that should be supported in the face of Israeli state terrorism. (Said's situation, of course, is very complex and cannot be discussed here in depth.) In this context, Said's status as a diasporic intellectual is very much defined by his actual political and ethical activities" (Pozo 2003). Further, San Juan reinforces his estimation of Said in a 2006 essay, entitled, "Edward Said's Affiliations: Secular Humanism and Marxism." In this piece, San Juan offers most eloquently his highest esteem and admiration, if only belatedly, of Said which should be seen as a culmination of a gradual evolution of regard from hard criticism[6] to acceptance and reconciliation, as signified in this essay's Abstract, as follows:

> Overall, Said, despite a resort to a militant species of liberal humanism, provides a critical perspective on the complicity of academic discourse with predatory neocolonial attacks on people of color everywhere, and on the value of popular-democratic ideals of democratic sovereignty and egalitarian community that can reconcile Europe and the Atlantic world with the revolutionary movements of "postcolonial" subalterns around the globalized planet. As a democratic, secular humanist, Said is an ally of the popular masses against the terror of corporate globalization. (San Juan 2006)

With the above-caveat concerning Said, it is well to keep in mind that many within the fields of the humanities and the social sciences still remain enamored with what is referred to here as neoliberal pedagogy, described above, and who also remain dismissive, often quite casually, of historical materialism as "class reductionist," "economistic," "deterministic," or "eurocentric," among other epithets as though it were worthless. Any of these epithets assumes that the standard, prevailing approaches associated, say, with the neoliberal pedagogy is the normal mode, in the Kuhnian sense, in explaining social reality, and that any other approach is heresy.

THE PROBLEMATIZATION OF RACE WITHOUT CLASS IN THE UNITED STATES

Perhaps the most prescient current criticism of postcolonialism's failure to relate the problem of imperialism and popular resistance to it, on one level, with the problem of racism and resistance to it in the United States, on another level, is articulated most cogently by scholar-activist, Cornel West. In response to the publication of Ta-Nehisi Coates' book, *Between the World and Me* (2015) and the accolade it has received particularly among many mainstream black intellectuals, West takes to task Coates' failure—despite his uniquely prominent position as a black writer in a profession (particularly as a national correspondent for the liberal-oriented *The Atlantic* magazine) dominated by whites—to level criticism against a black president who has used his power to wage war by drones abroad, who has supported the Zionist State of Israel in its slaughter of Palestinians, especially children, and, while the trend did not commence with his presidency, one who has nonetheless presided over the intensification of police militarization and who has sought to deflect the killing of black lives—either by white supremacists or by law enforcement agents—from the domestic terrorist label and redefining it as a gun control issue.[7] West likewise observes that many of those that have offered high praises to Coates' book, including Nobel Laureate Toni Morrison, have failed to do the same particularly in the appropriation of renowned and beloved black writer and activist, James Baldwin, with whom Coates has been compared. On July 16, 2015, West, believing that the comparison is unwarranted, posts the following message on his Facebook wall:

> In Defense of James Baldwin – Why Toni Morrison (a literary genius) is Wrong about Ta-Nehisi Coates. Baldwin was a great writer of profound courage who spoke truth to power. Coates is a clever wordsmith with journalistic talent who avoids any critique of the Black president in power. Baldwin's

painful self-examination led to collective action and a focus on social movements. He reveled in the examples of Medgar, Martin, Malcolm, Fannie Lou Hamer and Angela Davis. Coates's fear-driven self-absorption leads to individual escape and flight to safety – he is cowardly silent on the marvelous new militancy in Ferguson, Baltimore, New York, Oakland, Cleveland and other places. Coates can grow and mature, *but without an analysis of capitalist wealth inequality, gender domination, homophobic degradation, imperial occupation (all concrete forms of plunder) and collective fightback (not just personal struggle) Coates will remain a mere darling of White and Black Neo-liberals, paralyzed by their Obama worship and hence a distraction from the necessary courage and vision we need in our catastrophic times.* (italics added)

And, in clarification of his earlier comment, responding to criticisms that he may have been too harsh on Coates, West writes again on his Facebook page, four days later, excerpted as follows:

> My response to Brother Ta-Nehisi's new book should not be misunderstood. I simply tried to honestly evaluate the book at the level of Truth, Goodness and Beauty. Since I believe there will never be another Baldwin – just as there will never be another Coltrane, Morrison, Du Bois, Simone [as in Nina], Robeson or Rakim – the coronation of Coates as our Baldwin is wrong. His immense talents and gifts lie elsewhere and lead to different priorities. *He indeed tells crucial truths about the vicious legacy of white supremacy as plunder on a visceral level, yet he fails to focus on our collective fightback, social movements or political hope. Even his fine essays downplay people's insurgency and resistance. The full truth of white supremacy must include our historic struggles against it. His critical comments in his essays about the respectability politics or paternalistic speeches of the black president in power (absent in his book) do not constitute a critique of the presidency – pro- Wall Street policy as capitalist wealth inequality, drone policy as U.S. war crimes, massive surveillance as violation of rights, or defense of ugly Israeli occupation as immoral domination.* For example, none of the black or white neo-liberals who coronate Coates say that 500 Palestinian babies killed by U.S. supported Israeli forces in 50 days or U.S. drones killing over 200 babies are crimes against humanity. Yet they cry crocodile tears when black folk are murdered by U.S. police. Unlike Baldwin, Coates gives them this hypocritical way out – with no cost to pay, risk to take, or threat to their privilege because of his political silence on these issues.[8] (Italics added)

In fairness, Coates was interviewed by journalists Amy Goodman and Juan Gonzalez on the program, *Democracy Now!*, on July 22, 2015, and

Coates was able to, first, provide context to his work, and, second, to respond to some of the specific criticisms he has received for his new book, in his own words. First, in response to the query about his experience growing up in West Baltimore as a son of a former member of the Black Panther Party, and influence, if any, of the Civil Rights Movement on him, Coates responded:

> I am in some ways outside of the African-American tradition. The African-American tradition, in the main, is very, very church-based, very, very Christian. It accepts, you know, certain narratives about the world. I didn't really have that present in my house. As you said, my dad was in the Black Panther Party. The mainstream sort of presentation of the civil rights movement was not something that I directly inherited.
>
> And beyond that, you know, I have to say, that just as a young man and as a boy going out and navigating the world, the ways in which the previous generation's struggle was presented to me did not particularly make sense. And so, notions of nonviolence, for instance, when I walked out into the streets of West Baltimore, seemed to have very, very little applicability. *Violence was essential to one's life there. It was everywhere. It was all around us. And then, when one looked out to the broader country, as I became more politically conscious, it was quite obvious that violence was essential to America — to its past, to its present and to its future.* And so, there was some degree of distance for me between how — my politics and how I viewed the world at that time and what was presented as my political heritage. (Coates 2015, italics added)

And, on the broader issues of white supremacy, structural racism in the United States, and US imperialism, Coates offers further thoughts. Correlated to his experience as a student at Howard University, he commented:

> Well, one of the things that — you know, *this theme of the book of living under a system of plunder and about surviving and how you deal with that and how you struggle against it, within that are the beautiful things that black people have forged, you know, even under really, really perilous conditions.* For me, Howard University is one of the most loveliest [sic], for me personally. (Coates 2015, italics added)

On his meetings with and criticisms toward Obama, Coates explained:

> The first one [of a few meetings with Obama] was after I levied quite a bit of critique of his [Obama's] Morehouse speech, which I was not a fan of

and am not a fan of now. I think that the president—I thought then, and I think now, that *the president has a tendency, when it's convenient for him, to emphasize that he is the president of all America, and then, when it comes to issues of morality, to deliver a message that the president of all America has no right to deliver. The president of all America, the bearer of the heritage of America, the bearer of policy of America, which has — you know, for the vast, vast majority of its history has been a policy of plunder towards black people, has no right to lecture black people on morality. That's my position.* You know, I understand an African-American man wanting to have a conversation with young people. But as the president of America, as far as I'm concerned, you give up that right. You know, if there cannot be direct policy towards black people, then there should be no direct criticism towards black people either. (Coates 2015, italics added)

And when asked about "What would James Baldwin do [presumably today, if he were alive]?", after having been reminded that Baldwin gave John F. Kennedy "hell" (before his assassination) by presumably bringing up class issues, Coates offered something quite revealing, about his own particular "water's edge," metaphorically, where he would stop. Coates responded, with an apparent bit of agitation toward progressivism, much less socialism thus revealing a conservative if not reactionary streak, as follows: "But, you know,... *I was deeply concerned about the liberal and the progressive notion that one should pursue policy based on class and not really deal with race.*"[9] (Coates 2015, italics added)

Coates' orientation as reflected in this final quote indicates not an isolated case but, rather, a general pattern of thinking and attitudes among members of the black community, particularly those who have arrived at the mainstream status and have assumed presumably responsible leadership positions—those whom Glen Ford of the *Black Agenda Report* has frequently referred to as the "Black misleadership class"—to conform to standards of civility and personal responsibility for the consequences of their actions, standards which are assumed to be requisites for them to be acceptable as responsible negotiating partners, and powerbrokers in behalf of the black community, at the table with representatives of the corporate elites that have been—and remain—at the helm of political power in this country. Ford describes this demand for civility and its rationale in the context of the non-indictment of the police that shot dead a black youth—Michael Brown—and the ensuing protests as follows:

The corporate media, reflecting their owners' anxiety at the failure of Black people to revert to a state of passivity in Ferguson, Missouri, have arrived at a general consensus on two counts: the need to "demilitarize" the police (fewer bullets, smaller armored vehicles?) and, more immediately, to re-establish some semblance of "calm" (as in comatose) in the neighborhood and beyond.

Corporate-attuned Black powerbrokers and politicians deliver essentially the same message, counseling (quiet) introspection and a search for "solutions" (diversions) to the historical oppression in which they are deeply complicit.

But first, tensions must be reduced, to diffuse the confrontation – which, we are told, serves no one's interests but the "agitators and instigators" (who, apparently, have millions of dollars in derivatives wagers riding on urban chaos). (Ford)

The protests in Ferguson lent impetus to the emergence of an incipient, principally youth-led movement—known for its Twitter hashtag #BlackLivesMatter—against police brutality, a malignant social disease that reveals not only the violence that inheres in the state through the police but also its racial nature that continues to brutalize communities of color. Thus, calls for civility simply fall flat on their faces; they are regarded as mere calls intended to defang the protests and to blunt the anger of those that are being victimized. Further, calls for personal responsibility and self-reliance, such as that which the discredited comedian and presumably clean-cut television "Dad" Bill Cosby has made himself apparently acceptable and respectable to the white audience, are intended to shift the onus of failure on to victims of this long-standing social oppression and exploitation of blacks and communities of color in general, the assumption being that if they obey or play by the rules, educate themselves, and work hard, they will find success.

Giroux, in another essay, offers the following incisive assessment of the implications of the ethos of "personal responsibility" and "self-reliance" inculcated through various institutions, and serving as a complement to the work ethic used to persuade countless generations about the presumed worth of one's personal efforts and the promise of success, only to serve, in the end, as a handmaiden of neoliberal-oriented corporate power, in the following passages:

> Four decades of neoliberal policies have resulted in an economic Darwinism that promotes privatization, commodification, free trade, and deregulation. *It privileges personal responsibility over larger social forces,* reinforces the gap

between the rich and poor by redistributing wealth to the most powerful and wealthy individuals and groups, and it fosters a mode of public pedagogy that privileges the entrepreneurial subject while encouraging a value system that promotes self-interest, if not an unchecked selfishness.

.....

With its theater of cruelty and mode of public pedagogy, neoliberalism as a form of economic Darwinism attempts to undermine all forms of solidarity capable of challenging market-driven values and social relations, promoting the virtues of an unbridled individualism almost pathological in its disdain for community, social responsibility, public values, and the public good.

.....

One consequence is that social problems are increasingly criminalized while social protections are either eliminated or fatally weakened. Not only are public servants described as the new "welfare queens" and degenerate freeloaders but young people are also increasingly subjected to harsh disciplinary measures both in and out of schools, often as a result of a violation of the most trivial rules.4 Another characteristic of this crushing form of economic Darwinism is that it thrives on a kind of social amnesia that erases critical thought, historical analysis, and any understanding of broader systemic relations. *In this regard, it does the opposite of critical memory work by eliminating those public spheres where people learn to translate private troubles into public issues.* (Giroux 2014, italics added)

In the final analysis, this author is of the opinion that West's criticism of Coates, as quoted above, was not unwarranted. The criticisms leveled by Coates toward Obama and the degree of racist violence that he (Coates) has narrated may no doubt be genuinely felt; but his statement that he was "deeply concerned about the liberal and the progressive notion" may, in fact, reveal that he is an activist of the reactionary sort, reflecting the kind of phobic, irrational ideology that rejects historical materialism reminiscent during the Cold War era. Further, Coates' criticisms predictably fall short of what is needed to confront the racial state, failing essentially to relate this state with the material, social, and economic conditions—such as the inevitable link between race and class—spawned by the very nature of the capitalist system and the worldwide imperialist violence that it promotes, e.g., assault on the Palestinians through surrogate US ally, the Zionist State of Israel; Obama's authorization of additional lethal aid to the Zionist State as Israel's medieval-inspired assault and siege on Gaza was ongoing during the summer of 2014, to this day, and his (Obama's) signing of a new law placating the Jewish lobby and the Zionist State of Israel designed to render illegal participation by US-based corporations of the highly effective Palestinian-led Boycott, Divestment, and Sanctions (BDS) Movement against Israeli policies in the Occupied Palestinian Territories; or countless coups, assassinations, and destabilization campaigns against so-called undesirable regimes and leaders that the United States has sponsored throughout much of the Cold War period to this day. There is nothing civil about this imperialist behavior, and there is nothing civil either about police brutality and countless unlawful killings of innocent persons, often from communities of color, thus, implicating—and justifiably rendering suspect—the entire criminal justice system, often revealing its class nature and its politically inspired prosecutions against labor unions as well a s against progressive and left-oriented cause organizations. Calls for civility and invocation of personal responsibility and self-reliance, as discussed above, are, therefore, regarded as bearing no moral weight, but serving merely as mask to disguise the racial and violent nature of the state and doing nothing to allay fears or suspicions of the traditionally oppressed communities, much less alter or upset the present arrangement based on capital accumulation and labor exploitation.

This is the same arrangement currently being rejected by emergent new voices coming from perches not as comfortable as the ones being occupied by Coates, Morrison, Cosby, the corporate-backed Rev. Al Sharpton, or even by television talk show personality Oprah Winfrey. These new voices have a sharply critical tone to them and are not coming from the traditional black leadership class either, described above by Ford. The Rev. Osagyefo Uhuru Sekou, youthful activist-pastor of the Friendly Temple Missionary Baptist Church that hosted Michael Brown's funeral in August 2014, in a lecture at the Warner Pacific College in Portland, Oregon, offered the following candid description:

> Martin Luther King ain't coming back. Get over it. It won't look like the civil rights movement. It's angry. It's profane. If you're more concerned about young people using profanity than about the profane conditions they live in, there's something wrong with you. (van Gelder)

Rev. Sekou followed up on the above-comments during an interview, and further offered, among other insights, the following passages providing both the context and the nature of the emergent movement represented by these voices, as follows:

In the last decade, particularly in the age of Obama, the vast majority of the black leadership has been the punditry class—those of us, and I am guilty of this, who are on television, who write books, who give lectures, but don't necessarily experience on-the-ground direct confrontation with the state.

Now the leadership that is emerging are the folks who have been in the street, who have been tear-gassed. The leadership is black, poor, queer, women. It presents in a different way. It's a revolutionary aesthetic. It's black women, queer women, single mothers, poor black boys with records, kids with tattoos on their faces who sag their pants.

These folks embody intersectionality. Particularly in Ferguson, solidarity with Palestine was never a question. More than 250 Palestinians marched with us, and the local Palestinian solidarity committee was with us from day one.

And there is a suspicion of the state. As a result of that suspicion, a lot of folks have turned to cooperative models—talking about buying land, forms of entrepreneurship, a lot of discourse about self-healing — because there is such a disdain and distrust for the state. (van Gelder, italics added)

THE RECOVERY OF CLASS, AND THE CLASS BASIS OF RACISM

San Juan's interventions in debates pertaining to race and racism such as the one presently at hand have been numerous, vigorous, and profound. Perhaps the most significant o f these interventions in its generation, in which San Juan demonstrates his erudition and mastery of historical-materialist critique, is his 2002 book, entitled *Racism and Cultural Studies: Critiques of Multiculturalist Ideology and the Politics of Difference* (Duke University Press). One reviewer, Neferti Tadiar of Columbia University's Barnard College, writes of this book, included as blurb in the book's jacket, the following comment: "An important, stringent critique of the hegemonic versions of multiculturalism touted in both popular and academic spheres. San Juan provides a new reality to contend with – a new version of the present, one in which erased histories of racism, oppression, exploitation, and the struggle of marginalized groups are restored." Another reviewer, Jeffrey Cabusao, Professor of English and Cultural Studies at Bryant University, comments:

> Boldly pushing against the historical limitations of fashionable theoretical trends of the academy, San Juan urgently asks us to reclaim the rich and dynamic Marxist traditions (both Western and Third World Marxisms) of

theorizing the connection between cultural production and the struggle for radical social transformation (the twin tasks of ideological and material struggle). In *Racism and Cultural Studies* (*RCS*), San Juan offers a rigorous historical materialist method for regrounding the dominant "new times=new politics" post-al model of contemporary Cultural Studies. This alternative methodology, in *RCS*, shifts us from reified notions of difference to a dialectical regrounding in which difference is conceived as, in the words of Red Feminist Teresa Ebert, "difference within a material system of exploitation."4 This shifting of grounds enables San Juan to bring to the fore the importance of analyzing the complex ways in which difference – race, gender, sexuality – is historically produced and reproduced within class society. A leitmotif of this book is the advancement of Marx's challenge to idealism. It is not enough to interpret the world. We must collectively and creatively struggle for a radically transformed society in which difference will no longer be produced by racialized and gendered divisions of labor (exploitative social relations of production). Instead, genuine differences would emerge: each lives "according to her/his abilities and needs." (Cabusao 2005)

In this book, San Juan elaborates on several interrelated premises aspects of which he has previously began to develop at varying lengths through various media outlets. One of these premises, regarded as cardinal, as explained by reviewer Cabusao, is

> the notion that the U.S. nation-state is a racial polity, a thesis which philosopher Charles Mills proposed in *The Racial Contract* (1997).9 Within the U.S. racial polity, racism -- alongside its ideological twin, white supremacy -- functions as the organizing principle of the division of labor and unequal distribution of resources and wealth. This "racial divide constitutes 'a form of stratification built into the structure of U.S. society' as a Herrenvolk democracy."10 By returning us to the basics of understanding the centrality of white supremacy/racism in the development of U.S. capitalism, *RCS* [San Juan's *Racism and Cultural Studies*] offers an inventory and an advancement of dialectical methodological approaches that can be utilized to critique how the U.S. racial polity came to be, so that we can radically transform it. Given the expansive reach of U.S. Empire, one can no longer ignore how racism organizes global capitalism (international racialized and gendered divisions of labor, asymmetrical power relations between the global North and South) and sustains U.S. imperial hegemony around the globe. (Cabusao 2005)

It is worth it to recall at this juncture an article by Barbara Jeanne Fields, published in 1990, entitled "Slavery, Race and Ideology in the United

States of America." In that piece, Fields tried to explain that race was—and is—more than just a matter of race relations. In other words, inequality among races is a symptom of and traceable to the very nature of economic inequality. In the United States, this economic inequality has direct correlation with matters already brought up above, e.g., generations of slavery, colonial plunder, and the system of mass incarceration prevalent today. Fields laments those who persist in thinking of race as a mere matter race relations scholarship, or reducible to attitude. She writes:

> Probably a majority of American historians think of slavery in the United States as primarily a system of race relations — as though the chief business of slavery were the production of white supremacy rather than the production of cotton, sugar, rice and tobacco. One historian has gone so far as to call slavery 'the ultimate segregator'. He does not ask why Europeans seeking the 'ultimate' method of segregating Africans would go to the trouble and expense of transporting them across the ocean for that purpose, when they could have achieved the same end so much more simply by leaving the Africans in Africa. (Fields)

Fields then goes on to assess the implications of this hair-splitting process of isolating race from its historical, social, and economic context by citing comparable cases in history wherein connecting race to this proper context is absolutely essential. She writes:

> No one dreams of analyzing the struggle of the English against the Irish as a problem in race relations, even though the rationale that the English developed for suppressing the 'barbarous' Irish later served nearly word for word as a rationale for suppressing Africans and indigenous American Indians. Nor does anyone dream of analyzing serfdom in Russia as primarily a problem of race relations, even though the Russian nobility invented fictions of their innate, natural superiority over the serfs as preposterous as any devised by American racists. (Fields)

The essence of doing so would allow assignment of responsibility and accountability for what happened, e.g., the consequences of slavery and colonial plunder, just as what the Black Reparations Movement in the United States or, for that matter, what the reparatory justice movement in the Caribbean and similar such movements elsewhere across the former colonized areas of the globe, are all calling for, at minimum. The response of the United States and such former colonial powers as Great Britain,

France, and Belgium thus far has been less than noble; they have endeavored at great lengths to ignore these movements and to trivialize them, based on their notion that slavery and colonialism belong to the past; that blacks in the United States, having been long-freed from slavery, should be responsible for themselves; and that former colonies, having been freed from colonial control for at least a generation, should also now take responsibility for their own future. At the same time, they have also engaged in co-optative efforts designed to placate segments of the black community or the elite leadership class in the former colonies to blunt any demands for reparations, avoid any admission of wrong-doing, and evade any form of responsibility and accountability altogether, be it legal, moral, or ethical.

This pattern of evasion of responsibility on the part of the former colonial powers of Europe and, presently, the United States as an empire, is sadly replicated by continuing evasion of responsibility for horrendous consequences with genocidal implications of the US conduct of the war in Vietnam; in support of the 1965 military coup in Indonesia resulting in deaths of at least a million people; in the backing of the Indonesian military's invasion of East Timor, resulting in death and displacement of at least a third of that hapless island-country's population; the funding and training of death squads, paramilitary formations, and security agencies of oppressive regimes all throughout South and Central America throughout most of the Cold War period. In the botched but still ongoing so-called war on terror, several innocent persons have been swept up, summarily labeled terrorist or enemy combatants and subsequently inserted into US-maintained prison facilities such as at Abu Ghraib or Guantanamo[10] where they were then subjected to inhumane, and degrading treatment, or unspeakable treatment for a number of years, even decades. Many, nay, an overwhelming number of these have never been charged with any crime or wrong-doing, as illustrated in the specific case of Tariq Ba Odah, a young Pakistani man of twenty-three when he was ensnared by what his lawyer describes as a "bounty-based dragnet" for being at the wrong place at the wrong time following the illegal US invasion of Afghanistan in 2001 (Farah). Human rights organizations, like the Center for Constitutional Rights, have time and again called for them to be charged so they can defend themselves in a court of law or, otherwise, be released to freedom. The US government administrations since the presidency of George W. Bush to the present day, under 2009 Nobel Peace Prize awardee Barack Obama, have either refused to deal with this issue invariably arguing that there is bureaucratic red tape, or congressional opposition, or public outcry, or otherwise fear for that the innocent prisoners might do against the United States in an imagined retaliation for the injustice done to them while under detention!

Thankfully, we have 2005 Nobel laureate in Literature, Harold Pinter, in his Nobel lecture, entitled "Art, Truth, & Politics," courageously called at the highest profile possible the world's attention to these atrocities that might otherwise be forgotten. In contradistinguishing the record of the former Soviet Union, harshly recorded in the Western mainstream media, with that of the United States during the same post-World War II period, he declared, in part:

> But my contention here is that the US crimes in the same period have only been superficially recorded, let alone documented, let alone acknowledged, let alone recognised as crimes at all. I believe this must be addressed and that the truth has considerable bearing on where the world stands now. Although constrained, to a certain extent, by the existence of the Soviet Union, the United States' actions throughout the world made it clear that it had concluded it had carte blanche to do what it liked. (Pinter)

Pinter continued on discussing common methods the United States used, saying:

> Direct invasion of a sovereign state has never in fact been America's favoured method. In the main, it has preferred what it has described as 'low intensity conflict'. Low intensity conflict means that thousands of people die but slower than if you dropped a bomb on them in one fell swoop. It means that you infect the heart of the country, that you establish a malignant growth and watch the gangrene bloom. When the populace has been subdued - or beaten to death - the same thing - and your own friends, the military and the great corporations, sit comfortably in power, you go before the camera and say that democracy has prevailed. This was a commonplace in US foreign policy in the years to which I refer. (Pinter)

Then, citing specific examples, Pinter goes on:

> The United States supported and in many cases engendered every right wing military dictatorship in the world after the end of the Second World War. I refer to Indonesia, Greece, Uruguay, Brazil, Paraguay, Haiti, Turkey, the Philippines, Guatemala, El Salvador, and, of course, Chile. The horror the United States inflicted upon Chile in 1973 can never be purged and can never be forgiven.

Hundreds of thousands of deaths took place throughout these countries. Did they take place? And are they in all cases attributable to US foreign policy? The answer is yes they did take place and they are attributable to American foreign policy. But you wouldn't know it. (Pinter)

Characterizing US imperial demeanor in these and other instances, Pinter suggested that:

> It never happened. Nothing ever happened. Even while it was happening it wasn't happening. It didn't matter. It was of no interest. The crimes of the United States have been systematic, constant, vicious, remorseless, but very few people have actually talked about them. You have to hand it to America. It has exercised a quite clinical manipulation of power worldwide while masquerading as a force for universal good. It's a brilliant, even witty, highly successful act of hypnosis. (Pinter)

And, lastly, Pinter credits the United States for being a show in itself, saying:

> I put to you that the United States is without doubt the greatest show on the road. Brutal, indifferent, scornful and ruthless it may be but it is also very clever. As a salesman it is out on its own and its most saleable commodity is self-love. It's a winner. Listen to all American presidents on television say the words, 'the American people', as in the sentence, 'I say to the American people it is time to pray and to defend the rights of the American people and I ask the American people to trust their president in the action he is about to take on behalf of the American people.' (Pinter)

San Juan himself affirms the above-quoted passages. More importantly, he recovers the significance of class, long ignored by mainstream scholars of race who have sought to demonstrate its irrelevance by trivializing it to mean largely lifestyle or status. They have also sterilized the subject of race by assigning it under the benign rubric of "race relations" or "multicultural/intercultural relations," divorced from issues of capital accumulation and labor exploitation as well as the possibility that race may be used or manipulated as an instrument of these, all especially within the context of contemporary neoliberal globalization. San Juan articulates this essential point in a 2010 essay addressed to the Asian-American academic community, writing:

The gospel of neo-liberal globalisation, also known as "the Washington Consensus," took off with a retooling of methodological individualism in "rational choice theory" and officially sanctioned Establishment multiculturalism. *To maintain the hegemonic common sense of a racial hierarchy, the US dominant bloc requires a "buffer race" to split up the toiling majority, keeping blacks visible but subordinate, and thus deflect class conflict by preserving the civil-society consensus of white colour privilege* (Gran 1999). *To preserve the status quo, the identity of the white working class needs to be defined by race, not by class consciousness.* (San Juan 2010b, italics added)

Further, San Juan recovers, nay, insists on, the importance of history in terms of appreciating the unique origins and particularities of the current situation as well as the agency of the oppressed actors themselves in shaping their destiny, keeping in mind the forces arrayed against them, neither conceding that their history has been rewritten or erased by their oppressors, nor accommodating to any hybridity or decentering as a matter of compromise as postcolonialists are wont to do. In so doing, San Juan negates the validity to any critique that Marxism is deterministic or eurocentric when it comes to history and affirms the agency of its actors in responding to their unique and particular circumstances. This is exemplified in his critical re-reading of the past, preventing it from erasure or distortion, and contradistinguishing it from the current conventional interpretation of the system of slavery, an interpretation that would, almost as a jerk reaction or a default position, relegate slavery as a mere matter of social relations divorced from its economic roots that gave rise to inequality or, for that matter, political oppression. In the following passage from a 2005 essay in support of the black reparations movement, invoking reflections from black intellectuals and activists W.E.B. Du Bois, George Jackson, and Mumia Abu-Jamal on the black transition from slavery to bourgeois democracy, and drawing from insights from historical materialism, San Juan insists on an essential recalibration of the way justice for slavery's victims and their descendants may, nay, should, be properly conceived:

> How can restitution be made for past wrongs so as to undo what has been done to an entire people? What is problematic is the paradox of the solution: justice conceptualized as a fair exchange of values, the compensation for labor-power expropriated from the slave, follows of course from a liberal understanding of value as a product of free labor. However, it reveals in its fold the real inequality of the parties involved: the slave's labor was coerced, her/his freedom alienated from her/him. As everyone admits, this inequality

(impervious to market calculation) includes not only the deep psychological trauma of free persons being enslaved but also the disastrous social and political structures that have damaged the lives of the survivors—something "non-reparable or "incompensational" (Martin and Yaquinto 2004, 22). Can deprivation of freedom be repaired or rectified by an attempt at "equal" exchange? Can disparity of life chances be remedied by equality before the law of the market? (San Juan 2007, 41–42)

Prognosis

This chapter began with a discussion of the Cold War and the conditions it created in justifying and perpetuating US imperial hegemony in the global stage, the racial state, and its economic system based on accumulation. Academic disciplines not only were enjoined, many practitioners among them in their prominent positions, status, and access to and influence in mainstream journals, textbook writing, classrooms, and professional organizations, became Cold Warriors and apologists for the state. Playing one role or another and at varying degrees, these practitioners formed the core, throughout much of the Cold War and the post-Cold War periods, of what is referred to here as neoliberal pedagogy. This pedagogy predetermined the narratives in historical writing, and defined the broad parameters and purposes of research including the problems to be defined and the tools with which to solve them. Academic disciplines adjusted to and accommodated the demands of the state for ideological conformity which, in turn, imposed its definition of subversion for those who dared go beyond these parameters. To deny that there were no firings, demotions, non-hirings, and other forms of academic banishments against those who dared or otherwise thought prohibited thoughts would be disingenuous if not outright dishonest.

This conformity has been most evident in the social sciences as practitioners embraced a supposedly value-free approach to their respective disciplines, while regarding any alternate approach as value-laden, unscholarly, and most likely political, and therefore, to be rejected or proscribed. This is the fate that befell historical materialism, an approach avoided like plague having been associated with what was deemed as the worst features of orthodox Marxism including its presumed economic determinism, eurocentrism, and historicism precluding the agency of actors other than workers in a mature capitalist stage in bringing about their own emancipation.

The end of the Cold War and the concomitant collapse of actually existing socialist experiments in the former Soviet Union and in Eastern Europe brought about a sense of unabashed triumphalism in Western capitals—the end of history as one wrote—that seemed to validate their belief in the superiority of capitalism and its complementary political ideology of liberalism, both anchored on the belief in the primacy of the individual over society, against any competing ideology, in which presumably self-interested private individuals would compete to conserve and advance their gains over others and wherein the state, shedding its role in providing social services and upholding public interest, assumes its role as a protector of private gain and interests.

Within the US body politic, founded as it is on the blood and labor of slaves and the plunder of global resources through the institutions and mechanisms of the US-led neoliberal globalization, an elaborate web of market-oriented academic discourse evolved to dissimulate the racial nature of the state, the supremacist thinking that underlies it, and the persistence of a politico-economic system controlled by the Top One Percent of its households. As shown in an earlier discussion, this goes by the name of multiculturalism, a term with popular appeal but whose function in validating the power structure and in concealing the racial nature of the state is little understood. As understood by most, it has been taken as the basis of the policy of diversity, the acceptance of others, or the toleration of all kinds of differences. By its nature, therefore, it is insidious especially to those who have faith in it but who fail to recognize it as the mere exercise—to borrow San Juan's term—of the state's "plenary power" wherein the state forbids, on a formal-legal level, members of society to use force and violence against each other but which, in fact, reserves the prerogative to inflict the same on everybody and on any group at will and with the ultimate effect of maintaining, rather than challenging, the existing socioeconomic power structure favoring the aforesaid Top One Percent.

Insidious too is the promotion of the concept of personal responsibility as a correlate to the multicultural approach to interpersonal and interracial relations. An assumption of this concept is that the lot of each and every individual depends essentially on that person's determination to move beyond his/her current condition toward self-fulfillment. Rooted in the Protestant work ethic, it has been ingrained in popular consciousness but hammered particularly into the minds of minorities, particularly among blacks, by such popular television situation-comedy shows as "All in the Family" (1971–1979), and "The Cosby Show" (1984–1992), with the main characters of Archie Bunker and Mr. Huxtable, respectively, emphasizing the significance of traditional roles and values and, in the case of Dr. Huxtable, preaching the importance of fitting in on the part of an upper-middle-class Black family into US society. In real life, this has been the approach of such leading Black personalities like Bill Cosby, who played Dr. Huxtable, and Oprah Winfrey, who hosted a long-running Chicago-based television talk show, The Oprah Winfrey Show. The essence of the message of these programs places the onus for success or failure on the individual minority person and deflects any criticism from or attention to structural factors, conditioned by enduring sentiments of racism pervading interracial relations, all contributing to what mainstream sociologists have conveniently referred to as the culture of poverty. It is no surprise that this type of message also deflects proper attention to the role that the state has played in perpetuating this apparent sense of helplessness among members of minority communities, particularly among blacks. Through the enactment of a series of laws and policies that all but affirm the state's neoliberal character, it has presided over deregulatory programs that proved a boon to corporations enabling them to transfer wealth, much of which was derived from public funds, to private coffers with the government serving as a conduit, without as much requiring the corporate executives to earn their due by sweating it out under the hot sun, or rolling up their sleeves, and dirtying their fingernails like how the rest of average citizenry is made to believe to be the way to prosperity. This, in turn, becomes the justification for the enactment of mean-spirited austerity measures entailing curtailment of social programs on the argument that the government is not in the business of providing these services which, to begin with, should accrue to the individual, at least in the abstract, only if he/she goes out and find work and earns a wage to be able to afford these amenities.

This inculcation of personal responsibility, and the weight placed on it upon the individual, is sadly contrasted to the absence of acknowledgment of any official responsibility, much less accountability, for the legacy of the Atlantic slave trade and of the socioeconomic system of slavery especially in the American South upon which much of the early economic prosperity of this country rested and continues to rest; or, for the genocide against the indigenous population of the New World upon which much of their dispossession allowed the territorial expansion—along with the exploitation of resources therein—of what we know today as the United States; or, for the continuing plunder of much of the globe's resources, unprecedented in human history, under the guise of neoliberal globalization based, in reality, on a state-sanctioned economic system of private accumulation and profit.

If the boycott by the United States of the 2001 UN-sponsored World Conference Against Racism, held in Durban, South Africa, during the presidency of George W. Bush Jr., is any indication, any official acknowledgment is not forthcoming anytime soon, anticipating that the conference would take up the issue of reparations. This boycott was repeated in 2009 under the Obama Administration, partly in solidarity with the Zionist State of Israel, when a conference to review progress since the 2001 Durban Conference was held in Geneva, Switzerland in April 2009. In the case of the Zionist State, the boycott was an expression of displeasure over the anticipated discussion associating Zionism as a racist ideology.[11] The US boycott was criticized by Stan E. Willis, Director of the Chicago-based National Conference of Black Lawyers, who commented: "More than anything else, the symbolism of an African-American president rejecting a world gathering called to help wipe out racism is just stunning" (Muwakil).

From the legislative side, efforts at extracting any acknowledgment much less an apology fell apart when, in 2008 and 2009, respectively, the House and the Senate each but separately voted for an apology of its own but could not reconcile any common language that could be forwarded to the White House for the President's signature. But even then, there was not any assurance that the president would sign it into law.

The reparations movement, nonetheless, has gained momentum of its own in the spate of police killings and extra-judicial executions against unarmed black citizens and subsequent protests in Staten Island, New York, Ferguson, Missouri, and Baltimore, Maryland, among other cities across the country during the 2015–2016 period alone. These events led to the birth of the Black Lives Matter (BLM) Movement, discussed earlier, credited with having been instrumental, along with prominent members of the Black community, in persuading the United Nations (UN) to send a fact-finding mission to assess the human rights conditions in this country particularly as they pertain to Blacks. Thereafter, the UN Working Group of Experts on People of African Descent, notably chaired by Mireille Fanon Mende-France, daughter of author-activist Frantz Fanon, issued a preliminary report singling out slavery and its onerous legacy for the continuing sorry plight of citizens of African-American descent. It also urged the government of the United States to deliver on the demand for reparations as has been articulated by the reparations movement. Alongside this proposal, the report also urged the US Congress to enact the proposed legislation, entitled Commission to Study Reparation Proposals for African-Americans Act, and to set up a national human rights commission in a renewed effort to prod the government to acknowledge the Atlantic slave trade as a "crime against humanity" (UN Committee). In issuing the report, Mendes-France explained, in part: "Contemporary police killings and the trauma it creates are reminiscent of the racial terror lynchings in the past. Impunity for state violence has resulted in the current human rights crisis and must be addressed as a matter of urgency" (UN Committee). Further, the report addressed the "structural" origins of the continuing discrimination and oppression of the black community in this country. It reads, in part: "Despite substantial changes since the end of the enforcement of Jim Crow and the fight for civil rights, ideology ensuring the domination of one group over another continues to negatively impact the civil, political, economic, social and cultural rights of African-Americans today." I t ontinues: "The persistent gap in almost all the human development indicators such as life expectancy, income and wealth level of education and even food security… reflects the level of structural discrimination that creates de facto barriers for people of African descent to fully exercise their human rights" (UN Committee).

Interestingly, President Obama, in his "Farewell Address to the Nation," delivered on January 10, 2017 in his hometown of Chicago before a receptive crowd, painted a somber picture about his accomplishments while in office. Aside from affirming the exceptionalism of the United States especially in international affairs, in domestic matters, he acknowledged that modest goals had been attained, declaring: "Today, the economy is growing again; wages, incomes, home values, and retirement accounts are rising again; poverty is falling again" (Obama, "Farewell Address"). Despite this, Obama recognized that "stark inequality" exists and is "corrosive to our democratic principles." He added: "While the top 1% has amassed a bigger share of wealth and income, too many families, in inner cities and rural counties, have been left behind – the laid-off factory worker, the waitress and healthcare worker who struggle to pay bills – convinced that the game is fixed against them, that their government only serves the interests of the powerful – a recipe for more cynicism and polarization in our politics" (Obama, "Farewell Address").

Addressing the issue of race relations in particular, he distanced himself from what he referred to as a well-intended but unrealistic view of the United States as being in a "post-racial" stage following his election. This was largely because race, he asserted, "remains a potent and divisive force in our society," and that "we're not where we need to be" (Obama, "Farewell Address"). Ironically, he offered in this address support for that one policy that he could not enact—or against which he acted—as president: the matter of acknowledgment of slavery and its legacy albeit at the personal level. He further acknowledged that, for white Americans, this is particularly challenging because this would mean "acknowledging that the effects of slavery and Jim Crow didn't suddenly vanish in the '60s," especially when poll after poll shows that majority of white American respondents indicate no sense of racism or have no experience with racism, at least in the way that black Americans have.

Here, one gets the sense that while racism is a daunting and a persistent problem in race relations in this country, not all the immediate problems related to the inferior socioeconomic status being suffered by the black community may be attributed to racism. Indeed, many popular mainstream publications have offered their own respective assessments of the Obama years, much of which, negative, as a random albeit unscientific search on Google would reveal using the simple phrase "Black lives under Obama" in the searchline. Topping the list is a piece from *The Atlantic*, a centrist liberal-leaning magazine, entitled "How Barack Obama Failed Black Americans," by William A. Darity Jr., in its December 22, 2016 issue. Focusing, among others, on comparative incomes among black households and their white counterparts, Darity, who turns out to be Samuel DuBois Cook Professor of Public Policy at Duke University, writes:

> Estimates generated from the 2013 round of the Federal Reserve's Survey of Consumer Finances indicate that black households have *one-thirteenth* of the wealth of white households at the median. We have concluded that the average black household would have to save 100 percent of its income for three consecutive years to close the wealth gap. The key source of the black-white wealth gap is the intergenerational effects of transfers of resources. White parents have far greater resources to give to their children via gifts and inheritances, so that the typical white young adult starts their working lives with a much greater initial net worth than the typical black young adult. These intergenerational effects are blatantly non-meritocratic. (Darity)

Darity assesses further that

> Indeed, the history of black wealth deprivation, from the failure to provide ex-slaves with 40 acres and a mule to the violent destruction of black property in white riots to the seizure and expropriation of black-owned land to

the impact of racially restrictive covenants on homeownership to the discriminatory application of policies like the GI Bill and the FHA, created the foundation for a perpetual racial wealth gap. (Darity)

Another notable observation is one by Reginald Clark, in a piece entitled "The Expansion of Black American Misery under Barack Obama's Watch." Written for the *Black Agenda Report*, in its February 19, 2013 issue, Clark identifies two basic facts that have characterized race relations and, in particular, Black experience, in the United States under Obama, namely:

> 1. Black misery has been growing since 2009 under President Obama's economic and job creation policies. Black folks participation in the labor market has been steadily moving DOWNWARD during the Obama presidency—since 2009 when he was first inaugurated.
> 2. ALL other major racial groups have moved up albeit moderately since 2009! Blacks are the only group that has taken a definitive step BACKWARDS since then. Why? This article will argue that it is because for the past four years, until last week, Obama has declined to even put forth the idea that 'low income Black people need targeted help too!!! Needless to say, has not designed any job creation strategies or policies that would do something for the Blacks who supported him the most. (Clark)

Clark contends that President Obama's inability or unwillingness to design employment programs targeted at "stimulating the hiring practices in businesses that are located in geographic areas where Blacks mostly reside" has been the single most important factor contributing to Black underemployment, one that raised the rate of 16% in 2009 to 20% in 2012, representing a worsening by 25% overall of Black underemployment during Obama's first term. If one factors in, according to Clark, the at least 2 million Blacks currently incarcerated and without jobs, half of whom have been sentenced for non-violent offenses, the Black underemployment would be a staggering 30%. Thus, Clark concludes, "Black misery as a whole has increased in at least 10 other quality-of-life and socioeconomic areas as well: employment, family wages, home ownership, health care access, median net worth, poverty rate, college education attendance, college financial and retirement savings accounts and benefits and consumer debt" (Clark).

The above observations by Clark perfectly dovetail with those of Darity cited earlier. Darity adds that beyond the numbers indicating the perennial socioeconomic inferiority of Blacks in this country is the persistence of what he regards as a general perspective that "argues that an important factor explaining racial economic disparities is self-defeating or dysfunctional behavior on the part of blacks themselves" (Darity). Recalling President Obama's inability to bring meaningful relief to the Black community during his eight years in office, Darity is not coy about asserting that Obama himself has "trafficked" in this kind of perspective. He says:

> Of course there are some black folk who engage in habits that undermine their potential accomplishments, but there are some white folk who engage in habits that undermine their potential accomplishments as well. And there is no evidence to demonstrate that are (sic) proportionately more blacks who believe in ways that undercut achievement, especially since it is clear that *blacks do more with less*. Nevertheless, Obama consistently has trafficked heavily in the tropes of black dysfunction. Either he is unfamiliar with or uninterested in the evidence that undercuts the black behavioral deficiency narrative. (Darity)

Amplifying this author's concern expressed earlier about personal responsibility, Darity fears that the same message being conveyed by a black person like Obama, speaking from a position of authority, might be more damaging than helpful. Darity adds:

> I worried that it was possible for the symbolic and inspirational aspects of having a black president would be more than offset by the damage that could be done by the messages delivered by a black president. And it has been damaging to have Barack Obama, a black man speaking from the authoritative platform of the presidency, reinforce the widely held belief that racial inequality in the United States is, in large measure, the direct responsibility of the black folk. This has been the deal breaker for me: not merely is silence on white physical and emotional violence directed against black Americans, but t*he denial of the centrality of American racism in explaining sustained black-white disparity*. (Darity, italics added)

NOTES

1. In the Introduction to his aptly titled book, *Hegemony and Strategies of Transgressions* (SUNY Press, 1995, pp. 9–10), San Juan asks a series of questions addressed to practitioners in cultural studies, particularly to those in the postcolonial community, who may have been ambivalent about the moral efficacy of endorsing—tacitly or actively—the US empire's suppression of dissent at home and counterinsurgency against anti-imperialist movements

abroad; the same set of questions may be directed at liberal-oriented social science practitioners, particularly among those in the disciplines of political science and sociology, who have adapted or endorsed such approaches as conflict theory, pluralism, and functionalism, among others, and who have consciously stayed away from—if not outrightly rejected—the historical materialist frame of analysis. These questions are as follows: "Can a liberal democratic dispensation still claim moral legitimacy when its complicity with transnational corporate exploitation is witnessed daily? Is nationalism no longer valid, no longer a viable project for subalterns only now emerging (as flexible labor, traffic of exported bodies) into the arena of world history? Are 'peoples without history' forever condemned to 'postness' and the *Nachtraglichkeit* of the unrelenting forces of Western finance/knowledge capital? Is writing at the border/margin—always at the mercy of 'Cartesian imperialism' ('I invade you, therefore you exist')—a mode of collective resistance to reification and the religion of free trade? Or is it a symptom and effect of postmodern avantgardism, of 'the incredulity toward metanarratives'? In the world of nearly universal commodity fetishism, is the vernacular speech of people of color (not yet postmodernized by e-mail) an alter/native idiom that can catalyze the 'political unconscious' of the silent majority in the metropolitan centers? Can the ideals of pluralism and individualistic liberty in industrialized civil society suffice to empower the victims of racist/sexist power? Should we ('natives' of internal/external colonies, Fanon's 'wretched of the earth') repudiate both the Enlightenment paradigm and its antithesis, the ludic play of cyborgs and nomads, in favor of autochthonous programs enacted by 'specific intellectuals' and the *testimonios* of indigenous survivors?" (ibid.) Here, San Juan has specifically in mind Quiche Indian Rigoberta Menchu whose powerful *testimonio* as a survivor of the infamous US-sponsored El Mozote massacre, happening in December 1981, as part of a complex of atrocities waged by government-led and US-trained and -armed military and paramilitary forces suppressing the peasant-based rebellion in El Salvador, and spilling over into Guatemala, throughout much of the 1980s. San Juan later devotes a full section on Menchu's *testimonio* in Chapter One, "Interrogations and Interventions: Who Speaks for Whom?", in his *Beyond Postcolonial Theory* (St. Martin's Press 1998, pp. 33–39), wherein San Juan asks: "Since the genre of *testimonio* mediates the documentary sociohistorical context and authorial ego, reference and intentionality..., does Menchu's intertextual performance, her 'speaking truth to power', overcome the disengenousness (sic) of postmodernist aesthetics?" San Juan then assesses the value of Menchu's testimony—and the language used—as a valorous act of self-representation, as follows: "One can say that Menchu's *testimonio* evokes a reality-effect homologous to what she experienced. Whether the actual events occurred or not, what is certain is that the transcription of acts of barbarism tests the limit or ordinary language and the genre of classical expressive realism" (San Juan, *Beyond Postcolonial Theory*, p. 34).

Back to the subject of anti-imperialist and anti-capitalist revolutionary resistance in the Third World, all subject to comprehensive US suppressive program that includes, at one point or another, depending on circumstances, counterinsurgency, pro-insurgency, and low-intensity warfare, San Juan sees the conditions that gave rise to them, particularly the "uneven global arena" and the challenge of transforming it, as an opportunity to define and/or redefine, the *telos* not just of the individual practitioner but of whole disciplines themselves. San Juan had in mind Cultural Studies, and this author has in mind the social sciences. San Juan reasons that "[w]hat is at stake here is not just the discourse but the value of practical reason (employed by Third World activists) in questioning its limits and potential in relation to the agenda of progressive social transformation in the uneven global arena.... Here, I introduce the qualification that in the intractable and recalcitrant hinterlands..., the struggle is chiefly for bread, land, and shelter – for the integral and organic conditions of possibility for rational communicative actions free from the violence of capital, and more – for a significant measure of dignity appropriate for love and the needs of the species-being....I envisage the transition from Western 'hegemony' to the transformative and oppositional practices of all those 'others' inhabiting margins, pariah zones, quarantines, detention and deportation centers, internal colonies in North America and in Europe.... In this practice of conflating outside and inside..., what occupies center-stage are the creative and critical powers of people of color who have been victimized by transnational capital while producing/reproducing social wealth. Irrecusably, the future of over two-thirds of the planet's inhabitants is indivisible from their unremitting struggle for democratic empowerment, national self-determination, popular justice, and dignity. Their variegated, tortuous modes of combating class exploitation and national oppression comprise heterogeneous projects of resistance that ultimately reproduce the 'Third World' as a permanent political-cultural agency of local as well as intercultural transformation. *Whenever there is imperial domination in any form, historical experience teaches us that there will always be a 'Third World' subject of resistance and dialectical transcendence*" (San Juan, *Hegemony and Strategies of Transgressions*, pp. 8–9, italics added).

2. Here, while Horowitz apparently celebrates the "shrinking of the globe," the "universalization of culture," and the globalization of free trade, San Juan sees through Horowitz's rhetoric as "a mode of appropriation" which "*fetishizes and commodifies* others." "The self-arrogating universal," San Juan adds, "swallows the unsuspecting particulars in a grand hegemonic compromise. Indeed, retrograde versions of multiculturalism celebrate in

order to fossilize differences and thus assimilate 'others' into a fictive gathering which flattens contradictions pivoting around the axis of class. rationalization for the imposition of US imperial hegemony" (San Juan 2004). Indirectly, San Juan critiques Horowitz's assumption of a "universalized/universalizing culture" as a mere happenstance, or a "condition of human existence" that just happened to be when, in fact, as San Juan points out, it is "the effect of an enunciation of difference that constitutes hierarchies and asymmetries of power" (San Juan 2004).
3. San Juan notes a parallel reform-oriented approach on the part of Asian-Pacific Islander civil society activists and intellectuals in behalf of their respective Asian-Pacific Islander constituents. The assumption among these activists and intellectuals is that, by clamoring for expanded political and civil rights—rather than economic and social justice—the problem of economic inequality could somehow be vanquished. A pertinent quote from San Juan from a 2010 essay composed for the Asian-American audience, is as follows: "Takaki locates the problem in the linkage of 'democracy to national identity' [1994: 299], not to capitalism. Consequently, his solution to economic and racial inequality, including the intensifying exploitation of ethnicised or racialised workers, is the extension of rights and citizenship to everyone. There is a rich, flourishing archive of scholarly texts and discourses by Asian American lawyers [especially those engaged in 'critical race theory'] and activists devoted to this reform-minded approach, none of which has prevented the worsening inequality and anomic decay among Chinese, Filipinos, Vietnamese, Laotians, Kampucheans and Hmongs since the liberalisation of entry in 1965 [Hing 1998]. The prophylaxis of citizenship rights offered by Lowe, Takaki, Okihiro and others should be laid to rest by Natsu Taylor Saito's [2002; 2003] cogent argument that such belief in citizenship as the cure can only reinforce the state's systematic 'plenary power' over the others, especially in cases of immigrant persecution, dating back to the 1882 Exclusion Law. So we return to the analysis of the capitalist mode of production and reproduction as the enabling principle and legitimising guarantee of the racial polity [Meyerson 2000]" (San Juan 2010b).
4. Due to lack of space, San Juan's concluding sentiments on multiculturalism in response to an interview question by Michael Pozo on what students and professors in the field of cultural studies should think about on the subject, are worth noting, as follows:

> As I have argued in my earlier book, *Hegemony and Strategies of Transgression* (SUNY Press), multiculturalism has been appropriated to vindicate neo-liberal policies and instrumentalities. In short, the U.S. ruling class takes pride in the world hegemony of the United States because it is multicultural, diverse, open, sensitive to differences – difference as a guarantee of uniformity and democratic oneness. This

multiculturalism is an alibi for predatory globalization, which is the euphemism for the further extension of corporate exploitation everywhere. If this is multiculturalism, then we can all stop reading [Michel] Foucault and [Jacques] Lacan and instead go shopping and marvel at the infinite variety of multicultural goods – not just food but ideas, fashions, styles, images, simulacra, etc. [Jean] Baudrillard may still be right about the terrorism of the marketplace.

However, if multiculturalism signifies a sensitivity and openness to the Other so that the notion of identity is itself problematized – I am thinking here of Alain Badiou's critique of identity politics and alterity – I have no quarrel with such a program of genuine, creative multiculturalism.

Finally, I would like to reiterate that in all my works I try to apply a historical-materialist approach that considers human labor (both mental and physical) as the key to the critical transformation of society. It is a point of departure, not the answer to every question. In this I join other socialists and radicals working within the intellectual tradition of Benedict de Spinoza, Georg Lukacs, Antonio Gramsci, Rosa Luxemburg, Walter Benjamin, C.L.R. James, and others in advancing the cause of all those throughout the world who continue to be victimized by the "free market". Is there any other feasible alternative? (Pozo 2003, brackets added)

5. Through personal correspondence with this author, San Juan further clarifies and elaborates on his critique of postcolonialism and its practitioners, particularly with regard to their limitations with the historical materialist approach. San Juan writes: "Postcolonial studies" has been linked with Bhabha, Spivak and esp. the Australians Bill Ashcroft, etc. who exclude the Philippines and Latin American countries (except the Commonwealth Caribbean) from their research. So it is impossible to join Marxist critiques of imperialist/neocolonialist ideology and postcolonial views that the colonized peoples gained something from the colonizer, that is, they became mimicries or 'mimic men,' and thus were able to subvert the colonizer, or re-articulated the imperial discourse into something radical.

Postcolonial studies rejects the dialectic between modes of production and the cultural superstructures/ideology. They claim that culture either has nothing to do with modes of production; it has an autonomy that exceeds what they call economics or labor. In fact, Negri and Hardt (who echo some postcolonial dogmas) emphasize "immaterial labor" in the period of globalization, which means that "immaterial labor" refers to the realm of ideas, tastes, and attitudes. But what explains the changes in ideas, tastes, and attitudes? They avoid mentioning disparity of wealth, exploitation of the 99%, neocolonial interventions, etc. They might gesture to those, but they don't really integrate them as part of a structural or systematic explanation of historical changes. Their concept of historical change follows Foucault/Nietszche—change just drops from somewhere, irrational and mysterious.

My feeling is that while postcolonial studies, like women's studies, has become a safe comfortable domain of academic studies, it has lost relevance in understanding what's happening in the real world. Even Said rejected postcolonial studies because it cannot explain the US-Israeli destruction of Palestinian homeland and peoples.

"Some postcolonialists appeal to Fanon, C.L.R. James, even Cabral. But those guys rely on a strong Marxist framework, and are anchored to solid popular struggles in the colonies. While some Filipinos ape and echo Spivak and Bhabha, they cannot explain the severe impoverishment back home, and the continued domination of US ideas, values and tastes on the masses, through consumerism, mass media, fashions and styles, including of course academic modes of discourse and intellectual analysis." (San Juan 2015).

6. In a 1998 piece, entitled "The Limits of Postcolonial Criticism: The Discourse of Edward Said," San Juan suggested that Edward Said maintained a pretense to being a Marxist who has gone so far as to co-opt Marxists like Antonio Gramsci and C.L.R. James "to give an aura of leftism" but not for the purpose of "revitalizing historical materialism for revolutionary socialist goals." San Juan explains further: "The anti-Marxism of postcolonial theory may be attributed partly to Said's eclecticism, his belief that American left criticism is marginal, and his distorted if not wholly false understanding of Marxism based on doctrinaire anticommunism and the model of 'actually existing socialism' during the Cold War" (San Juan 1998).

7. Along these lines, noted public intellectual Henry Giroux notes: "State violence fueled by the merging of the war on terror, the militarization of all aspects of society, and a deep-seated and increasingly ruthless and unapologetic racism is now ubiquitous and should be labeled as a form of domestic terrorism. *Terrorism, torture, and state violence are no longer simply part of our history; they have become the nervous system of an increasingly authoritarian state*" (Giroux 2015, italics added).

8. Here, San Juan intervenes to clarify and provide context for James Baldwin's apparent conflicting positions on various situations and circumstances, creating an enigma that led some of his fellow contemporary Black leaders to criticize him including activists Eldridge Cleaver and Harold Cruse, while he himself felt critical of others, such as Aime Cesaire and his Negritude movement, and author Richard Wright. In a chapter on Baldwin in a 1995 book and by way of resolving this apparent enigma, San Juan explains: "Baldwin's predicament involves not a death-wish but the obsession with a dialectic of exchange where whites and blacks are positions imbricated in each other that

need to be sublated, not conflated, if racial conflict is to be resolved." Later in the chapter, San Juan acknowledges Baldwin's deep concern over the fate of his people, and elaborates as follows: "Baldwin now configures his people's situation in the context of the Cold War and the African anticolonial struggle. He identifies with the African desire for freedom, but refuses an Afrocentric transference. Here is where for Baldwin the American dream has turned into a nightmare 'on the private, domestic, and international levels,' where the United States has become the vindictive god of the Old Testament suppressing revolutions everywhere. Baldwin's belief in the United States as a possible utopian force is unshaken – but it is overturned by an existentialist faith that life is tragic. And this reality is for him what the black community represents. Whatever the ambiguities of Baldwin's formulations, his central argument is the fused or indivisible fate of all those caught in Du Bois' color boundary: 'The price of the liberation of the white people is the liberation of the blacks – the total liberation, in the cities, in the towns, before the law, and in the mind'… In this Imaginary register of the Double, Baldwin affirms the right of self-determination for all people of color as an organic part of a society-in-the-making, the New Jerusalem he envisioned arising from everyone taking responsibility for what's going on in the world. This was his utopian wager" (San Juan 1995).

9. Here is a sampling of James Baldwin's own words, transcribed by this author from an audio version of a speech delivered at the Claremont High School in Oakland, California in June 1963: "[I]n this country, every black man born in this country, until this present moment, is born into a country which assures him, in as many ways as it can find, that he is not worth the dirt he walks on. Every Negro boy and every Negro girl born in this country until this present moment undergoes the agony of trying to find in the body politic, in the body social, outside himself/herself, some image of himself or herself which is not demeaning. Now, many, indeed, have survived, and at an incalculable cost, and many more have perished and are perishing every day. If you tell a child and do your best to prove to the child that he is not worth life, it is entirely possible that sooner or later the child begins to believe it" (James Baldwin 20th Anniversary Commemoration….).

10. San Juan notes, in another 2009 essay, one of the revealing ironies in the convergence between the globalization of labor, particularly Filipino labor, the internationalization of US law, and the universalization of the so-called war on terror, and the ideology represented in the construction and maintenance of Guantanamo as a detention, prison, and torture facility. San Juan reacts to the impending visit to Guantanamo of Eric Holder, the top lawyer as Secretary of the Justice Department under much of the Obama Administration, in the following passage: "More revealing is Holder's planned visit to Guantanamo to inspect the facility for torturing 'unlawful combatants,'

which incidentally was partly built by cheap Filipino labor (Filipino contract labor also built US military barracks in Iraq. Guantanamo remains a symbol of what the U.S. stands for many "third world" countries or peoples who are considered enemies of democracy, the free market, and Samuel Huntington/Arthur Schlesinger's 'Western Civilization'" (San Juan 2009). The connections between Guantanamo and Abu Ghraib are palpable. Filipino contract workers—part of the global Filipino labor diaspora—have served in US military installations in Iraq and, in most probability including Abu Ghraib, as cooks, truck drivers, and maintenance workers. Also, as borne out by human rights lawyer Marjorie Cohn, torture, euphemistically referred to as enhanced interrogation methods developed at Guantanamo, have "migrated" to Abu Ghraib, as revealed by scandalous photos that leaked—and eventually partially released with official sanction by the Bush Administration in 2004. Subsequently, the first official internal investigation of human rights abuses at Abu Ghraib, as shown in these photographs, was led by US Army Major General Antonio Mario Taguba, of Filipino descent and a product of US military socialization in the Philippines. Taguba's findings, contained in a report that bore his name, i.e., the Taguba Report, implicated the Bush Administration in the same year with grave human rights abuses. In 2008, in the preface to the 2008 annual report by the Physicians for Human Rights, entitled *Broken Laws, Broken Lives*, Taguba expressed no doubt that the Bush Administration was guilty of committing, or has authorized the commission of, war crimes in the following passage: "[T]here is no longer any doubt as to whether the [Bush] Administration has committed war crimes. The only question that remains to be answered is whether those who ordered the use of torture will be held to account" (Physicians for Human Rights).

A caveat needs to be inserted at this juncture lest it be misinterpreted that Taguba's ascendancy and rise to one of the highest ranks in the US military would mean anything other than symbolic. The presence of Taguba, of course, would be promoted as a success of multiculturalism even though he was merely a token. San Juan has something so say on situations like this from a 2010 essay already quoted earlier but which is worth quoting from once more, as follows: "The fallacy of equating exploiter and exploited in order to ascribe agency/humanity to the subjugated but emotionally appealing victim vitiates many empirical studies of Filipino overseas migrant workers.... Supposedly novel in inventing agency for the colonised, this new epistemology in the disciplines of history and sociology interprets colonial domination as consensual negotiation between rulers and the ruled, reducing hegemony into an exercise in Habermasianesque rational communication. Polyculturalism thus becomes the alibi of imperialism that is suddenly capable of 'bad faith'" (San Juan 2010b).

The subject of state-sanctioned complex of torture, terror, and violence, including slavery obviously as a variant, and the justification thereof and resistance thereto, has, of course, been a recurrent theme in San Juan's writings including but not limited to, quite notably, his interrogation of the pathology and economic roots of torture and terror in Franz Kafka's outstanding body of works in a 2014 essay, entitled "Kafka & Torture: Deconstructing the Writing Apparatus of 'In the Penal Colony.'" In here, San Juan quotes Kafka as follows: "Capitalism is a system of dependencies, which run from within to without, from without to within, from above to below, from below to above. All is dependent, all stands in chains. Capitalism is a condition of the soul of the world." San Juan then stitches the essential threads connecting Kafka, Guantanamo, and Abu Ghraib in the following snippet: "Kafka's classic fable dramatizing corporeal hermeneutics might be salutary both to the victims and practitioners of torture (as Lundberg recently suggested [2013]), a heuristic baedeker to the ecology of a planet where prisons/penal institutions function as model internal colonies of which the Guantanamo Bay maximum-security cells comprise but one obsessive mirror-image. More instructive, the chief protagonist of Kafka's story, the explorer or traveler, is symptomatic of the vacillating if self-righteous mindset of liberals (should we say neoliberals?) whose weapon of methodological individualism becomes an apology for Abu Ghraib outrage, philanthropic rescue of veiled women, and mass drone killings. But let us first inquire into the contentious status of Kafka as the unrivaled icon of twentieth-century existentialist, apocalyptic modernism as well as fragmented, aleatory postmodernism" (San Juan 2014).

11. This US boycott, taken in sympathy with and effective support for the Zionist State's apartheid-like policies not only within the Zionist State itself, i.e., towards its own citizens of Palestinian descent with over sixty discriminatory statutes stacked against them, but also towards the Palestinians in the occupied territories under dispute which it continues to rule—or to besiege in the case of Gaza—militarily, enforcing, in the process, two sets of justice system—one for Jews preferentially and another for Palestinians discriminatorily—despite there being no war to fight and there being no army to fight against, except unarmed Palestinian civilians. With US support, the Zionist State has also successfully conflated anti-Zionism with anti-Semitism (exemplified by the introduction in 2017 in the US Senate of S.720, entitled Israel Anti-Lobby Act, as a means of deflecting criticisms against its expulsion and ethnic cleansing of the Palestinians and theft of their land and the resources therein, all in violation of existing international law. In a chapter examining the literary texts of FawazTurki, described by San Juan as "one of the most charismatic Third World intellectuals," San Juan sees hope in the "Palestinian courage and determination" that someday, the Palestinians will

"Return" to the land from which they have been rudely displaced beginning with the *nakba* (or *al-nakba*, catastrophe) brought about by the insertion of the Zionist State into Palestine in 1948 by largely European settlers aided by former colonial powers in the region, mainly Britain but also France. The "Return" has been and remains the theme of the largely peaceful weekly Palestinian Great March of Return which commenced in April 2018 that continues to this day. According to San Juan, Turki's "obsession with 'the Return' expressed itself in a seething anguish defined by communal rituals and shared familial memories." San Juan explains further the essence of this exile as follows: "The exile of the Palestinians embodies global contradictions that propel them forward, together with the entire Third World. Their hopes and dreams thus sprout from, and are rooted in, the concrete sociohistorical base of the Palestinian homeland" (San Juan 1994, pp. 63–64). Of Turki's poem, "Palestinians in Exile," San Juan's favorite among Turki's many poems, San Juan sees in it "the agony of desire for the Return metamorphoses into a craving for the beloved – a powerful erotic cry for a tryst long overdue, the unquenchable anguish 'between dream and nothingness' when chains and barbed wires will snap: 'Like lovers from Palestine,/agonizing over who is really in exile./they or their homeland" (San Juan 1994, p. 66).

References

Baraka, Ajamu, "Baltimore and the Human Right to Resistance", *Institute for Policy Studies*, April 30, 2015a. In: http://www.ips-dc.org/baltimore-and-the-human-right-to-resistance/.

———, "No 'Je Suis Charleston'?" *Counterpunch*, July 1, 2015b. In: http://www.counterpunch.org/2015/07/01/no-je-suis-charleston/.

Bauzon, Kenneth E., "Demonstration Elections and the Subversion of Democracy", *Argentine Center for International Studies (CAEI)*, IR Theory Program, December 2005. In: https://www.researchgate.net/publication/5005033_Demonstration_Elections_and_the_Subversion_of_Democracy.

———, "Secession in the Formal-Legalist Paradigm: Implications for Contemporary Revolutionary and Popular Movements in the Age of Neoliberal Globalization". Posted September 2014. In: https://www.academia.edu/8370651/Secession_in_the_Formal-Legalist_Paradigm_Implications_for_Contemporary_Revolutionary_and_Popular_Movements_in_the_Age_of_Neoliberal_Globalization.

———, *Liberalism and the Quest for Islamic Identity in the Philippines* (Durham, NC: Acorn Press in Association with Duke University Islamic and Arabian Development Studies, 1991), 219pp. Print.

Cabusao, Jeffrey Arellano, Review, "Racism and Cultural Studies: Critiques of Multiculturalist Ideology and the Politics of Difference", *Culture Logic, an Electronic Journal of Marxist Theory & Practice*, 8 (January 2005): 4. In: http://clogic.eserver.org/2005/cabusao.html.

Coates, Ta-Nehisi, Interview on *Democracy Now!* With Amy Goodman and Juan Gonzalez on July 22, 2015. In: http://www.democracynow.org/2015/7/22/between_the_world_and_me_ta.

Giroux, Henry A., "Neoliberalism as Public Pedagogy", *Academia.edu*. Posted on March 31, 2011. In: https://www.academia.edu/12795711/Neoliberalism_as_public_pedagogy.

———, "Neoliberalism's War on Democracy", *Truthout*, April 26, 2014. In: http://www.truth-out.org/opinion/item/23306-neoliberalisms-war-on-democracy#a6.

———, "The Racist Killing Fields in America: The Death of Sandra Bland", *Academia.edu*. Posted on July 19, 2015. In: https://www.academia.edu/14196417/The_Racist_Killing_Fields_in_America_The_Death_of_Sandra_Bland.

Pozo, Michael, "A Conversation with E. San Juan Jr.". With Introduction and Interview by Michael Pozo, *St. John's University Humanities Review*, 1, 2 (April 2003). In: http://facpub.stjohns.edu/~ganterg/sjureview/vol1-2/juan.html.

San Juan, E., Jr., *From the Masses, to the Masses: Third World Literature and Revolution* (Minneapolis, MN: MEP Publications/University of Minnesota, 1994), 197pp. Print.

———, *Hegemony and Strategies of Transgression: Essays in Cultural Studies and Comparative Literature* (Albany, NY: State University of New York Press, 1995), 286pp.

———, *Beyond Postcolonial Theory* (New York: St. Martin's Press, 1998), 325pp. Print.

———, "Race from the 20th to the 21st Century: Multiculturalism or Emancipation?" *Against the Current*, 78 (January–February, 1999). *Solidarity: A Socialist, Feminist, Anti-racist Organization*. In: https://solidarity-us.org/node/1757.

———, "Imperial Terror, Neo-Colonialism, and the Filipino Diaspora". A Lecture Delivered at the 2003 English Department Lecture series at St. John's University. *St. John's University Humanities Review*, 2, 1 (Fall 2003a). In: http://facpub.stjohns.edu/~ganterg/sjureview/vol2-1/diaspora.html.

———, "Marxism and the Race/Class Problematic". Originally published in *Cultural Logic* (2003b). In: http://clogic.eserver.org/2003/sanjuan.html.

———, "Post-9/11 Reflections on Multiculturalism and Racism", *Axis of Logic: Finding Clarity in the 21st Century Mediaplex* (November 13, 2004). In: http://www.axisoflogic.com/artman/publish/Article_13554.shtml.

———, "Edward Said's Affiliations: Secular Humanism and Marxism", *Atlantic Studies: Global Currents*, 3, 1 (2006): 43–61. In: http://www.tandfonline.com/doi/abs/10.1080/14788810500525481?journalCode=rjas20.

———, *In the Wake of Terror; Class, Race, Nation, Ethnicity in the Postmodern World* (Lanham, MD: Lexington Books, 2007), 232pp.

———, "Race and Class in Post-9/11 U.S. Empire", *Rizal Archive Blogspot*, April 30, 2009. In: http://rizalarchive.blogspot.com/2009/04/race-and-class-in-post-911-us-empire.html.

———, "African American Internationalism and Solidarity with the Philippine Revolution", *Socialism and Democracy*, 24, 2 (July 2010a): 32–65. In: http://www.tandfonline.com/eprint/Jqxa3MbH6e8pXFCcAHb9/full#.VcjchPlUWUF.

———, "From Genealogy to Inventory: The Situation of Asian American Studies in the Age of the Crisis of Global Finance Capital", *International Journal of Asia Pacific Studies*, 6, 1 (January 2010b): 47–75. In: http://ijaps.usm.my/wp-content/uploads/2012/06/Genealogy.pdf.

———, "History, Literature, and the Politics of Time". Presentation delivered at the University of the Philippines, Visaya, on February 4, 2014 (2014). In: http://rizalarchive.blogspot.com/2014/01/lualhati-bautistas-desaparecidos-andres.html.

———, Personal Email Correspondence with Kenneth E. Bauzon, June 29, 2015.

CHAPTER 8

Teleology in History and Intellectual Responsibility

> Contrary to some pundits of deconstruction, I believe that the subaltern… can perform the role of witnesses to "speak truth to power." For indigenous, oppressed peoples anywhere, the purpose of speech is not just for universally accepted cultural reasons – affirming their identities and their right to self-determination – but, more crucially, for their physical survival. Such speech entails responsibility, hence the need to respond to criticisms or questions about "truth" and its grounding. A warning by Walter Benjamin (1968) may be useful to clarify the notion of "truth" in lived situations where "facts" intermesh with feeling and conviction. In his famous "Theses on the Philosophy of History," Benjamin expressed reservations about orthodox historians such as Leopold von Ranke, whom Marx considered "a little root-grubber" who reduced history to "facile anecdote-mongering and the attribution of all great events to petty and mean causes." Benjamin speculated that the "truth" of the past can be seized only as an image, as a memory "as it flashes up at the moment of danger." I believe that this moment of danger is always with us when, in a time of settling accounts in the name of justice, we see the Mays [Note: In reference to US-based historian Glenn May and his ilk belittling the role of Andres Bonifacio in the Philippine Revolution, in his 1996 book Inventing a Hero: The Posthumous Re-Creation of Andres Bonifacio.] and their ilk suddenly come up with their credentials and entitlements in order to put the "upstart" natives in their proper place.
> E. San Juan, *After Postcolonialism…* (2000)

The Contemporary State of the World

After over five-hundred years of capitalist growth and expansion, over a hundred years of the United States as a global empire, over half a century of accelerated, post-World War II neoliberal hegemony, over two decades since the end of the Cold War, and over a decade since 9/11 and the declaration of the so-called war on terror, what are some of the identifiable markers that characterize the period in which we live, and the state of the planet we inhabit at this point in time, having been proclaimed supposedly as the endpoint of history? In plain language, what do we have to show for the much-vaunted progress anticipated as a result of Enlightenment-inspired Western-led science- and technology-based civilization?

Unprecedented Global Inequality

To find some answers, one may start with a recent publication from the United Nations Development Programme (UNDP), entitled *Humanity Divided; Confronting Inequality in Developing Countries* (2013). In its overview, the UNDP notes an interesting paradox in global development in that, while during the last few decades "the world witnessed impressive average gains against multiple indicators of material prosperity..., more than 1.2 billion people still live in extreme poverty. The richest 1 percent of the world population owns more than 40 percent of the world's assets, while the bottom half owns no more than 1 percent" (UNDP). The UNDP study goes on to offer the following sobering assessment:

> Nor are recent trends very encouraging. Over the last two decades, income inequality has been growing on average within and across countries. As a result, a significant majority of the world's population lives in societies that are more unequal today than 20 years ago. Remarkably, in many parts of the world, income gaps have deepened—and, with them, the gulf in quality of life between the rich and the poor—despite the immense wealth created through impressive growth performances. In fact, the sharpest increases in income inequality have occurred in those developing countries that were especially successful in pursuing vigorous growth and managed, as a result, to graduate into higher income brackets. Economic progress in these countries has not alleviated disparities, but rather exacerbated them. (UNDP)

Further, the UNDP study links inequality to the failure to enjoy—or, rather, the absence of—ancillary services which society needs to maintain a decent and meaningful existence. It also implicates it as a major factor in the perpetuation of conflict which, in turn, contributes to social disintegration. As the study reads, in part:

> The world is more unequal today than at any point since World War II. However, there are clear signs that this situation cannot be sustained for much longer. Inequality has been jeopardizing economic growth and poverty reduction. It has been stalling progress in education, health and nutrition for large swathes of the population, thus undermining the very human capabilities necessary for achieving a good life. It has been limiting opportunities and access to economic, social and political resources. Furthermore, inequality has been driving conflict and destabilizing society. When incomes and opportunities rise for only a few, when inequalities persist over time and space and across generations, then those at the margins, who remain so consistently excluded from the gains of development, will at some point contest the "progress" that has bypassed them. Growing deprivations in the midst of plenty and extreme differences between households are almost certain to unravel the fabric that keeps society together. This is especially problematic when we consider that, often, it is precisely those at the margins who tend to pay the biggest price for social unrest. But perhaps most important, extreme inequality contradicts the most fundamental principles of social justice, starting from the notion, enshrined in the Universal Declaration of Human Rights, that "all human beings are born free and equal in dignity and rights". (UNDP)

Lest the UNDP is mistrusted as a United Nations agency, reports from various other quarters during recent years and months have actually been echoing or complementing the same concern. One such report is by OXFAM International which, at the end of 2014, issued a timely report entitled *Even It Up; Time to End Extreme Inequality*. A press release issued in January 2015 headlined "Richest 1% will own more than the rest by 2016" (OXFAM 2014). The press release reads, in part:

> ...the richest 1 percent have seen their share of global wealth increase from 44 percent in 2009 to 48 percent in 2014 and at this rate will be more than 50 percent in 2016. Members of this global elite had an average wealth of $2.7 million per adult in 2014.
> Of the remaining 52 percent of global wealth, almost all (46 percent) is owned by the rest of the richest fifth of the world's population. The other 80 percent share just 5.5 percent and had an average wealth of $3.851 per adult – that's 1/7000th of the average wealth of the 1 percent. (OXFAM 2014)

And, in the Executive Summary of the report itself, OXFAM emphasizes the inevitable link between economic inequality, on the one hand, and global poverty, on the other; further, it makes reference to the all-important "rules and systems" that have resulted to these conditions, indicating that these are a man-made set of phenomena and not a result of some sort of "Invisible Hand." The summary reads, in part, as follows:

> Crucially, the rapid rise of extreme economic inequality is standing in the way of eliminating global poverty. Today, hundreds of millions of people are living without access to clean drinking water and without enough food to feed their families, many are working themselves into the ground just to get by. ...
> [P]overty and inequality are not inevitable or accidental, but the result of deliberate policy choices. Inequality can be reversed. The world needs concerted action to build a fairer economic and political system that values everyone. The rules and systems that have led to today's inequality explosion much change. (OXFAM 2014)

Five years since the above-cited OXFAM report was issued, OXFAM issued another study, entitled *Public Good or Private Wealth* (2019) wherein it states:

> The number of billionaires has doubled since the financial crisis and their fortunes grow by $2.5bn a day, yet the super-rich and corporations are paying lower rates of tax than they have in decades. The human costs – children without teachers, clinics without medicines – are huge. Piecemeal private services punish poor people and privilege elites. Women suffer the most, and are left to fill the gaps in public services with many hours of unpaid care". (OXFAM 2019)

Again, if one looks at and collates readily available data, including those presented above, it is not hard to confirm that, in fact, since the early 1980s, we have seen the income of the bottom 90% of the globe's population decline steadily, and that this decline continues, while that of the top 1% has accelerated at an obscene rate, and continues to grow.

The Environmental Crisis

Perhaps a problem of greater magnitude and urgency than inequality and poverty is the one concerning the environment. The term "global environmental problem" is a comprehensive, catch-all phrase that encompasses all ancillary problems related to human-induced destruction, degradation, abuse, misuse, and benign neglect of the environmental commons, and how these problems constitute a large part of what has been termed the post-industrial or, sometimes by others, the post-capitalist age.

However, although the problem of global warming has been mentioned as a major concern—attributed largely to the use of fossil fuel whose unchecked carbon emission into the atmosphere has been identified by scientists as a major factor in such phenomena as atmospheric temperature rise; unprecedented rise in sea level threatening coastal areas and island-nations; melting of the Arctic ice cap, and the onset of extreme weather patterns affecting parts or regions of the globe unaccustomed to these new weather patterns, e.g., unseasonable extreme heat or extreme cold, thus contributing, further, to the onset of diseases, acidification of oceans, the destruction of crops, unseasonal migration of wildlife, food riots, and of the emergence of what has been labeled as climate refugees, among others, there are, in fact, various other areas of concern, much of which are likewise human-induced. These would include the clearcutting of forests, mountaintop removal, monoculture agricultural practices, chemical-dependent industrial agriculture, commercial deep-sea trawling, pollution/depletion of freshwater supply, soil erosion, deforestation, desertification, population pressure on food sources, proliferation of landfills, rise of slum cities, and many, many others all of which cumulatively and ultimately contribute to the imbalance of the ecosystem or compromise biodiversity or impair the economic viability especially of the poorer members of the community to survive, or rise in violence in presumably safe communities.

Canadian journalist and activist Naomi Klein has called attention to much of these concerns in her recent book, *This Changes Everything: Capitalism vs. the Climate* (2014). Klein elaborates on much of the problems identified above, and she also raises a number of very important points regarding the factors giving rise to them. One of these is what she refers to as the extractivist model of economic development, a version of capitalism in which, Klein argues, the profit-motive is dependent on "the large-scale removal (or 'extraction') of natural resources for the purposes of exporting raw materials." By its very nature, extractivism is "nonreciprocal dominance based on relationship with the earth. It is the opposite of stewardship, which involves taking but also taking care that regeneration and future life continue" (Klein). Klein's assertion on the role of extractivism as an approach that privileges private profit over environmental sustainability in explaining the despoliation of the environment, unfortunately, is merely the frontal manifestation of a philosophy, ingrained at the heart of capitalism's contemporary morphed manifestation, neoliberalism, which essentially elevates the commodification and exploitation of the commons to a new level, i.e., through a full-court press using as instruments a set of integrated neoliberal global institutions—trading, financial, media, legal, private economic, and/or foreign policy (such as the World Economic Forum, the Trilateral Commission, and the Bilderberg Group), and including use of such covert agents as economic hit-men, including outright sanctions and/or force, on recalcitrant countries, as described earlier, among others; and legitimized and validated, further, by a set of governing principles, rules, and practices—all to facilitate and accelerate private gain and, by extension, the global hegemony of the industrial and military powers of North America, Western Europe, and Japan. Unfortunately, those who adhere to this system, representing largely the corporate community and governments under its sway, have been dominant particularly in asserting the primacy of this system. Their domination and control over the media have made it possible for their own narrative—that this system redounds to the benefit of all in society—to suffuse to the rest of society with hardly any challenge.

Giving recognition to this travail has not just been Klein or the thousands of environmentalists who participated in the mammoth march for the environment—dubbed as the People's Climate March—in New York City in September 2014. In fact, no less than Pope Francis himself has taken notice of this, in his courageous encyclical, entitled *Laudato Si'* (in medieval Italian, meaning "Praise be to you!"), with the subtitle "On care of the Common Home," issued in May 2015. With the assistance of the pontifical academies and a significant number honorary experts and climate scientists from around the globe invited into help formulate the final draft, Pope Francis notes the plunder that has taken in the air, the soil, and the water, in paragraph 2 of this encyclical as follows:

> We have come to see ourselves as her lords and masters, entitled to plunder her at will. The violence present in our hearts, wounded by sin, is also reflected in the symptoms of sickness evident in the soil, in the water, in the air and in all forms of life. This is why the earth herself, burdened and laid waste,

is among the most abandoned and maltreated of our poor; she "groans in travail" [*Rom* 8:22]. (Pope Francis)

On the particular issue of climate change, Pope Francis notes that this is one of the most important challenges facing mankind today. He notes that its worst impact is felt in developing countries where "many of the poor live in areas particularly affected by phenomena related to warming, and their means of subsistence are largely dependent on natural reserves and ecosystemic services such as agriculture, fishing and forestry." He also notes the rise in human migration, referred to in the mainstream media as climate refugees, "from the growing poverty caused by environmental degradation [but which] are not recognized by international conventions as refugees [and] bear the loss of the lives they have left behind."

On a number of references, Pope Francis leaves no doubt about the culpability of the dominant economic system—capitalism and its neoliberal manifestation, along with its concomitant principles and policies—in creating and exacerbating much of the environmental problems mankind faces today. Several particular passages are herewith quoted to illustrate this point. In paragraph 32, Pope Francis notes that "[t]he earth's resources are also being plundered because of short-sighted approaches to the economy, commerce, and production." In paragraph 45, he refers in particular to class divisions signified by the rise of gated communities and declares: "In some places, rural and urban alike, the privatization of certain spaces has restricted people's access to places of particular beauty. In others, 'ecological' neighbourhoods have been created which are closed to outsiders in order to ensure an artificial tranquility. Frequently, we find beautiful and carefully manicured green spaces in so-called 'safer' areas of cities, but not in the more hidden areas where the disposable of society live." In paragraph 52, he acknowledges what many victims of structural adjustment programs imposed by the World Bank and the IMF have already known for years, and that is that "[t]he foreign debt of poor countries has become a way of controlling them..," complemented by another phrase, from paragraph 56 in which he states that "economic powers continue to justify the current global system wherein priority tends to be given to speculation and the pursuit of financial gain, which fail to take the context into account, let alone the effects on human dignity and the natural environment." And, finally, in defense of the commons, described earlier in this essay as under steady assault toward commodification on the part of the free marketeers,

Pope Francis makes the important affirmation in, paragraph 93, quoted in part below, that:

> Whether believers or not, we are agreed today that the earth is essentially a shared inheritance, whose fruits are meant to benefit everyone. For believers, this becomes a question of fidelity to the Creator, since God created the world for everyone. Hence every ecological approach needs to incorporate a social perspective which takes into account the fundamental rights of the poor and the underprivileged. The principle of the subordination of private property to the universal destination of goods, and thus the right of everyone to their use, is a golden rule of social conduct and "the first principle of the whole ethical and social order".[71] The Christian tradition has never recognized the right to private property as absolute or inviolable, and has stressed the social purpose of all forms of private property. Saint John Paul II forcefully reaffirmed this teaching, stating that "God gave the earth to the whole human race for the sustenance of all its members, *without excluding or favouring anyone*". (Pope Francis)

It should be pointed out here that Pope Francis is not disavowing capitalism per se. He has received sustained criticisms from various quarters for his stance on specific ancillary issues, e.g., population control; source and degree of carbon emission particularly on the respective roles of humans; of science; of theology; and of government; among others. Vocal criticisms have come particularly from climate change deniers, free market advocates, and politicians and pundits who assert that Pope Francis should not get involved in matters of public policy. Again, in paragraph 93, he affirms—in agreement with Pope John Paul II before him—that "the Church does indeed defend the legitimate right to private property," but that this defense of private property is premised on the idea—as a matter of "first principle"—and here, directly referring to the inequitable distribution of the world's income favoring the globe's Top 1%—that "there is always a social mortgage on all private property, in order that goods may serve the general purpose that God gave them" (As noted in Note [74] of Laudato Si). Consequently, he maintained, "it is not in accord with God's plan that this gift be used in such a way that its benefits favour only a few." The issues that he touched upon in his encyclical are issues for mankind as a whole to deal with on an urgent basis, that these are moral issues, and that governments alone would be unable, nay, helpless, to tackle these issues by themselves without them (a) deriving support and legitimacy from society at large, and, (b) reorienting their direction and priorities.

Unfortunately, even as the Pope rallies the global community to support his environmental initiative, corporate interests are cashing in on the growing popularity of this movement by inserting themselves, for example, in the UN decision-making process in the pursuit of the UN's Sustainable Development Goals (SDGs), particularly concerning such critical issues as poverty, hunger, and climate change, appearing progressive but, in fact, setting back the process by coopting it. To observers like this writer, the Pope's encyclical is an essential complement to international initiatives such as those being taken by intergovernmental organizations like the UN. However, *Insurge Intelligence*, a crowd-funded, grassroots-oriented independent media project, reports of a concerning—or disconcerting—development, as follows:

> But records from the SDG process reveal that insiders at the heart of the UN's intergovernment engagement negotiations have criticised the international body for pandering to the interests of big business and ignoring recommendations from grassroots stakeholders representing the world's poor.
>
> Formal statements issued earlier this year as part of the UN's Post-2015 Intergovernmental Negotiations on the SDGs, and published by the UN Sustainable Development Division, show that UN 'Major Groups' representing indigenous people, civil society, workers, young people and women remain deeply concerned by the general direction of the SDG process — whereas corporate interests from the rich, industrialised world have viewed the process favourably.
>
> Among the 'Major Groups' engaged in the UN's SDG process is 'Business and Industry.' Members of this group include fossil fuel companies like Statoil USA and Tullow Oil, multinational auto parts manufacturer Bridgestone Corporation, global power management firm Eaton Corporation, agribusiness conglomerate Monsanto, insurance giant Thamesbank, financial services major Bank of America, and hundreds of others from Coca Cola to Walt Disney to Dow Chemical.
>
> These interests have showered the UN's SDG agenda with glowing praise — calling only for the need for further engagement with business and industry.
>
> In its 24th July statement before one UN SDG review meeting, the <u>Global Business Alliance</u> — set-up by corporations to represent their mutual commitment to "market-based solutions" — proudly told delegates that the process "amplifies our traditional role in economic growth and innovation" and commended the SDG draft:
>
> "An important role for business is recognized throughout". (Ahmed)

Thus, it seems evident that even the best intentions by leading personalities and institutions like Pope Francis and the UN, respectively, are not immune from subversion or cooptation by the "few" whom he criticized in his encyclical as being intent on preserving their control over the levers of economic power and, by extension, political power. It is this seemingly incorrigible profit-orientation of the capitalist system that has led Pope Francis to make the following statement, made in Bolivia during a visit there in July 2015, highly critical of this economic system and, in so doing, associated himself with an important characterization made by an important figure of the Church, Basil of Caesarea:

> Time, my brothers and sisters, seems to be running out; we are not yet tearing one another apart, but we are tearing apart our common home. Today, the scientific community realizes what the poor have long told us: harm, perhaps irreversible harm, is being done to the ecosystem. The earth, entire peoples and individual persons are being brutally punished. And behind all this pain, death and destruction there is the stench of what Basil of Caesarea called "the dung of the devil". An unfettered pursuit of money rules. The service of the common good is left behind. Once capital becomes an idol and guides people's decisions, once greed for money presides over the entire socioeconomic system, it ruins society, it condemns and enslaves men and women, it destroys human fraternity, it sets people against one another and, as we clearly see, it even puts at risk our common home. (Plis; "Unbridled capitalism...")

This is particularly true over the issue of migration which Pope Francis has referred to with particular concern in his encyclical. While part of this "few" may be directly implicated in the devastation of the environment, another part of this same group may also be held responsible for creating and sustaining the conditions that allowed for global migration—and exploitation—of labor at various stages in the evolution of the global economic system. San Juan describes this pattern as follows:

> After about four centuries of the worldwide circulation of commodities - including the hugely profitable trade in slaves from Africa that inaugurated, for Marx, the "rosy dawn" of capitalism - the stage was set for more intense capital accumulation based no longer on commercial exchange and the regional discrepancies in the price of goods but on the process of production itself. "Place" gave way to space; lived time divided into necessary, surplus, and "free" segments. Linked by relations of exchange governed by

the logic of accumulation centered in Europe and later in North America, the trajectories of peoples of color, the "people without history" in Eric Wolfs reckoning, entered the global labor market with the expansion of industrial capitalism, the commercialization of agriculture, urbanization, and the concomitant dislocation and displacement of populations from their traditional homelands. (San Juan 1997)

San Juan explains that the demand for the global labor market has not abated. If at all, it has intensified but that the problems attendant to it, as shall be explained below, have also exacerbated. San Juan adds:

> We are still in the epoch of transnational migrations and the traffic in bodies. The breakup of the Soviet Union and Yugoslavia, plus the exacerbated ethnic/racial conflicts in their wake, promise mutations less tractable than the configurations of earlier boundary shifts. (San Juan 1997)

Recapping Neoliberalism's Rules, and Implications

Neither time nor space would allow at this time to rehearse fully the rules and systems alluded to in the OXFAM study. These have been discussed, to an extent, in a preceding chapter above. Suffice it to highlight at this point the following features of contemporary neoliberal globalization as having played, in this author's view, the most significant role in creating this inequality and, hence, the endemic global poverty that we see all around. The principles of neoliberal globalization include: (a) privatization; (b) deregulation; (c) trade liberalization; and, (d) militarization. Very simply, these principles favor the rich and the powerful, either as persons or as artificial, man-made, fictional entities, e.g., corporations. The principle of privatization is designed to divest public, service-delivery institutions, e.g., government and/or any of its public service delivery organs (health care, housing, education, etc.) of their functions and transfer the same to private, profit-oriented entities that claim to deliver these services under the guise of efficiency but for a fee. It fulfills the function of commodifying the commons for the profit of the few and at the expense of the many. Additionally, these entities, in claiming to provide these services, more often than not also claim the privilege of receiving subsidies from the government presumably to aid them in providing these services.

The principle of deregulation, on the other hand, is designed to eliminate rules and regulations, which may have been originally put in place, through the democratic process, in order to safeguard public health, public safety, public welfare, including that of the natural environment, but which the business/corporate community has complained against as being too onerous to enforce, or that they cut into their profits, or, otherwise provide, in their view, undue encumbrance to their competitiveness. Deregulation also comes in two other guises: (a) one, as simply non-enforcement of an existing rule or a regulation by an agency that has been lobbied against (heavily in many cases) by private, often pro-corporate lobbying groups, and, (b) enforcement of a rule that has been enacted despite public interest, in order to cater to private interest. The deregulation that we have witnessed over the last forty years has been possible only because the state itself has been transformed into a neoliberal one, coming under the control of officials whose election into office have heavily depended on corporate campaign contributions with little or no restrictions under the guise of free speech, one which serves largely as a conduit for public funds for private benefit.

Trade liberalization, as third principles herein identified is supposed to combat protectionism, deemed to be a bad word as i t is sen as a barrier to free trade. The assumption here is that there should be free and unhampered exchange of goods and services—but not labor—across national borders. Thus, trade barriers, direct or indirect, should be eliminated with the consequent effect that domestic laws, rules, and regulations originally intended to protect and shield domestic producers from foreign competition, or to protect certain domestic industries as a means of helping them grow and flourish, or to protect and conserve certain domestic resources from foreign exploitation, are now up for elimination. To enforcers of global trading rules within the WTO, this is seen as a positive step toward the harmonization of domestic laws with global trading rules. However, one does not need to think hard that the implication of this principle is dire for domestic producers, now denied any protection or any assistance from their government who would now have to compete with well-funded, well-organized foreign competitors that may, more likely than not, receive subsidies from their own government, e.g., the United States, that subsidizes its corporations, and provides them with cheap loans for their investments and operations through the Export-Import Bank, and low-cost insurance through the OPIC, all designed for no other purpose than to pry open the so-called emerging economies of the Third World for exploitation and use (Bauzon 2000).

Finally, the principle of militarization is not a formally recognized principle of neoliberal globalization, but it is, in practice, the ultimate hammer over the heads of states that defy the above-principles. Militarization and neoliberal globalization have been intertwined, by law, as dictated to by Article XXI of the WTO's Charter (WTO Charter, Article XXI). This article provides so-called exceptions to member states allowing them to allocate domestic budget for purposes of arms production and defense. In effect, it allows member states to provide subsidies to their arms industry if the intended goal is to enhance that member state's security. However, because the interpretation is loose as to what "security" means, this has given advantage to the traditional military powers, whose respective military establishments have been among the worst polluters and transgressors of sovereignty of weaker states, and violators of human rights around the world, led by the United States to build their arsenal, feed money into their respective military-industrial complexes, and traffic in arms worldwide, contributing to endless cycle of conflicts. "Security" has, in fact, the common alibi used by the United States to apply a whole range of options involving the use of force from the routine application of sanctions and embargoes against states not so much for violations of international law but because the latter's policies do not conform with those of the United States, to assassinations of leaders or otherwise the overthrow of their governments through coups or outright invasions simply because they have resources coveted by the United States. The casualness with which the United States has exercised these options around the world as though god-given prerogative especially since the end of World War II is matched by the hubris with which the US Special Operations Command has published, in May 2019, a document entitled *Support to Resistance: Strategic Purpose and Effectiveness*, through the Joint Special Operations University (O'Connor). Note that the traditional meaning of the term "resistance," as understood in the report, has been hijacked and its meaning subverted so that it would mean resistance not to US imperialism as in the case with anti-colonial and anti-capitalist movements traditionally but, rather, in reactionary support of this imperialism; it is a coopted resistance in the service of imperialism on the part of an assortment of surrogate groups, e.g., the Contras in Nicaragua, the Taliban and the *al-Qaeda* in Afghanistan, and the right-wing UNITA [*Unico Nacional para Independencia Total de Angola*] faction in Angola, etc., that it has funded, trained, armed, managed, and directed which the United States has, at one time or another, used and, in some cases, continues to use, as tools with which to undermine, intimidate, pressure, or, otherwise, overthrow a regime it does not like or which shows any hint at all of challenging America's hegemony. Another Orwellian feature of this notion of resistance is that it is, in fact, being used offensively against targets that have not harmed the United States but which are self-determining and, without much intending to other than wanting to be left alone and forge their own future, happen to stand in the way of America's predatory imperialist agenda. This attests to the subjective construction of terrorism or the enemy so that its definition suits one's expedient needs at a given moment in time. By this Orwellian definition—which would otherwise be deemed as terrorism by the targeted sovereign and legally constituted states and as construed under universally accepted principles of international law—these identified patterns of US behavior are normalized, and the US expects the rest of the world to go along. It matters little whether the International Court of Justice (or World Court in popular parlance) has already rendered a decision in 1986 in a case filed before it by the Sandinista Government of Nicaragua, which, in effect pronounced the United States as both a terrorist state and a terrorist-aiding state by its establishment, management, and arming of the Contra thugs during the 1980s; the Contras have engaged in untold acts of violence, e.g., destruction of civilian infrastructure, disruption of agricultural production, assassination of public officials, and Sandinista supporters and sympathizers, including in drug trafficking to boot, all designed to undermine the Sandinista government (International Court of Justice). By the above-mentioned study's definition, the list of countries targeted for disruption includes Russia and China today because these two countries, according to the report's principal author, "have boldly demonstrated expansionist tendencies," assuming that America's own expansion throughout the past century and more is normal, a prerogative that belongs only to itself and no other (As quoted in O'Connor).

US Militarism and the Threat of Nuclear Annihilation

It is not an exaggeration to say that, at this stage of human history, the other danger that poses the greatest challenge to human survival—in addition to the environmental crisis discussed above—remains the threat of reckless and final war imposed by the United States on the rest of the world, simply because it can, or as an irrational response to a perceived foreign threat. Neoliberal rules have allowed this happen, it is an instinctive behavior on the part of empires at their peak in their drive for economic and geostrategic dominance, and there is no single state—neither Russia nor China, whose respective military is largely designed for defensive purposes—that can deter it. This threat of a nuclear holocaust is recognized by no less than Renata Dwan, currently the Director of the UN Institute for Disarmament Research who warned that "[a] nuclear doomsday looms closer as the risk of atomic war is at its highest since World War Two" ("Risk of Nuclear War").

Providing much validation to the history recounted in this work, a history punctuated by the deliberate and sustained drive of the US empire for expansion and hegemony, an empire that is neither accidental nor abstract. The fact that a resident in the White House today promises to make this empire great again is incidental; the "greatness" envisioned in this slogan has been and remains founded on the same principles and practices that brought about what Marx, the great seer, has described as the "rosy dawn" of capitalism complete with its accouterment of violence, and its victims—including the would-be victims—have therefore no illusion about their fate. Neoliberal globalization, as has been described throughout this work and recapped in this concluding chapter, is set up comprehensively to accomplish these. Its comprehensive set of principles, rules, institutions, and practices are designed to privatize and commodify the commons without regard for the common good but all for accumulation of private profit; they are especially stacked against the multitude, mainly those in the Third World but also against the bulk of the population in the First and Second Worlds whose prosperity, confidence, and security they have enjoyed since the end World War II have now been steadily eroded and undermined by the unprecedented greed they have witnessed in their lifetime, thanks to relentless and systematic drive to privatize public assets and services, and deregulate and nullify commonsensical laws. For those still with fond hope and trust that this empire as currently constituted will somehow reform itself and adhere to its supposed founding enlightened liberal and humane principles, Francis Boyle, Professor of International Law at the University of Illinois, Urbana-Champaign, offers a needed historical context—and advice—with palpable comparisons between current and previous US behavior as follows:

Historically, the latest eruption of American militarism in the 21st century is akin to that of America opening the 20th Century by means of the U.S.-instigated Spanish-American War in 1898. The then Republican administration of President William McKinley grabbed their colonial empire from Spain in Cuba, Puerto Rico, Guam, and the Philippines, inflicted a near-genocidal war against the Filipino people; while at the same time illegally annexing the Kingdoms of Hawaii and subjecting the Native Hawaiian people... to genocidal conditions. Additionally, McKinley's military and colonial expansion into the Pacific was also designed to secure America's economic exploitation of China pursuant to the euphemistic rubric of the "open door" policy.

....

Today a century later, the serial imperial aggression launched, waged, and menaced by the neoconservative Republican Bush, Junior administration, then the neoliberal Democratic Obama administration and now the reactionary Trump administration threaten to set off World War III". (Boyle)

The institutional support that provides the enforcement mechanism for the aforementioned neoliberal rules and principles has been placed at the virtual disposal of the United States. These include: (a) the World Trade Organization as the clearinghouse for all global trading activities, providing even mechanisms for conflict resolution which serve as unelected, pseudo-judicial body whose decisions are final even against sovereign governments; (b) regional trading organizations, e.g., the North American Free Trade Agreement (NAFTA) between the United States, Canada, and Mexico; and the contemplated, highly secretive, and much-criticized Trans-Pacific Partnership (TPP); (c) the World Bank and the IMF which impose conditionalities, under the guise of so-called Structural Adjustment Programs (SAPs), on borrowing countries while providing a pretext for the pre-determination of domestic economic policies and, thus, preempt the sovereignty, of the borrowing country, from the outside.

The rules of neoliberal globalization are contained in the charters of various trading regimes agreed upon by the participating member states. These are enforceable as law on all member states of, say, the WTO, or any regional trading organization like the NAFTA, or on any state that has officially signed to borrow funds and agree to the terms of the Structural Adjustment Program (SAP) offered by a public global financial organization, e.g., the World Bank, and the International Monetary Fund (IMF); or any banking consortium, e.g., the European Central Bank (ECB), or the Paris Club. In practice, these SAPs have become a Trojan Horse that allowed these lending institutions to predetermine and preempt the sovereign internal decision-making process of borrowing states because not only do these SAPs bind the latter states to agree beforehand to the conditionalities, e.g., deregulation of utilities, privatization of services, sale of public assets, administrative and governmental reforms, etc., they also agree beforehand to regular monitoring and oversight to ensure compliance.

Further, the nature of the SAPs is dictated by the general policy direction preferred by the leading members of these funding institutions due to built-in rules that favor the wealthy members whose voting rights within these institutions are guaranteed under the so-called weighted voting system. This system assures the same percentage of votes as the percentage of financial contributions by the members to the general fund. This perennially favors the wealthy members while it also perennially subjects weaker borrowing states to bondage. Periodic debt servicing remittances by the weaker borrowing states ensure sacrificing social programs under threat of delinquency or bankruptcy. During the 1970s and 1980s, when money was relatively cheap to lend, many loans were taken out by authoritarian leaders, many friendly to the United States and who were encouraged to purchase military hardware to boost their rule, benefiting the US-based arms industry in the process. When many of these dictators were overthrown, succeeding governments, e.g., Corazon Aquino of the Philippines in 1986, was reticent to declaring these debts odious and, instead, carried on with loan re-payments, saddling generations of their citizens yet to be born with these debts.

While the neoliberal globalization's premise is unhampered free trade, presuming the supremacy of the market over politics from which it sees itself—when convenient—as divorced from, it abides by the orthodox economic principle of comparative advantage. The principle sounds fair and benign on the surface as it advices parties to a transaction to take advantage of the resources they have the most of. For instance, because Third World countries have plenty of natural resources or labor, they should take advantage of these to forge ahead. Likewise, because the First World countries have plenty of capital, heavy equipments, and high-tech products to export, they should also take advantage of these resources. While the logic seems neat, in practice, it condemns the poorer partner to the transaction to eternal subordination. The partnership is never equitable and will never be equitable. This is made worse by the prerogative taken by powerful countries—while telling the poorer states not to subsidize their industries and ignore whatever development priorities they might have—to assert their global economic hegemony through various means including subsidies to their corporations either through outright grants or, indirectly, through cheap loans through the Export-Import Bank or cheap insurance of their assets through the publicly funded Overseas Private Investment Corporation (OPIC). These subsidies distort the market in that it gives undue advantage to the favored corporations over their foreign competitors.

Prying Open "Emerging Markets": Corporations as Imperial Tools

The powerful states led by the United States also actively promote the products of their national companies. For example, the US government routinely provides humanitarian assistance to disaster or poverty-stricken areas of the world in the form of grains. Often, these grains are genetically modified food products produced by their food-producing companies, e.g., Monsanto, Con Agra, Cargill, ADM (Archer Daniels Midland), benefiting these companies when new orders come in or when farmers in those countries begin using these grains for their farms, binding them to an agreement to respect the patent rights of the grain-producing company(ies), or committing them to purchase grains for future planting seasons. This is where the intellectual property rights (IPRs) enforced by the WTO favor and strengthen these corporations, making them dominant actors in the international politics. Because they are profit-seeking organizations, they sell their products to segments of the population who can pay, not to those who cannot. They serve their shareholders, not the general public, and not the poor in the Third World. Thus, their slogan of "feeding the world" (taken from ADM's "We feed the world" motto) is false on its face.

The dominance today of the global food producers is manifest in the prevailing verticalized food production system dominated at the top by global food giants. These giant corporate food producers virtually dictate prices that are more often than not detached from the real value of the food or of the labor that produced it. Small farmers at the base of the verticalized food production produce at the specification of the corporation with which they are aligned. They survive because they are assured of a market for their product. Independent farmers, many or whom are organic farmers, are not aligned with a corporation and, thus, accept the challenges or suffer the difficulties that come with independence, or even the possibility of bankruptcy. Because government subsidy is based on acreage, the corporate farm—which relies on heavy machinery, large acreage, and chemical food and pesticide products—gets the subsidies while small farmers do not even though their techniques are more environmentally sustainable.

Further, the dominance of these giant food-producing corporations is a legacy of the Green Revolution, with its avowed aim of "food security" was promoted and funded by private philanthropic organizations like the Ford and Rockefeller Foundations during the 1960s and 1970s. Under the cover of the slogan to feed the world, it funded grain and seed research institutes like the International Rice Research Institute (IRRI) in Laguna Province, Philippines, founded in 1960, and the International Maize and Wheat Improvement Center (or CIMMYT in its Spanish initials), established initially in a collaboration between the Mexican government and academic- and corporate-based researchers under the auspices of the Rockefeller Foundation in 1966, both under the scientific leadership and guidance of Norman E. Borlaug who, in 1970, was awarded the Nobel Peace Prize for his efforts. The supposed goals were manifold including: (a) discover high-yielding rice varieties; (b) discover varieties resistant to insects; (c) discover varieties for upland farming requiring less water; and (d) train farmers in the use of new technologies, among others. In the end, because cultivation of the discovered, i.e., genetically engineered, "miracle rice" was capital intensive, many farmers in the Philippines and elsewhere were not able to realize the promise of prosperity. They could not afford to purchase hand-held tractors, those who had these new equipments could not afford to buy spare parts, while others could not afford to buy the requisite fertilizers and/or pesticides. Many who had initially borrowed money to invest in equipment or fertilizer went under when crops failed. Who the Green Revolution benefited, however, were the corporate food producers, the producers of mechanized farm products, and biotech companies that began to proliferate worldwide, boosted by the promise of patents being awarded to them upon discovery of new forms of "life" such as by tinkering with the genetic composition of seeds and, in the process, undermined food sovereignty in the Third World. This paved the way for a trend identified by Indian scientist-activist Vandana Shiva as "biopiracy," or the theft of indigenous knowledge from all over the world, engaged in not only by food producers but by pharmaceutical companies as well (Shiva).

Contesting Empire and the Role of Emancipatory Movements

These are just a few among many that ills the current neoliberal order. It is unlikely that under the current global structure of power, things will change for the benefit of who Spinoza referred to as the multitude. There is an encouraging sign that various manifestations of resistance to this order are having localized success, e.g., the protest against water privatization in Cochabamba, Bolivia; the armed rebellion by the Mayan Indians in southern Mexico, under the leadership of the Zapatista National Liberation Front against land privatization sanctioned under NAFTA; the urban protest called the Battle of Seattle that disrupted a WTO Ministerial Conference; the seed bank project inspired by Shiva in India; and the protests against World Bank-funded dam construction project in South Africa, among many others. However, what is lacking is a comprehensive understanding about the nature of the problem with its roots in extraction for value accumulation. As San Juan explains:

> Globalization as the transnationalized domination of finance capital exposes its historical limit in the deepening class inequality of a polarized antagonism-laden world. While surplus extraction in the international labor market remains basic to the logic of accumulation, the ideology of neoliberal exchange has evolved, after 9/11, into the unilateral 'American Exceptionalist' discourse of the 'war on terrorism' and the more contentious 'clash of civilizations'. Contradictions in specific loci of social struggles inform the imperialist project of resolving the crisis of finance capital by eliminating any obstacle (such as nation-state fiscal controls, trade tariffs, etc.) to its unlimited sway. Prompted by this exigency, the U.S. ruling class is desperately striving to impose hegemonic control over multiple nations, states, and peoples in an increasingly contested space, imposing its own "American Way of Life". (San Juan 2007a, xxiii–xxiv)

While no easy and immediate solutions appear on the horizon to resolve, the prospect of organic protracted resistance at the grassroots exemplified by the struggle of Ho Chi Minh against French colonialism in Indochina, Amilcar Cabral against Portuguese colonialism in Africa, Aime Cesaire against French colonialism in the Caribbean, and Frantz Fanon against racism in general provide hope and inspiration not lost to San Juan.

It is apropos to conclude this work with reassuring thoughts from no less than San Juan himself. San Juan upholds the prerogative of peoples around the world to engage in continued resistance as a matter of right, in juxtaposition to the imperialism by the United States which it asserts as its manifest destiny. Thus, San Juan valorizes the anti-imperialist struggle in the Philippines as exemplary to others, in the following fashion:

> In sum, Filipino nationalism constantly renews its emancipatory drive by forging or revitalizing new political subjects (such as women, church workers, indigenous, or ethnic minorities) at varying historical conjunctures. It is organically embedded in a long-sustained tradition of emancipatory movements whose origin evokes in part the Enlightenment narrative of popular sovereignty as mediated by homegrown protagonists interacting with external influences. The paradigm of national liberation thus bears a complex genealogy of native and borrowed constituents in permanent synergy. In sites of actualization are the local events of mass protests and individually differentiated resistance against persisting U.S. domination complicit with comprador oligarchy. In effect, the body politic if the Filipino 'nation' remains in the process of being invented primarily through diverse modes of opposition against corporate transnationalism and its commodifying destructiveness. It is therefore fashioning without interruption appropriate forms of cultural identity and autonomous political subjectivity. It selects from past legacies and present contingencies and is open to solidarity and collaboration with all progressive, egalitarian struggles of peoples of color and working people everywhere for a more just, equal, war-free sustainable world in place of the exhausted, life-denying dystopia of globalizing capital. (San Juan 2007b, xxviii–xxix)

References

Bauzon, Kenneth E., "Political Forecasting and the Third World Economies: A Critical Assessment", *Kasarinlan: Philippine Journal of Third World Studies*, 15, 1 (2000): 23–64. In: https://www.academia.edu/3382032/Political_forecasting_and_the_Third_World_economies_a_critical_assessment.

Klein, Naomi, *This Changes Everything: Capitalism vs. The Climate* (New York: Simon & Schuster, 2014), 576pp.

OXFAM International, *Even It Up: Time to End Extreme Inequality*, Report (Oxford, UK: Oxfam GB, October 2014), 136pp. In: https://www.oxfam.org/sites/www.oxfam.org/files/file_attachments/cr-even-it-up-extreme-inequality-291014-en.pdf.

———, *Public Good or Private Wealth? OXFAM Briefing Paper* (London, UK: Oxfam GB, January 2019), 106pp. In: https://oxfamilibrary.openrepository.

com/bitstream/handle/10546/620599/bp-public-good-or-private-wealth-210119-en.pdf?utm_source=indepth.

San Juan, E., Jr., *After Postcolonialism: Remapping Philippines-United States Confrontations* (Lanham, MD: Rowman & Littlefield, 2000), 272pp. Recipient, The Gustavus Myers Center for the Study of Human Rights in the United States Outstanding Book on Human Rights for 2001. Recipient, The Association of Asian American Studies Book Award for 2001.

———, *In the Wake of Terror; Class, Race, Nation, Ethnicity in the Postmodern World* (Lanham, MD: Lexington Books, 2007a), 232pp.

———, "Jose Rizal: Re-discovering the Revolutionary Filipino Hero in the Age of Terrorism", Afterword (Modified, 2011d) to *Rizal in Our Time: Essays in Interpretation* (Pasig City, Philippines: Anvil Publishing, 1997), 144pp. In: https://www.univie.ac.at/ksa/apsis/aufi/rizal/RediscoveringRIZAL.pdf.

———, *U.S. Imperialism and Revolution in the Philippines* (New York: Palgrave Macmillan, 2007b), 265pp. Print.

United Nations Development Programme (UNDP), *Humanity Divided; Confronting Inequality in Developing Countries* (New York: November 2013). In: http://www.undp.org/content/dam/undp/library/Poverty%20Reduction/Inclusive%20development/Humanity%20Divided/HumanityDivided_Full-Report.pdf.

References

Ackerman, Seth, "Yes, Racism Is Rooted in Economic Inequality", *Jacobin*, July 29, 2015. In: https://www.jacobinmag.com/2015/07/hillary-clinton-democratic-primary-sanders-netroots/.

Aguinaldo, Emilio, "Inaugural Address", *Official Gazette*, Government of the Philippines, January 23, 1899. In: http://www.gov.ph/1899/01/23/inaugural-address-of-president-aguinaldo-january-23-1899/.

———, *Reseña Verídica* (Tarlak, Islas Filipinas: Imprenta Nacional a cargo del Sr. Zacarias Fajardo, 1899). In: http://www.gutenberg.org/files/14307/14307-h/14307-h.htm.

Ahmed, Nafeez, "UN Plan to Save Earth Is 'Fig Leaf' for Big Business: Insiders—Why the New Sustainable Development Agenda Is 'Fundamentally Compromised' by Corporate Interests", *Insurge Intelligence*. Posted September 4, 2015. In: https://medium.com/insurge-intelligence/un-plan-to-save-earth-is-fig-leaf-for-big-business-insiders-2b91c106bb03.

Alexander, Michelle, *The New Jim Crow: Mass Incarceration in the Age of Colorblindness*, With New Foreword by Cornel West (New York: The New Press, 2012), 36pp.

Allen, James Edgar and John J. Reidy, *The Battle of Bayan and Other Battles, Being a History of the Moro Campaign from April 17 to Dec. 30, 1902: A Record of Events Occurring during a Period of Eight Months' Service in the Lake Region of Mindanao—Also Letters of Congratulation from His Excellency the President of the United State, Major General Adna R. Chaffee, and Others* (Manila: E. C. McCullough & Co., 1903). In: https://ia800202.us.archive.org/7/items/battleofbayanoth00alleiala/battleofbayanoth00alleiala.pdf.

"Annexation", *United States Magazine and Democratic Review*, July–August 1845, 6pp. Full text available in https://pdcrodas.webs.ull.es/anglo/OSullivanAnnexation.pdf.

Balce, Nerissa, "The American Vampire and the Filipino Journalists: Philippine Libel Laws Then and Now", *Interaksyon*, February 22, 2014. In: http://www.interaksyon.com/lifestyle/essay-the-american-vampire-and-the-filipino-journalists-philippine-libel-laws-then-and-now.

———, *Body Parts of Empire: Abjection, Filipino Images and the American Archive* (Ann Arbor, MI: University of Michigan Press, Forthcoming).

———, "The Filipina's Breast: Savagery, Docility and the Erotics of the American Empire", *Social Text*, 24, 2 (Summer 2006): 89–110. In: https://nerissabalce.files.wordpress.com/2008/11/balce_the-filipinas-breast.pdf.

Baraka, Ajamu, "Baltimore and the Human Right to Resistance", *Institute for Policy Studies*, April 30, 2015a. In: http://www.ips-dc.org/baltimore-and-the-human-right-to-resistance/.

———, "No 'Je Suis Charleston'?" *Counterpunch*, July 1, 2015b. In: http://www.counterpunch.org/2015/07/01/no-je-suis-charleston/.

Bartolovich, Crystal, "Introduction: Marxism, Modernity, and Postcolonial studies", in *Marxism, Modernity, and Postcolonial Studies*, edited by Crystal Bartolovich and Neil Lazarus (Cambridge, UK: Cambridge University Press, 2002), 304pp. In: http://catdir.loc.gov/catdir/samples/cam033/2001052881.pdf.

Bauzon, Kenneth E., "Demonstration Elections and the Subversion of Democracy", *Argentine Center for International Studies (CAEI)*, IR Theory Program, December 2005. In: https://www.researchgate.net/publication/5005033_Demonstration_Elections_and_the_Subversion_of_Democracy.

——— (With Charles Frederick Abel), "Dependency: History, Theory, and a Reappraisal", in *Dependency Theory and the Return of High Politics*, edited by Marianne Tetreault and Charles Fredrick Abel (Westport, CT: Greenwood Press, 1986), 270pp. In: https://www.academia.edu/3382095/Dependency_History_Theory_and_a_Reappraisal.

———, "Knowledge and Ideology in Philippine Society", *Philippine Quarterly of Culture and Society*, 19, 3 (September 1991): 207–234. In: http://www.jstor.org/stable/29792059?seq=1#page_scan_tab_contents.

———, *Liberalism and the Quest for Islamic Identity in the Philippines* (Durham, NC: Acorn Press in Association with Duke University Islamic and Arabian Development Studies, 1991), 219pp. Print.

———, "Neo-Marxism: End of a Career or Start of a New One?" *Kasarinlan: Philippine Journal of Third World Studies*, 6, 4/7/1 (December 1999): 113–126. In: https://www.academia.edu/3382023/Neo-Marxism_End_of_a_Career_or_a_Start_of_a_New_One.

———, "Political Forecasting and the Third World Economies: A Critical Assessment", *Kasarinlan: Philippine Journal of Third World Studies*, 15, 1 (2000):

23–64. In: https://www.academia.edu/3382032/Political_forecasting_and_the_Third_World_economies_a_critical_assessment.

———, "Secession in the Formal-Legalist Paradigm: Implications for Contemporary Revolutionary and Popular Movements in the Age of Neoliberal Globalization". Posted September 2014. In: https://www.academia.edu/8370651/Secession_in_the_Formal-Legalist_Paradigm_Implications_for_Contemporary_Revolutionary_and_Popular_Movements_in_the_Age_of_Neoliberal_Globalization.

———, "Situating Communities of Color in the United States: Critical Reflections on the Paradigms of Multiculturalism and Diversity", Paper prepared for delivery at the International Conference on Multiculturalism, Nation-State and Ethnic Minorities in Canada, the United States, and Australia, Tsukuba-shi, Ibaraki-ken, Japan, December 9–11, 2000. In: https://www.academia.edu/8209807/Situating_Communities_of_Color_in_the_United_States_Critical_Reflections_on_the_Paradigms_of_Multiculturalism_and_Diversity.

———, "Social Knowledge and the Legitimation of the State: The Philippine Experience in Historical Perspective", *Political Communication*, 9, 1 (July–September 1992): 173–189. In: https://www.academia.edu/3395861/Social_knowledge_and_the_legitimation_of_the_state_The_Philippine_experience_in_historical_perspective.

———, "The Tradition of Sociopolitical Inquiry", in *Liberalism and the Quest for Islamic Identity in the Philippines* (Durham, NC: Acorn Press in Association with the Islamic and Arabian Development Studies, Duke University, 1991), 219pp. In: https://www.researchgate.net/publication/264936329_The_Tradition_of_Sociopolitical_Inquiry_%28Chapter%29.

———, "Themes from the History of Capitalism to the Rise of the US Empire in the Pacific, with Annotations from Selected Works of E. San Juan, Jr.", *Kritika Kultura*, 26 (2016): 408–443. In: https://www.researchgate.net/publication/301338166_THEMES_FROM_THE_HISTORY_OF_CAPITALISM_TO_THE_RISE_OF_THE_US_EMPIRE_IN_THE_PACIFIC_With_Annotations_from_Selected_Works_of_E.

Beaud, Michel, *A History of Capitalism 1500–2000*, 2nd Edition (New York: Monthly Review Press, 2002), 356pp.

Beede, Benjamin R., ed., *The War of 1898 and U.S. Interventions, 1898 to 1934: An Encyclopedia* (London, UK: Routledge, 1994), 778pp.

Berge, William H., "Voices for Imperialism: Josiah Strong and the Protestant Clergy", *Border-States: Journal of the Kentucky-Tennessee American Studies Association*, 1 (1973). In: https://spider.georgetowncollege.edu/htallant/border/bs1/berge.htm.

Boyle, Francis, "Unlimited Imperialism and the Threat of World War III: U.S. Militarism at the Start of the 21st Century", *Global Research*, December 25, 2012.

In: https://www.globalresearch.ca/unlimited-imperialism-and-the-threat-of-world-war-iii-u-s-militarism-at-the-start-of-the-21st-century/5316852.

Bratton, John and David Denham, *Capitalism and Classical Social Theory*, 2nd Edition (Toronto, ON: University of Toronto Press, 2013), 432pp.

Braudel, Fernand, *Civilization and Capitalism 15th–18th Century*, Volume I. *The Structures of Everyday Life—The Limits of the Possible*. Translation from the French, Revised by Sian Reynolds (New York: Harper & Row Publishers, 1979), 623pp.

———, *Civilization and Capitalism 15th–18th Century*, Volume 2. *The Wheels of Commerce*. Translation from the French by Sian Reynolds (New York: Harper & Row Publishers, 1979), 670pp.

Buat, Musib M., "Are the Moros Filipinos?" *Moro Herald*, November 25, 2008. In: http://www.moroherald.com/2008/11/25/are-the-moros-filipinos/.

Cabusao, Jeffrey Arellano, "Nature, Society, and Filipino Transformative Writing: An interview with Cultural Theorist and Poet E. San Juan, Jr.", *Center for Art and Thought*. In: http://www.centerforartandthought.org/work/contributor/jeffrey-arellano-cabusao.

———, "The Responsibility of Filipino Intellectuals in the Age of Globalization and Empire: An Interview with E. San Juan, Jr. and Delia D. Aguilar", *Culture Logic, an Electronic Journal of Marxist Theory & Practice* (2008–2009 double issue, April 2010): 1–21. In: http://clogic.eserver.org/2009/Cabusao.pdf.

———, Review, "Racism and Cultural Studies: Critiques of Multiculturalist Ideology and the Politics of Difference", *Culture Logic, an Electronic Journal of Marxist Theory & Practice*, 8 (January 2005): 4. In: http://clogic.eserver.org/2005/cabusao.html.

Clark, Reginald, "The Expansion of Black American Misery Under Barack Obama's Watch", *Black Agenda Report*, February 20, 2013. In: https://www.blackagendareport.com/content/expansion-black-american-misery-under-barack-obama%E2%80%99s-watch.

Coates, Ta-Nehisi, *Between the World and Me* (New York: PenguinRandom House, 2015a), 176pp.

———, Interview on *Democracy Now!* With Amy Goodman and Juan Gonzalez on July 22, 2015. In: http://www.democracynow.org/2015/7/22/between_the_world_and_me_ta.

Constantino, Renato, *The Miseducation of the Filipino* (Quezon City, Philippines: Foundation for Nationalist Studies, January 1970). In: https://nonlinearhistorynut.files.wordpress.com/2010/02/miseducation-of-a-filipino.pdf.

Darity, William, Jr., "How Barack Obama Failed Black Americans", *The Atlantic*, December 22, 2016. In: https://www.theatlantic.com/politics/archive/2016/12/how-barack-obama-failed-black-americans/511358/.

Dirlik, Arif, "The Postcolonial Aura: Third World Criticism in the Age of Global Capitalism", *Critical Inquiry*, 20, 2 (Winter 1994): 328–356. In: http://jan.ucc.nau.edu/sj6/dirlikpocoaura.pdf.

Dowd, Douglas Fitzgerald, U.S. Capitalist Development Since 1776: Of, by, and for Which People? (Armonk, NY: M. E. Sharpe, 1993), 561pp.

Duka, Cecilio D., *Struggle for Freedom: A Textbook on Philippine History* (Quezon City, Philippines: Rex Bookstore, 2008), 427pp.

Dumindin, Arnaldo, "Philippine-American War, 1899–1902". In: http://philippineamericanwar.webs.com/.

Dyer, Thomas G., *Theodore Roosevelt and the Idea of Race* (Baton Rouge, LA: Louisiana State University Press, 1992), 182pp.

Edgerton, Robert B., *Hidden Heroism: Black Soldiers in America's Wars* (New York: Basic Books, 2002), 296pp.

Eperjesi, John R., *The Imperialist Imaginary: Visions of Asia and the Pacific in American Culture*. Foreword by Donald E. Pease (Lebanon, NH: University Press of New England, 2005), 211pp. Print.

Farah, Omar, "Tariq Ba Odah's Eight-Year Hunger Strike at Guantanamo Bay", *Rolling Stone Magazine*, July 6, 2015. In: http://www.rollingstone.com/politics/news/tariq-ba-odahs-eight-year-hunger-strike-at-guantanamo-bay-20150706.

Ferguson, Niall, *Colossus: The Price of America's Empire* (New York: Penguin Press, 2004), 384pp.

Fields, Barbara Jeanne, "Slavery, Race and Ideology in the United States of America", *New Left Review*, I/181 (May–June 1990). In: http://newleftreview.org/I/181/barbara-jeanne-fields-slavery-race-and-ideology-in-the-united-states-of-america.

Foner, Eric, "The Continental Revolution—The Gliding of American Capitalism Happened on Both Sides of the Continent", *The Nation*, June 1, 2017. In: https://www.thenation.com/article/frontiers-american-capitalism/.

Ford, Glen, "Ferguson and the War on Black America", *The Progressive*, August 2014. In: http://www.progressive.org/news/2014/08/187830/ferguson-and-war-black-america.

Francis, Pope, "Encyclical Letter Laudato Si' of the Holy Father Francis on Care for Our Common Home", *The Vatican*, May 24, 2015. In: http://w2.vatican.va/content/francesco/en/encyclicals/documents/papa-francesco_20150524_enciclica-laudato-si.html.

Francisco, Luzviminda, "The First Vietnam: The U.S.-Philippine War of 1899", *History as Weapon.com* (1973). In: http://www.historyisaweapon.com/defcon1/franciscofirstvietnam.html.

Franco, Jean, "Killing Priests, Nuns, Women, Children", in *On Signs,* edited by Marshall Blonsky (Baltimore, MD: Johns Hopkins University Press, 1985).

268 REFERENCES

Friedman, Thomas L., "A Manifesto for the Fast World", *New York Times Magazine*, March 28, 1999. In: https://www.nytimes.com/books/99/04/25/reviews/friedman-mag.html.

———, *The World Is Flat—A Brief History of the Twenty-First Century* (New York: Farrar, Straus and Giroux, 2005), 488pp.

Fulton, Robert A., *Moroland: The History of Uncle Sam and the Moros 1899–1920* (Bend, OR: Tumalo Creek Press, 2016 ed.). In: http://www.morolandhistory.com/00.Text%20Document/a_brief_history_of_.htm; http://www.morolandhistory.com/00.Text%20Document/a_brief_history_of_.htm#_American_Troops_arrive.

Funston, Frederick, *Memories of Two Wars: Cuban and Philippine Experience* (New York: C. Scribner's Sons, 1911), 472pp.

Garamone, Jim, "Joint Vision 2020 Emphasizes Full-Spectrum Dominance", *DoD News*, June 2, 2000. In: http://www.defense.gov/news/newsarticle.aspx?id=45289.

Gartzke, Erik and Dominic Rohner, "The Political Economy of Imperialism, Decolonization and Development", Center for Institutions, Policy and Culture in the Development Process, Working Paper Series No. 406 (Zurich, Switzerland: University of Zurich, April 2010), 55pp. In: http://www.econ.uzh.ch/ipcdp/Papers/ipcdp_wp406.pdf.

Giroux, Henry A., "Neoliberalism as Public Pedagogy", *Academia.edu*. Posted on March 31, 2011a. In: https://www.academia.edu/12795711/Neoliberalism_as_public_pedagogy.

———, "Neoliberalism's War on Democracy", *Truthout*, April 26, 2014. In: http://www.truth-out.org/opinion/item/23306-neoliberalisms-war-on-democracy#a6.

———, "The Racist Killing Fields in America: The Death of Sandra Bland", *Academia.edu*. Posted on July 19, 2015. In: https://www.academia.edu/14196417/The_Racist_Killing_Fields_in_America_The_Death_of_Sandra_Bland.

Grattan, Sean, "The Indignant Multitude: Spinozist Marxism After Empire", *Mediations: Journal of the Marxist Literary Group*. PDF Edition, 25, 2 (Spring 2011). In: http://www.mediationsjournal.org/articles/the-indignant-multitude.

Halstead, Murat, *The Story of the Philippines: The El Dorado of the Orient* (Chicago, IL: Our Possessions Publishing, 1898), 459pp. In: https://ia601408.us.archive.org/21/items/storyphilippine02halsgoog/storyphilippine02halsgoog.pdf.

Hardt, Michael and Antonio Negri, *Commonwealth* (Harvard University Press, 2009), 434pp. PDF version available in: http://www.thing.net/~rdom/ucsd/biopolitics/Commonwealth.pdf.

———, *Commonwealth* (Cambridge, MA: Belknap Press, 2010), 448pp. PDF version available in: http://www.thing.net/~rdom/ucsd/biopolitics/Commonwealth.pdf.

———, *Empire* (Cambridge, MA: Harvard University Press, 2000), 478pp. PDF version available in: http://www.angelfire.com/cantina/negri/HAREMI_printable.pdf.

———, *Multitude: War and Democracy in the Age of Empire* (New York: Penguin Books, 2004), 448pp. PDF version available in: http://rebels-library.org/files/multitude.pdf.

Henrickson, Kenneth E., Jr., *The Spanish-American War* (Westport, CT: Greenwood Press, 2003), 178pp. In: https://books.google.com/books?id=Qv5srwHj4XsC&pg=PA73&lpg=PA73&dq=spanish+american+war,+Hendrickson&source=bl&ots=DnB2Tu_mBs&sig=2EB5RVdL5NY8pEyz1U-Uk8g_1cI&hl=en&sa=X&ved=0CEEQ6AEwBmoVChMI77H5xcWsxwIVS1s-Ch26HAD9#v=onepage&q=spanish%20american%20war%2C%20Hendrickson&f=false.

Higginbotham, F. Michael, *Ghosts of Jim Crow—Ending Racism in Post-racial America* (New York: New York University Press, 2013), 316pp.

"History of Masonry in the Philippines, 1890–1900", *Philippine Center for Masonic Studies* (2006). In: http://www.philippinemasonry.org/1890---1900.html.

"History of Silliman University: Silliman's Journey of Over a Century", Silliman University. In: http://su.edu.ph/page/10-history#.

Horowitz, Irving Louis, *The Decomposition of Sociology* (New York: Oxford University Press, 1993), 282pp.

Hume, David, *Essays: Moral, Political, and Literary*. Edited by Eugene F. Miller (Indianapolis, IN: Liberty Fund, 1985), Part II, Essay I: Of Commerce, p. 252. In: https://oll.libertyfund.org/titles/hume-essays-moral-political-literary-lf-ed.

Idle No More, "The Manifesto". In: http://www.idlenomore.ca/manifesto.

Ince, Onur Ulas, "Between Commerce and Empire: David Hume, Colonial Slavery and Commercial Incivility", *History of Political Thought*, 39, 1 (Spring 2018b): 107–134. In: http://www.ulasince.com/wp-content/uploads/2018/02/Ince-2018-Between-Commerce-and-Empire.pdf.

———, "Between Equal Rights: Primitive Accumulation and Capital's Violence", *Political Theory*, 46, 6 (2018): 885–914. In: http://www.ulasince.com/wp-content/uploads/2018/12/Ince-2018-Between-Equal-Rights.pdf.

———, *Colonial Capitalism and the Dilemmas of Liberalism* (Oxford, UK: Oxford University Press, 2018a), 232pp.

———, "Development", in *Concepts in International Law*, edited by Jean d'Aspermont and Sahib Singh (Cheltenham, UK: Edward Elgar, 2017). Pre-proof version. In: http://box5163.temp.domains/~ulasince/wp-content/uploads/2017/10/Ince-Development-REVISED2.pdf.

———, "Enclosing in God's Name, Accumulating for Mankind: Money, Morality, and Accumulation in John Locke's Theory of Property", *Review of Politics*, 73 (2011): 29–54. In: http://box5163.temp.domains/~ulasince/wp-content/uploads/2017/10/Ince-2011-Money-and-Accumulation-in-Locke.pdf.

———, "John Locke and Colonial Capitalism: Money, Possession, Dispossession". Paper prepared for delivery at the 111th Annual Meeting of the American Political Science Association, San Francisco, CA, September 2–6, 2015. In: https://www.academia.edu/15120203/John_Locke_and_Colonial_Capitalism_Money_Possession_and_Dispossession.

———, "Primitive Accumulation, New Enclosures, and Global Land Grabs: A Theoretical Intervention", *Rural Sociology*, 79, 1 (2014): 104–131. In: http://box5163.temp.domains/~ulasince/wp-content/uploads/2017/10/Ince-2014-Primitive-Accumulation.pdf.

———, "Property", in *Encyclopedia of Political Thought*, edited by Michael Gibbons (Oxford, UK: Wiley-Blackwell, 2014), pp. 3008–3017. In: http://box5163.temp.domains/~ulasince/wp-content/uploads/2017/10/Ince-2014-Property-Wiley-EPTH.pdf.

International Court of Justice, Case Concerning Military and Paramilitary Activities in and Against Nicaragua (Nicaragua v. United States of America), Merits, Judgment of 27 June 1986. In: https://www.icj-cij.org/files/case-related/70/070-19860627-JUD-01-00-EN.pdf.

"James Baldwin 20th Anniversary Commemoration: Remembering the Life and Work of the Legendary Writer and Civil Rights Activist", *Democracy Now!* December 7, 2007. In: www.democracynow.org/2007/12/7/james_baldwin_20th_anniversary_commemoration_remembering.

James, Joy, ed., *The Angela Y. Davis Reader* (Blackwell Publishing, 1998), 380pp.

Johnson, Nathanael, "Here's Why Hawaii's Anti-GMO Laws Matter", *Grist*, November 20, 2014. In: http://grist.org/food/heres-why-hawaiis-anti-gmo-laws-matter/.

Kho, Madge, "The Bates Treaty", *Philippine Update* (n.d., ca. 1973). In: http://www.philippineupdate.com/Bates.htm.

Klein, Naomi, *This Changes Everything: Capitalism vs. The Climate* (New York: Simon & Schuster, 2014), 576pp.

Kuhn, Thomas S., *The Structure of Scientific Revolutions*, 3rd Edition (Chicago, IL: The University of Chicago Press, 1996), 212pp.

Macpherson, C.B., *The Political Theory of Possessive Individualism* (Oxford, UK: Oxford University Press, 1962).

Magdoff, Harry, *The Age of Imperialism: The Economics of U.S. Foreign Policy* (New York: Monthly Review Press, 1969), 208pp. Print.

Maggor, Noam, *Brahmin Capitalism: Frontiers of Wealth and Populism in America's First Gilded Age* (Cambridge, MA: Harvard University Press, 2017), 304pp.

Malcolm, George A., "The Malolos Constitution", *Political Science Quarterly*, 36, 1 (March 1921): 91–103. In: http://www.jstor.org/stable/2142663?seq=1#page_scan_tab_contents.

Martin, Michael T. and Marilyn Yaquinto, *Redress for Historical Injustices in the United States: On Reparations for Slavery, Jim Crow, and their Legacies* (Durham, NC: Duke University Press, 2007), 702pp.

Marx, Karl, *Capital: A Critique of Political Economy*, Volume 1, English Edition (Moscow: Progress Publishers, 1887). In: https://www.marxists.org/archive/marx/works/1867-c1/ch31.htm.

McCoy, Alfred W., *Policing America's Empire—The United States, the Philippines, and the Rise of the Surveillance State* (Madison, WI: The University of Wisconsin Press, 2009), 659pp. Print.

McKenna, Thomas M., *Muslim Rulers and Rebels: Everyday Politics and Armed Separatism in the Southern Philippines* (Oakland, CA: University of California Press, 1998), 343pp.

McKinley, William, "Benevolent Assimilation Proclamation", *Humanities Web*. In: http://www.humanitiesweb.org/human.php?s=h&p=c&a=p&ID=23008.

Mill, John Stuart, *The Subjection of Women*, Reprint Edition (Mineola, New York: Dover Publications, 1997), 112pp. Available online in: https://www.marxists.org/reference/archive/mill-john-stuart/1869/subjection-women/.

Morris, Edmund, *The Rise of Theodore Roosevelt*, The Modern Library Edition (New York: Random House, 2001), 920pp. Print.

Ngozi-Brown, Scot, "African-American Soldiers and Filipinos: Racial Imperialism, Jim Crow and Social Relations", *The Journal of Negro History*, 82, 1 (1997): 42–53.

Obama, Barack, "Farewell Address", *The Los Angeles Times*, January 10, 2017. For full, unedited text, please see: https://www.latimes.com/politics/la-pol-obama-farewell-speech-transcript-20170110-story.html.

O'Connor, Tom, "U.S. Special Forces School Publishes New Guide for Overthrowing Foreign Governments", *Newsweek*, May 8, 2019. In: https://www.newsweek.com/us-guide-overthrow-government-special-forces-school-1419837?fbclid=IwAR2_5j2q8CFNux3Fax7mYMoQFGywz3eQuVo6TLXOFfePmE-4lSviqdXHbCc .

Opisso, Antonio M., *Review of the Philippines to the End of the Commission Government—A Study in Tropical Democracy* (Indianapolis, IN: The Bobbs-Merrill, 1917), 541pp. Reviewed in *American Society of International Law*, 12, 2 (April 1918): 427–433. In: http://www.jstor.org/stable/2188164?seq=1#page_scan_tab_contents.

"Our Imperial Imperative", Interview with Niall Ferguson. *Atlantic Unbound*, May 25, 2004. In: https://www.theatlantic.com/past/docs/unbound/interviews/int2004-05-25.htm.

OXFAM International, *Even It Up: Time to End Extreme Inequality*, Report (Oxford, UK: Oxfam GB, October 2014), 136pp. In: https://www.oxfam.org/sites/www.oxfam.org/files/file_attachments/cr-even-it-up-extreme-inequality-291014-en.pdf.

———, *Public Good or Private Wealth? OXFAM Briefing Paper* (London, UK: Oxfam GB, January 2019), 106pp. In: https://oxfamilibrary.openrepository.com/bitstream/handle/10546/620599/bp-public-good-or-private-wealth-210119-en.pdf?utm_source=indepth.

———, "Richest 1% Will Own More Than All the Rest by 2016", Press Release, January 19, 2015. In: https://www.oxfam.org/en/pressroom/pressreleases/2015-01-19/richest-1-will-own-more-all-rest-2016.

Paraiso, Bryan Anthony C., "Promise of Philippine Independence Foiled by American Duplicity", *National Historical Commission, Republic of the Philippines*, March 22, 2013. In: http://nhcp.gov.ph/promise-of-philippine-independence-foiled-by-american-duplicity/.

Perkins, John, *Confessions of an Economic Hit Man* (New York: Plume, 2005), 303pp. Print.

Pershing, John J., *My Life Before the World War, 1860–1917: A Memoir* (Lexington, KY: University Press of Kentucky, 2013), 744pp. Preview in: https://books.google.com/books?id=aNfrnkW2AF4C&pg=RA1-PT371&lpg=RA1-PT371&dq=John+Pershing,+Lanao&source=bl&ots=sYTL48pIpS&sig=NRM03opHR349EwCFsGEwW91MEu4&hl=en&sa=X&ved=0ahUKEwiq4O2Og4XVAhXDHT4KHVEvDx4Q6AEIQjAE#v=onepage&q=John%20Pershing%2C%20Lanao&f=false.

Philbrick, Nathaniel, *Sea of Glory: America's Voyage of Discovery—The U.S. Exploring Expedition, 1834–1842* (New York: The Penguin Group, 2003), 452pp. Print.

"Philippine Declaration of Independence". In: http://fileserver.net-texts.com/asset.aspx?dl=no&id=26668.

The Philippine History Site, "The Philippine Revolution". In: http://opmanong.ssc.hawaii.edu/filipino/republic.html.

"The Philippine War—A Conflict of Conscience for African Americans", *National Park Service, Presidio of San Francisco, National Park Service* (n.d.). In: http://www.nps.gov/prsf/learn/historyculture/the-philippine-insurrectiothe-philippine-war-a-conflict-of-consciencen-a-war-of-controversy.htm.

Physicians for Human Rights, *Broken Laws, Broken Lives: Medical Evidence of Torture by US Personnel and Its Impact* (Cambridge, MA, June 2008), 121pp. In: http://brokenlives.info/?page_id=69.

Pinter, Harold, "Art, Truth & Politics", Nobel Lecture. *The Nobel Foundation* (2005). In: http://www.nobelprize.org/nobel_prizes/literature/laureates/2005/pinter-lecture-e.html.

Plis, Ivan, "No, Pope Francis Didn't Call Capitalism 'The Dung of the Devil'", *The Daily Caller*, July 10, 2015. In: http://dailycaller.com/2015/07/10/no-pope-francis-didnt-call-capitalism-the-dung-of-the-devil/.

Pobre, Cesar P., *History of the Armed Forces of the Filipino People* (Quezon City, Philippines: New Day Publishers, 2000), 731pp.

Polanyi, Karl, *The Great Transformation: The Political and Economic Origins of Our Time*, Foreword by R.M. McIver (Boston, MA: Beacon Press, 1957).

Potok, Mark, *The Year in Hate and Extremism, Annual Report 2014*, Southern Poverty Law Center. In: http://www.splcenter.org/Year-in-Hate-and-Extremism.

Pozo, Michael, "A Conversation with E. San Juan Jr.". With Introduction and Interview by Michael Pozo, *St. John's University Humanities Review*, 1, 2 (April 2003). In: http://facpub.stjohns.edu/~ganterg/sjureview/vol1-2/juan.html.

"Risk of Nuclear War Now Highest Since World War 2: UN", *TeleSur*, May 21, 2019, In: https://www.telesurenglish.net/news/Risk-of-Nuclear-War-Now-Highest-Since-World-War-2-UN-20190521-0026.html?fbclid=IwAR0s2NW0yDO4DYeVWAGytH3oxAhf99ncY6IUjC6HJ_ZbUirzmBk5H0zUXz8.

Roma-Sianturi, Dinah, "'Pedagogic Invasion': The Thomasites in Occupied Philippines", *Kritika Kultura*, 19 (February 2009).

San Juan, E., Jr., "Abu Sayyaf & Bangsamoro Struggle: Background to Mamasapano", *The Philippines Matrix Project*. Posted April 10, 2015a. In: https://philcsc.wordpress.com/2015/04/10/abu-sayyaf-bangsamoro-struggle-background-to-mamasapano-e-san-juan-jr/?fb_action_ids=10205120043074181&fb_action_types=news.publishes&fb_ref=pub-standard.

———, "African American Internationalism and Solidarity with the Philippine Revolution", *Socialism and Democracy*, 24, 2 (July 2010a): 32–65. In: http://www.tandfonline.com/eprint/Jqxa3MbH6e8pXFCcAHb9/full#.VcjchPlUWUF.

———, *After Postcolonialism: Remapping Philippines-United States Confrontations* (Lanham, MD: Rowman & Littlefield, 2000a), 272pp. Recipient, The Gustavus Myers Center for the Study of Human Rights in the United States Outstanding Book on Human Rights for 2001. Recipient, The Association of Asian American Studies Book Award for 2001.

———, "Afterword: From Development to Liberation—The Third World in the 'New World Order'", in *Development and Democratization in the Third World: Myths, Hopes and Realities*, edited by Kenneth E. Bauzon (Washington, DC: Crane Russak/Taylor & Francis, 1992), pp. 297–310.

———, "An African American Soldier in the Philippine Revolution: An Homage to David Fagen", *Cultural Logic* (2009a). In: http://clogic.eserver.org/2009/SanJuan.pdf.

———, "Antonio Gramsci on Surrealism and the Avantgarde". Originally published as International Gramsci Society Online article, January 2005a. In: http://www.internationalgramscisociety.org/resources/online_articles/articles/san_juan_01.shtml.

———, "Asian American Dereliction, Self-Deception, Servility—With Reflections on Jessica Hagedorn's Dream Jungle and Bienvenido Santos' What the Hell for You Left Your Heart in San Francisco", *The Philippines Matrix Project, Interventions Toward a National-Democratic Socialist Transformation*, March 3, 2009b. In: https://philcsc.wordpress.com/2009/05/03/asian-american-dereliction-self-deception-servility/.

———, "BALAGTAS: Proyekto Tungo Sa Diyalektikong Analisis at Materyalismong Interpretasyong ng Florante at Laura". Posted August 17, 2013a. In: https://philcsc.wordpress.com/2013/08/17/balagtas-a-dialectical-and-materialist-approach-in-filipino-e-san-juan-jr/.

———, "Benedict Spinoza and Racism in the U.S.", Academia (n.d.). In: https://www.academia.edu/771780/BENEDICT_SPINOZA_AND_RACISM_IN_THE_U.S.

———, *Between Empire and Insurgency—The Philippines in the New Millenium: Essays in History, Comparative Literature, and Cultural Politics* (Quezon City, Philippines: University of the Philippines Press, 2015b), 318pp.

———, "Beyond Identity Politics: The Predicament of the Asian American Writer in Late Capitalism", *American Literary History*, 3, 3 (Autumn 1991): 542–565. In: http://access.sjcny.edu:2137/stable/490015?Search=yes&resultItemClick=true&&searchUri=%2Faction%2FdoAdvancedResults%3Fgroup%3Dnone%26amp%3Bc6%3DAND%26amp%3Bq4%3D%26amp%3Bc3%3DAND%26amp%3Bf2%3Dall%26amp%3Bf4%3Dall%26amp%3Bf0%3Dall%26amp%3Bf3%3Dall%26amp%3Bc5%3DAND%26amp%3Bla%3D%26amp%3Bq0%3DAtlantic%2BStudies%26amp%3Bf6%3Dall%26amp%3Bisbn%3D%26amp%3Bc4%3DAND%26amp%3Bq2%3D%26amp%3Bsd%3D%26amp%3Bacc%3Don%26amp%3Bq6%3D%26amp%3Bf1%3Dall%26amp%3Bq1%3DE.%2BSan%2BJuan%252C%2BJr.%26amp%3Bed%3D%26amp%3Bq5%3D%26amp%3Bf5%3Dall%26amp%3Bwc%3Don%26amp%3Bc1%3DAND%26amp%3Bc2%3DAND%26amp%3Bq3%3D%26amp%3Bpt%3D%26amp%3Bsi%3D51&seq=1#page_scan_tab_contents.

———, *Beyond Postcolonial Theory* (New York: St. Martin's Press, 1998), 325pp. Print.

———, "C.L.R. James: Beyond Post-colonial Theory", *The Philippines Matrix Project*. Posted on January 12, 2015c. In: https://philcsc.wordpress.com/2015/01/; https://philcsc.wordpress.com/2015/01/12/c-l-r-james-beyond-post-colonial-theory/?fb_action_ids=10204551439419445&fb_action_types=news.publishes&fb_ref=pub-standard.

———, "Contemporary Global Capitalism and the Challenge of the Filipino Diaspora", *Global Society*, 25, 1 (January 2011a): 7–27. In: https://www.academia.edu/4982257/GLOBAL_CAPITALISM_AND_THE_FILIPINO_DIASPORA.

———, *Crisis in the Philippines: The Making of a Revolution* (South Hadley, MA: Bergin & Garvey Publishers, 1986), 265pp. Print.

———, ed., *Critics on Ezra Pound* (Coral Gables, FL: University of Miami Press, 1972), 128pp.

———, "Critique of Imperial Cultural Studies and the Task of Indigenization in the Philippines", *The Philippines Matrix Project, Interventions Toward a National-Democratic Socialist Transformation*, February 28, 2013b. In: https://philcsc.wordpress.com/2013/02/28/critique-of-imperial-cultural-studies-and-the-task-of-indigenization-in-the-philippines-e-san-juan-jr/.

———, "The Cult of Ethnicity and the Fetish of Pluralism: A Counter-hegemonic Critique", *Cultural Critique*, 18 (Spring 1991): 215–229. In: http://access.sjcny.edu:2137/stable/1354100?Search=yes&resultItemClick=true&&searchUri=%2Faction%2FdoAdvancedSearch%3Fgroup%3Dnone%26amp%3Bc6%3DAND%26amp%3Bq4%3D%26amp%3Bc3%3DAND%26amp%3Bf2%3Dall%26amp%3Bf4%3Dall%26amp%3Bf0%3Dall%26amp%3Bf3%3Dall%26amp%3Bc5%3DAND%26amp%3Bla%3D%26amp%3Bq0%3DAtlantic%2BStudies%26amp%3Bf6%3Dall%26amp%3Bisbn%3D%26amp%3Bc4%3DAND%26amp%3Bq2%3D%26amp%3Bsd%3D%26amp%3Bacc%3Don%26amp%3Bq6%3D%26amp%3Bf1%3Dall%26amp%3Bq1%3DE.%2BSan%2BJuan%252C%2BJr.%26amp%3Bed%3D%26amp%3Bq5%3D%26amp%3Bf5%3Dall%26amp%3Bwc%3Don%26amp%3Bc1%3DAND%26amp%3Bc2%3DAND%26amp%3Bq3%3D%26amp%3Bpt%3D&seq=1#page_scan_tab_contents.

———, "Cultural Politics, U.S. Imperialist War of Terror, and Socialist Revolution in the Philippines", *Institute for Political Economy*, July 20, 2011b. In: http://politicaleconomy.info/index2.php?option=com_content&do_pdf=1&id=57.

———, "Cultural Studies Amongst the Sharks: The Struggle Over Hawaii", *Third Text*, 16, 1 (2002a): 71–78. In: http://www.tandfonline.com/doi/abs/10.1080/09528820110120731#.VeuOC5dUWUE.

———, "Cultural Studies, Ethnic Writing, and Indigenization in the Philippines", *The Philippines Matrix Project, Interventions Toward a National-Democratic Socialist Transformation*, December 8, 2012a. In: https://philcsc.wordpress.com/2012/12/08/cultural-studies-ethnic-writing-and-indigenization-in-the-philippines/.

———, "Cultural Studies, Frantz Fanon, and the Problem of Indigenization in the Philippines", *Philippines Cultural Studies Center*, October 4, 2012b. In: http://philippinescsc.blogspot.com/2012/10/cultural-studies-frantz-fanon-and.html.

———, "Culture and Revolution", *Conjuncture,* 5, 5 (May 1992): In: https://www.academia.edu/15972838/CULTURE_AND_REVOLUTION?auto=view&campaign=weekly_digest.

———, "Dialectics and History: Power, Knowledge, Agency in Rizal's Discourse", *The E. San Juan, Jr. Archive,* August 9, 2006a. In: http://rizalarchive.blogspot.com/2006/08/rizals-discourse.html.

———, "Edward Said's Affiliations: Secular Humanism and Marxism", *Atlantic Studies: Global Currents,* 3, 1 (2006b): 43–61. In: http://www.tandfonline.com/doi/abs/10.1080/14788810500525481?journalCode=rjas20.

———, "Excavating the Bulosan Ruins: What Is at State in Rediscovering the Anti-Imperialist Writer in the Age of U.S. Global Terrorism", *The Philippines Matrix Project, Interventions Toward a National-Democratic Socialist Transformation.* Reposted from *Kritika Kultura,* 23 (2014a), April 6, 2014. In: https://philcsc.wordpress.com/2015/04/06/excavating-the-bulosan-ruins-reposted-from-kritika-kultura-23-2014/.

———, "Fanon and C.L.R. James: Lessons from Anti-postcolonial Revolutionaries", *The Philippines Matrix Project.* Posted October 10, 2014b. In: https://philcsc.wordpress.com/2014/10/10/fanon-c-l-r-james-lessons-from-anti-postcolonial-revolutionaries/.

———, "The Filipino-American War of 1899–1902 and Its Contemporary Resonance", Remarks prepared for delivery at the Bryn Mawr College, Pennsylvania, March 18, 1998, on the occasion of the program, "The Spanish-American-Cuban-Filipino War of 1898 and Its Legacy", *Austrian-Philippine Homepage* (1998a). In: http://www.univie.ac.at/voelkerkunde/apsis/aufi/history/sonny3.htm.

———, "Filipino OFWs Versus the Neoliberal Ideology of Transnationalism: Interrogating Transnationalism—The Case of the Filipino Diaspora in the Age of Globalized Capitalism". Posted July 20, 2012c. In: https://philcsc.wordpress.com/2012/07/20/filipino-ofws-versus-the-neoliberal-ideology-of-transnationalism/.

———, "From Genealogy to Inventory: The Situation of Asian American Studies in the Age of the Crisis of Global Finance Capital", *International Journal of Asia Pacific Studies,* 6, 1 (January 2010b): 47–75. In: http://ijaps.usm.my/wp-content/uploads/2012/06/Genealogy.pdf.

———, "From Race to Class Struggle: Re-problematizing Critical Race Theory", *Michigan Journal of Race and Law,* 11, 1 (2005b): 75–98. In: https://repository.law.umich.edu/mjrl/vol11/iss1/5.

———, *From the Masses, to the Masses: Third World Literature and Revolution* (Minneapolis, MN: MEP Publications/University of Minnesota, 1994), 197pp. Print.

———, "Going Back to Class? The Re-emergence of Class in Critical Race Theory," *Michigan Journal of Race and Law,* 75 (Fall 2005b). In: https://

litigation-essentials.lexisnexis.com/webcd/app?action=DocumentDisplay&crawlid=1&doctype=cite&docid=11+Mich.+J.+Race+%26+L.+75&srctype=smi&srcid=3B15&key=aba0e1b588afc0b0b64700544fcd28fe.

———, *Hegemony and Strategies of Transgression: Essays in Cultural Studies and Comparative Literature* (Albany, NY: State University of New York Press, 1995), 286pp.

———, "History, Literature, and the Politics of Time". Presentation Delivered at the University of the Philippines, Visaya, on February 4, 2014 (2014c). In: http://rizalarchive.blogspot.com/2014/01/lualhati-bautistas-desaparecidos-andres.html.

———, "Imperial Terror, Neo-Colonialism, and the Filipino Diaspora". A Lecture Delivered at the 2003 English Department Lecture Series at St. John's University. *St. John's University Humanities Review*, 2, 1 (Fall 2003a). In: http://facpub.stjohns.edu/~ganterg/sjureview/vol2-1/diaspora.html.

———, *In the Wake of Terror: Class, Race, Nation, Ethnicity in the Postmodern World* (Lanham, MD: Lexington Books, 2007a), 232pp.

———, "The 'Invincible' Abu Sayyaf and Permanent U.S. Intervention in the Philippines: Reflections on the Bangsamoro Struggle for Self-Determination". (2015d). In: https://www.academia.edu/11887241/ABU_SAYYAF_and_BANGSAMORO_STRUGGLE_A_Background_to_the_Mamasapano_Encounter.

———, "Jose Rizal: Re-discovering the Revolutionary Agent Behind the National Hero", *The Philippines Matrix Project, Interventions Toward a National-Democratic Socialist Transformation*, May 26, 2011c. In: https://philcsc.wordpress.com/2011/05/26/the-revolutionary-rizal-slaves-of-yesterday-tyrants-of-today/.

———, "Jose Rizal: Re-discovering the Revolutionary Filipino Hero in the Age of Terrorism", Afterword (Modified, 2011d) to *Rizal in Our Time: Essays in Interpretation* (Pasig City, Philippines: Anvil Publishing, 1997), 144pp. In: https://www.univie.ac.at/ksa/apsis/aufi/rizal/RediscoveringRIZAL.pdf.

———, "Kafka & Torture: Deconstructing the Writing Apparatus of 'In the Penal Colony'". Posted January 2014d. In: https://www.academia.edu/11779952/KAFKA_AND_TORTURE.

———, "The Limits of Postcolonial Criticism: The Discourse of Edward Said", *Against the Current*, 77 (November–December 1998b). *Solidarity: A Socialist, Feminist, Anti-racist Organization*. In: https://solidarity-us.org/node/1781.

———, "Man Is a Political Animal" (Poem), *Philippine Collegian*, July 25, 1957.

———, "Marxism and the Race/Class Problematic". Originally published in *Cultural Logic* (2003b). In: http://clogic.eserver.org/2003/sanjuan.html.

———, "Migration, Ethnicity, Racism: Narrative Strategies in Asian American Writing", *Migracijske tcmc!* 3, 3 (1997): 189–216. In: hrcak.srce.hr/126628?lang=en.

———, "The Multiculturalist Problematic in the Age of Globalized Capitalism", *Social Justice*, 27, 1 (2000b): 61–75. In: http://www.socialjusticejournal.org/archive/79_27_1/79_05SanJuan.pdf.

———, "Nation-State, Postcolonial Theory, and Global Violence", *Social Analysis: The International Journal of Social and Cultural Practice*, 46, 2 (Summer 2002d): 11–32.

———, "Nationalism, the Postcolonial State, and Violence", *The Philippines Matrix Project, Interventions Toward a National-Democratic Socialist Transformation*, December 3, 2014e. Originally published in *Left Curve*, 26. In: https://philcsc.wordpress.com/2014/12/03/violence-nationalism-the-postcolonial-state-essay-by-e-san-juan-jr/.

———, "Notes on U.S. Genocide in the Philippines", *The Philippines Matrix Project*. Posted June 16, 2013c. In: https://philcsc.wordpress.com/2013/06/16/notes-on-u-s-genocide-in-the-philippines/.

———, "On Frantz Fanon and C.L.R. James: Beyond Transnationalism", *The Philippines Matrix Project, Interventions Toward a National-Democratic Socialist Transformation*, August 6, 2014. In: https://philcsc.wordpress.com/2014/08/06/on-frantz-fanon-c-l-r-james-beyond-transnationalism-by-e-san-juan-jr/.

———, "Overseas Filipino Workers: The Making of an Asian-Pacific Diaspora", Originally published in *The Global South*, 3, 2 (2010c): 99–129. In: https://www.academia.edu/1738367/FILIPINO_WRITERS_IN_THE_UNITED_STATES_THE_FILIPINO_DIASPORA.

———, "The Paradox of Multiculturalism: Ethnicity and Identity in the Philippines". (1999a). In: https://www.univie.ac.at/ksa/apsis/aufi/ethno/paradox.htm.

———, Personal Email Correspondence with Kenneth E. Bauzon, June 29, 2015e.

———, "Peirce/Marx: Interface of Pragmaticism and Marxism", *The Philippines Matrix Project, Interventions Toward a National-Democratic Socialist Transformation*, February 14, 2013d. In: https://philcsc.wordpress.com/2013/02/14/peircemarx-interface-of-pragmaticism-marxism-e-san-juan-jr/.

———, *The Philippine Temptation: Dialectics of Philippines-U.S. Literary Relations* (Philadelphia, PA: Temple University Press, 1996).

———, "Postcolonialism, Uneven Development, and Imperialism: The Example of Amilcar Cabral", in *Marxism, Modernity, and Postcolonial Studies*, edited by Crystal Bartolovich and Neil Lazarus (Cambridge, UK: Cambridge University Press, 2002b), pp. 221–239. In: https://www.academia.edu/10130036/POSTCOLONIALISM_UNEVEN_DEVELOPMENT_and_IMPERIALISM_The_Example_of_Amicar_Cabral--by_E_San_Juan_Jr.

———, "Post-9/11 Reflections on Multiculturalism and Racism", *Axis of Logic: Finding Clarity in the 21st Century Mediaplex* (November 13, 2004b). In: http://www.axisoflogic.com/artman/publish/Article_13554.shtml.

———, "Preparing for the Time of Reparation: Speculative Cues from W.E.B. Du Bois, George Jackson, and Mumia Abu-Jamal", *Souls*, 7, 2 (2005): 63–74.

———, "Problematizing Multiculturalism and the 'Common Culture'", *MELUS*, 19, 2, "Theory, Culture, and Criticism" (Summer 1994): 59–84. In: http://access.sjcny.edu:2137/stable/467725?Search=yes&resultItemClick= true&&searchUri=%2Faction%2FdoAdvancedSearch%3Fgroup%3Dnone% 26amp%3Bc6%3DAND%26amp%3Bq4%3D%26amp%3Bc3%3DAND% 26amp%3Bf2%3Dall%26amp%3Bf4%3Dall%26amp%3Bf0%3Dall%26amp% 3Bf3%3Dall%26amp%3Bc5%3DAND%26amp%3Bla%3D%26amp%3Bq0% 3DAtlantic%2BStudies%26amp%3Bf6%3Dall%26amp%3Bisbn%3D%26amp% 3Bc4%3DAND%26amp%3Bq2%3D%26amp%3Bsd%3D%26amp%3Bacc% 3Don%26amp%3Bq6%3D%26amp%3Bf1%3Dall%26amp%3Bq1%3DE. %2BSan%2BJuan%252C%2BJr.%26amp%3Bed%3D%26amp%3Bq5%3D% 26amp%3Bf5%3Dall%26amp%3Bwc%3Don%26amp%3Bc1%3DAND%26amp% 3Bc2%3DAND%26amp%3Bq3%3D%26amp%3Bpt%3D&seq=1#page_scan_ tab_contents.

———, "Problems in the Marxist Project of Theorizing Race", in *Racism: Essential Readings*, edited by Ellis Cashmore and James Jennings (London: Sage, 2001), 422pp. In: https://books.google.com/books?id=Mms33VopsQQC& pg=PA225&lpg=PA225&dq=E.+San+Juan,+Jr.,+Marxism&source=bl&ots= bvkqbUURvu&sig=L1riVtuSHcfX_QXuzoDWgYC4WHo&hl=en&sa=X&ei= bVGHVcPvIoaXyQTU2YCQAw&ved=0CCgQ6AEwAjgK#v=onepage&q=E. %20San%20Juan%2C%20Jr.%2C%20Marxism&f=false.

———, "Prospects for Transformation in the Philippines in the Next Millenium", *Austrian-Philippine Home Page*, 1998. In: https://www.univie.ac.at/ ksa/apsis/aufi/history/sonny2.htm.

———, "Race and Class in Post-9/11 U.S. Empire", *Rizal Archive Blogspot*, April 30, 2009c. In: http://rizalarchive.blogspot.com/2009/04/race-and-class-in-post-911-us-empire.html.

———, "Race from the 20th to the 21st Century: Multiculturalism or Emancipation?" *Against the Current*, 78 (January–February, 1999b). *Solidarity: A Socialist, Feminist, Anti-racist Organization*. In: https://www.solidarity-us. org/node/1757.

———, *Racial Formations/Critical Transformations: Articulations of Power in Ethnic and Racial Studies in the United States* (Amherst, NY: Humanity Books/Prometheus Books, 1992), 163pp. Recipient, 1993 National Book Award in Cultural Studies from the Association for Asian American Studies. Recipient, the Gustavus Myers Center for the Study of Human Rights in the United States Outstanding Book on Human Rights for 1992.

———, *Racism and Cultural Studies: Critiques of Multiculturalist Ideology and the Politics of Difference* (Durham, NC: Duke University Press, 2002c), 428pp. In: https://www.dukeupress.edu/Racism-and-Cultural-Studies/.

---, "Racism and Race in the USA (ca. 1995, 2005)", *The Philippines Matrix Project, Interventions Toward a National-Democratic Socialist Transformation*, Match 7, 2009. In: https://philcsc.wordpress.com/2009/03/07/racism-race-in-the-usa-circa-1998-2005/.

---, "Re-visiting Race and Class in Post-9/11 United States of America", *The E. San Juan, Jr. Archive*, April 30, 2009d. In: http://rizalarchive.blogspot.com/2009/04/race-and-class-in-post-911-us-empire.html.

---, "Re-visiting the Singularity of the National Liberation Struggle in the Philippines", *The Philippines Matrix Project, Interventions Toward a National-Democratic Socialist Transformation*. Posted September 2006c. In: http://rizalarchive.blogspot.com/2006/09/national-liberation-struggle-in.html.

---, "Reading the Stigmata: Filipino Bodies Performing for the U.S. Empire", *Countercurrents*, April 25, 2015f. In: http://www.countercurrents.org/sanjuan250415.htm.

---, "Reflections on Hegemonic Cultural Studies and the Problem of Indigenization in the Philippines", *The Philippines Matrix Project*. Posted November 12, 2012d. In: https://philcsc.wordpress.com/2012/11/12/reflections-on-hegemonic-cultural-studies/.

---, "Remebrance (sic) of Things Almost Past by an English Major in U.P. (1954–58)", *Manila Times*, March 4, 2012e (Brackets added). In: https://www.pressreader.com/@Sonny_Juan/csb_L0zQjf3TvXh9jl-DbkbdJQjA9ao HqRUmY4P7WHqRRbHnAaDAfuG0og0W4cXya27B?fbclid=IwAR0WOOy Gz70ZRWVidDp8xqCpEdYWPdHY1rU3YH9aZnV0ij76tyMIQ-VMzwk.

---, "Sisa's Vengeance: Rizal and the Mother of All Insurgencies", *Kritika Kultura*, 17 (2011e): 23–56. In: http://kritikakultura.ateneo.net/images/pdf/kk17/sisa.pdf.

---, "Speculative Notes by a Subaltern Amateur in Cultural Studies", *JOMEC Journal: Journalism, Media and Cultural Studies* (June 2012f). In: http://www.cardiff.ac.uk/jomec/jomecjournal/1-june2012/sanjuan_subaltern.pdf.

---, "Spinoza and the War of Racial Terrorism", Originally published in *Left Curve, No. 27, and as Chapter in Working Through the Contradictions: From Cultural Theory to Critical Practice* (Lewisburg, PA: Bucknell University Press, 2004b). In: http://www.leftcurve.org/LC27WebPages/Spinoza.html. Also available in: https://philcsc.wordpress.com/2014/11/17/spinozas-philosophy-the-body-race-freedom-by-e-san-juan-jr/.

---, *Toward Filipino Self-Determination: Beyond Transnational Globalization* (Albany, NY: State University of New York Press, 2009e), 200pp. In: http://www.sunypress.edu/p-4865-toward-filipino-self-determinat.aspx.

---, "Toward a Materialist Cultural Politics", *The Philippines Matrix Project*. Posted September 4, 2012g. In: https://philcsc.wordpress.com/2012/09/04/toward-a-materialist-cultural-politics/.

———, "Tracking the Spoors of Imperialism and Neocolonialism in the Philippines: Sketch of a Synoptic Reconnaissance", *Portside*, February 2, 2015g. In: http://portside.org/print/2015-02-02/tracking-spoors-imperialism-neocolonialism-philippines-sketch-synoptic-reconnaissance.

———, "A Tradition of Dehumanizing: The CIA's Psycho-War and Torture Schemes in the Philippines", *Global Research*, May 2, 2010d. In: http://www.globalresearch.ca/a-tradition-of-dehumanizing-the-cia-s-psycho-war-and-torture-schemes-in-the-philippines/18939.

———, *U.S. Imperialism and Revolution in the Philippines* (New York: Palgrave Macmillan, 2007b), 265pp. Print.

———, "Violence, Nationalism, and the Postcolonial State", *The Philippines Matrix Project*. Posted December 3, 2014f. In: https://philcsc.wordpress.com/2014/12/03/violence-nationalism-the-postcolonial-state-essay-by-e-san-juan-jr/?fb_action_ids=10204226505936311&fb_action_types=news.publishes&fb_ref=pub-standard.

———, "War in the Filipino Imagination: Filipino Writers in the United States Wrestling with the Minotaur", *The Philippines Matrix Project, Interventions Toward a National-Democratic Socialist Transformation*, December 13, 2011. In: https://philcsc.wordpress.com/2011/12/13/war-memories-in-filipino-writing-in-the-united-states/.

———, "Who's Afraid of Jessica Hagedorn? Notes on Filipina Writer in America", *The Philippines Matrix Project, Interventions Toward a National-Democratic Socialist Transformation*, October 6, 2008. In: https://philcsc.wordpress.com/2008/10/06/whos-afraid-of-jessica-hagedorn-notes-on-a-filipina-writer-in-america/.

———, *Working Through Contradictions: From Cultural Theory to Critical Practice* (Cranbury, NJ: Associated University Presses, 2004c), 426pp. In: https://books.google.com/books?id=POQd0XbRsOQC&dq=San+Juan,+David+Fagen&source=gbs_navlinks_s.

Schirmer, Daniel B. and Stephen Rosskamm Shalom, Editors, "The Philippine-American War" (Editors' Introduction), in *The Philippine Reader: A History of Colonialism, Neocolonialism, Dictatorship, and Resistance* (Boston, MA: South End Press, 1987), pp. 8–19. In: https://books.google.com/books?id=TXE73VWcsEEC&pg=PA9&lpg=PA9&dq=mock+battle+for+Manila,+Spain,+United+States&source=bl&ots=9855VslcAG&sig=DByMdbBDVSWMv676gLi57_lnQ8Q&hl=en&sa=X&ved=0CB0Q6AEwADgKahUKEwiM5uyV07HHAhVIbj4KHR0iA40#v=onepage&q=mock%20battle%20for%20Manila%2C%20Spain%2C%20United%20States&f=false.

Shiva, Vandana, *Biopiracy: The Plunder of Nature and Knowledge* (Boston, MA: South End Press, 1997), 148pp.

Shohat, Ella, "Notes on the 'Post-colonial'", *Social Text*, 31/32 (1992): 99–113. In: https://racismandnationalconsciousnessresources.files.wordpress.com/2008/11/ella-shohat-notes-on-the-post-colonial.pdf.

Spinoza's Political Treatise: A Critical Guide. Edited by Yitzhak Y. Melamed and Hasana Sharp (Cambridge, UK: Cambridge University Press, 2018). In: https://www.academia.edu/36492836/Spinozas_Political_Treatise_A_Critical_Guide.

Staples, Steven, "The Relationship Between Globalization and Militarism", *Social Justice Magazine*, 27, 4 (2000). In: http://www.thirdworldtraveler.com/Globalization/Globalization_Militarism.html.

Steel, Ronald, *Pax Americana: The Cold War Empire—How It Grew and What It Means* (New York: The Viking Press, 1967), 371pp. Print.

Strong, Josiah, *Our Country: Its Possible Future and Its Present Crisis* (Charlotte, NC: Baker & Taylor for the American Home, 1885), 229pp.

Thornley, Andrew, *The Inheritance of Hope: John Hunt, Apostle of Fiji*, Translated into Fijian by Tauga Vulaono (Suva, Fiji: Institute of Pacific Studies, The University of the South Pacific, 2000), 531pp. Print.

Tigar, Michael E. and Madeleine R. Levy, *Law and the Rise of Capitalism*, New Edition (New York: Monthly Review Press, 2000), 348pp.

Treadgold, Donald W., *The West in Russia and China: Russia, 1472–1917* (Cambridge, UK: Cambridge University Press, 1973), 363pp.

Twain, Mark, *To the Person Sitting in Darkness* (New York: Anti-Imperialist League of New York, 1901). In: http://xroads.virginia.edu/~drbr/sitting.html.

"Unbridled Capitalism Is the 'Dung of the Devil', Says Pope Francis", *The Guardian*, July 9, 2015. In: https://www.theguardian.com/world/2015/jul/10/poor-must-change-new-colonialism-of-economic-order-says-pope-francis#img-2.

United Nations Development Programme (UNDP), *Humanity Divided: Confronting Inequality in Developing Countries* (New York, November 2013). In: http://www.undp.org/content/dam/undp/library/Poverty%20Reduction/Inclusive%20development/Humanity%20Divided/HumanityDivided_Full-Report.pdf.

United States Department of State, Office of the Historian, "Milestones: 1866–1898: Mahan's The Influence of Sea Power Upon History: Securing International Markets in the 1890s". In: https://history.state.gov/milestones/1866-1898/mahan.

Van Gelder, Sarah, "Rev. Sekou on Today's Civil Rights Leaders: 'I Take My Orders from 23-Year Old Queer Women'", *Yes! Magazine*, July 22, 2015. In: http://www.yesmagazine.org/peace-justice/black-lives-matter-s-favorite-minister-reverend-sekou-young-queer.

Veric, Charlie Samuya, "Culture from Imperialism: American Colonial Education in the Philippines", in *Back to the Future: Perspectives on the Thomasite Legacy to Philippine Education*, edited by Corazon D. Villareal (Manila, Philippines: American Studies Association of the Philippines in Cooperation with the Cultural Affairs Office, US Embassy, 2003), 417pp.

Wallerstein, Immanuel, *The Modern World System: Capitalist Agriculture and the Origins of the European World Economy in the Sixteenth Century* (New York: Academic Press, 1974).

Walzer, Michael, *Just and Unjust Wars: A Moral Argument with Historical Illustrations*, 4th Edition (New York: Basic Books, 1977), 361pp. Print.

West, Cornel, "In Defense of James Baldwin—Why Toni Morrison (A Literary Genius) Is Wrong About Ta-Nehisi Coates", *Facebook.com*, July 16, 2015. In: https://www.facebook.com/drcornelwest?fref=nf.

———, "My Response to Brother Ta-Nehisi's New Book Should Not Be Misunderstood", *Facebook.com*, July 20, 2015. In: https://www.facebook.com/drcornelwest?fref=nf.

Whitney, Mike, "The Pentagon's '2015 Strategy' for Ruling the World", *Global Research*, July 5, 2015. In: http://www.globalresearch.ca/the-pentagons-2015-strategy-for-ruling-the-world/5460404.

Williams, Thomas and James Calvert, *Fiji and the Fijians: Mission History*, Volume 2. Edited by George Stringer Rowe (London, UK: William Nichols, 1858), 435pp. Print.

Worcester, Dean C., *The Philippines: Past and Present*, Volumes 1–2 (New York: Macmillan, 1914). In: http://www.gutenberg.org/files/12077/12077-h/12077-h.htm.

World Trade Organization Charter (WTO), Article XXI, Security Exceptions. In: https://www.wto.org/english/res_e/booksp_e/gatt_ai_e/art21_e.pdf.

Zinn, Howard, *A People's History of the United States, 1492–Present* (New York: Harper Perennial Modern Classics, 2005), 729pp.

Index

A
aboriginal population. *See* indigenous peoples
Abu Ghraib, 152, 217, 235n10
Abu-Jamal, Mumia, 220
affirmative action, 197
Afghanistan, 253
Africa, 9, 27, 32, 64n1, 116, 260. *See also* South Africa
  anti-colonialism in, 173, 234n8
  North, 54
  Portuguese colonialism in, 260
  segregation in, 216
  South, 32
  underdevelopment of, 180
  U.S. intervention in, 173
African Americans. *See also* Obama, Barack; racism
  church-based tradition of, 209
  discrimination against, 202
  opposed to Philippine-American war, 110, 112–116
  rights of, 224–226
  as soldiers, 110–116
  as underclass, 173
  U.S. president, 224, 225–228
Afrikaaners, 32
Agent Orange, 67n5
Aguinaldo, Emilio, 78
  capture of, 79, 105, 128
  and Dewey, 83, 87–89
  exile in Hong Kong, 79–80
  as head of provisional government, 101
  as Philippine leader, 78–80
  manipulation and betrayal of, 81–84
  proclamation of independence, 85–86
  return from exile, 81–82
  revolutionary government of, 87–88
Ahab, Captain, 34
Alangkat uprising, 163n6
Alden, James, 38–41, 44, 46
Alexander, Michelle, 198–199
Alfonso XIII (King of Spain), 118
Algeria, 54
Ali, Datu, 127
Ali rebellion, 127

INDEX

Allen, James Edgar, 130–146
al-Nakba, 237n11
al-Qaeda, 253
Alyosha. See Karamazov, Alyosha
America. See North America; South America; United States
American Board of Commissioners for Foreign Missions, 16
American Pacific Orientalism, 157
American Squadron, 49
Ampuan-Agaus, Datu, 147
Anderson, Anderson, 26
Anderson, Thomas MacArthur, 81
Angola, 173
anti-capitalism, 13, 230n1, 253. See *also* capitalism
anti-colonialism, 116. See *also* colonialism
anti-imperialism, 115–116, 228–230n1. See *also* imperialism
Anti-Imperialist League, 92, 110
anti-Semitism, 236n11
anti-Zionism, 236n11
apartheid, 25, 173
Apology Resolution, 61
Aquino, Corazon, 257
Arrighi, Giovanni, 32, 182n1
Artacho, Isabelo, 79
Asia. See *also* China; Japan
  East, 150
  Indochina, 172
  South, 178
  Southeast, 178
Asian Americans, 174, 219
Asian Development Bank, 13
Asian-Pacific Islanders, 231n3
Asiatic mode of production, 28n2
Atlantic slave trade. See slave trade
austerity, 223
Australia, 47

B

Bacolod, Sultan of, 139–141
Badiou, Alain, 232n4
Balce, Nerissa, 156–160
Baldwin, Frank D., 129–131, 134–138
Baldwin, James, 207, 233n8
Balzac (Honore de), 156
Baraka, Ajamu, 199, 201–202
barbarism, 7, 53, 204, 230n1
barbarization, 184n3
Basil of Caesarea, 250
Bates, John C., 116, 119, 121–123
Bates Treaty, 17, 122–124, 128
Battle of Bacolod, 147, 148
Battle of Bayan, 131–138
Battle of Bud Bagsak, 148, 149, 163n7
Battle of Little Big Horn, 67n5
Battle of Manila, 110
Battle of Manila Bay, 56, 60, 77, 81
Battle of Seattle, 260
Baudelaire (Charles Pierre), 156
Baudrillard (Jean), 232n4
Bautista, Ambrosio Rianzares, 85
Bayan, Sultan of, 129, 130–134, 136
Beaud, Michel, 24
Beede, Benjamin, 129
behavioralism, 193
Belgium, 54, 184n2, 217
Bell, J. Franklin, 107
benevolent assimilation, 89, 97n5, 119, 125, 151
Benevolent Assimilation Proclamation, 109–112, 119
Benjamin, Walter, 232n4
Berge, William H., 63
Berlin Conference, 32
Beveridge, Alfred, 109
Bhabha, Homi, 203–205
Bilderberg Group, 246
Binidayan Fort, 131–134
biodiversity, 245
biopiracy, 259

biotech industry, 71n9, 259
#Black Lives Matter (BLM) Movement, 211, 224
Black Panther Party, 209
Black Reparations Movement, 216, 220, 224
Blount, James H., 87, 158
Boer Wars, 32
Bolivia, 13, 178, 250, 260
Bolshevik Revolution (1917), 27
Bonifacio, Andres, 77–78, 95n2
Bonifacio, Ciriaco, 79
Bonifacio, Procopio, 79
Borlaug, Norman E., 259
Bourdieu, Pierre, 69n7, 183n1
bourgeois class, 27n1, 165n9, 192, 220
Boycott, Divestment, and Sanctions (BDS) Movement, 213
Boyle, Francis, 255
Braudel Center, 24
Braudel, Fernand, 23
Brazil, 178, 218
Bretton Woods, 172
Britain, xv, 28n2, 32, 55
British East India Company, 9
British-French wars, 32
British West Indies Company, 55
Brothers Karamazov, 8
Brown, Michael, 210
Brown v. Board of Education, 197
Buat, Musib M., 118
Buayan (Rajah), 118
Bud Bagsak, 163n7. *See also* Battle of Bud Bagsak
Buffalo Soldiers, 110, 115
Bukharin, Nikolai, 31–33, 182n1
Burger, Warren, 197
Burke, Edmund, 9
Bush Administration, 235n10, 256
Bush, George W., 152, 217
Butig-Maciu expedition, 141, 142–148

Butig, Sultan of, 140

C
Cabral, Amilcar, 13, 29n2, 187n6, 260
Cabugatan of Maciu (Sultan), 140, 142
Cabusao, Jeffrey, 214
Calderon, Felipe, 101
Calvert, James, 35, 48
Camp Vicars, 136–139, 142, 147
Canada, 32, 70n9, 179
capital accumulation, 20n2, 31–33, 89, 160n1, 172, 182n1, 205, 213, 224
  by dispossession, 29n2
  hegemony based on, 172–175
capitalism, 23, 179, 182n1, 194–198, 205, 222, 231n3. *See also* anti-capitalism; post-capitalism
  collective, 32
  and democracy, 5, 200
  and environmental sustainability, 246
  evil of, 194
  global, 2, 7, 15, 161n2
  and hegemony, 28n1
  Kafka's view of, 236n10
  and liberalism, 7
  logic of, 201
  mature, 27
  merchant, 180
  nature of, 180
  neoliberal, 18, 247
  and slavery, 26, 69n7
  and the state, 26–27, 182n1
  in Western Europe, 172–174
  as world-system, 3, 32, 180, 201
Caribbean, 15, 260
Carmack, Edward Ward, 88
Carson, Arthur, 64
Cartesian dualism, 5
  imperialism, 229n1
Castle, Samuel Northrup, 16

Cazneau, Jane McManus Storm (Cora Montgomery), vii, 62
Cebull, Richard, 196
Center for Constitutional Rights, 217
Central America, 217
  counterinsurgency in, 3, 185n4
  U.S. intervention in, 172
Central American Free Trade Agreement – Dominican Agreement (CAFTA – DR), 3
Cesaire, Aime, 233n8, 260
Chaffee, Adna R., 126, 130–135, 137–139
Chile, 172, 177, 218
China, 16, 32, 65n2, 118, 150, 174, 256
CIMMYT (*Centro Internacional de Mejoramiento de Maiz y Trigo*), 259
Citizen's Committee of Public Safety, 16
civilizing mission, 5, 25, 65n3, 69n8, 157
civil rights movement, 199, 209
Civil War, 25, 66n5
Clark, Reginald, 226–227
Clark, William, 39–43
clash of civilizations, 260
class conflict, 27
class displacement, 192
class, recovery of, 214–220
class reductionism, 192
class struggle, 29n5
Clay, Henry, vii
Clinton, William Jefferson "Bill,", 61
Coates, Ta-Nehisi, 207–213
coercive pacification, 163n7
Cohn, Marjorie, 235n10
Cold War, 20n1, 172, 212, 221, 222
  knowledge production in, 191–194
collateral damage, 151
Colombo Plan, 172

colonialism, 14–15, 23, 25, 166n10, 180, 203–204. *See also* anti-colonialism
  "compadre,", 57–59
  conflated with progress, 8
  education and, 153–160
  and empire, 6
  and Enlightenment, 4, 19
  European, 19, 24, 181–182, 204–205, 216
  and exploitation of resources, 5
  justification for, 109
  neo-, 161n2, 166n9, 203–207
  in the Philippines, 157–160
  and racism, 24–25
  United States, 46, 151, 155–156, 159
  victims of, 204–205
  and violence, 53, 157
  Western, 19
colonial plunder, 215–217
colonization, 8, 64n1
  by Britain, 28n2, 32
  by France, 32
  and migrant workers, 154
  by the Netherlands, 32
  by Portugal, 9
  by Spain, 17
  by the U.S., 66n4
commercial civility, 6–8
Commission to Study Reparation Proposals for African-Americans Act, 225
commodification, 211, 246, 247
commons (global), 5, 9, 180, 245–246, 247
Communist Party of the Philippines (CPP), 183n2
Compadre colonialism, 57
conatus, principle of, 10
conditionalities, 256
conflict theory, xi, 193–194

Congo, 173
Congo Free State, 54
Constantino, Renato, 153–154
consumerism, 54, 165n9
Contras, 252–254
Cooke, Amos Starr, 16
corporate personhood, 198
Cortes (Spanish), 79
Cosby, Bill, 211, 223
Cosby Show, The, 222
counterinsurgency, 3, 17, 228n1
  in Central America, 3, 185n4, 217
  in the Philippines, 17, 110, 149, 155, 184n2
  U.S., 151, 159
  in Vietnam, 54, 67n5
criminal justice system, 213
Crusaders, 8
critical race theory, xi
Cuba
  strategic hamleting in, 54
  subjugation of, 182
  U.S. aid to revolutionaries, 15, 17, 59
  as U.S. possession, 60, 89–90, 116
  and the USS *Maine*, 59–60
Cuban revolution, 59
cultural studies, 71n9, 183n1, 228n1, 231n4
cultural theory, 51, 164n8
culture(s). *See also* multiculturalism; polyculturalism
  American, 58, 68n6, 202
  civic, 156, 199, 200
  and colonialism, 159–160
  common, 13, 53, 200
  Filipino, 97n6, 102, 160
  hegemonic, 73n9
  indigenous Pacific, 156
  Moro, 122–125
  Native American, 131
  non-Western, 19
  plural, 202
  political, 202
  popular, 68n6
  of poverty, 223
  primitive, 157
  universalized/universalizing, 231n2
  Western, 172
  world, 195
Curry, Manly B., 155
Custer, George A., 67n5
cybernetics, 193

D

Dacula, Datu, 129
Dahl, Robert, 193
Darity, William A., Jr., 226–228
Darwin, Charles, 25, 191, 192
Darwinism, 63
  economic, 212
  social, 159, 200–203
Davenport, Kiana, 71n9
Davis, Angela, 27, 208
Davis, George Whitfield, 126–137
death squads, 172, 217
debt servitude, 177
deconstruction, 234n10
de Dios, Emilio Riego, 80
demilitarize. *See* militarization
democracy
  and capitalism, 5, 184n3, 195, 201, 205
  direct, 14
  enemies of, 235n10
  and imperialism, 57, 201
  liberal, 195
  and national identity, 231n3
  neoliberal, 200
  in the Philippines, 55, 166n10, 172
  popular, 14, 69n9
  programs, 175
  Spinoza's views on, 11, 12, 14

in the U.S., 193, 200
democratization, 184n2
De Molay, Order of (Philippines), 155
Department of Homeland Security (DHS), 200
dependency theory, 180, 186n5
deregulation, 180, 184n3, 211, 251, 252, 257
De Ruyter, Michiel, 10
desegregation, 197–198
determinism, 5, 25, 207, 221–222
Dewey, George, 56, 60, 64, 80–81, 88–92
  plausible deniability of, 88–93
de Witt, Cornelius, 10
de Witt, Johan, 10
Dirlik, Arif, 2–3
diversity, 194
domain assumptions, 193
Dostoyevsky, Fyodor, 8
Doty, Roxanne Lynn, 108
Douglass, Frederick, 110
Dred Scott case, 25
drones, 197, 207–208, 236n10
Du Bois, W.E.B., 26, 208, 220, 234n8
Dutch. *See* Netherlands
Dwan, Renata, 255
Dyer, Thomas, 61

E
Eadie, Pauline, 165n9
Eastern Europe, 222
Easton, David, 193
East Timor, 217
Ebert, Teresa (Red Feminist), 215
economic hit man. *See* economic jackal
economic inequality, 215–228, 231n3
economic jackal, 4, 55, 66–68n5
economics, 195
economism, 192, 207
Edgerton, Robert B., 111–113

education, colonial, 153–160
Ejercito Zapatista Liberacion Nacional (EZLN), 178. *See also* Zapatista National Liberation Front
Elliott, Charles Burke, 56
El Mozote massacre, 229n1
El Salvador, 218
Emmons, George, 40–42
empire
  American, 12–19, 52, 56, 59, 61, 62–64, 181, 210, 216, 219, 228, 256
  British, 7, 51
  class, 201, 231n2, 231n4
  colonial, 8, 163n6
  colonization and, 8
  corporate, 229n1, 232n4
  and the Enlightenment, 4–9
  from Enlightenment to neoliberal globalization, 9–14
  evil, 174
  European, 7, 15, 193–194
  global, 242
  and global commerce, 7, 77
  and global sovereignty, 11
  neoliberal, 196
  North American, 194
  in the Philippines, 151, 162n4, 163n7, 166n10
  racial nature of, 182
  Spanish, 69n8, 96n3
  US, x, 14, 151, 164n8, 255
  visualization of, 157–160
enemy combatants, 197
Enlightenment, 95n2, 229n1
  and empire, 4–9
  and progress, 5, 8, 14
Eperjesi, John R., 51
ethnic cleansing, 182n1
eurocentric, 2, 5, 27, 29n2, 53
eurocentrism, 207, 221

Europe. *See also* specific European countries by name
  Eastern, 222
  Western, 246
European Central Bank (ECB), 256
European Council, 184n2
exceptionalism, 33–34, 53, 54, 55–57, 199–202, 225
Exclusion Law, 231n3
executive powers, 197
existentialism, 236n10
exploitation, 27, 186n6, 191, 214, 246
  colonial and neocolonial, 203
  corporate, 229n1
  global, 180
  of labor, 164n9, 184n9, 205, 213, 232n4
  of labor power, 173
  of persons of color, 230n1
  politics of, 191
  racial, 31
  of resources, 180, 222, 252
  sexual, 87
  of the Third World, 252
Export-Import Bank, 252
expressive realism, 230n1
extractivism, 245

F
Fagen, David, 114–116
Fall, Bernard, 151
Fanon, Frantz, 224, 260
Ferrer, Felix, 79
field manuals (US military), 17
Fields, Barbara Jeanne, 215–216
Fiji islands, 15, 34–53
Filipino-American War. *See* Philippine-American War
Filipino diaspora, 164n9, 184n3
First World, 4, 257
Flores, Ambrosio, 155

Foley, Barbara, xi
food production, 258
Ford Foundation, 259
Ford, Glen, 210
foreign assistance (1969), 176
Foreign Assistance Act (1947), 172
formalism, xi
Forsyth, William D., 129
Foucault (Michel), 232n4, 232n5
France, vii, 217
  in Algeria, 54
  colonialism in Indochina, 172
  colonialism in the Caribbean, 260
Francisco, Luzviminda, 103–104, 151
Franco, Jean, 185n4
Freeman, Needhom N., 121
free markets, 5, 155, 165n9, 180, 194, 232n4, 235n10, 247
free trade, 3, 8, 127, 151, 175, 187n6, 211, 229n1, 230n2, 257
Free Trade Zones, 164n9, 187n6
Freire, Paulo, 206
Friedman, Thomas L., 177–182, 184n3
full spectrum dominance, 174
Fulton, Robert A., 120, 123–127, 140–142
functionalism, xi, 193
Funston, Frederick, 105

G
G8 Ministerial Conference, 13
Gast, John, 146
Gatewood, Willard, Jr., 113
Gaza. *See* Palestine and Palestinians
Genetically Modified Organisms (GMO), 70n9
genocide, 66n4, 157, 182n1, 191
  cultural, 66n4, 71n9
Giroux, Henry A., 195, 211, 233n7

global financial institutions, 68n5. *See also* International Monetary Fund (IMF); World Bank (WB)
globalization. *See also* neoliberal globalization
  corporate, 206
  and industrialization, 173
  of labor, 234n10
  as normal, 178
  predatory, 232n4
  processes of, 11
  San Juan's definition of, 182n1, 184n3, 184–186n4, 261
  and U.S. intervention, 172
  U.S.-led, 176, 222
global warming, 245–249
Gonzalez, Juan, 208
Goodman, Amy, 208
Gouldner, Alvin W., 193
Government of the Republic of the Philippines (GRP), 161n2, 183n2
Gowing, Peter, 120
Gramsci, Antonio, 232n4, 233n6
Gratz v. Bollinger, 197
Grayson, William, 103
Greece, 172, 218
Green Revolution, 258
Guam, 60, 89, 256
Guantanamo Bay, 59
Guantanamo detention camp, 152, 234n10
Guatemala, 172, 218, 229n1
Guevara, Che, 13
Guevara, Sulpicio, 85

H
Habermanesque, 235n10
habitus, 69n7, 95n2, 174, 191–194
Haiti, 218
Halstead, Murat, 90
hamleting, 54, 106

Hardt, Michael, 11–14
harmonization rules, 4
Harvey, David, 185n4
Hawaiian Islands, 16, 61, 70n9, 256
Hay, John, 150
Hearst, William Randolph, 59
hegemony
  based on capital accumulation and labor extraction, 172–175
  based on racial hierarchy, 220
  global, 4, 11, 174, 246
  neoliberal, 161n2, 242
  of the U.S., 3, 11–12, 220, 231n2, 233n5, 260
Hendrickson, Kenneth E., 81–82
Henry, Wilkes, 40, 44, 46
Higginbotham, F. Michael, 196
historical determination, 205
historical materialism, 220
historical materialist approach, 23, 24, 94n1, 207, 214, 220, 221, 232n4
historiography, Marxist, 180
Ho Chi Minh, 13
Holder, Eric, 234n10
Holland. *See* Netherlands
Holliday, Preston, 111
Hong Kong, 60, 79–80, 154
Horowitz, Irving Louis, 194–199, 231n2
Hudson (Captain), 36
Hukbalahap Movement (*Huk*), 95n2, 161n2
humanitarian interventionism, 59
humanities, 207
human rights, 14, 186n6, 202, 224, 235n10
Hume, David, 6–9
Hunt, Hannah, 47
Hunt, John, 47, 50
Huntington, Samuel, 235n10

I

Idle No More (INM) Movement, 71n9
ilustrado, 78, 79, 106
imperialism, 3, 4, 9, 14, 204, 261. *See also* anti-imperialism
  American, 181, 205
  in behalf of the Anglo-Saxon race, 63
  British, 28n2
  in China, 65n2
  by European powers, 68n7
  failure of postcolonialism with regard to, 207
  in the Pacific, 60–63, 156
  United States, 12, 14, 16, 19, 47, 57, 205, 209, 219–221
  victims of, 151, 204–2065
  Western, 19, 151
imperialist imaginary, 52
Ince, Onur Ulas, 6–8
India, 28n2
Indian Removal Act, vii
Indian Wars, 181
indigenous peoples, 5, 15, 24, 26, 53, 204, 223, 261
  as aboriginal savages, 62
  in the Algerian Sahara, 54
  in America, vii, 9, 67n5
  in Canada, 70n9
  and colonization, 51
  as peoples of color, 206
Indochina, 172
Indonesia, 217, 218
  US intervention in, 172
insurectos, 109. *See also* insurgent
Insurge Intelligence, 249
insurgent, 82, 90, 102, 115, 158
Intellectual Property Rights (IPRs), 258
International Court of Justice (World Court), 254
International Maize and Wheat Improvement Center. *See* CIMMYT (Centro Internacional de Mejoramiento de Maiz y Trigo)
International Monetary Fund (IMF), 166n9, 172, 177, 179, 256
International Rice Research Institute (IRRI), 2589
intersectionality, 214
Intramuros, 17, 81
investor rights, 4
Invisible Hand, 8, 181, 244
Iran, 172
Iraq, 109, 177, 235n10
Irish resistance, 26
Israel Anti-Lobby Act (S.720), 236n11
Israel, Zionist State of, 207, 212, 224, 236n11
Italy, 172–174

J

Jackson, George, 220
Jamaica, 54
James, C.L.R., 68n6, 232n4, 233n5
Jameson, Frederic, 203
Japan, 47, 150, 154, 174, 184n3, 246
Jaudenes, Fermin, 90
Jim Crow, 198, 226
John Paul II (Pope), 248
Johnson, L.M., 87
Johnson, Robert, 42
Joint Special Operations University, 253
Joint United States Military Advisory Group (JUSMAG), 152
"Joint Vision 2020" (US DoD), 174
Jolo Archipelago. *See* Sulu Archipelago

K

Kafka, Franz, 236n10
Kamlon insurrection, 163n6

Karamazov, Alyosha, 8
Karnow, Stanley, 58, 151
Katipunan, 78, 95n2, 155
Kennedy, John F., 210
kerekere, 50
Kho, Madge, 117, 118, 120
Kipling, Rudyard, 107
Kiram, Mohammad Jamalul I (Sultan), 118
Klein, Naomi, 245
knowledge production, and the Cold War, 191–194
Knox, Samuel, 37
Kobbe, William, 116
Krag rifles, 129
Kudarat, Sultan, 125
Kuwait, 155

L
labor
  Filipino, 235n10
  international division of, 3, 164n9, 180, 185n3, 186n6
  migrant, 3, 165n9, 187n6
labor exploitation, 184n3, 186n6, 213, 219, 250
labor export, from the Global South, 165n9
  from the Philippines, 3
labor extraction, 172, 181
labor migration, 3, 65n2
labor power, 28n2, 29n5, 173, 192
Lacan (Jacqus), 232n4
Lake Lanao Expedition, 136–144
Lakota Indians, 67n5
Lanao Expeditionary Force, 134–138
Lanao Lake region, pacification of, 125–135, 148
Land Defenders, 70n8
Latin America. *See* South America
Latin America Free Trade Area (LAFTA), 186n5

Lenin, Vladimir I., 33
liberal democracy, 195
liberal idealism, 27
liberalization, 150
  of trade, 2–7, 180, 251–254
Lincoln, Abraham, 25
Lions Club (Philippines), 156
Lith, Richard, 49
Llanera, Marciano, 80
Locke, John, 5–8, 24
Logia Modestia, 155
London Missionary Society, 47
low-intensity warfare, 112, 185n4, 230n1
Lukacs, Georg, 232n4
Luxemburg, Rosa, 232n4
Lyon, Paul, 157

M
Mabini, Apolinario, 85, 101
Macabebes, 152
MacArthur, Arthur, 105–110, 154
Maciu, Sultan of, 139–147
MacNair, W.B., 145
Magdalo, 78
Magdiwang, 78
Magna Carta (1215), 8
Maguindanao Sultanate, 17, 118, 125–138, 162n3
Mahan, Alfred Thayer, 16, 61, 62
Maine, USS (battleship), 59–61
Majul, Cesar Adib, 118
Malcolm, George A., 102
Malinowski, Bronislav, 192
Malolo Massacre, 16, 33–53
Manicheanism, 205
manifest destiny, vii, 15, 53, 62, 89–90, 261
Manila Bay, 56, 60, 64, 77
Maporo (Datu), 163n6
Marable, Manning, 203

Maranao Sultanate, 17, 129–134
Marcuse, Herbert, 203
marginalization, 191
Maria Cristina falls, 147
Marks, George P., III, 111
Marshall Plan, 172
Marxism, xii, 2, 9, 194, 203, 220
  orthodox, 221
Marxism-Leninism, 179
Marxist dogmatism. *See* Marxism
Marxist scholarship, 203
  sociologists, 194
  tradition, 2
Marx, Karl, 9, 25–27, 28n2, 32, 64n1, 94n1, 193, 255
Masonic Movement (Philippines), 155
Massacre at Bud Bagsak, 124, 149, 163n7
Massacre at Wounded Knee, 67n5
Massacre of Bud Dajo, 124
materialism, historical, 12, 203, 212, 220, 233n6
materialist critique, historical. *See* materialism, historical
Maura Law (1893), 119
McArthur, Arthur, 109
McCoy, Alfred, 160, 166n10
McKinley, William, 55, 92, 105, 108, 119, 123, 126, 160n1
  Benevolent Assimilation Proclamation, 119, 160n1
McNair, W.S., 131
Melville, Herman, 34, 68n6
Menchu, Rigoberta, 229n1
Mende-France, Mireille Fanon, 224
mercantile trade, 6, 8
Merritt, Wesley, 81, 90–91, 125
Mexico, vii, 13, 256
  privatization in, 13, 178–179
Middle East, 154, 173, 206
migrant labor, 3, 155, 187n6
  remittances by, 3

workers, 154
militarism, 256
militarization. *See* neoliberal globalization
Military Bases Agreement, 152
military doctrines, 174–175
military operations, 174–175
Mill, John Stuart, 25
Milliken v. Bradley, 197
Mindanao Sultanate. *See* Maguindanao Sultanate
Miranda rights, 197
missionaries, 16, 35, 51
  in Fiji, 45–51
  in Hawaii, 16
  to the Philippines, 64, 159
mode of production, 23, 29n2
modernism, xi, 20n1, 236n10
modernist project, 20n1
modernization model, 172
modern state system, 53
money, as representation of value, 6
Monroe Doctrine, 16, 60
Montenegro, Antonio, 80
Montesquieu, Charles de Secondat, 8
Montgomery, Cora (Jane McManus Storm Cazneau), vii, 62
Morga, Antonio, xiii
Moro, Aldo, 12
Moroland, 17
  declaring independence from Spain, 117–121
  historical background, 162n3
  integration into Philippines, 150–151
  pacification of, 17, 116–151, 162n5
  U.S. sovereignty over, 117, 120, 122, 126
Moro Problem, 127
Moro Province Legislative Council, 122
Morrison, Toni, 207, 213

Movimento dos Trabalhadores Rurais Sem Terra (MST), 179
Muda, Rajah, 134
multicultural/intercultural relations, 219
multiculturalism, xi, 173, 200, 222
   fetish of, 199–203
   paradigm of, 199
   terminology of, 13
multiculturalism, 201–219, 230n2, 232n4
multitude, 9–14, 255
Mutual Defense Treaty, 152

N
Nakba. See al-Nakba
national borders, 182n1
National Conference of Black Lawyersna, 223–224
National Democratic Front, 184n2
nationalism, 19, 53, 182n1, 206, 229n1
   civic, 200
   Filipino, 261
National Military Strategy (2015), 174–175
Native Americans, vii, 6, 66n4, 131
natural selection, 25
naval imperialism, 62
Navigation Laws (British), 8
Negri, Antonio, 11–14
Negritude, 233n8
neocolonialism. *See* colonialism
neofunctionalism, 193
neoliberal globalization, 55, 150, 178–179, 182n1, 222–224, 251–259
   and capitalism, 247
   contemporary, 11, 18, 55, 219, 251
   hegemony of, 242
   institutional structures of, 13, 176–179
   militarization of, 177, 233n7
   pedagogy, 200, 221
   as predatory, 232n4
   principles of, 14, 176–182, 251–254
   resistance to, 13, 178–179
   rules of, 251–258
   and uneven development, 180–182
neoliberalism, 2, 176, 180, 195, 196, 198, 212, 246
neoliberal order, 164n9
neoliberal pedagogy, rise of, 194–199
Netherlands
   colonization by, 32
   as co-sponsor of peace process (Philippines), 184n2
   Dutch civilizing expeditions, 54
   Dutch descent, 32
   Dutch East India Company, 10
   Dutch Golden Age, 10
   Dutch Republic, 10
   Orange monarchists, 10
New People's Army (NPA), 183n2
Newtonian presumption, 191
Newton, Isaac, 192
"New World Order", 155
New Zealand, 47
nihilism, 14
Nixon, Richard, 176
North America, 50, 194, 246. *See also* Canada; United States
North American Free Trade Agreement (NAFTA), 256, 260
North Atlantic Treaty Organization (NATO), 175
Norway, 184n2

O
Oahu Jack, 37, 39, 41
Obama Administration, 224, 234–235n10
Obama, Barack, 196, 199, 202, 209, 212, 214, 217, 225–228, 256

INDEX

Occupied Palestinian Territories, 213, 236–237n11
O'Connell, Paddy, 36
O'Connor, Tom, 254
Odah, Tariq Ba, 217
Olivares, Jose de, 157
"Open Door" policy, 150–151, 256
Operation Phoenix, 66–67n5
Operation Rolling Thunder, 66–67n5
Opium Wars, 32, 65n2, 175
Orientalism, American Pacific, 158
Orwellian, 254
O'Sullivan, John, vii
Otis, Elwell, 103, 105, 117, 126, 148, 158
Overseas Filipino Workers (OFWs), 164–166n9, 234–236n10
   Filipino contract workers, 234–236n10
Overseas Private Insurance Corporation (OPIC), 252
Overseas Private Investment Corporation (OPIC), 176, 258
OXFAM International, 243, 244

P
pacification
   coercive, 163n7
   of Lanao Lake region, 125–138, 147, 148
   of Moroland, 116–151, 162–163n5
   of the Philippines, 55, 58, 101–110
   racial dimensions of, 110–116
Pact of Biak-na-Bato, 79–81
Paduka Batara (Sultan), 118
Pakistan, 172
Pakistani, 217
Palestine and Palestinians, 205, 214, 236–237n11
Palestinian Great March of Return, 236–237n11

Panama Canal, 15, 60
Pandapatan Fort, 132
Pandapatan, Sultan of, 134
Pandita of Nuzca, 147
Papalangi, 35, 36
Paraguay, 218
Paraiso, Bryan Anthony C., 82
paramilitary organizations, 172, 185–186n4, 197
Parents Involved in Community Schools v. Seattle School District No. 1, 197–198
Paris Club, 256
Parsons, Talcott, 192
paternalistic principles, 150
Paterno, Pedro, 79–80, 113
Pearl Harbor, 16, 61
"pedagogic invasion", 56
pedagogy
   neoliberal, 207, 221
   public, 196, 212
pénétration pacifique, 54
peninsulares, 79
People's Climate March, 246
Perkins, John, 55
Permanent Court of Arbitration, 33
Perry, Matthew, 47
Perry, Oliver Hazard, 37
Pershing, John J., 136–151, 163n6
Pershing Lake Lanao Expedition, 140–144, 147–148, 163n6
personal responsibility, 210–211, 222, 228
Philbrick, Nathaniel, 33–46
Philippine-American War, 55, 106–108, 158
   casualties of, 102, 108, 112, 148, 151, 155
   desertion of U.S. soldiers, 110, 113–114
   incident at San Juan Bridge, 103
   pacification campaign, 61–112

U.S. atrocities, 107, 114, 151
Philippine Commissions, 55, 123–124, 158
Philippine Constabulary, 17
Philippine Constitution (1935), 152
Philippine flag, 87
Philippine National Anthem, 87
Philippine Organic Act (1902), 55
Philippine Revolution, 17, 59, 77–78, 85, 93n1, 94–95n2, 153
   Aguinaldo's government, 79, 85
   Dewey's plausible deniability, 88–93
   execution of Bonifacio, 78–79, 96n4
   manipulation and betrayal of Aguinaldo, 81–84
   in opposition to the cacique mentality, 94–95n2
   at the point of US intervention, 77–81
   proclamation of independence, 85–88, 152
Philippine revolutionaries, 77, 78, 95n2, 96n3, 102–106
Philippines, 16, 17, 218
   counterinsurgency in, 109, 152
   Green Revolution in, 259
   McKinley's assimilation policy, 108–110
   migrants from, 3
   pacification of, 17, 54, 109, 117
   racial dimension of pacification, 110–116
   resistance in, 161n2
   Spanish sovereignty in, 119
   U.S. occupation of, 57, 89–92, 127–134
   U.S. intervention in, 62, 77–93
   U.S. surveillance system, 158
Philippine Scouts, 152
photography, ethnographic, 157
Physicians for Human Rights, 234–235n10

Piang, Datu, 127, 129
Pinter, Harold, 217–219
Platt Amendment (1903), 15
Platt, Orville, 15
plenary power, 222, 231n3
Plessy decision, 25, 111
pluralism, 173, 193, 199–203
pluralist analysis, 193
policy of attraction, US, 163n7
political forecasting, 18
political science, 10, 192–193
political theory, 5
polo services, 95–96n3
polyculturalism, 234–235n10
Portugal, colonization by, 9, 55
   Inquisition in, 9
positivist logic of representation, 53
post-capitalism, 245. *See also* capitalism
postcolonialism, 2–4, 28–29n2, 186–187n6, 203
postcolonial stage, 186–187n6
postcolonial studies, 28n2
postcolonial theory, 233n6
post-marxism, 28–29n2
postmodernism, 20n1, 175, 236n10
   transnational, 19
postmodernity, 185–186n4
postmodern times, 185–186n4
Powell doctrine, 183–184n2
Powell, Colin, 183–184n2
power
   executive, 197
   hierarchies and asymmetries of, 230–231n2
   plenary, 222, 231n3
Power, Samantha, 65–66n3
Pozo, Michael, 50, 206
Pratt, E. Spencer, 83
Pratt, Edward B. (Captain), 116
Presbyterian Board of Foreign Mission, 64
principalia, 95–96n3

privacy rights, 197
privatization, 5, 150, 177, 178, 251, 260
  in Hawaii, 16
  of the military, 108
pro-democracy groups, 197
Progressive Era, 157
progressivism, 210, 213
Project for a New American Century (PNAC), 175
proletarian class, 27, 28–29n2, 78
Propaganda Movement, 93–94n1
protectionism, 176–179
Protestant work ethic, 222
Public Law, 61, 69–73n9
Puerto Rico, 60, 89, 116, 256
Pulitzer, Joseph, 59

Q
Quemada, 54

R
race
  and class, 26
  without class, 207–221
race relations, 25, 216, 219, 225–228
racial hierarchy, 173, 197, 220, 230–231n2
racial inequality, 216, 225, 231n3
racial theory, 159
racism, xi, 5, 24, 64, 103, 196, 199, 205, 223–224
  class basis of, 214–221
  and colonialism, 5, 24–25
  as domestic terrorism, 233n7
  eradication of, 199, 222, 228–230n1, 233n8
  ideology of, 224
  structural, 198, 202, 209, 220, 223, 225
  and Zionism, 236n11

Rajah Bungso-Lopez Treaty, 118
Rakitin, Mikhail Osipovich, 8
rational choice theory, 220
reconcentrado, 54, 106, 113, 138
Red Brigades, 12
Rehnquist, William, 197
Reidy, John J., 130–138, 143–147
Reparations movement, 216, 220, 224
Republic of the Philippines (GRP), 161n2, 183n2
Rice, George D., 136
Rice, Mark, 159
Ringgold, Cadwalader, 41–43, 49
risk analysis, 18
Rivera, Primo de, 80
Rizal, Jose P., xii–xiii. *See* 93–97nn1–6
Roberts, John, 197
Rockefeller Foundation, 259
Rodney, Walter, 180
Roma-Sianturi, Dinah, 56
Roof, Dylann, 199
Roosevelt Administration, 123
Roosevelt, Theodore, 60–62, 107, 109, 111, 115, 124, 134
Root, Elihu, 15, 107, 126, 130
Rotary Club, 156
Rough Riders, 60, 111, 115
Russia, 26, 150, 216, 254

S
Said, Edward, 19, 71n9, 204, 206
Saito, Natsu Taylor, 231n3
Sakdalista, 95n2
Saleeby, Najeeb, 120, 122
Sandwich Islands. *See* Hawaiian Islands
San Juan, E., Jr., ix–xi
  on the anti-colonial character of of the Philippine resistance, 115–116
  on anti-imperialist and anti-capitalist resistance, 230n1

on the anti-imperialist themes of Melville's *Moby Dick*, 68n6
on the apologists for US colonialism in the Philippines, 57–59
on Asian-Pacific Islanders, 231n3
on black American soldiers, 110, 113
on Bonifacio, 95n2
on the bourgeois nationalization of the state, 28n1
on capitalism as a world system, 201
on capitalism as system of capital accumulation, and labor exploitation, 205
on class reductionism, 192
on Cold War displacement of class, 191–194
on colonization, 51
on the contemporary "state,", 182n1
on counterinsurgency nature of US assistance, 183n2
on cultural genocide, 66n4
on cultural studies, 72n9, 228n1
on the emancipatory role of knowledge production, 19
on Fanon, 229n1
on the feminist praxis in Filipino writing, 154
on the Filipino diaspora, 164n9
on finance capitalism, 260
on Frederick Douglass, 110
on genocidal US counterinsurgency, 113
on globalization and labor, 234n10
on Hawaii, 31, 69n9
on history, 19
on the internationalization of US domestic law, 234n10
on Jose Rizal, 93n1
on labor exploitation, 184n3, 205
on labor power, 65n2
on Marxism and history, 28n2, 220
on McKinley's rationale for conquest, 92–93
on mercantile trade, 64n1
on merchant capitalism, 180
on Moroland, 162n5, 163n6
on multiculturalism, 231n4
on national liberation, 19, 179
on the nation-state, 53–55
on neoliberal democracy, 200
on the Opium Wars, 65n2
on the Philippines, 55–58, 92–93, 93n1, 110, 115, 152, 160n1
on postcolonial "ethical utopianism", 179
on postcolonialism, 203–206
on the Propaganda Movement, 93n1
on questioning US suppression of dissent, 228n1
on race and racism, 214
on religion as means of exacting consent, 50
on resistance in the Philippines, 161n2
on the slave trade, 26, 68n7
on Spain, 97n6
on Spinoza, 13
as theoretical wedge, 201
on uneven development, 186–187n6
on the universaliation of the US "war on terror", 234n10
on the universalization of culture, 230n2
on the US annexation of the Philippines and the conscience of humanists, 151
on the US "civilizing mission", 69n8
on the US claim to exceptionalism, 56
on U.S. colonialism, 97n5, 167n10
on the US interruption of the Philippine Revolution, 93n1
on utilitarian doctrine, 54

on the valor of anti-imperialist resistance, 260–261
on value accumulation, 260
and violence, 53
on violence in international relations, 66n3
on the violence of US colonial rule, 163n6
on white supremacy, 202
Sandinista Government of Nicaragua, 254
Schirmer, Boone D., 90
Schlesinger, Arthur, 235n10
School of the Americas, 185n4
Schuck, Charles (son), 120
Schuck, Charlie (father), 120–121
Schuck, Edward, 121
Schuck, Herman, 121
Schuck, William, 121
Schurman Commission, 87, 106, 158
Schurman, Jacob, 55
Scott, Hugh L., 123
"security exceptions", 176
seed bank, 260
segregation, 29n5, 111, 191
Sekou, Osagyefo Uhuru, 213
self-determination, right to, 152, 206
Semitism, anti-, 236n11
Shalom, Stephen Rosskamm, 90
Sharpley-Whiting, T. Denean, 156
Sharpton, Al, 213
Sherman, William Tecumseh, 148
Shiva, Vandana, 259, 260
Shohat, Ella, 2
Silliman, Horace B., 64
Silliman Institute. *See* Silliman University
"Silliman spirit", 64
Silliman University, 64, 158
Singapore, 82
Sison, Jose Maria, 161n2, 184n2

slavery, 6–9, 26, 27, 181, 215–217, 220, 223, 224, 226
slaves, African, 55, 64n1, 77, 160n1, 250
slave trade, 26, 32, 64n1, 68n7
Atlantic, 223–225
liberal critique of, 7
Smith, Adam, 8
Smith, "Howlin' Jake,", 107
Snowden, Edward, 160
Social Darwinism, 159, 200
socialism, 27, 115, 194
actually existing, 233n6
social justice, 231n3
social knowledge, 191–194
social sciences, 18, 193–195, 206–209, 221–224, 229n1
social theory, 5, 26, 194
social thought, 5
sociology, 193–196, 235n10
Sojourner's Club, 155
South Africa, 32, 173, 224
South America, 217
as Latin America, 204
South Asia, 178
Southeast Asia, 178
sovereignty, 4, 11, 17, 59, 70–71n9, 97n5, 116–118, 166n10, 256
Soviet Union, 218
and the Cold War, 172, 174
as "evil empire,", 174
Spain. *See also* Philippine Revolution; Spanish-American War
Cuban revolution against, 15, 59–61
Philippine revolution against, 60
in the Philippines, 16
surrender of, 90, 91
treaties with Sultanates, 118
as weakened international power, 97n6
Spanish-American War, 16, 33, 55, 62, 77, 81, 91

302 INDEX

Spanish Armada, 56, 60
Spanish South Pacific Squadron, 60
Spinoza, Baruch (Benedict de), 9–14, 232n4, 260
Spivak, Gayatri, 204
Steinberg, David Joel, 57
Strong, Josiah, 63–64
Structural Adjustment Programs (SAPs), 3, 177, 247, 256
structural dependence, 186n5
structural-functionalism, 58, 193
subaltern studies, 174
subsidies, 258
Sultan Kudarat-Lopez Treaty, 118
Sulu Archipelago, 116, 120
Sulu Sultanate, 17, 118, 121, 122, 162n4
  pacification of, 123, 125–129
Sumner, Samuel S., 138, 141
Supreme Court decisions, 197–198
surplus labor, 27
surplus value, 29n2, 31, 53, 180
surveillance, 18, 115–116, 158–160, 187n6, 208
Sustainable Development Goals (SDGs), 249
systems analysis of politics, 193

T
Tadiar, Neferti, 214
Taft Commission, 56, 87, 106, 158
Taft, William Howard, 55, 105–108, 123–124
Taguba, Antonio Mario, 234–236n10
Taguba Report, 234–236n10
Taliban, 253
Tejeros Convention, 78
terrorism, 182n1, 185n4, 233n6
testimonio, 228–229n1
Texas, annexation of, vii, 62
Thatcher, Margaret, 178

Third Expeditionary Force (North Dakota), 155, 234–235n10
Third World, 2, 19, 20n1, 26, 172–174, 203, 228–230n1, 255, 259
  emerging markets in, 3, 252
  as enemy of democracy, 234–235n10
  exploitation of, 252
  neocolonial exploitation in, 203
  postmodernism in, 20n1
  uneven development of, 180–182, 186–187n6
  U.S. intervention in, 172
  and western hegemony, 228–230n1
Thirty Meter Telescope, 69–73n9
Thirty Years War, 31, 182–183n1
Thornley, Andrew, 49, 50
Tigar, Michael E., 8
Tirona, Daniel, 78
Top One Per cent, 164n9, 222, 244
torture, 97n4, 113, 152, 178, 233–234n8
trade (commerce), 8, 13
  foreign, 6
  liberalization of, 3, 180, 251, 252
  mercantile, 6, 8
transnational corporation (TNC), 3
Trans-Pacific Partnership (TPP), 3, 256
Treaty of Paris (1898), 55, 60, 89, 91, 116–118, 122, 123, 125, 126
Treaty of Utrecht, 25
Treaty of Westphalia, 31, 32, 182–183n1
Trias, Mariano, 80
Trilateral Commission, 246
Trotskyism (American), 68n6
Truman Doctrine, 172
Tuaregs, 54
Tui Cakau (Chief), 48–50
Turkey, 218
Turki, Fawaz, 236–237n11
Twain, Mark, 92, 97n5, 151

Tyler Doctrine, 16, 61
Tyler, John, 16, 61

U

Uali of Butig (Sultan), 140
Udasan, Datu, 129
Ukraine, 177
Umbra, Datu Amirul, 129
Underwood, Joseph, 38–40, 43–46
Uniao Nacional para a Independencia Total de Angola (UNITA), 253
Unilinear view of history, 26
United Nations (UN), 172, 224, 65–66n3
United Nations Development Programme (UNDP), 242
United Nations Institute for Disarmament Research, 255
United States
  agenda in the Middle East, 65–66n3
  aid to Cuban revolutionaries, 15, 59–61
  as a settler state, 202
  as superpower, 174–175
  criticism of (by Harold Pinter), 217–219
  emergence as an empire, 14–16, 157
  exceptionalism of, 33, 53–59, 202, 225, 260
  exploration of the Pacific, 33–53
  hegemony of, 14, 206, 221, 231–232n4, 254
  imperialism as predatory, 254
  Malolo Massacre as predictive of future military demeanor abroad by the, 65–66n3
  occupation of Philippines by, 57, 89–93, 125–137
  problem of race without class in, 207–213
  unilateralism, 18
  westward expansion of, vii, 62

Universal Declaration of Human Rights, 243
universal ecclesiastical authority, 31
universalization of culture, 230–231n2
"unlawful combatants", 234–236n10
unmanned aerial vehicles (UAVs), 197. *See also* drones
UN Working Group of Experts on People of African Descent, 224
UN World Conference Against Racism, 224
Uruguay, 218
U.S. Agency for International Development (USAID), 197
U.S. Asiatic Squadron, 60
U.S. Department of Defense, 174
U.S. Department of State, Office of the Historian, 62
U.S. Department of the Treasury, 172
U.S. Exploring Expedition, 33–35
U.S. Navy, exploration of the Pacific by, 33–49
U.S. Special Operations Command, 253
utilitarian individualism, 200
utilitarianism, 54
Uttu, Datu, 127, 128

V

Veidovi (Fijian Chief), 36–39, 45–47
verticalized global food production system, 13, 258
Vicars, Thomas A., 136
Vietnamization program, 66–68n5
Vietnam War, 54, 66–68n5, 151, 217
violence
  as barbarism, 7, 228–230n1
  and colonialism, 54
  and colonization, 53
  and imperialism, 212
  pathology of, 33–53, 235–236n10

racialized, 151–153
and religion, 65–66n3
state, 26–27, 33–49, 53, 65–66n3, 151–153, 182–183n1, 222, 233
and Zionism, 212–213

W

Walker, William, 55
Wallerstein, Immanuel, 23
Walzer, Michael, 59
warfare. *See also* war on terror; specific wars by name
   low-intensity, 112, 174, 218, 184–185n4, 228–230n1
   permanent, 174–175
War of the Spanish Succession, 25
war on terror, 18, 47, 152, 175, 181, 182–183n1, 234–236n10
Washington Consensus, 164–166n9
"water cure", 113
Wesleyan Methodist Missionary Society, 47
West, Cornel, 207, 208
Western Europe, 7
Westphalian state system, 4, 31, 32, 182–183n1
White Man's Burden, 5, 25, 151
white supremacy, 111, 202, 216, 199–202
Wildman, Rounsenville, 82, 88
Wilkes, Charles, 48, 49, 52–53
Wilkes Treaty, 162n4
Williams, John, 47
Williams, Thomas, 35
Willis, Stan E., 224

Winfrey, Oprah, 213, 223
Wolf, Eric, 64–65n1
women
   black, 156–158
   commodification of, 154–156
   as migrant workers, 154–156, 184–185n3
Wood, Leonard, 81–82, 122–124
Worcester, Dean C., 83, 87, 158–160
World Bank (WB), 3, 13, 164–166n9, 177, 179, 185–186n4, 256, 260
World Conference Against Racism, 224
World Economic Forum (WEF), 179, 246
world hypotheses, 193
world systems theory, 24, 180
World Trade Organization (WTO), 3, 13, 165–166n9, 176, 178–179, 182–183n1, 256

X

xenophobia, 191

Z

Zapatista National Liberation Front, 178, 260. *See also* Ejercito Zapatista Liberacion Nacional (EZLN)
Zimbabwe, 173
Zinn, Howard, viii, 110
Zionism
   anti, 236n11
Zionist State of Israel, 207, 212–213, 236n11. *See also* Israel
Zizek, Slavoj, 201
Zola (Emile), 156